ELEMENTS
OF
FAMILY LAW

AUSTRALIA
The Law Book Company
Sydney

CANADA
The Carswell Company
Toronto, Ontario

INDIA
N.M. Tripathi (Private) Ltd.
Bombay
and
Eastern Law House (Private) Ltd.
Calcutta
M.P.P. House
Bangalore
Universal Book Traders
Delhi

ISRAEL
Steimatzky's Agency Ltd.
Tel-Aviv

PAKISTAN
Pakistan Law House
Karachi

ELEMENTS
OF
FAMILY LAW

by

STEPHEN M. CRETNEY, MA, DCL, FBA

One of Her Majesty's Counsel
Solicitor, Professor of Law
in the University of Bristol

LONDON
SWEET & MAXWELL
1992

Published in 1992
by Sweet & Maxwell Ltd.
South Quay Plaza, 183 Marsh Wall, London E14 9FT
Computerset by
PB Computer Typesetting, Pickering, N. Yorks.
Printed in England by
Clays Ltd., St. Ives plc

A CIP catalogue record for this book
is available from the British Library

ISBN 0 421 450304

The illustration which appears on the cover is "Prince James Francis
Edward Stuart (1688–1766) and his sister Louisa Maria Theresa
(1692–1712)" by Nicolas de Largillière, reproduced by courtesy of the
National Portrait Gallery, London.

Extracts from The Warnock Committee Report on Human Fertilisation
and Embryology and the Government White Paper—Children Come
First. © Crown copyright.

For
ALC
MCAC
EAFC

PREFACE

My objective in writing this book remains to serve the needs of those students who seek a clear and concise guide to the basic principles or central core of English family law and who are prepared to accept that such a guide can only be provided at the cost of some sacrifices both in range and depth of coverage. I had always believed that the book might best be used in conjunction with a selection of primary materials; and happily an admirable selection is readily accessible in Hoggett and Pearl's *The Family, Law and Society, Cases and Materials* (2nd ed., 1991). I have given relevant references to that work at the end of each Chapter of the text; and I have also included a number of other suggestions for further reading.

Some parts of the text follow the pattern of *Principles of Family Law* (5th ed., 1990); but the sections of that work dealing with Children were written entirely by its co-author, Professor Judith Masson, and accordingly the corresponding parts of this book are completely new. It is difficult to achieve in a short book the balanced approach to discussions of policy issues which can properly be expected in texts aiming to be comprehensive; and I have therefore been less hesitant than in the past to express my own views on a number of matters which are, or which I believe should be, controversial.

I remain convinced of the need for law students to study the law in its social and economic context; but I am even more convinced that students must understand that the law—concerned as it is with the question of the right of the State to coerce the unwilling—is a rigorous intellectual discipline in its own right. The family lawyer certainly needs to understand the language, skills and approaches of others professionally concerned with the family; but it is surprising— particularly in the light of the disturbing facts revealed by the Cleveland and other enquiries—that little emphasis seems to be given to the need for all concerned to understand at least the fundamental principles of the law. I hope that this book will be of some value in that respect.

I have included the facts of many decided cases in the text in an attempt to convey to the reader something of the reality of the subject. References are given to the Family Law Reports ("FLR"), but alternative citations may be found in the Table of Cases.

I have been much helped in preparing this edition by comments on sections of the text made by Gillian Douglas, Senior Lecturer in Law at the Cardiff Law School, and by Gwynn Davis, Senior Research Fellow in the Law Faculty at Bristol University. The whole text has been skilfully reduced to immaculate typescript by Mrs. Wendy Brett. I am grateful to them all.

Amongst the mass of new statutory material dealt with in this edition will be found the provisions of the Human Fertilisation and Embryology Act 1990 which seek to identify a child's parents; and it therefore seemed not inappropriate to choose for the cover illustration the subject of the most celebrated maternity dispute in English history. The birth of a son to the wife of King James II—one of the principal events precipitating what generations of schoolboys were taught to call the Glorious Revolution—took place in the presence of some 30 witnesses (including the Lord Chancellor, the Lord President and Lord Privy Seal) but this did not suffice to quell rumours that the lawful heir to the throne was a suppositious child smuggled into the Royal bed in a warming-pan. All lawyers know that truth may be elusive; but the reader of this text will perhaps find in it other illustrations—albeit less constitutionally important—of the reality that law making is essentially a political process depending more on the tides of fashion and on what people wish to believe rather than on objective truth—if indeed there be such a thing.

I hope the law is correctly stated on the basis of the sources available to me today, April 4, 1992.

STEPHEN CRETNEY
The feast of St. Isidore of Seville, 1992

CONTENTS

CONTENTS

Low comm

CONTENTS

TABLE OF CASES

TABLE OF CASES

TABLE OF CASES

TABLE OF STATUTES

United Kingdom Statutes

TABLE OF STATUTES

PART I—MARRIAGE AND ITS TERMINATION

INTRODUCTION

The traditional concern of English family law is with marriage and its consequences. Marriage was and is important for the lawyer because marriage creates a legal status in the sense in which that word was explained by Lord Simon of Glaisdale in *The Ampthill Peerage* [1977] AC 547, 577: "the condition of belonging to a class in society to which the law ascribes peculiar rights and duties, capacities and in-capacities." If a couple are married they automatically have certain rights and duties; and, in principle, the nature and quality of their relationship is irrelevant: a wife who (as in *Re Rowlands, dec'd* [1984] FLR 813) has not lived with her husband for more than 40 years is nonetheless still in principle entitled to succeed to her husband's property on his intestacy.

The significance of marriage as creating a legal status is dramatically illustrated by the case of *Re Collins (dec'd)* [1990] 2 FLR 72:

> Mrs Collins left her husband—a man with a record of violent crime—shortly after their marriage in 1978. She was given leave to bring divorce proceedings within three years of the marriage on the ground that the case was one of exceptional hardship or depravity. A decree nisi was granted but the decree had not been made absolute at the date when Mrs Collins died. Accordingly she was in law still married; and her husband became entitled on her intestacy to the whole of her estate.

Conversely, if a couple are not legally married, neither partner is automatically entitled to the legal rights which flow from the status of marriage. It is irrelevant that they have been living together happily for many years, and that they have for long been regarded as a married couple by all their friends and relatives. For example:

> In *Burns* v. *Burns* [1984] FLR 216 a man and a woman lived together for 19 years. Mrs Burns (as she was known) gave up her job to look after Mr Burns and their two children. Although she put her earnings into the housekeeping, and bought domestic appliances and other household goods, she was held to have no claim to the house or any of the assets (and see *Windeler* v. *Whitehall* [1990] 2 FLR 505, para. 9–01 below).

It is true that legislation now sometimes gives rights to those who have lived together as husband and wife; but an understanding of

1

marriage and its legal consequences must have priority in any understanding of English family law, precisely because marriage of itself does create legal rights and obligations.

The law's concentration on marriage as the basis upon which legal rights are founded no longer reflects social reality. In recent years, there has been a very sharp increase in extra-marital cohabitation; and it has been estimated that some 900,000 people were cohabiting in 1986/1987. It is widely recognised that living together before marriage is now almost the norm—in 1972, 16 per cent. of women who married had previously cohabited with their future husband; but by 1987 the proportion reached around 50 per cent.—but what is perhaps most striking is the remarkable increase in the proportion (now 28 per cent.) of children born outside marriage often (it would seem) to couples living together in a stable relationship.

These demographic trends raise profoundly difficult issues of social and legal policy. How far should the law make special provision assimilating the position of those who are married and those who are merely cohabiting? This is, perhaps the most important issue of policy in contemporary family law; but before that issue can be sensibly discussed it is necessary to understand the law governing marriage and its consequences. The first part of this book therefore deals with the creation (Chapter 1), annulment (Chapter 2) and dissolution of marriage (Chapters 3-5). Chapter 6 deals with the remedy of judicial separation, and also (for reasons explained in the text) with legal remedies against domestic violence.

Chapter 1

FORMATION OF MARRIAGE

Introduction

If marriage is regarded in social rather than legal terms it is (as the **1–01** historian L. Stone has pointed out) a complex and often lengthy process; but in legal terms marriage comes into existence in a moment and is independent of the parties' social relationship. This is not to say that the law has not had to resolve difficult social and moral issues. Is marriage to be (as it is in English legal theory) the voluntary union for life of a woman and a man to the exclusion of all others, or is a person to be allowed to have several spouses at the same time—and if so, how many? And what do we mean by "a man" and a "woman?" Can a transsexual marry? Can a 15-year-old marry? What formalities have to be completed to create a marriage?

Not surprisingly, although virtually all legal systems do have **1–02** ground rules governing such matters, the content of those rules differs greatly from country to country, and from time to time. For example, until the enactment of Lord Hardwicke's Marriage Act in 1753, English law required no *formal procedures* at all for the creation of a marriage. If a couple agreed between themselves that they were married, that sufficed to create what is correctly called a "common law marriage"—*i.e.* a marriage as valid as if it had been celebrated by the Archbishop of Canterbury in Westminster Abbey in the presence of a large congregation. This state of affairs continued in Scotland (a fact which originally accounted for the popularity of Gretna Green as a place for runaway marriages) until as recently as 1940, and it still exists in some parts of the world. But English law now prescribes quite elaborate formalities with which those who wish to be legally married must comply. For example:

> In *Rignell* v. *Andrews* [1991] 1 FLR 332 a man had lived with a woman for 11 years and she had changed her surname to his. He claimed that she was accordingly his "common law wife," and that he was entitled to the higher rate of personal allowance for income tax purposes available to a man whose "wife" was living with him. The claim was unsuccessful. The judge held that the term "wife" meant a woman who had entered into a marriage with a man, and was not apt to cover a woman who was merely cohabiting with a man, however permanent or close the relationship. The word "marriage" did not include the relationship inaccurately referred to as a "common law marriage."

Again, there have been remarkable changes in the English rules **1–03** about *who can marry whom*? It was only in 1929 that Parliament

3

decided that in this country a 15-year-old child was not to be allowed to marry; and the rules about marriages between relatives have been changed as recently as 1986 by the Marriage (Prohibited Degrees of Relationship) Act which, as we shall see (para. 2–10 below) even allows a person in certain circumstances to marry his mother-in-law or her father-in-law.

The basic rule
1–04   The basic rule of English law is that a marriage can be created between any two people who have the necessary *legal capacity* and comply with the *stipulated formal requirements*. The text deals first (in this Chapter) with formalities. Chapter 2 then deals with the rules about capacity.

FORMALITIES—THE MARRIAGE CEREMONY

1–05   One thing which can be said with certainty about the English law is that it is complex—so much so that the Law Commission said that it was "not understood by members of the public or even by all those who have to administer it": Law Com. No. 53, Annex, para. 6. It would serve no useful purpose to try to explain in an elementary textbook the details of the law as contained in the Marriage Acts 1949 to 1986. All that can be done is to highlight some of the main characteristics of the law. Much of the complexity is caused by the fact that English law gives intending spouses a very wide choice of marriage ceremony: they can marry according to the rites of the Church of England; they can, subject to conditions, marry according to the rites of other religions; or they can marry in a purely secular procedure in a Register Office.

(i) Parental consent sometimes required
1–06   If either party to an intended marriage is under 18 the consent of that person's parents or guardians is normally required. If the child is in Local Authority care under a care order, the Local Authority's consent is required in addition; and if the court has made a residence order under the provisions of the Children Act (see para. 13–09 below) the consent of the person with whom the child is to live under the terms of that order is required in substitution for that of the parents and guardians. The court can override a refusal to give the necessary consent.

A marriage solemnised without the requisite consent will be valid; but the parties may be liable to prosecution for making a false statement.

4

(ii) Requirements for banns, licence or certificate

The law stipulates certain preliminaries to the wedding in order to 1–07
give an opportunity for people to claim that there is (in the language
of the Book of Common Prayer) some "just cause or impediment."
The formalities required depend on whether or not the marriage is to
take place according to the rites of the Church of England.

(a) *Anglican marriages*

If there is to be an Anglican ceremony, Banns will usually be called. 1–08
But alternatively the parties may obtain a Common Licence from the
Church Authorities, or a Special Licence issued on behalf of the
Archbishop of Canterbury. Banns are the cheapest preliminary, but
involve the longest delay. A Special Licence is at the other extreme. It
can authorise a marriage at any time and in any place. At one time
the cost was such as to make it available only to the affluent, but the
fee has not kept pace with changes in the value of money, and more
than 1,500 marriages by special licence take place each year.

(b) *Preliminaries to other forms of marriage*

If there is to be a civil ceremony, or a non-Anglican religious 1–09
ceremony, the parties may obtain a Superintendent Registrar's
Certificate—which can be regarded as an equivalent to banns in so
far as it is the cheapest procedure but requires the longest waiting
time. A Superintendent Registrar's Certificate and Licence—often
(incorrectly) called a "special licence"—costs rather more, but permits
marriage after the expiration of one whole day from the giving of the
notice. In either case, prescribed information has to be given and
recorded in a marriage notice book which is open to public
inspection. And there are special preliminaries to facilitate the
marriage of the terminally ill, the housebound, prisoners, and people
in mental hospitals.

(iii) The marriage ceremony

The legislation permits four types of ceremony. First, marriage 1–10
according to the rites of the Church of England. Secondly, the secular
ceremony in a register office. Thirdly, marriages according to the rites
of the religion concerned in a registered place of religious worship;
and finally Quaker and Jewish marriages. The only feature which is
common to all types of ceremony is that the parties must at some
stage express their consent to the marriage in a prescribed form of
words.

(a) *The Church of England*

The marriage must be celebrated by a clergyman in the presence of 1–11
two or more witnesses. The clergyman will use the rite laid down in
the Book of Common Prayer or authorised alternative form of service.
Two thirds of all marriages with a religious ceremony are performed
according to the rites of the Church of England.

(b) Register Office wedding

1–12 The Register Office ceremony is simple in the extreme, and must be entirely secular. The parties declare that they know of no lawful impediment to the marriage, and "call upon these persons here present to witness that I, AB, do take thee, CD, to be my lawful wedded wife (or husband)." The ceremony takes place in the office, "with open doors" and two or more witnesses must be present.

Responsibility for the provision of Register Offices falls on Local Authorities, and a government discussion paper stated that "while many of these are in pleasant buildings with good facilities and agreeable surroundings, there are some which are less attractive and fail to meet the public's expectations of a suitable place for a marriage."

Notwithstanding these shortcomings, nearly half of all marriages now take place in register offices. But a very high proportion—some 70 per cent.—of marriages in which both parties are marrying for the first time are solemnised with some form of religious ceremony. The refusal of many churches to marry the divorced, rather than principled preference for secularism may thus account, at least in part, for the apparent popularity of register office weddings.

(c) Marriages in a registered place of religious worship

1–13 These provisions were originally intended to allow Roman Catholic churches and non-conformist chapels to be used for marriages; but it is possible for any building which is a place of meeting for religious worship to be registered for this purpose. But what is "religious worship" for this purpose? The courts have held that the expression does not extend to the practices of scientologists: *ex parte Segerdal* [1970] 2 QB 697. But there is no doubt that Sikh and Hindu Temples, and Mosques, are entitled to be registered (although it seems that only a few—54 Mosques and 94 Sikh Temples—are registered).

The building is registered by the Registrar-General; but the form of the ceremony—which will usually be conducted by a minister of the religion concerned—is a matter for the parties and the body controlling the building, subject to one vital qualification. This is that at some stage in the proceedings the parties must make the statements set out in para. 1–12 above in either English or Welsh. (There is no requirement that they understand the language used.)

(d) Jewish and Quaker weddings

1–14 The celebration of Jewish and Quaker marriages has, ever since Lord Hardwicke's Act, been entirely a matter for the religions concerned. There is no requirement that such marriages take place in public in a registered building, or that they be performed by an authorised person; and the state's role is limited to requiring that an appropriate preliminary should have taken place, and that any such marriage be registered.

(iv) Registration

All marriages celebrated in this country must be registered. This   **1–15**
provides proof that the ceremony took place, and also facilitates the
collection of demographic information.

PROPOSALS FOR REFORM

In 1990, the government published a White Paper, *Registration,*   **1–16**
Proposals for Change [Cm. 939] containing numerous proposals for
reform. Many of the proposals are intended to remove the anomalies
in the existing system governing formalities—for example, it would
no longer be possible to shorten the waiting time necessary before a
marriage can be solemnised simply by obtaining a licence. But the
government also made a number of proposals of much greater
impact—for example, that a choice of building, including stately
homes or hotels, should be available.

SUGGESTIONS FOR FURTHER READING

Hoggett and Pearl, pp. 1–19, 30–34.
Registration: Proposals for Change, HMSO, Cm. 939 (1990).
A. Bradney, "How Not to Marry People" (1989) 19 Fam Law 408.
J. A. Priest, "Buttressing Marriage" (1983) 13 Fam Law 119.

Chapter 2

CAPACITY TO MARRY—ANNULMENT

INTRODUCTION—VOID AND VOIDABLE MARRIAGES

2–01 Who can marry whom; and what is to happen if someone goes through a marriage ceremony although the rules prohibit the marriage? To take an example, what is the position if a woman who has not seen her husband for 20 years, and has been told that he is dead, remarries. Is the second marriage valid if it turns out that the first husband was in fact still alive?

The simplest answer to this question would be that the rules simply prevent the second "marriage" from coming into existence, so that neither party would have any consequential legal rights and duties. No doubt there would be a procedure whereby the unfortunate parties could, to avoid any trouble for the future, get an official document certifying that the second "marriage" was "null and void to all intents and purposes whatsoever." And this is indeed precisely how the law worked for many years in this country. But things are now rather different. This is because of the development of the law of nullity (or annulment) of marriage, which we must now try to explain.

Void and voidable—the distinction and its consequences
2–02 A confusing feature of the law is that (for historical reasons concerned with the relationship between the common law courts and the ecclesiastical courts) English law treats some marriages affected by irregularity as being *voidable* and some as *void*. The main differences between the two categories are as follows:

(a) A decree of nullity can be pronounced in relation to a void marriage at any time, even after the death of the parties. A decree can only be granted annulling a voidable marriage during the lifetime of both parties.
(b) If the marriage is void, then no valid marriage ever existed. But if the marriage is voidable, it is valid unless and until annulled.
(c) If the marriage is void, any "interested person" may take proceedings; whereas only the parties to a voidable marriage can take proceedings to have it annulled.

But even void marriages may have legal consequences
2–03 This basic distinction between the voidable marriage (which is perfectly valid unless and until it is annulled) and the void marriage, (which does not exist and requires no decree to bring it to an end) is comprehensible enough. However, the distinction has in recent years

8

become somewhat blurred because many of the legal consequences of a valid marriage have, in order to avoid hardship, been attached even to void marriages provided that a decree of nullity is obtained. Hence, although it is never necessary to obtain a decree annulling a void marriage, it may be very much in a petitioner's interest to do so. This can be, illustrated by considering the case of a woman who has entered into a bigamous marriage. That "marriage" is void. Any children will, in principle, be illegitimate. Neither of the parties to the "marriage" will have any legal right to succeed to property on the intestacy of the other. Neither of the parties will have any statutory or other rights to be provided with housing by the other partner. Neither will be entitled to bring legal proceedings to compel the other to provide financial support. If one of them becomes dependent on Income Support, the Department of Social Security will have no right to claim reimbursement of the amounts paid out (as it would if the one were a "liable relative" of the other).

Instances of such "marriages" are not uncommon in the Law Reports. For example:

> In *Re Spence (dec'd)* [1990] 2 FLR 278, Addie Elizabeth married Frederick William Love in 1895, and Mr Love survived until 1953. Unfortunately the marriage appears not to have been happy and Mrs Love left her husband. She set up home with Thomas Spence, and had two sons by him. In 1934 she went through a ceremony of marriage with Mr Spence; but since Mr Love was still alive at that time the purported "marriage" to Mr Spence was void. Nourse L.J. said a void "marriage, both as a matter of language and by definition . . . is a nullity. It is only an idle ceremony. It achieves no change in the status of the participants. It achieves nothing of substance." Hence, the sons were illegitimate and (as the law then stood: see para. 11–13 below) not regarded as legally related to one another for succession purposes.

So far, this may seem logical, if harsh. But suppose that Addie Elizabeth's relationship with Thomas Spence had also been unhappy. Since her "marriage" was void, she could have petitioned for a decree of nullity; and the court would have had power to make precisely the same orders for financial relief for her and for the children as if she had been legally married. Bringing proceedings to establish that there is no marriage thus, paradoxically, creates the legal consequences that would flow from dissolving a valid marriage.

THE SIGNIFICANCE OF NULLITY

At one time the law of nullity was important as a technique for **2–04** dealing with the legal consequences of the breakdown of a matrimonial relationship. This was because until 1857 there was no judicial divorce, and nullity was the only way (short of an Act of Parliament) of getting legal release from an unhappy relationship. Moreover, until the coming into force of the Divorce Reform Act 1969 the "guilty" party to a marriage could not divorce the "innocent" partner, so that in some cases a man who was anxious to remarry might petition for nullity if his partner refused to divorce him. Today, however, nullity is of little importance in this context: if a marriage has irretrievably broken down, one party will sooner or later be able to get a divorce. Indeed, in 1990 there were only 430 nullity decrees, compared with 157,344 divorces. But nullity cannot be ignored: it remains of fundamental conceptual importance because it is the law of nullity which effectively determines who may marry whom. A brief account of the modern law therefore follows.

THE MODERN LAW OF NULLITY

Law now statutory

2–05   The law governing nullity—for long derived from the practice of the ecclesiastical courts—was comprehensively reformed by the Nullity of Marriage Act 1971; and the legislation is now consolidated in the Matrimonial Causes Act 1973. The conceptual framework derived from the canon law is still apparent, and the doctrines of the ecclesiastical courts may thus still be relevant in deciding, for example, what is meant by "consummation" of a marriage; but statute now constitutes an exhaustive codification of the law.

The law is discussed under three heads:

(a)   the grounds on which a nullity petition may be presented;
(b)   the bars to the making of nullity decrees;
(c)   the effects of a nullity decree.

I. THE STATUTORY GROUNDS

Void marriages

2–06   The modern law preserves the distinction—resulting from its historical development of the law—between void and voidable marriages. The grounds on which a marriage is void are (MCA 1973, s.11): (i) parties within prohibited degrees; (ii) either party under 16; (iii) non-compliance with formalities; (iv) marriage bigamous; (v) parties not male and female.

Voidable marriages

2–07   The grounds on which a marriage is voidable are (MCA 1973 s.12): (i) incapacity to consummate; (ii) wilful refusal to consummate; (iii) lack of consent; (iv) venereal disease, pregnancy by third party, and mental illness.

A. VOID MARRIAGES

1. Prohibited Degrees

Consanguinity and affinity

In order to understand the law and the policy to which it gives 2–08 effect, we must first clarify the distinction between rules dealing with relationships of consanguinity (that is to say, marriage between blood relations, such as parent and child or brother and sister) and those based on affinity.

Relationship by affinity is a relationship created by marriage. Relatives by affinity are called "affines," and consist of the spouse (or former spouse) of one's own relatives, and relatives of one's spouse (or former spouse). The term thus extends to in-laws and to step-relations.

The prohibitions

English law prohibits marriage with a parent, child, grandparent, 2–09 brother or sister, uncle or aunt, nephew or niece. (Unlike some other Western systems of law it has no restriction on marriage between cousins.)

There are sound genetic reasons for forbidding marriage between close blood relations, since there is a higher chance of mutant genes being present in common in two persons with a close common ancestor. But even this issue is not altogether clear-cut because the characteristics which appear in the offspring of a union between blood relatives may be either favourable or unfavourable. This is, after all, the secret of breeding racehorses.

Biological objections of this kind cannot apply to prohibitions on marriage between affines. Historically these prohibitions originate in the traditional doctrine of the church whereby marriage makes man and woman one flesh. Thus, if it is wrong to marry my sister it must be equally wrong to marry my wife's sister. Since my sister is within the prohibited degrees of consanguinity, my sister-in-law (that is to say, my wife's sister) was for the church within the (correspondingly prohibited) degrees of affinity.

More recently, justification for prohibiting marriages between affines has been based on broader considerations of social policy, and in particular on the argument that disturbing sexual relationships should be excluded from the home circle. Yet many of these considerations are difficult to apply consistently without causing hardship. Should a man be allowed to marry his step-daughter, for example? At first glance, the answer might seem very clear: surely the law should protect girls from the danger of sexual exploitation by those in authority over them, and not allow a man to look on a young girl as a potential bride when his true role has been that of a father?

But suppose that the facts are that a man married a widow whose daughter was an adult living away from home; and suppose that he first met (and fell in love with) the daughter only after her mother's death? Is there any justification for not allowing them to marry?

Over the years, the law has been progressively relaxed. The increase in divorce and remarriage since the end of World War II much increased the risk that a couple who have never in fact been members of the same family unit would be debarred from marriage by reason of a relationship through marriage; and this was one of the factors which led to the liberalization of law by the Marriage (Prohibited Degrees of Relationship) Act 1986.

The 1986 Reforms

2–10   The basic principle of the 1986 legislation is that marriage with relatives by affinity is now *permitted*; but in two cases marriage to an affine is permitted only subject to conditions. The rules can best be understood by examples.

(i) *Marriage to a step-child.* Marriage to a step-child is only permitted if two conditions are satisfied. First, at the time of the marriage both parties must be 21 or over. Secondly, the step-child must not have been a child of the step-parent's family at any time whilst the step-child was under 18. (For present purposes it is sufficient to say that a child of the family is somebody who has been treated as a child of a particular marriage: see further para. 14–03 below.) The policy of the law is clearly that marriage should not be permitted where one of the parties has effectively acted as the other's father or mother during the step-child's childhood.

(ii) *Marriage to a son or daughter-in-law.* A man may only marry his daughter-in-law (or a woman her son-in-law) if both parties are 21 or over; and the child's spouse (through whom the "in-law" relationship arises) and that spouse's mother (or father) are dead.

The drafting of the legislation is complex, and the above summary is incomplete. Moreover, although the underlying policy is clear enough, the legislation does not always give effect to it. Thus, the policy is clearly that a man may not, for example, marry his step-daughter if he has had a parental relationship with her, but that he should be permitted to do so in other cases; and that a man should not be allowed to marry his daughter-in-law if he has been responsible for breaking up her marriage to his son. But the Act would, it seems, permit a marriage between a man and his daughter-in-law even if the man's most recent marriage (to a woman who was not the son's mother) was ended by a divorce founded on his adultery with the daughter-in-law the discovery of which so overwhelmed the son that he committed suicide.

Adoption

There are two rules which have a special bearing in cases where a 2–11
child has been adopted—*i.e.* has become legally the child of adoptive
parents, and ceased to be the child of the original birth parents. First
of all, the child remains within the same prohibited degrees in
relation to his natural parents and other relatives as if he had not
been adopted. Hence, a marriage between a couple who are in fact
brother and sister will be void even though neither of them knows
about the relationship. (There are now special provisions in the
legislation entitling a person to have access to the recorded facts
about the birth, so that the risk that a marriage will be celebrated in
ignorance of the biological relationship has been to some extent
reduced: see Adoption Act 1976, s.51, para. 11–13 below.)

The second rule relevant to cases where a child has been adopted is
that an adoptive parent and the adopted child are deemed to be
within the prohibited degrees, and they continue to be so
notwithstanding that the child is subsequently adopted by someone
else. This clearly reflects the policy that the law should discourage
sexual relationships within the home circle.

There are no other express prohibitions arising by reason of
adoption.

Prohibited degrees and the crime of incest

Since 1908 it has been a criminal offence for a man knowingly to 2–12
have sexual intercourse with his daughter or certain other relations.
However the class of relations is more narrowly defined than for the
purpose of the prohibited degrees of marriage: a man may, without
infringing the criminal law, have intercourse with his aunt or niece,
for example, notwithstanding the fact that they are within the
prohibited degrees.

2. Minimum Age

No marriage under 16

A marriage is void if either party is under 16. This rule (which 2–13
applies whether or not either knew the facts) should be distinguished
from the rule which requires parental consent where a person
intending to marry is under 18. If a 17-year-old girl gets married
without her parents' consent, the marriage will be perfectly valid,
because failure to comply with the parental consent rule has no effect
on the validity of the marriage. But in contrast a marriage between a
boy of 17 and a girl who everyone thinks to be 16 is void if it is
subsequently established that she was in fact one day short of her
sixteenth birthday—and it makes no difference that both sets of
parents consented to the marriage. In fact, the average age of
marriage in this country has moved upwards over the years: the
median age of brides is now over 25, and (in 1987) only 13 per cent.
of all brides married as teenagers—16 years earlier the corresponding

proportion had been 27 per cent. Presumably, very few people would want to return to the pre-1929 position (when marriages of 12-year-old girls were permitted). But it is not quite so plain that an under-age marriage should be void (as distinct from voidable). If a couple marry, genuinely but mistakenly believing that they are both of marriageable age, it is harsh to hold the marriage void—perhaps many years later. Moreover if a couple have lived together for many years believing their marriage to be valid, it would seem to be quite wrong to let a third party challenge it—perhaps to get a financial benefit under the succession laws. These criticisms may have particular force in cases where the wife was born outside this country, there is no formal record of her birth, and no one realised that she had in fact been under 16 at the time of the marriage.

3. Defective Formalities

2–14   In general only deliberate disregard of the marriage formalities will invalidate a marriage—the Marriage Act 1949 provides that if the parties "knowingly and wilfully" disregard certain requirements the marriage shall be void. In contrast the Act stipulates that evidence of certain irregularities (for example, failure to obtain parental consent) is not to be given in proceedings touching the validity of the marriage. Hence, such defects cannot invalidate the marriage. But the Act is silent as to the consequences of certain irregularities—for example, the requirement that the marriage be celebrated with open doors, and that certain prescribed words be used. It seems probable that such irregularities would not affect the validity of the marriage.

Although the formal requirements for the preliminaries to and solemnisation of marriage are complex, there is no evidence that the complexity results in defects which affect the validity of the marriage.

4. Bigamy

2–15   A purported marriage is void if it is proved that at the time of the ceremony either party was already lawfully married to a third party ("X"). The fact that the parties on reasonable grounds believe X to be dead makes no difference: if it is subsequently established that X was in fact alive at the time of the ceremony the "marriage" will be void. In practice, difficulties quite often arise because there is no evidence as to whether X was alive at the date of the ceremony or not; but these cases can often be resolved by applying a presumption that a person is dead if there is no evidence that he was alive throughout a continuous period of seven years: see *Principles of Family Law*, (5th ed. 1990), p. 78.

The question whether a marriage is void for bigamy is answered once and for all by reference to the facts as they existed at the date of the ceremony which is under consideration. A marriage which was void because at that time one of the parties was married remains void even if the lawful spouse dies the day after the bigamous ceremony.

5. Parties of Same Sex

General principle
The Act provides (s.11(c)) that a marriage is void if the parties are not respectively male and female. In *Talbot* v. *Talbot* (1967) 111 SJ 213 a widow went through a marriage ceremony with a "bachelor" who was (it subsequently transpired) a woman; and (unsurprisingly) the "marriage" was held void. But the interpretation of this apparently simple provision can give rise to difficulties. 2–16

Transsexuals
Transsexuals are people who have the physical attributes of one sex (for example, male genitalia) but nevertheless feel themselves to be members of the other. Medical science can now provide help for this problem, and treatment may be available at specialist clinics under the National Health Service. The treatment may take the form of sex reassignment therapy, usually involving hormone treatment, the surgical removal of the male genitalia, and the construction of an artificial vagina; and a person who has successfully undergone such treatment will be treated as a woman for many official purposes—national insurance records will be amended, and a passport will be issued in a female name, for example. But will a marriage by such a person to a man be valid? 2–17

The orthodox view is that, for the purposes of the marriage laws a person's sex is fixed for all time at birth; and that the only relevant tests of sexual identity are biological. In this view a person born with male genitalia and a male chromosomal structure is a "man" for the purpose of the marriage laws, notwithstanding the fact that the patient had, after the reassignment therapy, lived and been accepted as a woman, possessed most of the external attributes of a woman and had in most ways become philosophically, psychologically and socially a woman. On this view, therefore, a person classified as a male at birth in accordance with the principles set out above will not be able to marry as a woman—the successful sex reassignment therapy being irrelevant. The leading case on the subject is *Corbett* v. *Corbett* [1971] P 83:

> April Ashley had undergone a sex change operation, lived as a woman, and indeed worked successfully as a female model; she had also been recognised as a woman for national insurance and passport purposes. It was held, applying the principles stated above, that she remained a man and that her marriage to the petitioner was accordingly void.

The decision in the April Ashley case was based on the common law (under which the question was whether the parties were properly 2–18

15

described as a "man" and a "woman"). The Matrimonial Causes Act, however, uses the words "male" and "female"; and it may be possible to argue that these terms refer to a person's gender (that is to say, the sex to which he or she psychically belongs); and that accordingly the question whether a person is "male" or "female" is not to be resolved solely by reference to tests of biological sexuality. However, such arguments have not carried much weight with the courts. In *R* v. *Tan and Greaves* [1983] QB 1053 the Court of Appeal, accepting the reasoning in the *Corbett* case, concluded that a transsexual who had undergone sex reassignment therapy was a "man" for the purpose of offences penalising living on the earnings of prostitution; and there is at least one reported case in which a degree of nullity has been granted under the 1973 Act in respect of a "marriage" between persons one of whom had undergone sex reassignment therapy: see [1990] Fam Law 455.

Transsexuals feel that English law prevents their forming any legally recognised marital relationship: they are treated as men for the purpose of determining whether a union with a man can constitute a valid marriage; and the treatment which they have undergone may make it legally impossible for them to contract a marriage with a woman, because they will be unable to consummate such a marriage: see para. 2–22 below. Perhaps not surprisingly, therefore, the provisions of the European Convention on Human Rights—and specifically Article 12 which protects the right to marry, and Article 8, which protects the right to respect for private life—have been invoked: see *Rees* v. *United Kingdom* [1987] 2 FLR 111; *Cossey* v. *United Kingdom* [1991] 2 FLR 492. Both applications failed: the European Court on Human Rights accepts that the right to marry protected by the Convention is a traditional marriage between persons of opposite biological sex. The Court has also rejected complaints that the Registrar General's refusal to alter the birth register to reflect the applicant's change of sexual identity constituted a breach of the right guaranteed by Article 8 to respect for private life. But it is noteworthy that the evidence before the court indicated a general move towards greater legal recognition of gender reassignment, and that the court's judgment stressed the need for States which adhered to the Convention to keep their law under review.

Nullity decrees for homosexual "marriages"?

2–19   The Matrimonial Causes Act states that a "marriage" is void if the parties are not respectively male and female. It may, therefore, be the case that a decree would only be granted if there were at least something which plausibly looked like a "marriage" in the traditional heterosexual sense—for example where there is some reasonable doubt as to the sex of the parties. The matter is important since, if the court were to grant a decree of nullity in respect of a union between a couple who were undoubtedly of the same sex the court would also have power to make orders for financial provision and property adjustment: see para. 2–49 below.

6. Polygamous Marriages

20 MCA 1973, s.11(d) provides that an actually or potentially polyga- **2–20**
mous marriage entered into after July 31, 1971 is void if either party
to the marriage was at the time domiciled in England and Wales. The
interpretation of this provision is complex and outside the scope of
this book.

B. VOIDABLE MARRIAGES

1. Incapacity to Consummate

21 MCA 1973, s.13(1) provides that a marriage shall be voidable if it has **2–21**
not been consummated owing to the incapacity of either party to
consummate it. This is a statutory codification of a basic principle of
the canon law: although marriage was formed simply by consent, it
was an implied term of the contract that the parties had the capacity
to consummate it; and physical capacity was thus as much a basic
requirement of marriage as the intellectual capacity to consent. The
law is still influenced by its origins in the canon law.

Salient features of the law
22   The main principles of the law can be summarised: **2–22**

(i) *What is "consummation"?* Consummation means sexual intercourse which is "ordinary and complete": there must be both erection
and penetration for a reasonable length of time. It is not necessary for
either party to have an orgasm; nor are sterility or barrenness
relevant.

(ii) *May be psychological.* Although some cases of incapacity are
based on physical abnormality, many derive from psychological
causes. This question of causation is irrelevant in deciding the issue of
capacity. It follows from this that it is immaterial that the impotence is
only *quoad hunc* or *hanc*—*i.e.* that the respondent is capable of having
intercourse with other partners. It also follows that a spouse who
suffers from invincible repugnance to the act of intercourse with the
other will, for this purpose, be regarded as incapable of consummat-
ing the marriage. But it would seem that some element of psychiatric
or sexual aversion is necessary and that a rational decision not to
permit intercourse is insufficient:

In *Singh* v. *Singh* [1971] P 226, the petitioner was a 17-year-old Sikh girl
who reluctantly went through a marriage ceremony arranged by her

17

parents with a man that she had never previously met. Karminski L.J. said that she "never submitted to the physical embraces of the husband, because ... it does not appear that she saw him again." Since she did not want to be married to him it was "understandable that she did not want to have sexual intercourse with him" but (the judge said) this was "a very long way from an invincible repugnance."

(iii) *Pre-marital intercourse irrelevant.* The fact the parties have had normal intercourse prior to the marriage ceremony is irrelevant to the issue of whether the marriage has been consummated.

(iv) The incapacity must be *permanent and incurable.* It will be deemed to be incurable if any remedial operation is dangerous, or if the respondent refuses to undergo an operation.

(v) *Evidence required.* It is for the petitioner to prove that the incapacity exists. The court has power to order a medical examination, and may draw adverse inferences against a party who refuses to be examined.

(vi) *Either party can petition.* Before the enactment of the Nullity of Marriage Act 1971 a spouse who relied on his or her own incapacity would fail if, at the time of the marriage, the petitioner knew of the incapacity, or if it would in all the circumstances have been unjust to allow the petition to succeed. But there is nothing in the Act to suggest that this particular rule survives; and it seems that a petitioner who knows of his or her incapacity will be entitled to a decree unless the respondent can establish the modern statutory bar of approbation as laid down in the Matrimonial Causes Act 1973: see para. 2–42 below.

(vii) *Must have existed at time of marriage?* It was a basic requirement of the canon law that the incapacity exist at the date of the marriage. This rule reflected the vast theoretical difference between recognising that the marriage was a nullity in cases where incapacity could be said to prevent a marriage coming into existence at all and dissolving a valid marriage by a divorce decree because of some supervening cause.

Has this been changed by the modern legislation, which does not in terms require that the incapacity should have existed "at the time of the celebration of the marriage?" Does this mean—for example—that a wife whose husband is made impotent as a result of a car accident on the way from the church to the honeymoon could now petition successfully for nullity? It seems clear that the statutory codification of the law was not intended to effect any change; and the courts might well interpret the provision in the light of the classical distinction between nullity and divorce, and thus refuse a decree in such a case.

2. Wilful Refusal to Consummate

Anomalous but useful. MCA 1973, s.12(b) provides that a marriage is voidable if it has not been consummated owing to the wilful refusal of the respondent to consummate it. Conceptually, wilful refusal (which is something which occurs after marriage) should not be a ground for nullity; and it has only been recognized as such by English law since 1937. However, in practice wilful refusal is found very useful: 490 out of the 570 petitions seeking annulment of a voidable marriage recorded in 1988 were founded on wilful refusal, and there is some indication (see the comments on *A* v. *J* *(Nullity Proceedings)* [1989] 1 FLR 110, para. 2–25 below) that the courts may be influenced in adopting a realistic interpretation of the law by the fact that divorce will now in almost every case be available after a period of time. 2–23

The main features of the law are:

(i) *Must be refusal*
A decree will only be granted if an examination of the whole history of the marriage reveals "a settled and definite decision" on the part of the respondent, "come to without just excuse." A husband (it has been held) must use appropriate tact, persuasion and encouragement and his wife will not be guilty of wilful refusal if he has failed to do so. Moreover: 2–24

> In *Potter* v. *Potter* (1975) 5 Fam Law 161, CA a wife was refused a decree because the husband's failure to consummate resulted from a natural and not deliberate "loss of ardour" after a prolonged history of sexual difficulties.

(ii) *Without excuse*
If the respondent can show a "just excuse" for his refusal to consummate he is not guilty of wilful refusal: 2–25

> In *Ford* v. *Ford* [1987] Fam Law 232 a marriage had taken place whilst H was serving a sentence of five years' imprisonment. H and W were left alone on visits for periods of up to two hours and W had heard from other visitors that it was not unusual in such circumstances for intercourse to take place. The judge held that H's refusal to have intercourse in prison (in breach of the Prison Rules) would not by itself have justified a finding that he had wilfully refused to consummate the marriage; but a degree was granted on the basis of evidence of other incidents.

The question of whether there is a just excuse for refusal to consummate a marriage has become of some importance since in the

Sikh and some other ethnic minority community traditions it is the practice for the parties to go through a civil marriage ceremony, and thereafter for a religious ceremony to take place. By Sikh religion and practice, the religious ceremony is essential to the recognition of the marriage; and it has been held that a husband's failure to organise the religious ceremony is not merely a just excuse for the wife's refusing to consummate the marriage, but itself amounts to a wilful refusal on his part to consummate. This can be illustrated by reference to the case of *Kaur* v. *Singh* [1972] 1 WLR 105:

> A marriage was arranged between two Sikhs. A civil ceremony took place, but the husband refused to make arrangements for the religious ceremony, notwithstanding the fact that it was his duty to do so. It was held that the wife was entitled to a decree on the grounds of his wilful refusal to consummate the marriage.

The more recent case of *A* v. *J* *(Nullity Proceedings)* [1989] 1 FLR 110 appears to go even further:

> A marriage was arranged between two highly educated persons of Indian origin and a civil marriage took place at a Register Office. Shortly after the civil marriage the husband flew to the United States where he held a post as a Research Fellow. During the few days when the couple were together in England there was (as the judge put it) "very little one-to-one association between them during a period when one might have expected them to be experiencing their first fine careless rapture"; and during the husband's time in the United States the exchanges between the couple were few and far between. Finally the wife said that she thought it would be better to call off the religious ceremony which had been fixed for some four months after the civil ceremony. It was held that the husband was entitled to a decree of nullity on the ground of the wife's wilful refusal to consummate the marriage. Her failure to accept the husband's apologies for his cruel behaviour, her refusal to consider a reconciliation, and her adamant insistence on an indefinite postponement of the religious ceremony were sufficient. The judge commented:

> "It is unfortunate that these (Nullity Proceedings) had to be fought out, for the simple fact is that the couple have never lived together, not even for a week. They have lived apart since their civil wedding which was over 2 years ago. The marriage had irretrievably broken down, indeed has never started up ... " (at p. 111)

(iii) *What is consummation?*

2–26   The House of Lords has said that this word must be interpreted as understood in common parlance, and in the light of social circumstances known to exist when the legislation was passed.

> In *Baxter* v. *Baxter* [1948] AC 274, HL, it was held that a wife's refusal to allow intercourse unless her husband used a condom was not a refusal on her part to consummate the marriage.

There are conflicting decisions as to whether a marriage is consummated by *coitus interruptus*; but the issue is probably now irrelevant since an insistence by one party in this practice would almost certainly found a divorce petition based on "behaviour": MCA 1973, s.1(2)(b); para. 4–16 below.

3. Lack of Consent: Duress, Mistake, Insanity, etc.

No marriage without consent
For the Canon Law, marriage was created by the consent of the   2–27
parties, and without true consent there could be no marriage. As a result of a somewhat controversial provision in the Nullity of Marriage Act 1971, a marriage celebrated after July 31, 1971 is no longer void, but is voidable if either party did not validly consent to it, whether in consequence of duress, mistake, unsoundness of mind or otherwise: MCA 1973, s.12(c).

The mental element in marriage—the dilemma
Cases of lack of consent usually involve situations in which there   2–28
has in fact been an *expression* of consent. For example, a man may admit that he spoke the words of consent but say that he only did so because his bride's father was standing behind him with a shotgun. In such cases it can be argued that the apparent consent is not real, and that there should in principle be no marriage; but it would obviously give rise to great uncertainty if an apparently valid marriage could be avoided by subsequently claiming the existence of a state of mind or belief which was not evident at the time of the ceremony.

The solution
English law seeks to resolve this juristic dilemma by, on the one   2–29
hand, refusing to allow private reservations or motives to vitiate an ostensibly valid marriage, whilst, on the other hand, accepting that there may be cases in which there has been no consent at all. The law is somewhat complex; and the cases can best be considered under the three heads specifically referred to in the legislation: (a) insanity; (b) duress and fear; (c) mistake.

(a) *Insanity*
Marriage (according to a 19th century judge) is a very simple   2–30
contract, which it does not require a high degree of intelligence to understand: Sir James Hannen P in *Durham* v. *Durham* (1885) 10 PD 80, 81. Mental illness or deficiency will only affect the validity of consent if either spouse was, at the time of the ceremony incapable of understanding the nature of marriage and the duties and responsibilities it creates. Such incapacity is hard to establish; and it is difficult to believe that petitions will now be brought on this ground. If either party to the marriage wants to terminate it, he will usually be

able to rely on the alternative "mental illness" ground introduced by legislation precisely because it was so difficult to establish lack of consent: see para. 2–38 below. Since the marriage would in any event now only be voidable (rather than void) relatives whose succession rights had been prejudiced would no longer be able to claim, after the death of one of the parties, that the marriage had been invalid.

(b) Duress and fear

2–31　　The question is whether there has been a real consent. Hence (it has been said) "where a formal consent is brought about by force, menace or duress—a yielding of the lips, not of the mind—it is of no legal effect." The main conditions seem to be as follows:

2–32　　　　**(i) Must be overriding fear.** This principle is most clearly illustrated by an American "shotgun" marriage case, the marriage was void because (said the judge) "if there had not been a wedding, there would have been a funeral" (*Lee* v. *Lee* (1928) 3 SW 2d 672). In contrast if the marriage were deliberately contracted out of a sense of obligation to family or religious tradition it could not be annulled on this ground:

> In *Singh* v. *Singh* [1971] P 226, the bride had never seen her husband before the marriage, and only went through the ceremony out of a "proper respect" for her parents and Sikh traditions; but the court refused to annul the marriage because there was no evidence of fear.

2–33　　　　**(ii) Test subjective.** The case law used to support the view that only a threat of immediate danger to life, limb or liberty could suffice to justify the granting of a decree of nullity on this ground. But the reality is that a weak-minded person's will may be overcome by threats which would have had no impact on a stronger character. Accordingly, the view adopted by the Court of Appeal in *Hirani* v. *Hirani* (1982) 4 FLR 232 that the test is simply whether the threats or pressure are such as to destroy the reality of the consent and to overbear the will of the individual is much to be welcomed.

　　In the Irish decision of *W(C)* v. *W* [1989] IR 696:

> A pregnant woman was pressurised by her parents to get married. She was told by her employer that she would lose her job if she remained unmarried. She was granted a decree of nullity.

2–34　　　　**(iii) Fear must arise from external circumstances, but not necessarily from acts of the other party.** Thus:

> In *Szechter* v. *Szechter* [1971] P 286 threats to life and liberty arising from the policies of a totalitarian regime were held to suffice: the parties

married so that they would be allowed to leave the country and thus avoid imprisonment.

This seems a somewhat doubtful decision, however, since, although the parties were no doubt frightened, their decision to marry was a conscious and a rational one. Indeed, they wanted to be married so that they could enjoy the legal consequences of matrimony.

(iv) Does it make any difference if the threats are justly 2–35 **imposed?** Suppose that a man is told he will be prosecuted for unlawful sexual intercourse unless he marries the girl with whom he is alleged to have had intercourse (as in *Buckland* v. *Buckland* [1968] P 296). On one view such a petition will fail if the petitioner is guilty; a decree may be obtained only if the accusation is false, or if the petitioner was threatened with a more severe penalty than the courts impose (as in an American case where the man was told that having sexual intercourse with a minor was "a hanging matter"). But it is submitted that this view of the law is illogical and contrary to principle. The justice of the threat has nothing to do with the subjective question of consent.

(c) *Mistake and fraud*

Generally neither mistake nor fraud avoids a marriage. The maxim 2–36 "caveat emptor" ("let the buyer beware") applies, it has been said, just as much to marriage as it does to other contracts. Even fraud is not a vitiating factor if it induces consent, but only if it procures the appearance without the reality of consent. Hence, a marriage into which a woman tricked a man by concealing the fact that she was pregnant by a third party was valid at common law. (Since 1937 it has been possible, subject to certain conditions, to have a marriage annulled on the ground that the respondent was pregnant by a third party: see para. 2–38 below.)

Mistake is only relevant if it vitiates consent. The cases fall into three groups:

(i) Mistake as to the person as distinct from his attributes. If I 2–37 marry A under the belief that she is B this is sufficient to invalidate the marriage; but if I marry A erroneously believing her to be a rich heiress the marriage will be unimpeachable.

(ii) Mistake as to the nature of the ceremony. False beliefs that the petitioner was appearing in a police court, or that the ceremony was a betrothal or religious conversion ceremony (*Mehta* v. *Mehta* [1945] 2 All ER 690) have been held sufficient to invalidate the marriage. The fact that one of the parties was so drunk (or under the influence of drugs) that he did not know what he was doing at the time is also sufficient: *Sullivan* v. *Sullivan* (1812) 2 Hag Con 238, 246.

(iii) But mistake about legal consequences of marriage insufficient.- Thus:

In *Way* v. *Way* [1950] P 71 a petition failed where H wrongly assumed that his Russian wife would be allowed to leave the Soviet Union and live with him.

Again:

In *Messina* v. *Smith* [1971] P 322 W went through a marriage ceremony, knowing that it was such a ceremony, and that the purpose of it was to enable her to obtain British nationality and a British passport and thereby protect herself against the risk of deportation for offences incidental to her carrying on her trade of prostitution. A petition to annul the marriage failed. The parties did intend to acquire the status of married persons, and it was immaterial that one or both of them may have been mistaken about, or unaware of, some of the incidents of that status.

4. Venereal Disease, Pregnancy by Another and Mental Illness

2–38 The remaining grounds on which a marriage may be voidable were primarily intended to deal with problems caused by the absence of any matrimonial relief for fraudulent or wilful concealment of material facts—for instance, a man who discovered that his wife was carrying another man's child had no ground of matrimonial relief: deceit was not a ground for annulment, and the pregnancy did not establish that she had, since the marriage, committed adultery. New grounds were accordingly created in 1937. They are now:

(i) that at the time of the marriage the respondent was suffering from *venereal disease* in a communicable form. (It is unclear whether AIDS is a venereal disease for this purpose: it was felt necessary to amend the National Health Service (Venereal Disease) Regulations 1968 No. 1624 to include all sexually transmitted diseases, and not merely those commonly known as Venereal Disease: see *X* v. *Y and others* [1988] 2 All ER 648); or

(ii) that at the time of the marriage the respondent was *pregnant* by some person other than the petitioner; or

(iii) that at the time of the marriage either party, though capable of giving a valid consent, was suffering (whether continuously or intermittently) from *mental disorder* within the meaning of the Mental Health Act 1983, of such a kind or to such an extent as to be unfitted for marriage. (This provision is intended to cover the case where, although the afflicted party is capable of giving a valid consent to the marriage, the mental disorder makes him or her incapable of carrying on a normal married life. A petitioner may rely on his or her own mental disorder for the purpose of a petition on this ground.

II. BARS

If one of the grounds set out above is established, the petitioner will   2–39
usually be entitled to a decree. However, if the marriage is voidable, the petition may still fail if one of three bars contained in MCA 1973 s.13 is established. (There are now no bars to the granting of a decree where the marriage is void.) The three bars are:

(1) Time
In the case of proceedings on the ground of (a) lack of consent, (b)   2–40
venereal disease, or (c) pregnancy by a third party it is an absolute bar that proceedings were not instituted within three years of the marriage. (The court may however allow a petitioner who has, during the three year period, suffered from mental disorder to start proceedings after that period if it is in all the circumstances just to do so.)

(2) Knowledge of defect
A petition founded on (a) venereal disease or (b) pregnancy by a   2–41
third party will fail unless the petitioner can satisfy the court that, at the time of the marriage, the petitioner was ignorant of the facts alleged. It is not sufficient that the husband knew that the wife was pregnant, he must also have known that she was pregnant by another man.

(3) "Approbation"
MCA 1973, s.13(1) provides that the court shall not grant a decree   2–42
of nullity on the ground that a marriage is voidable if the respondent satisfies the court:

> "(a) that the petitioner, with knowledge that it was open to him to have the marriage avoided, so conducted himself in relation to the respondent as to lead the respondent reasonably to believe that he would not seek to do so; and

> (b) that it would be unjust to the respondent to grant the decree."

This bar replaces the complex and uncertain bar of approbation which was inherited from the ecclesiastical courts. Three separate matters must be proved:

(i) *conduct* by the petitioner in relation to the respondent which resulted in the respondent reasonably believing that the petitioner would not seek to have the marriage annulled;

(ii) *knowledge* by the petitioner, at the time of the conduct relied on, that the marriage could be annulled; and

(iii) *injustice* to the respondent if a decree were to be granted.

The case of companionship marriages

2–43   Suppose that an elderly widower marries a spinster on the understanding that they are not to have sexual relations—that their marriage is to be "for companionship only." After living with her for some years, the husband changes his mind and seeks to have sexual relations. The wife (who had at the husband's request given up a job carrying pension rights on the marriage) refuses. Will she be able successfully to defend a nullity petition alleging wilful refusal? It would seem that if the wife could prove that the husband knew that nullity was available in cases of non-consummation she might do so, since in this case the loss of pension rights could probably constitute injustice to her: *cf. Scott* v. *Scott* [1959] 1 All ER 531; and (on pension rights) para. 4–62 below.

Not a public interest bar

2–44   The law is now only concerned with the conduct of the parties towards the other, and with injustice to the respondent. It is not concerned with representations which have been made to third parties, or with considerations of public policy:

> In *D* v. *D (Nullity: Statutory Bar)* [1979] Fam 70 it was held that the fact that a couple adopted a child (and thus represented to the court considering the adoption application that they were husband and wife) did not debar one of them from subsequently petitioning on the ground of wilful refusal. The fact that it might be thought contrary to public policy to allow either subsequently to assert that the marriage was a nullity was no longer relevant.

III. EFFECTS OF A DECREE

Historical evolution

2–45   At one time a *void* marriage had no legal consequences. Hence, for example, any children born to the parties would necessarily be illegitimate; neither party to the relationship would be entitled to acquire the other's British citizenship or to inherit on the other's intestacy; and a man could not be required to maintain a woman who had been living with him in the belief that they were married. In the eyes of the law they were not, and never had been, more than a man and mistress.

The same consequences followed even if the marriage was only *voidable*. This was because, although the marriage was valid until annulled, the decree, when made operated retrospectively: the marriage *became* void *ab initio*, *i.e.* from the outset.

Modern law
Over the years the law has been reformed, and the position is now 2–46 radically different:

(a) *Voidable marriages—decrees not retroactive*
Under the law as it stood before 1971 the parties to a voidable 2–47 marriage were validly married until annulment, but once a decree absolute had been pronounced they were deemed never to have been married.

> Thus in *Re Rodwell* [1970] Ch 726 the deceased's daughter could only qualify as a "dependant" within the meaning of the Inheritance (Family Provision) Act 1938 if she had "not been married." The daughter's voidable marriage had in fact been annulled; and Pennycuick J. held that because of the retrospective effect of the decree she qualified as a person who had not been married.

This rule was abolished in 1971 on the basis that it was anomalous, inconvenient and uncertain; and a voidable marriage which is annulled is now treated as if it had existed up to the date of the decree. It has, however, become apparent that the new rule may have unfortunate consequences:

> In *Ward* v. *Secretary of State for Social Services* [1990] 1 FLR 119 the widow of an army officer went through a ceremony of marriage. The marriage turned out to be a disaster. The husband—as the petitioner discovered for the first time after the ceremony—was a manic depressive and behaved in an aggressive way towards her. Within less than a week, the marriage (which had never been consummated) had effectively come to an end. In due course a decree of nullity was granted on the ground that the marriage had not been consummated. It was held that the petitioner had ceased to be the army officer's widow, and was thus no longer entitled to a widow's pension.

(b) *Legitimacy of children*
Children of *voidable* marriages are legitimate because the marriage is 2–48 treated as valid. Even the child of a *void* marriage will be "treated as" the legitimate child of his parents provided that at the time of the act of intercourse resulting in his birth (or at the time of the celebration of the marriage if later) both or either of the parties reasonably believed that the marriage was valid. It is immaterial whether the belief that the marriage was valid was due to a mistake of law: see Legitimacy Act 1976, s.1(3) as amended by the Family Law Reform Act 1987, s.28.

However, a child will only be treated as legitimate under these provisions if the birth occurred *after* the void marriage: *Re Spence (dec'd)* [1990] 2 FLR 278.

(c) *Financial provision for parties*

2–49　　If the marriage is *voidable*, the parties financial rights are the same before annulment as if the parties had been validly married; and the court has the same financial powers on granting a decree of nullity as it has on divorce: see para. 9–26 below.

If the marriage is *void* the parties are not married; and they have no legal rights as husband and wife. But if a decree of nullity is obtained, the court will have exactly the same powers to order one party to make financial provision for the other as it would have if a valid marriage had been dissolved. Thus, in *Cossey* v. *The United Kingdom* [1991] 2 FLR 492, 496, a transsexual obtained a decree of nullity precisely because she had been advised that this was the only means open to her of obtaining financial relief. Again a "wife" or "husband" who has obtained such a decree can apply to the court for reasonable provision out of the other's estate after the death: see para. 7–43 below.

It is the decree which creates these rights to apply to the court; and this could cause hardship to a woman who, for example, only discovered that her "marriage" was void for bigamy after her husband's death. Such a woman had no right to succeed as her "husband's" widow on his intestacy; and it would be too late for her to obtain a decree. To deal with this problem a person who in good faith entered into a void marriage with a person now deceased has been given a right to apply to the court for reasonable provision out of the deceased's estate, exactly as if the applicant were the deceased's widow or widower, or had obtained a decree of nullity carrying with it the right to be considered for financial provision: Inheritance (Provision for Family and Dependants) Act 1975, s.25(4); see further para. 7–43 below.

CONCLUSION—DO WE NEED THE LAW OF NULLITY?

2–50　　The law of nullity has lost much of its practical importance because many of the legal consequences of marriages have now been attached even to a void marriage; while virtually all marriages can sooner or later be dissolved by divorce if either party wishes it. The law has been totally transformed since the days before the Divorce Reform Act 1969 when a divorce could be obtained only if one party could prove that the other had committed a matrimonial offence, and nullity was the only alternative legal way of escape. As Anthony Lincoln J. put it in *A* v. *J (Nullity Proceedings)* [1989] FLR 110, 111:

"Nullity proceedings are nowadays rare, though not wholly extinct. It is unfortunate that these had to be fought out ... there would have been no difficulty in pronouncing mutual decrees nisi, dissolving the marriage, if the necessary consent [to a divorce] had been forthcoming."

In view of the inevitable unpleasantness of nullity proceedings (which may involve medical examinations and will normally involve a full hearing) it is sometimes suggested that the concept of the voidable marriage might be abolished; instead the parties should be left to obtain a divorce based on the breakdown of their marriage. This has been done in Australia; but the Law Commission (for reasons which some have found unconvincing) rejected such a solution for this country.

SUGGESTIONS FOR FURTHER READING

Hoggett and Pearl, pp. 18–30.
Law Commission Report No. 33, *Nullity of Marriage* (1970).
No Just Cause, The Law of Affinity in England and Wales: Some Suggestions for Change (Church Information Office Publishing, 1984).
L. Mair, *Marriage* (1971).
S. Wolfram, *In-Laws and Out-Laws: Kinship and Marriage in England* (1985).
K. O'Donovan, "Transsexual Troubles. The Discrepancy between Legal and Social Categories" in S. Edwards, *Sex, Gender and the Law* (1985).
J. Taitz, "A Transsexual's Nightmare: The Definition of Sexual Identity in English Law [1988] 1 JLF 139.
C. Cossey, *My Story* (1991).

Chapter 3

THE MODERN LAW OF DIVORCE—INTRODUCTION

NATURE OF DIVORCE

3–01 Marriage, as we have seen, for the lawyer simply creates a legal status from which certain legally enforceable rights and duties arise. Divorce, from the same perspective, simply terminates that legal status: thereafter, neither party has the legal rights or owes the legal duties of a spouse. Divorce brings to an end a legal relationship, but it has no direct bearing on personal relationships.

This distinction between the lawyer's and the lay person's perspective can best be understood by considering the implications of an example. Suppose that a couple have cohabited for only a few days after marriage and that thereafter they have for many years, lived separate and apart, consumed with mutual hatred and bitterness. So far as the law is concerned they remain a married couple entitled to the rights flowing from the legal relationship of man and wife. (It should be noted that the law has no procedure whereby husband and wife can be compelled to live together, much less to provide the mutual society, help and comfort for which the institution of marriage was traditionally ordained.) Conversely, divorce does not necessarily bring the parties' personal relationships to an end. Indeed the fact that there will often be children to be cared for is one of the strongest arguments used in favour of a divorce procedure which will minimise the risk of damaging the ability of the spouses to continue to act as parents.

Historical evolution of the law

3–02 The modern law of divorce cannot be understood without some knowledge of its historical development.

Until the Reformation, English law followed the canon law of the Catholic Church in not permitting divorce (in the sense in which that word is used today). But by the 18th Century a procedure for divorce by private Act of Parliament had been developed. In 1857 the Matrimonial Causes Act 1857 created the Court for Divorce and Matrimonial Causes, and gave it power to dissolve marriages if the petitioner could prove adultery, that he was free of any matrimonial guilt, and that there was no connivance or collusion between the parties. Divorce was thus, in theory at least, a legal remedy only available to an injured and legally guiltless spouse.

There were, over the years, amendments to the law, and the grounds for divorce were somewhat widened in 1937; but it was still (in theory, at least) not possible to obtain a divorce by consent. More important, it was not possible to obtain a divorce against an "innocent" spouse—unless he or she was incurably insane. A man might have left his wife 20 or 30 years ago and committed himself to another woman by whom he had children. But he would not be able to marry her so long as his first wife refused to divorce him and (by abstaining from committing any matrimonial offence) did not herself provide any grounds for divorce. Such "stable illicit unions" not only caused unhappiness to the adults concerned, but condemned their children to the category of bastards—with all the legal disadvantages then flowing from illegitimacy.

Pressures for reform

The administration of the law also involved much unpleasant-   3–03
ness—for example a petitioner who had committed adultery was not guiltless, and could thus only obtain a divorce if the court "exercised its discretion" in the petitioner's favour. This involved filing a so-called "discretion statement" containing full details of the petitioner's transgressions. As recently as 1969, the Court of Appeal held that it was not sufficient for a solicitor to make sure the petitioner understood the meaning of "adultery" (unlike the petitioners who told judges: "I did not think it was adultery during the daytime"; "I thought it meant drinking with men in public houses"; "it is not adultery if she is over 50": see *Barnacle* v. *Barnacle* [1948] P 257.) The solicitor also had to warn the client of the need to disclose adultery committed at any time before the case was actually heard: *Pearson* v. *Pearson* [1971] P 16. Not surprisingly, therefore, there was strong pressure for change not only from those who wished to be able to remarry, but also from within the legal profession.

Bills designed to allow divorce on proof of seven years separation attracted considerable support, but the crucial breakthrough came with the publication in 1966 of *Putting Asunder*, the report of a Committee set up by the Archbishop of Canterbury. This report was effectively the catalyst for the divorce reforms effected by the Divorce Reform Act 1969. It favoured as the lesser of two evils the substitution of the doctrine of breakdown for that of the matrimonial offence; but the Archbishop's Committee thought that in order to answer the question whether the marriage had indeed broken down the court should carry out a detailed inquest into "the alleged fact and causes of the 'death' of a marriage relationship." The Committee also proposed that the court should be obliged to refuse a decree (notwithstanding proof of breakdown) if to grant it would be contrary to the public interest in justice and in protecting the institution of marriage.

The field of choice

The Lord Chancellor immediately referred the report to the newly   3–04
established Law Commission. The Commission took as its starting point that a good divorce law should seek "(i) To buttress, rather than

to undermine, the stability of marriage; and (ii) when, regrettably, a marriage has irretrievably broken down, to enable the empty legal shell to be destroyed with the maximum fairness, and the minimum bitterness, distress and humiliation." The Commission rejected the view that a divorce law, which is directed essentially towards dissolving the marriage bond, could do nothing towards upholding the status of marriage. The Commission considered that the law could "and should ensure that divorce is not so easy that the parties are under no inducement to make a success of their marriage and, in particular, to overcome temporary difficulties. It can also ensure that every encouragement is afforded to a reconciliation and that the procedure is not such as to inhibit or discourage approaches to that end."

Inquisitorial approach rejected

3–05   The Commission favoured reform; but it did not accept the proposal made by the Archbishop's group that divorce should be available only after the breakdown of the marriage had been established by a full inquest into the marriage. The Commission thought that such an inquiry into causes might be humiliating and distressing to the parties, so that one of the criteria for reform would not be met. Moreover it would be impracticable to have an inquest in all cases without a vast increase in expenditure of money and human resources. Possible alternatives were discussed; and eventually agreement was reached between the Commission and the Archbishop's group on the principles ultimately embodied in the Divorce Reform Act 1969. This principle is that breakdown should be the sole ground for divorce; but breakdown is not to be the subject of a detailed inquest by the court; instead it is to be inferred, either from the commission of certain facts akin to the old matrimonial offences or (i) from two years' separation if the respondent consents, or (ii) from five years' separation if the respondent does not consent.

SOURCES OF THE LAW

3–06   The *Divorce Reform Act 1969* (which came into force on January 1, 1971) radically reformed the law. That Act was subsequently consolidated in the Matrimonial Causes Act 1973 which made no substantial change in the law. The Matrimonial and Family Proceedings Act 1984 made a number of significant procedural and other amendments, but it did not change the law governing the ground for divorce itself. The Children Act 1989 has made many important changes affecting the consequences of divorce in so far as they relate to the arrangements to be made for children, and the Act prompted significant change in the administration of family law—but although these developments may well have a significant impact on the nature of the divorce process none of them affect the ground for divorce itself.

DIVORCE NOW DOMINATED BY PROCEDURE

The special procedure
Under a statutory provision dating back to 1857, the divorce court is   **3–07**
required to inquire into the facts alleged: MCA 1973, s.1(3); and until 1973 all divorce cases were heard in open court. The court could not grant a decree without hearing the oral testimony of the petitioner; but in practice the position is now very different. Under the so-called "special procedure" which was first introduced in that year with a view to achieving simplicity, speed and economy (Latey J., *R v. Nottinghamshire County Court, ex parte Byers* [1985] FLR 695) there will usually be no oral proceedings at all unless the respondent takes steps to defend the proceedings and it seems that it is now virtually impossible for the court to discharge the inquisitorial function imposed on it by statute (but compare *N. v. N. (Divorce: Agreement not to Defend)* [1992] 1 FLR 266 for a different view).

In outline, the "special procedure" is as follows. The petitioner completes a standard form of petition, which must be lodged together with an affidavit verifying the truth of the answers to a standard form of questionnaire. These documents are then considered by a District Judge (formerly called a Registrar) in private; and if the District Judge is satisfied that the petitioner has sufficiently proved the contents of the petition and is entitled to a decree he will make and file a certificate to that effect. There is no machinery for investigating the truth of the allegations unless there are circumstances which give rise to suspicion: see *Callaghan v. Hanson-Fox and Another* [1991] 2 FLR 519, para. 3–08 below (where a respondent to a petition founded on living apart subsequently claimed that at all material times he had been living with the petitioner and continued to do so until her death). In reality the District Judge can do no more than read the few documents before him; and District Judges have been urged not to take an over-meticulous or over-technical approach: *ex parte Byers*, above.

The decree is then pronounced in open court, either by a Circuit Judge or District Judge, usually in the form "I pronounce decree nisi in cases 1 to 50."

The great majority of divorce cases are dealt with in this way. Almost no cases are actually fought out: in 1990 only four divorces were granted after trial. There are a number of reasons for the very small number of contested cases. First, if either party wants a divorce he or she will today in practice sooner or later be able to obtain one; and a solicitor is therefore likely to advise a client not to oppose the grant of the decree, but perhaps rather to bargain for satisfactory financial and other arrangements as the price for not putting the petitioner to the trouble and expense of dealing with a defended case. Secondly the cost of litigation usually makes it "unrealistic, if not impossible," for most couples to pursue their suits to a fully contested hearing; and if it is clear that the marriage has irretrievably broken down, legal aid is not usually available to a respondent to enable him or her to defend a divorce petition. (Dicta in the Court of Appeal to the effect that legal aid should be granted if there are serious allegations which the respondent should be allowed to meet do not seem to have had any significant impact on practice: *McCarney* v. *McCarney* [1986] 1 FLR 312.) Finally, as the Booth Report put it, the court itself "discourages defended divorce not only because of the futility of trying a contention by one party that the marriage has not broken down despite the other party's conviction that it has, but also because of the emotional and financial demands that it makes upon the parties themselves and the possible harmful consequences for the children of the family."

Hence, as a result of the widespread use of the "special procedure," divorce, although in legal theory still the outcome of a judicial process, has in uncontested cases few of the attributes traditionally associated with adjudication. This development has profound consequences for the administration of the law: many of the problems which case law had exposed on the working of the legislation do not in practice arise, and it is therefore possible, at least in an elementary text, to deal with the law comparatively briefly. Nevertheless, the reader must resist the temptation to regard the substantive law as irrelevant: there are still a few defended cases; whilst the "facts" from which the divorce court may infer irretrievable breakdown are also relevant in proceedings for financial relief in the magistrates' court: see para. 9–06, and even in undefended cases under the "special procedure," the petitioner may encounter difficulties if those concerned are ignorant of the underlying legal rules. Indeed, it is now being suggested that the confusing nature of the divorce process under the special procedure itself exacerbates the emotional distress incidental to divorce; and this has been one of the factors which led to suggestions that the substantive law of divorce be further reformed. Consideration of this issue must be postponed until the present law and procedure have been outlined in the next two chapters. However, a brief summary of the divorce process may be helpful at this stage.

THE DIVORCE PROCESS: A SUMMARY

3–08 A person who wants a divorce must present a petition to the court, but this cannot be done before the expiration of one year from the date of the marriage. That petition must allege that the marriage has irretrievably broken down; and the petitioner must satisfy the court of one or more of five specified facts from which the court is empowered to infer such breakdown. If the petitioner does prove one of the facts, then, unless the other spouse (called "the respondent") satisfies the court that the marriage has not irretrievably broken down or successfully opposes the grant of the decree on the ground that the dissolution of the marriage would cause the respondent grave financial or other hardship, the court will grant a decree of divorce. Thereafter the court will deal with financial issues, and with the arrangements to be made for the upbringing of the children. New procedures introduced in the light of the Children Act 1989 mean that it is no longer necessary for either party to appear when the arrangements for the children are considered by the court; and it is hardly an exaggeration to say that divorce now involves less formality than marriage.

For historical reasons, the divorce decree will in the first instance be a decree nisi ("unless"); and the marriage will not be dissolved until the court grants a decree absolute (normally, on the petitioner's application, six weeks or more after decree nisi. The respondent may apply for the decree to be made absolute; but it is a matter for the court in its discretion to decide whether or not to grant the application: *Smith* v. *Smith* [1990] 1 FLR 438). The fact that the marriage remains in being until decree absolute is vividly illustrated by the case of *Dackham (Dackham Intervening)* v. *Dackham* [1987] 2 FLR 358, CA:

> After decree nisi, a Registrar apparently purported to grant a decree absolute in circumstances in which he had no jurisdiction to grant such a decree. Some time thereafter, the petitioner died, and the Court of Appeal held that, since the prescribed formalities had not been concluded, the marriage had not been dissolved, and the couple were accordingly still married at the date of the petitioner's death. The court emphasised that the rules governing the making of a decree absolute were of fundamental importance, because a decree was good against the whole world, and affected the parties' status. Once it has been granted it is binding on the parties and indeed on everyone else.

Other cases demonstrate the same approach. For example:

> In *Callaghan* v. *Hanson-Fox and Another* [1991] 2 FLR 519, a man allowed a divorce to be granted to his wife. The decree was made absolute, and shortly thereafter she died. He then claimed that the facts stated in the petition were false and that the decree had been obtained by fraud. The court refused his application to set the decree aside, for the reasons set out in the last two sentences of the summary of *Dackham's* case, above.

SUGGESTIONS FOR FURTHER READING

Hoggett and Pearl, pp. 184–193.
J. Burgoyne, R. Ormrod and M. Richards, *Divorce Matters* (1987).

R. Phillips, *Putting Asunder, A History of Divorce in Western Society* (1988).

L. Stone, *The Family, Sex and Marriage in England* 1500–1800 (1977).

L. Stone, *Road to Divorce; England 1530–1989* (1990).

Law Commission Report No. 192, *The Ground for Divorce* (1990), Appendix C (on the "special procedure").

Report of the Matrimonial Causes Procedure Committee (*The Booth Report*) HMSO (1985).

Chapter 4

THE MODERN LAW OF DIVORCE—SUBSTANTIVE LAW

Bar on Petitions within One Year of Marriage

Between 1937 and 1984 no petition for divorce could be presented **4–01** before the expiration of the period of three years from the date of marriage unless it was shown that the case was one of exceptional hardship suffered by the petitioner or one of exceptional depravity on the part of the respondent. In 1984 Parliament accepted that this provision was unsatisfactory not least because it involved the making of distressing and humiliating allegations in a substantial num-ber—1,604 in 1983—of cases. But it was thought desirable to retain some restriction on the availability of divorce early in marriage so as—symbolically at least—to assert the state's interest in upholding the stability and dignity of marriage, and to prevent divorce being apparently available within days of the marriage ceremony. It is therefore provided (MCA 1973, s.3) that no petition for divorce shall be presented to the court before the expiration of the period of one year from the date of the marriage.

It is important to note that this rule prevents divorce proceedings being started within one year of the marriage; but it does not affect the ground upon which divorce may be obtained. It is specifically provided that the rule does not prevent the presentation of a petition based on matters (such as, for example, the respondent's adultery or behaviour) which occurred before the expiration of that period. Conversely, the mere fact that a year has elapsed since the celebration of the marriage does not entitle the petitioner to a decree of divorce. In order to obtain such a decree a petitioner must establish the ground for divorce, as explained below.

Other remedies dealt with later in this book—such as judicial separation or ouster orders under the Domestic Violence and Matrimonial Proceedings Act—can be used to provide legal redress in the first year of the marriage.

Irretrievable Breakdown Misleadingly Described as the Ground for Divorce

In legal theory, there is now one ground, and one ground only, on **4–02** which the court has power to dissolve a marriage, and that is that the marriage has broken down irretrievably: Matrimonial Causes Act 1973, s.1(1). But the statement that breakdown is the sole ground for divorce is for two reasons misleading:

4–03   (i) The court may not dissolve a marriage, however clear it may be that it has broken down irretrievably, unless the petitioner satisfies the court of one or more of five "facts," (three of which are similar to the old matrimonial offences of adultery, cruelty and desertion).

> For example, in *Buffery* v. *Buffery* [1988] 2 FLR 365, CA, the parties to a 20 year marriage had grown apart, no longer had anything in common, and could not communicate. The Court of Appeal accepted that the marriage had broken down. Notwithstanding the fact that the court considered that the husband had been somewhat insensitive about money matters, it was held that the wife had failed to establish the "behaviour" fact (see para. 4–16 below). Accordingly, a decree could not be granted.

Again:

> A decree was refused in *Richards* v. *Richards* [1972] 1 WLR 1073 where the husband (who suffered from mental illness) assaulted the wife and was moody and taciturn. In the end, she left him. The judge found that the marriage had irretrievably broken down. Nevertheless, a decree was refused. The wife had not established the "behaviour" fact.

4–04   (ii) The statement that breakdown is the sole ground for divorce might lead one to think that the court would investigate whether or not there had been such a breakdown. But in practice there is no such investigation, and a decree will almost invariably be granted on proof of one of the facts. This is because:

(a) Although the specified facts are in theory merely the necessary evidence from which the court may infer breakdown, proof of any of the five specified facts will raise a strong presumption that there has been a breakdown which is irretrievable: see para. 3–08 above. The Act in practice puts the burden of proving that there has *not* been an irretrievable breakdown on the respondent; and this burden is almost impossible to discharge. For example:

> In *Le Marchant* v. *Le Marchant* [1977] 1 WLR 559 a decree was granted notwithstanding the wife's denial that the marriage had broken down irretrievably and her protestations that she still loved her husband.

In the rare cases in which there is doubt as to whether or not the marriage has irretrievably broken down the only practicable solution will be for the court to adjourn the proceedings to enable attempts to be made to effect a reconciliation.

(b) The second reason why the court will rarely be in a position to consider the question of irretrievable breakdown stems from the almost universal use of the "special procedure" explained above. It is true that a respondent may in theory defend the case simply on the issue of whether the marriage has in truth irretrievably broken down; but in practice it may be difficult to get legal aid for this purpose: see para. 3–07 above.

THE FIVE FACTS

One or more of the "facts" specified in section 1(2) of the Matrimonial **4–05**
Causes Act 1973 must be proved if the court is to hold that the marriage has irretrievably broken down. They are:

(a) That the respondent has committed adultery and the petitioner **4–06**
finds it intolerable to live with the respondent.
(b) That the respondent has behaved in such a way that the petitioner cannot reasonably be expected to live with the respondent.
(c) That the respondent has deserted the petitioner for a continuous period of at least two years immediately preceding the presentation of the petition.
(d) That the parties to the marriage have lived apart for a continuous period of at least two years immediately preceding the presentation of the petition and the respondent consents to a decree being granted.
(e) That the parties to the marriage have lived apart for a continuous period of at least five years immediately preceding the presentation of the petition.

1. Adultery

Simple adultery insufficient
To establish this fact it is necessary to show not only (i) that the **4–07**
respondent has in fact committed adultery, but also (ii) that the petitioner finds it intolerable to live with the respondent.

(a) *The fact of the respondent's adultery*
Adultery involves voluntary or consensual sexual intercourse **4–08**
between a married person and a person (whether married or unmarried) of the opposite sex not being the other's spouse.

Sexual intercourse. This term has the same meaning as in the crime **4–09**
of rape, that is to say that there must be some penetration, however brief, of the female genitalia by the male member. Thus, a woman

who is artificially inseminated without her husband's consent is not guilty of adultery; and it seems that a married man who has sexual relations with a partner who has undergone a sex-change operation involving the construction of an artificial vagina would probably not be guilty of adultery: see para. 2–17 above. It is clear that "indecent familiarities" (such as mutual masturbation) do not constitute adultery, nor does sexual activity between two persons of the same sex. However, in such cases a petition based on "behaviour" (see para. 4–16 below) might be appropriate.

4–10   *Intercourse must be voluntary or consensual.* This means that a wife who is raped, or who has insufficient mental capacity to consent to intercourse either because she is too young or because she is mentally handicapped cannot be guilty of adultery. Drunkenness may, it seems, negative consent if it is "excusable," *e.g.* where a woman had been given a "laced" drink against her will.

Proof of adultery

4–11   This used to cause many difficulties; and the standard of proof was said to be high. But, since October 1991, it has not been necessary for the petitioner to identify the adulterer (FPR 1991, r. 2.7), and provided that the respondent admits the adultery alleged there is no effective way in which the matter can be investigated. This change in the rules means that petitioners are no longer tempted falsely to state that they are unaware of the adulterer's identity: see *Bradley* v. *Bradley (Queen's Proctor Intervening)* [1986] 1 FLR 128 (where the falsehood was discovered).

(b) *The petitioner finds it intolerable to live with the respondent*

4–12   The policy of the Divorce Reform Act was that adultery was relevant only in so far as it was a symptom of marital breakdown; and the Act was influenced by the philosophy that adultery should "not in itself ... be regarded as demonstrating breakdown unless the petitioner can in addition satisfy the court that the act of adultery is so offensive and deeply wounding to him or her that any further married life with the respondent is unthinkable."

In practice the Act does not achieve this objective. In *Cleary* v. *Cleary and Hutton* [1974] 1 WLR 73 the Court of Appeal held that the "fact" is established if the petitioner genuinely finds it intolerable to live with the respondent, even if the adultery has not played any significant part in the breakdown of the marriage. The court refused to construe the section as if it required proof "that the respondent has committed adultery by reason of which the petitioner finds it intolerable to live with the respondent." Moreover, it is clear that the test of whether the petitioner finds it intolerable to live with the respondent is subjective, not objective. It is sufficient if the petitioner does in fact find it intolerable to live with the respondent; it is immaterial that a reasonable person might not find it so.

No link between requirements

The view that no link between the two requirements need be 4–13
shown can in theory lead to some apparently bizarre results. For
example, in *Roper* v. *Roper* [1972] 1 WLR 1314, 1317 Faulks J.
suggested that a wife might even divorce a husband who had
committed a single act of adultery because he blew his nose more
than she liked. But the no-link interpretation gives effect to the plain
words of the section; and it is consistent with the aim of the
legislation that breakdown of marriage should be the sole ground for
divorce. Breakdown is not, but adultery is, a justiciable issue. Once
adultery has been established, the court draws the inference of
irretrievable breakdown unless there is evidence to the contrary. The
only reason why a literal construction of the Act seems strange is that
it produces results unjust to a party who wishes to preserve the
existence of the marital status. But the law is not now concerned with
such considerations. The fact that the divorced spouse is "wholly
innocent" and the petitioner "wholly responsible" for the breakdown
is not a reason for keeping in existence the empty legal shell of a
marriage which has in fact broken down.

Six months living together a bar

If one spouse knows that the other has committed adultery, but has 4–14
continued thereafter to live with him or her for six months or more, a
divorce petition cannot be based on that act of adultery: MCA 1973,
s.2(1). Conversely, if they have lived together for less than six months
that fact is to be disregarded "in determining ... whether the
petitioner finds it intolerable to live with the respondent." The object
of this rule was to make it clear that a couple could seek a
reconciliation without running the risk that by living together the
innocent party would be held to have forgiven the adultery.

Reasons why adultery popular

A petitioner seeking to establish the "adultery" fact may simply 4–15
state in the petition that the respondent has committed adultery. The
Rules (Family Proceedings Rules 1991, r. 2.34(3)) require the petitioner
to file an affidavit in support, in which the petitioner has to give the
reasons for believing that the respondent has committed the adultery
alleged, and to state whether the petitioner finds it intolerable to live
with the respondent, to give the date on which the petitioner first
knew that the respondent had committed that adultery, and whether
the petitioner and the respondent have thereafter lived in the same
household (these latter questions being relevant to the six month
provision referred to above). The court has no way of investigating
whether uncontested allegations of adultery are true (although it
appears that it was—before the change in the Rules referred to at
para. 4–11 above—the practice of some District Judges to require
further evidence where the name of the alleged adulterer was not
given). In practice, therefore, the adultery "fact" permits immediate

divorce by consent; and this may be one of the reasons why it is so much used—in 1988 there were 50,250 petitions, *i.e.* more than 27 per cent. of the total. (The most recently published statistics—for 1990—provide no information on the "facts" alleged in divorce or nullity petitions thus perhaps providing further evidence that the choice of "fact" is no longer regarded as particularly significant.)

2. Respondent's Behaviour

4–16   MCA 1973, s.1(2)(b) allows the court to infer breakdown on proof of the "fact" that "the respondent has behaved in such a way that the petitioner cannot reasonably be expected to live with him."

Most commonly used fact
4–17   This fact is relied on more than any other: in 1988 as many as 88,260 divorce petitions (out of a total of 182,804—*i.e.* nearly half the total number of petitions) were based on it; and it may be significant that the great majority of petitioners relying on this fact (over 86 per cent.) are wives. The extensive reliance on this fact is regrettable, since the need to allege such behaviour is inconsistent with the policy of enabling marriages which have irretrievably broken down to be dissolved with the "minimum bitterness, distress and humiliation."

Allegations sometimes trivial
4–18   The rules require a petitioner to give brief particulars of the individual facts relied on and there may be some temptation to include in the petition a lengthy catalogue of incidents. Sometimes these allegations may be trivial:

> In *Livingstone-Stallard* v. *Livingstone-Stallard* [1974] Fam 47, CA, the court had to consider the parties' methods of washing their underwear.

> In *Richards* v. *Richards* [1984] FLR 11, HL it was alleged that the husband never remembered the wife's birthday or wedding anniversary, did not buy her Christmas presents, failed to give her flowers on the birth of their child and failed to notify her parents of the event, refused to take her to the cinema, and refused to dispose of a dog which had caused considerable damage to the matrimonial home.

But even such allegations may cause great distress—particularly if the respondent believes that the petitioner has been truly responsible for the breakdown.

But often serious
4–19   Physical violence (for example, blacking the wife's eye on two occasions and striking her in the face on another: *Bergin* v. *Bergin* [1983] FLR 344) is a common complaint. Sometimes it is coupled with other delinquencies (such as drunkenness and alcoholism: *Ash* v. *Ash*

[1972] Fam 135) or making unjustifiable remarks to the husband's superiors with results potentially damaging to his career: *Bateman* v. *Bateman* [1979] Fam 25. The courts also find themselves considering details of the parties' sexual behaviour:

> In *Mason* v. *Mason* (1980) 11 Fam Law 143, CA, it was held that a wife's refusal to permit intercourse more than once a week did not, in all the circumstances, amount to behaviour from which the irretrievable breakdown of the marriage could be inferred.

Petitions may allege such matters as the practice of perversions, and the making of excessive sexual demands; and sometimes there is an element of mental unbalance on the part of the respondent:

> In *O'Neill* v. *O'Neill* [1975] 1 WLR 1118 the husband, a retired airline pilot, had a withdrawn personality and the marriage had never been entirely satisfactory; but the "last straw" for the wife was that for two years the husband carried out a prolonged renovation programme in the flat which they had bought, and this involved mixing cement on the living room floor, having no door on the lavatory for eight months, and so on.

Problems of interpretation

The interpretation of this "fact" has caused some difficulties; and it cannot be said that discussion of them is entirely academic since it seems that petitions based on this "fact" are more likely than others to be defended. The more important doctrinal points which emerge from the case law may be summarised as follows: 4–20

(a) *Two distinct requirements*

The petitioner must establish, first, that the respondent has behaved in a certain way; and secondly, that on the basis of such facts as are proved about the respondent's behaviour the petitioner cannot reasonably be expected to live with him or her.   4–21

(b) *"Unreasonable behaviour" incorrect*

This abbreviation is often used; but it is wrong to do so. In Eekelaar's words, it "is not the behaviour that needs to be unreasonable, but the expectation of cohabitation." For example: 4–22

> In *Bannister* v. *Bannister* (1980) 10 Fam Law 240 the wife's undefended petition alleged that the husband had not taken her out for two years, did not speak to her except when it was unavoidable, stayed away for nights giving her no idea where he was going, and had been living an entirely independent life ignoring her completely. She failed at first instance because the judge considered that this did not constitute "unreasonable behaviour," but the Court of Appeal allowed the wife's appeal on the ground that the husband's behaviour did make it unreasonable to expect the wife to live with him.

(c) *Test objective; but reasonableness judged through eyes of the parties*

4-23   The test is objective in so far as the question to be answered is: can the petitioner "reasonably be expected" to live with the respondent? The test is not "has the respondent behaved reasonably?"

The court must consider the particular parties to the suit before it, not "ordinary reasonable spouses." It seems to follow that a violent petitioner may reasonably be expected to live with a violent respondent; a petitioner who is addicted to drink can reasonably be expected to live with a respondent similarly addicted; a taciturn and morose spouse can reasonably be expected to live with a taciturn and morose partner; a flirtatious husband can reasonably be expected to live with a wife who is equally susceptible to the attractions of the other sex; and if each is equally bad, at any rate in similar respects, each can reasonably be expected to live with the other." In *Ash* v. *Ash* [1972] Fam 135 (from which this citation is taken):

> The husband accepted that he had been violent and had tendencies to alcoholism and to drunkenness (which he attributed to the availability of an expense account, to the demands of his work, and to his wife's lack of understanding); but the court concluded that she could not reasonably be expected to live with her husband.

On the other hand:

> In *Pheasant* v. *Pheasant* [1972] Fam 202 the husband's complaint was simply that the wife was not able to give him the spontaneous, demonstrative affection which he said his nature demanded and for which he craved; and he claimed that this made it impossible to live with her. It was held that he had failed to establish the behaviour "fact," since the wife had been guilty of no breach of any of the obligations of marriage. The couple had simply (it would seem) become incompatible, and that—perhaps strangely if the sole ground for divorce is really that the marriage has irretrievably broken down—does not suffice.

(d) *Right-thinking person test*

4-24   Value judgments about the nature of marriage are obviously involved in making such assessments; and the Court of Appeal (*O'Neill* v. *O'Neill* [1975] 1 WLR 1118) has favoured an approach which puts the issue in terms of a direction to a jury:

> "Would any right-thinking person come to the conclusion that this husband has behaved in such a way that his wife cannot reasonably be expected to live with him, taking into account the whole of the circumstances and the characters and personalities of the parties?"

This will necessarily involve the court taking a view about the obligations and standards of behaviour implicit in marriage—a task which some may think not altogether appropriate.

(e) *Respondent need not be morally culpable*

This point may be particularly relevant where the behaviour in question results from mental illness; and there are some cases in which it is clear that, whatever the excuse, the petitioner cannot reasonably be expected to live with the other: **4–25**

> In *White* v. *White* [1983] Fam 54 for example, it was alleged that the husband was, by his own account, intending to kill himself by jumping from a balcony. However, he then heard a message from God telling him not to kill himself but to kill his wife instead. He told the wife that he would obtain a shotgun, use it to blow her head off and then play football with the severed head. On such facts a decree would be granted, and it would be immaterial that the husband was affected by mental illness to such an extent as not to be responsible for his actions.

> In *Katz* v. *Katz* [1972] 1 WLR 955 the husband was a manic depressive who had been an in-patient at a mental hospital. He constantly criticised the wife, and this coupled with other abnormal behaviour resulted in her suffering acute anxiety which culminated in a suicide attempt. She was granted a decree.

But the cases provide no clear answer to the question of principle: what is it reasonable to expect one spouse to tolerate?

> In *Thurlow* v. *Thurlow* [1976] Fam 32 where a husband was granted a decree against his epileptic and bed-ridden wife, it was said that the court would take full account of the obligations of the married life, including "the normal duty to accept and share the burdens imposed upon the family as a result of the mental or physical ill-health of one member."

But the task is a balancing one and the fact that the health of the petitioner or that of the family as a whole is likely to suffer is a powerful factor influencing the court in favour of granting a decree. (Indeed, the Rules require the petitioner to state the effect which the respondent's behaviour has had on the petitioner's health: see FPR Form M7(b).) Similar considerations would presumably apply if the respondent's behaviour is caused by physical disease such as disseminated sclerosis, or cerebral thrombosis. The courts (see for example *O'Neill* v. *O'Neill* [1975] 1 WLR 1118) have deprecated reference to the wording of the marriage service in the Book of Common Prayer (which includes an undertaking to take the other "for better or for worse, in sickness and in health"); but it is not clear that the test of "reasonableness" can be applied without some view as to the nature of the obligations of marriage.

(f) *Behaviour may be either positive or negative*

However, in practice the fact may be more readily established in cases where the behaviour is positive. Rees J. said in *Thurlow* (above) that spouses may often, but not always, be expected to tolerate more **4–26** in the way of prolonged silences and total inactivity than of violent language or violent activity. Just as unjustified refusal of sexual intercourse, and incorrigible or inexcusable laziness which led to financial stress affecting the wife's health were held to constitute the matrimonial offence of cruelty under the old law, so they would constitute "behaviour" for the purposes of the present "fact": see *Carter-Fea* v. *Carter-Fea* [1987] Fam Law 130, CA (husband unable to deal with family finances). Nevertheless, there must be something which can properly be described as "behaviour." This again may be relevant in cases of illness: in *Thurlow* v. *Thurlow* the court referred to a hypothetical case of a spouse reduced to a human vegetable as the result of a road accident, and removed at once to hospital to remain there for life. The petitioner could (it was said) face "very considerable difficulties in establishing that there was any, or any sufficient behaviour towards him."

(g) Living together after conduct in question

4-27   Can the respondent say that the fact that the petitioner has gone on living in the same household proves that the petitioner *can* live with him? The Act contains a provision (s.2(3)) which is intended to facilitate reconciliation by enabling the parties to live together for a short period without losing the right to seek divorce if the attempt is unsuccessful. In deciding whether the petitioner can reasonably be expected to live with the respondent the court must disregard cohabitation for up to six months. Longer periods do not constitute an absolute bar; and the longer the period the more difficult it will be to show that the petitioner cannot reasonably be expected to live with the respondent. But the petitioner is entitled to rebut such an inference.

> In *Bradley* v. *Bradley* [1973] 1 WLR 1291 the trial judge refused to grant a decree to a wife who was still living in a four-bedroomed council house with the husband and seven children; but the Court of Appeal held that she should be allowed to prove that, although she was in fact living with her husband, it was unreasonable to expect her to continue to do so. As Scarman L.J. pointed out, there could be reasons (particularly concern for the interests of the children) which might explain her continued residence with him.

The dilemma of the behaviour fact

4-28   The existence of the behaviour "fact" presents something of a problem. On the one hand its existence is difficult to reconcile with the policy of the law in minimising the bitterness, distress and humiliation incidental to the breakdown of a marriage; on the other hand, so long as it exists, it seems wrong that those who are confronted by a behaviour petition which, under the traditional practice of the legal aid authorities (see para. 3-07 above), they are often unable to defend, should be "publicly maligned with no effective means of reply."

3. Desertion

To make out the desertion "fact" (MCA 1973, s.1(2)(c)) two things must be proved. First, that the respondent has deserted the petitioner; and secondly that the respondent has done so for a continuous period of two years which immediately preceded the presentation of the petition. **4-29**

Unimportant in practice
The desertion fact is in practice of little importance, being relied on in only a tiny proportion (1.19 per cent. in 1988) of all divorce petitions. This is because if a couple have lived apart for two years and both consent to a divorce that is sufficient to establish a "fact" evidencing breakdown; if they have lived apart for five years that is of itself a "fact." In consequence it will only be necessary to rely on the desertion "fact" in two cases: first, where the couple have lived apart for at least two (but not five) years and the respondent is unwilling to agree to a divorce; secondly, where they have lived apart for five years, but the petitioner fears that the grant of a decree based on that fact might be opposed on one of the "hardship" grounds considered at para. 4-56 below. **4-30**

Law excessively complex
Desertion is one of the traditional matrimonial offences; and the divorce courts for long adopted a restrictive attitude to the concept, for fear that too wide a definition would lead to what statute now in fact (if not strict legal theory) permits, *i.e.* divorce by consent after a period of separation. The effect of the courts' struggles with changing policy considerations over the years was to introduce what Lord Diplock (*Hall* v. *Hall* [1962] 1 WLR 1246, 1254) called "metaphysical niceties" into the law; and in consequence it is difficult to make clear statements of principle without over-simplification. Nevertheless, the attempt must be made. **4-31**

First requirement: the respondent has deserted the petitioner
The main elements of desertion are: (i) the fact of separation; (ii) the intention to desert. The intention to desert involves: (a) lack of consent to the separation on the part of the petitioner; (b) lack of any justification for the separation; and (c) the respondent having the mental capacity to form the intent. **4-32**

(a) *The fact of separation*
Factual separation is an absolute pre-requisite to desertion; and the typical case of desertion is where one spouse leaves the matrimonial home. However "desertion is not the withdrawal from a place, but **4-33**

from a state of things," as Lord Merrivale put it in *Pulford* v. *Pulford* [1923] P 18, 21. What is required is a separation of households, not a separation of houses. This has two important consequences:

4–34   (i) Factual separation *can be established even if the parties are living under the same roof*. The question has been reduced to whether or not there has been any sharing (however minimal) of a common life—for example, sharing a common living room, or taking meals together. If so, the parties are not separated:

> In *Le Brocq* v. *Le Brocq* [1964] 1 WLR 1085 the wife excluded her husband from the matrimonial bedroom by putting a bolt on the inside of the door. There was no avoidable communication between them, but the wife continued to cook the husband's meals, and he paid her a weekly sum for housekeeping. Hence he failed to establish the *factum* of desertion: there was, as Harman L.J. put it, "separation of bedrooms, separation of hearts, separation of speaking: but one household was carried on ... "

4–35   (ii) *Existence of matrimonial home not essential*. Failure without good cause, to establish a matrimonial home may by itself lead to the inference of desertion; and if husband and wife cannot agree on where the matrimonial home should be—for example, the husband wishes to take a job in Penzance whereas his wife wishes to continue living in Newcastle—the court will have to decide whether one of them is being unreasonable. A husband no longer has any absolute right to decide where he and his wife should live: *Dunn* v. *Dunn* [1949] P 98.

(b) *The intention to desert—animus deserendi*
4–36   The mental element required is an intention, inferred from the words and conduct of the spouse alleged to be in desertion, to bring the matrimonial union permanently to an end: *Lang* v. *Lang* [1955] AC 402, PC. It follows that not every separation will constitute desertion, since: (i) the separation may be consensual; (ii) there may be good cause for the separation; or (iii) the respondent may lack the mental capacity necessary to form the intention to desert. It is necessary to say a few words about each of these requirements.

4–37   (i) *Separation consensual*. Desertion is a matrimonial offence; and one party cannot complain about an agreed separation. However, the fact that one spouse is glad that the other has gone does not mean that there is consent to the separation.

4–38   (ii) *Good cause*. The respondent may be justified in leaving the petitioner against the latter's will, either (i) by necessity; or (ii) because of the petitioner's behaviour. The question is really whether the respondent has a "reasonable excuse" for leaving. Thus, in G v. G [1964] P 133 where the husband's behaviour terrified the children, it was held that the wife was justified in not allowing him into the matrimonial home even though by reason of mental illness he was not morally responsible for his actions. Again "grave and weighty" behaviour (for example adultery, cruelty, or unjustifiable refusal of sexual intercourse by the petitioning spouse) justified the respondent in leaving; and in *Quoraishi* v. *Quoraishi* [1985] FLR 780:

> the Court of Appeal held that a husband's conduct in taking a second wife (as he was permitted to do by his personal law) in the circumstances justified his first wife in leaving him. His petition for divorce was rejected, and a marriage which had evidently irretrievably broken down was kept legally in existence.

(iii) *Mental incapacity.* Mental illness may prevent the formation of   **4–39** the intention to desert. It is a question of fact (the onus of proof being on the petitioner) whether it has done so. If by reason of insanity one spouse had deluded beliefs about the conduct of the other, the rights of the parties in relation to an allegation of desertion are to be adjudicated on as if that belief were true:

> In *Perry* v. *Perry* [1964] 1 WLR 91 the wife (quite wrongly) believed that her husband was trying to murder her. She left him. If the deluded belief had been true she would have been justified in doing so; and so she was not in desertion.

Constructive desertion—driving spouse out
Under the pre-1969 law it was recognised that the spouse who left   **4–40** might have been driven out by the other's behaviour; and in such cases the spouse who remained would be held to have *constructively* deserted the other.

Under the modern law, a spouse who leaves in such circumstances   **4–41** will be able to prove the "behaviour" fact (para. 4–16 above) and will thus not need to wait for two years before petitioning. But suppose that one spouse simply orders the other to leave—as in *Khan (Sajid)* v. *Khan (Sajid)* [1980] 1 WLR 355 where the husband was alleged to have said "I am telling you in front of your father, you are not to come back again?"

It has been held in *Morgan* v. *Morgan* (1973) 117 SJ 223 that such cases should continue to be dealt with as cases of constructive desertion (rather than "behaviour"); with the result that no petition can be presented for two years from the date of the separation.

Second requirement: respondent has deserted petitioner for a   **4–42** continuous period of two years immediately preceding the presentation of the petition

Two main points have to be noted about calculating the necessary period of desertion:

(a) *Desertion an inchoate offence*

4-43   Desertion can be terminated (for example, by the party in desertion making an offer to return and thus demonstrating that he or she no longer has the necessary intention to desert) at any time before the filing of the petition; and in such a case, no decree can be granted. Again desertion will be terminated if it becomes consensual (for example by the parties making a separation agreement) or if supervening events remove the duty to cohabit (for example, if a decree of judicial separation is made).

(b) *Continuous does not mean continuous*

4-44   Although the Act stipulates that the respondent must be shown to have deserted the petitioner for a continuous period of two years, it also provides that in deciding this issue "no account shall be taken of any one period (not exceeding six months) or of any two or more periods (not exceeding six months in all) during which the parties resumed living with each other, but no period during which the parties lived with each other shall count as part of the period of desertion. ... " However, it is still necessary to show an aggregate of two years' desertion; and any period or periods of resumed living together is deducted in calculating the overall period. For example, if H deserted W in January 1990, W could petition in July 1992 notwithstanding the fact that they had resumed living together for six months. But on such facts W could not petition in January 1992.

4. Living Apart

The real breakdown facts

4-45   The provisions of sections 1(2)(d) and 1(2)(e) of the Act constituted the real novelty of the 1969 Divorce Reform legislation; and they best justify the claim that the law is now based on the irretrievable breakdown of marriage. As Ormrod L.J. said in *Pheasant* v. *Pheasant* [1972] Fam 202, 207, "separation is undoubtedly the best evidence of breakdown, and the passing of time, the most reliable indication that it is irretrievable." Moreover, it is only in cases based on the living apart facts that (as the Booth Committee put it, para. 2.9) the spouses are no longer required at the outset of proceedings to "think in terms of wrongdoing and blameworthiness."

Section 1(2)(d) requires proof that the parties have lived apart for a continuous period of at least two years immediately preceding the presentation of the petition and that the respondent consents to a decree being granted. Section 1(2)(e) merely requires proof that the parties have lived apart for a continuous period of at least five years immediately preceding the presentation of the petition. In effect, therefore, these provisions permit divorce by consent and also divorce by repudiation: provided that the parties have lived apart for five years one spouse can have the marriage terminated whatever the other may think about it.

However little use is made of these morally neutral "facts" in practice—in 1988 some 17 per cent. of petitions (30,860 out of 182,804) were founded on two years living apart and rather more than 5 per cent. (9,830 petitions) on five years living apart.

The period required

In both cases the Act requires that the separation be "continuous"; **4–46** but in pursuance of the policy of encouraging reconciliation no account is to be taken of any period or periods (not exceeding six months in all) during which the parties resumed living with each other. However, no period during which the parties lived with each other is to count as part of the period for which they lived apart.

Meaning of "living apart"

The courts have held that living apart involves both (a) a physical **4–47** and (b) a mental element:

(a) Physical separation

A couple can be treated as living apart even if they are still living **4–48** under the same roof. This notion is familiar from the law of desertion (see para. 4–34 above) and it has also been accepted that a couple can be regarded as "separated" for tax purposes notwithstanding the fact that they are living in the same house: *Holmes* v. *Mitchell* [1991] 2 FLR 301. The divorce legislation specifically provides (s.2(6)) that "a husband and wife shall be treated as living apart unless they are living with each other in the same household, and references in this section to the parties to a marriage living with each other shall be construed as references to their living with each other in the same household"; and the result of this provision is that husband and wife are to be treated as living apart, even if they are living under the same roof, *unless* it can be said that they are still living in the same household. The question to be asked is whether there is any community of life between them. In practical terms, the question is whether one party continues to provide "matrimonial services" for the other, and is there any sharing of domestic life? If, therefore, the wife still does her husband's ironing or cooks his meals, or if the husband and wife share the same living room, eat at the same table (or perhaps watch television together) they are still to be regarded as living in the same household:

> In *Mouncer* v. *Mouncer* [1972] 1 WLR 321 the parties had for some time been on bad terms—to the extent that the wife petitioned for divorce on the ground of cruelty in 1969. An attempt at reconciliation was made, but this was not wholly successful. Nevertheless the divorce suit did not go ahead, the parties continued to live under the same roof (although in

separate bedrooms), they usually took their meals together, and the wife did most of the household cleaning. In 1971 the husband left the house, and petitioned for divorce. Although the wife consented, it was nonetheless held that living apart for two years had not been made out. The spouses had continued to live as a single household "from the wholly admirable motive of caring properly for their children," but this could not affect the fact that there had been no sufficient separation of households.

4–49   *As husband and wife.* There may be exceptional cases in which the parties live under the same roof and the one cares for the other, but in some capacity other than that of a spouse. Thus:

In *Fuller* v. *Fuller* [1973] 1 WLR 730 husband and wife separated in 1964. The wife lived with another man as his wife, and took his name. In 1968 the husband had a serious heart attack, and the medical advice was that he could not live on his own again. He therefore moved into the house occupied by the wife and her partner, and lived as a lodger in a back bedroom, being provided with food and laundry by the wife in return for a weekly payment. The Court of Appeal held that the parties were not living with each other in the same household. "Living with each other" connoted something more than living in the same household; the parties must also be living with each other as husband and wife, rather than as lodger and landlady.

(b) *The mental element in living apart*

4–50   In the case of *Santos* v. *Santos* [1972] Fam 247 the Court of Appeal held that living apart can for the purposes of this "fact" only start when one party recognises that the marriage is at an end—that is to say, when the spouses are, in common parlance, "separated," rather than simply living apart by force of circumstances. Until that date (so the court held) the spouses are not "living apart," although they may "be apart." This requirement of a mental element means that a decree would not be granted in cases such as the following:

H is sentenced to ten years' imprisonment. After he has been confined for five years, W (who until then has stood by him) falls in love with X whom she wishes to marry. H does not want a divorce. W cannot petition until five years after she decided the marriage was at an end.

H, with W's agreement, took up employment abroad in 1989. He has now met another woman whom he wishes to marry. W recognises that the marriage has irretrievably broken down, and is prepared to consent to a divorce. She cannot however petition under section 1(2)(d) (although if H admits adultery she will be able to petition under section 1(2)(a)).

4–51   **But intention need not be communicated.** How does a petitioner prove that he has formed the necessary intention? In *Santos* the Court of Appeal held that it was not necessary for one spouse to communicate a decision that the marriage was at an end to the other. For example:

> H has been a patient in a mental hospital for more than ten years. W decided more than five years ago that she would never resume married live with H, but has not told him because she knew that to do so would upset him, and also because she did not wish to remarry. However, she has now met someone she does wish to marry; and there is no hope of H ever recovering sufficiently to leave hospital. W can immediately petition for divorce under section 1(2)(e) although H has had no ground to suspect that the marriage was in difficulties.

Approach inconsistent with special procedure. The Court of   **4–52**
Appeal's decision was based on the assumption that consensual divorces based on separation require close judicial scrutiny; but this reasoning has been completely undermined by the adoption of the special procedure. It is true that the petitioner is required to state on oath "the date when and the circumstances in which you came to the conclusion that the marriage was in fact at an end" (FPR 1991, Form M7(e)); and the District Judge will need to be satisfied that the documentation has been correctly completed. However, it will not be possible for any probing of that evidence to take place; and accordingly in practice the only result of the *Santos* decision is to complicate the law, and no doubt to confuse petitioners who do not have access to legal advice and who may thus not realise the importance of stating that they had come to the conclusion, more than two or five years ago, that the marriage was over.

DIFFERENCES BETWEEN TWO AND FIVE YEAR PERIODS

There are two main differences between the living apart facts. First,   **4–53**
where the petition is based on two years living apart the respondent must consent to a decree being granted; secondly, where the petition is founded solely on five years living apart the court may in certain circumstances withhold a decree if it is satisfied that the dissolution of the marriage would cause grave financial hardship to the respondent.

The respondent's consent
The forms seek to ensure that the respondent will understand the   **4–54**
consequences (specifically in relation to succession and pension rights and rights of occupation under the Matrimonial Homes Act 1983: see para. 7–34 below) of consenting to a decree being granted: FPR 1991, Form M5, para. 5. The Notice of Proceedings asks whether the respondent consents to a decree being granted, and warns that the

court will grant the decree unless it considers that the marriage has not broken down irretrievably.

Respondent's withdrawal of consent

4–55   The respondent's consent may be conditional—*e.g.* on no order for costs being made—and any consent may be withdrawn, for any or no reason, before the decree nisi is pronounced. Moreover, the Act (s.10(1)) empowers the court to rescind the decree at any time before decree absolute if it is satisfied that the petitioner misled the respondent (whether intentionally or unintentionally) about any matter which the respondent took into account in deciding to consent. The question appears to be entirely subjective: did this particular respondent in fact take the matter into account (not, would a reasonable respondent have done so)? Thus, if H leads his wife to believe that he wants a divorce so that he can marry X (when in fact he does not intend to do so), or that if he is divorced he will marry not X but Y (when he intends to marry X), or that his mistress is pregnant (when she is not), or that she is not pregnant (when she is), application could be made to have the decree rescinded. But in practice there are very few applications to rescind decrees under this provision.

Refusal of decree because of hardship

4–56   At the time of the 1969 reforms there was a lot of concern about the plight of the "innocent" wife who could not have been divorced under the offence based law. Section 5 MCA 1973 is intended to provide some protection in such cases; but the legislation is restrictively drafted and has itself been given a restrictive interpretation by the courts. The case law is not without significance, since the Law Commission have recently proposed the retention of a "hardship" bar in any reformed divorce law: see para. 5–12 below.

When defence available

4–57   The Act provides that the court may dismiss a petition founded solely on the five year living apart "fact" if two distinct conditions are satisfied: (a) that dissolution will result in "grave financial or other hardship to the respondent" and (b) "that it would in all the circumstances be wrong to dissolve the marriage."

(a) *Hardship*

4–58   There are two elements: first, the hardship (whether financial or otherwise) must be "grave"; secondly it must result from the dissolution of the marriage (rather than from the fact that it has broken down).

4–59   **(i) Must be grave**. In *Reiterbund* v. *Reiterbund* [1975] Fam 99, CA, it was said that this word has its ordinary meaning; and the hardship must therefore be important, or very serious. It is not sufficient to show that a spouse will lose something; and a spouse is not entitled to be compensated pound for pound for everything that he or she will lose in consequence of the divorce:

> Mrs Reiterbund was a 52-year-old wife who would lose her entitlement to the state widows' pension if her 54-year-old husband died before she reached the age of 60. But the court refused to withhold a divorce. On the evidence the risk of her husband dying in the next eight years was not great, and secondly, even if he did, Mrs Reiterbund would not suffer any great loss: she would receive exactly the same income under the supplementary benefit system as under the widow's pension scheme.

(ii) Need not be financial. It is, in theory, open to a respondent **4–60** to establish grave hardship other than financial hardship; but in fact there has been no reported case in which such a defence has succeeded. In particular the courts have taken a robust approach to pleas based on religious belief. It is not enough for the respondent to show that divorce is contrary to his or her religion and that divorce will cause unhappiness and a sense of shame; there must be evidence of some specific hardship flowing from the divorce:

> In *Rukat* v. *Rukat* [1975] Fam 63 the wife (a Sicilian) had married the husband in 1946. In 1947 she returned with their child to Sicily, where she had subsequently lived with her parents. Although there had been various unsuccessful attempts at reconciliation, the wife had then lived as a separated woman in Sicily for more than 25 years. She claimed that because of the social structure in Sicily a divorce would have serious repercussions for her own and her child's position, that she would not be accepted in her community, and that she would be unable to return to live where her property was and where her parents and child lived. A decree was nevertheless granted because the wife had failed to establish that anyone in Sicily would know there had been a divorce or that any adverse consequences would follow from the divorce (as distinct from the separation).

(iii) Must result from divorce, not from breakdown. The **4–61** respondent must prove that her position as a divorced spouse is worse than it would be as a separated spouse. This is difficult to do. It is, for example, true that many divorced people suffer serious financial problems; but the court has wide powers to make financial orders on divorce, and the problems usually stem from the fact that the marriage has broken down and that there is insufficient money to keep two households, rather than from the fact that the marriage has been legally dissolved by divorce.

(iv) The problem of pensions. Exceptionally, the divorce court **4–62** has virtually no powers to reallocate contingent pension rights on divorce: see para. 9–35 below; and most of the cases in which the "hardship" defence has been successfully raised accordingly involved the loss of such benefits—the Act defines "hardship" as "including" the loss of the chance of acquiring any benefit which the respondent might acquire if the marriage were not dissolved. For example:

> In *Parker* v. *Parker* [1972] Fam 116 a wife aged 47 was entitled, contingently on surviving her husband, to a pension under the police pension scheme. It was held that this loss of possible future security after the death of her husband, was a grave hardship considered in the light of her probable financial stringency at that time.

More generally:

> In *Le Marchant* v. *Le Marchant* [1977] 1 WLR 559 the Court of Appeal held that the loss of a contingent right to an index-linked pension (*i.e.* one which gives a high degree of protection against inflation) was prima facie grave financial hardship to a wife.

4–63   **(v) Burden on respondent to provide acceptable alternative.** In such cases, it will be possible for the husband to compensate the wife for the lost entitlement. For example:

> In *Le Marchant* v. *Le Marchant* [1977] 1 WLR 559 he agreed to make an outright transfer of the matrimonial home to the wife and a cash payment of £5,000 on his impending retirement; he also agreed to take out a life policy under which £5,000 would be payable to the wife if she survived the husband. That would give her £10,000 if the husband predeceased her which she could invest in stocks and shares or in buying an annuity; and this was held adequately to compensate her for the loss of an index-linked pension of £1,300 per annum.

4–64   (b) *"Wrong in all the circumstances"*
If, but only if, the court is satisfied that such hardship will result, it will proceed to the next stage, and consider whether it would "in all the circumstances" be wrong to dissolve the marriage. The Act specifically directs attention to a number of matters to be considered. These include the conduct of the parties to the marriage:

> In *Brickell* v. *Brickell* [1974] Fam 31 the court took into account the fact that the "innocent" wife had in the past deserted her husband and damaged his business. The court granted a decree notwithstanding the fact that the dissolution would cause the wife grave financial hardship.

The Act also directs attention to the *interests of the parties* to the marriage (so that it will usually be a material factor that the petitioner wishes to re-marry); the *interests of any children* (including, for example, the petitioner's children by the woman he intends to marry) and the *interest of any other persons* concerned—for example, the woman whom the husband will marry if he is freed to do so.

Balancing hardship against policy of law. Having considered these   4-65
circumstances, the court must then balance the policy embodied in
the modern divorce law, which (as Finer J. put it in *Reiterbund* v.
Reiterbund [1974] 1 WLR 788, 798) "aims, in all other than exceptional
circumstances, to crush the empty shells of dead marriages" against
the "grave financial or other hardship" which will be caused to the
respondent. As is clear from *Brickell* v. *Brickell* (above) it may well not
be "wrong" to destroy the empty legal shell, even at the expense of
grave hardship to the respondent.

In the light of these factors it is not surprising that there have been   4-66
few cases in which a decree has been refused; but *Julian* v. *Julian*
(1972) 116 SJ 763 will serve as an example of such a case:

> The husband was 61 and the wife 58. Neither was in good health. The
> wife was receiving periodical payments from the husband which could be
> increased to £946 per annum, but they would cease if the husband
> predeceased her. The wife would lose her right to a police widow's
> pension of £790 per annum. The only financial provision the husband
> could make for her after his death was an annuity of £215. It was held
> that the loss of the widow's pension constituted grave financial hardship.
> The court also held that it would be wrong in all the circumstances to
> dissolve the marriage: it could not be said to be hard on the husband to
> deprive him of the chance to remarry given his age, health and
> circumstances.

Conclusion—scope of defence limited but perhaps adequate

In practice, the hardship defence seems likely to be used primarily   4-67
to protect middle-aged and elderly wives against the loss of pension
rights, and then only very sparingly. The reality seems to be that the
extent of the mischief at which the provision was aimed—that to
permit divorce on the basis of five years' separation would be to
establish a "Casanova's charter," under which husbands would "put
away" their blameless wives—has been shown to be exaggerated. In
1984, for example, of the 10,780 petitions based solely on the
separation fact, more were presented by wives (5,810) than by
husbands (4,970); and only 17 per cent. of all divorced women were
45 or over. In the circumstances section 5 might be thought to be an
adequate response to the problem.

Other protection for respondents in separation cases

MCA 1973, s.10(2) contains a complex provision which is intended   4-68
to secure the financial position of a spouse who is divorced on either
of the two "living apart" facts. A respondent may apply to the court
after the granting of a decree nisi for consideration of his or her
financial position after the divorce. In such a case the court must not
make the decree absolute unless it is satisfied that the financial
arrangements are "reasonable and fair" or "the best that can be made
in the circumstances." This provision was originally enacted when the
court had less extensive financial powers than it now enjoys. It is

today comparatively rarely invoked, but it may still be applied in certain circumstances. For example:

> In *Garcia* v. *Garcia* [1992] 1 FLR 256, CA, the court held that it had power to refuse to make absolute a decree nisi granted to a husband based on five years living apart. The wife alleged that he had failed to make the stipulated payments under a Spanish agreement for the maintenance of the child. It is true that the legislation refers to financial provision for the respondent, but the Court of Appeal seems to have considered that the position of the spouse and parent should be considered together.

SUGGESTIONS FOR FURTHER READING

Hoggett and Pearl, pp. 194–217, 221–222.
G. Davis and M. Murch, *Grounds for Divorce* (1988).
Law Commission Report No. 6, *Reform of the Grounds of Divorce—The Field of Choice* (1966).
Law Commission Report No. 116, *Time Restrictions on Presentation of Divorce and Nullity Petitions* (1982).

Chapter 5

DIVORCE—FURTHER REFORM?

INTRODUCTION—THE DIVORCE RATE AND ITS SIGNIFICANCE

The divorce rate in England and Wales is now one of the highest in **5–01** Europe, and it has increased more rapidly than in almost any other Western country. In 1966 there were 3.2 divorces per thousand married persons, in 1971 there were 6.0; in 1981 11.9, whilst in 1987 there were 12.7. The divorce rate has thus doubled since the introduction of the reformed Divorce Law and quadrupled over the last 20 years. Should this be a cause for concern? The view that the figures are a clear sign of national moral decay ... (George Brown [1991] Fam Law 128) may seem extreme; but it is difficult to refute the argument that many of the predictions made in the 1960s about the likely trend of divorce rates have been dramatically falsified: see Deech (1991) 106 LQR 229.

It may be that the question of whether or not a high divorce rate should be a cause for concern is essentially one of social policy on which lawyers, as such, should not be expected to have any particular expertise; but lawyers can certainly be expected to assess the effectiveness of the legal system in meeting the declared objectives underlying the legislation. In this context, it is notable that even those who accept the underlying policy of the present law—that is to say, that divorce should be available if a marriage has irretrievably broken down—have come to question whether the law in practice meets the objectives formulated by the Law Commission in 1966 (*i.e.* to buttress rather than to undermine the stability of marriage, whilst enabling the empty legal shell of a marriage which has irretrievably broken down to be destroyed: see para. 3–04 above). This questioning has been a factor in highlighting the importance of the procedures whereby divorce is granted, and has encouraged experimentation into the use of conciliation or mediation as a method of resolving issues arising on marital breakdown.

The first part of the Chapter considers the attempts which have been made to promote reconciliation and to improve the divorce process by encouraging the parties to reach an agreed solution to the problems arising out of divorce. The second part considers criticisms of the substantive law. Finally the text discusses proposals for further reform made by the Law Commission in 1990.

I. THE DIVORCE PROCESS—RECONCILIATION AND CONCILIATION

Reconciliation

For many years, reconciliation—that is bringing parties to a **5–02** marriage which appears to have broken down together and restoring a functioning matrimonial relationship between them—was seen as a primary objective of a humane divorce law; and the Divorce Reform Act 1969 was described in its long title as an Act to "facilitate reconciliation in matrimonial causes." The 1969 Act introduced for the first time the notion of reconciliation as an institutionalised feature of matrimonial litigation, but it has to be admitted that the statutory provisions—such as requiring a solicitor to file a certificate stating whether the possibility of reconciliation had been discussed—had an exceedingly limited effect in practice; and it increasingly came to be thought that reconciliation (in the sense of "reuniting persons who are estranged") had little chance of success once divorce proceedings had been started. Moreover, the extension of the so called special procedure seems to have virtually destroyed any potential there might be in statutory provisions empowering the court to adjourn proceedings if there appeared to be a reasonable possibility of reconciliation, since the District Judge will (as the Law Commission has put it) "rarely be able to detect a chance of reconciliation simply from the documents in front of him": Law Com. No. 170 (1988), para. 3.09.

Conciliation

5–03   The emphasis therefore shifted towards provision of facilities for conciliation ("the process of engendering common sense, reasonableness and agreement in dealing with the consequences of estrangement"). Expert help might not save the marriage, but it could—so it was thought—often help the parties to a marriage to resolve issues relating to finance and the upbringing of children with the minimum of anxiety for themselves or their children. The National Family Conciliation Council—which formulates standards of practice, issues guidance about conciliation, and organises training—has defined the primary aim of conciliation as being to help couples involved in the process of separation and divorce to reach agreements or reduce the area or intensity of conflict between them, especially in disputes concerning their children. Conciliation (in the Council's view) has both short term and long term objectives. The short term objective is to help the parties reach a workable settlement which takes account of the needs of the children and adults involved; but the longer term objective is to help both parents maintain their relationship with their children and to achieve a co-operative plan for their children's welfare.

Conciliation therefore calls into question the appropriate function of the court system, since it seeks to diminish the part played by contentious litigation in resolving family disputes and thereby to minimise the bitterness incidental to the break-up. As the Booth Committee—established to examine procedures—put it in 1985 (para. 3.10), it is "of the essence" of conciliation that responsibility should remain at all times with the parties themselves; and that the role of the neutral conciliator should be simply to assist the parties. In this view, contested legal proceedings are not to be seen as the norm, but are "only appropriate where parties have been unable to reach agreement after being given every assistance and encouragement to do so." The Committee, in strongly supporting the use of conciliation in matrimonial proceedings (para. 3.11), claimed that conciliation puts the responsibility for reaching agreement about the consequences of the breakdown onto the parties who should not expect simply to leave matters to lawyers.

This emphasis on the need for responsibility rather than reliance on state intervention through the legal system had considerable appeal in the intellectual and social climate of the 1980s; but conciliation, with its heavily child-centred and social-work orientated approach to families and their problems, also seemed a promising option to many Welfare Officers and other non-lawyers who were, in practice, to assist the parties; and the concept also had a strong appeal to the many settlement-orientated solicitors who were involved in divorce cases.

But how precisely does conciliation function in the divorce process? Unfortunately, there is no single model and the vast literature on the subject does not always throw much light on the content of the conciliation process, or indeed its "effectiveness." However, two main models of conciliation have emerged in this country. Their salient features may be summarised as follows:

In court conciliation

These developments have focused primarily on the use of a "pre- 5–04 trial review" to encourage parties to realise that a settlement is preferable to a solution imposed by the court after a forensic contest. The pre-trial review (which is commonly used in litigation in order to define the issues and expedite the trial process) was first specifically adapted to promoting conciliation, in the sense of achieving settlements, in cases where the petition was being defended.

Subsequent experience suggested that the pre-trial review could be adapted, with encouraging results to many cases in which there appeared to be a conflict between the parties, and particularly to cases in which there was a conflict about the children. These schemes normally involve a "conciliation appointment" before a District Judge, which is also attended by a Court Welfare Officer. The nature of the application and the matters in dispute are outlined by the parties or their advisers. If the dispute continues, the parties and their advisers will be given the opportunity of retiring to a private room together with the welfare officer in an attempt to reach agreement. There are various provisions designed to safeguard the parties' position if no agreement results: see *Practice Direction (Family Division: Conciliation Procedure)* [1982] 1 WLR 1420.

The dangers—pressurising the parties

A number of variants on this model of in-court conciliation can be 5–05 found in experiments in different parts of the country, but most of the schemes have in common the involvement of both the District

Judge and the welfare officer. This may be an effective method of producing agreement, since the District Judge is invested with the symbolic authority of the court (albeit he has no power to impose a solution on the parties at the conciliation appointment itself, and that he will not personally adjudicate on the case should the appointment be unsuccessful). But the question whether the parties should be exposed to what they may perceive as pressure to settle is controversial.

Another danger—confusing the role of the welfare officer

5–06   In-court conciliation involves some risk that the role of the welfare officer will be misunderstood. In fact, conciliation is a wholly different function from reporting (see para. 13–34 below) and should be carried out by different people. But cases have been reported in which an officer who has failed to bring about a successful conciliation has nonetheless purported to write the welfare report—a practice which is wholly wrong: see *Re H (Conciliation: Welfare Reports)* [1986] 1 FLR 476. A welfare officer who carries out conciliation has no authority over the parties at the conciliation appointment or indeed subsequently; but, however scrupulous the officer may be to observe the proper distinction, there is still a danger that the parties will believe that the officer has power to influence the court in favour of the solution which appears best to him or her.

Out of court conciliation

5–07   The "in-court" conciliation schemes outlined above are only available to parties who have started the litigation process; yet it is generally recognised that (in the words of the Booth Committee: para. 3.12) "early intervention can be a major factor in developing a positive and conciliatory approach," and that accordingly the prospects of success are highest at a very early stage in the breakdown. There has, accordingly, been an enormous growth of interest in conciliation and great enthusiasm for the concept; and schemes have been established in many areas. There is much variety of practice; but there is broad agreement that conciliation is to be seen as a process whereby the parties are encouraged to negotiate with the assistance of a third party over the issues that divide them. That third party (the conciliator) will usually be a trained social worker; and joint or separate meetings (sometimes including the children) may be held over many weeks. The conciliator has no stake in the dispute, and is not identified with any of the competing interests involved. The conciliator may add proposals to those which have been volunteered by the parties, but it is a fundamental principle that the conciliator should have no power to impose a settlement on the parties, who remain responsible for their own decisions on the issues which have been in dispute. The conciliator is responsible for the *process*, but not for the *outcome* of that process: see NFCC *Statement of Aims and Objectives*.

Conciliation must be distinguished from the process of *counselling*—which may be intended simply to help the parties adjust to the ending of their marriage and its consequences—and there is a school of thought which holds that it should also be distinguished from therapeutic intervention using techniques influenced by psychoanalytic doctrines.

Conciliation is also wholly different in concept from *arbitration*, a process in which the parties agree to be bound by the decision of the arbitrator whom they have selected, whether they agree with that decision or not.

There is much controversy about the *"effectiveness"*—a question begging term—of conciliation, and recently doubts have begun to be expressed about the extent to which the reality reflects the theoretical notions discussed above. In particular, Dingwall and Greatbatch ([1990] Fam Law 410) have suggested (on the basis of an analysis of what actually happens in conciliation sessions conducted at five centres) that conciliators had far more power to influence the way in which negotiations were conducted, and indeed their eventual outcomes, than had previously been recognised; and it has been suggested—contrary to the avowed philosophy of the conciliation movement—that neither the process nor the outcomes of conciliation are controlled exclusively by the couple concerned.

Another area in which there have been differences of outlook relates to the *matters which are appropriate* for reference to conciliation. Until recently, out-of-court conciliation services have tended to focus on the making of arrangements relating to the upbringing of children; but in recent years a Family Mediation Association has been established involving a lawyer mediator and a social work counsellor or conciliator, who together seek to assist the parties to agree on all matters relating to the dissolution of their marriage, including financial matters: see L Parkinson [1990] Fam Law 477. Attempts are also being made to evaluate the prospects for so-called *comprehensive conciliation* (*i.e.* an attempt to deal comprehensively with *all* the issues arising on breakdown).

The future for conciliation

Conciliation services have been plagued by lack of secure funding. Responding in part to considerable pressure exercised by the conciliation movement, various officially supported enquiries have been made. In particular, funding was provided for a Conciliation Project Unit at the University of Newcastle-upon-Tyne which reported to the Lord Chancellor in 1989 on the *Costs and Effectiveness of Conciliation in England and Wales.* The report concluded that conciliation did indeed generate "important social benefits," that conciliation should be recognised as an alternative mechanism to formal adjudicatory procedures for the resolution of disputes, and that couples should be encouraged to reach their own agreements in a setting which would assist civilised discussion and provide an

5–08

appropriate degree of informality. However, the report did not favour court-based conciliation schemes (although it did accept the advantages of the pre-trial review system as a means of defining issues in dispute and as providing an opportunity to draw the parties' attention to the availability of conciliation). The Report considered that a network of local services, independent of courts and probation service—to be termed the Family Advisory Counselling and Conciliation Bureau—should be established; and that these services would provide advice, counselling and conciliation. However, to the disappointment of many concerned, the report not only failed to provide detailed costings of some of the options which it considered to be promising, but also concluded that existing conciliation schemes added significantly to the overall resource cost of settling disputes. It seems that, although these and other proposals are "still being considered," the Government has no plans to introduce a national conciliation service: see *Law Society's Gazette*, December 4, 1991, p. 8.

II. Defects of the Substantive Law

5–09   It soon became apparent that the Divorce Reform Act had not been as effective in eradicating bitterness, distress and humiliation from the divorce process as had been hoped; and in the late 1970s powerful criticisms began to be made of the procedural aspects of divorce. It was said (for example) that the inevitable unhappiness associated with most matrimonial proceedings was "considerably magnified by the adversarial nature of the court proceedings and of the preliminaries thereto." These criticisms were influential in promoting the concept of conciliation; but they also led Government to establish a Committee under an experienced Family Division Judge (Booth J.) with a brief to propose procedural changes. This the committee did; but perhaps its real significance lies in having put reform of the substantive law once more on the agenda. The Committee concluded that "the bitterness and unhappiness of divorcing couples is frequently exacerbated and prolonged by the fault element in divorce and that this is particularly so where the fact relied upon is behaviour, whether or not the suit is defended." (para. 2.10). So the wheel turned full circle: the merits of the substantive law again came to be called into question and once again the Law Commission undertook a review of the law.

The Law Commission's view: divorce law confusing and unjust
5–10   The Law Commission published a Discussion Paper, *Facing the Future*, in 1988; and a Report with draft legislation, *The Ground for Divorce*, in 1990. The Report concluded that the present law falls "far short" of its original objectives. Far from minimising bitterness and hostility, the law (and above all the "behaviour" fact) provoked

unnecessary hostility and bitterness, particularly when incidents relied on in the petition were "exaggerated one-sided or even untrue." (Law Com. No. 192, 1990, para. 2.17). The law was also confusing, misleading, and not understood by those involved. In particular, although in theory the law was based upon irretrievable breakdown, it seemed in practice to depend on the making of allegations about past behaviour. Underlying these criticisms, the Commission found (para. 2.2) that the law was seriously defective in doing

—"nothing to give the parties an opportunity to come to terms with what is happening in their lives, to reflect in as calm and sensible way as possible upon the future, and to re-negotiate their relationship."

The Commission thought that the law should concentrate on bringing parties to an understanding of the practical reality of divorce—what it would be like "to live apart, to break up the common home, to finance two households where before there was only one, and to have or to lose day to day responsibility for the children ... " (para. 2).

The Commission considered that the present law failed to reflect the reality of divorce as a process: divorce is not a final product but part of "a massive transition" for the parties and their children; and it is crucial in the interests of the children as well as the parties that the transition be as smooth as possible in order to make the quality of the parents' post divorce relationship with the children as good as possible.

III. THE OPTIONS FOR REFORM

How, then, should the law be changed? The Commission rejected a **5–11** number of possible options for reform—return to a wholly fault-based system, divorce after a full enquiry into whether the relationship had indeed irretrievably broken down, divorce by unilateral notice, divorce by mutual consent, divorce based on living apart for a period of time—and preferred a divorce law which regarded divorce not as a separate event but as part of a process of facing up to and resolving its practical, social and emotional consequences over a period of time. Under this procedure—perhaps to be called *Divorce on Consideration and Reflection*—irretrievable breakdown would remain the sole ground for divorce. But divorce would be granted only after a fixed period set aside for consideration both of the alternatives and of the practical consequences involved.

The Commission considered that the Consideration and Reflection model shared many of the advantages of divorce after a fixed period of separation. In particular, such a law would avoid the injustices and other problems associated with the retention of fault. The Commission considered that the lapse of a substantial period of time provided solid evidence of a permanent breakdown in the marital relationship; and that the proposal would restrain hasty or rash applications and ensure that couples gave some consideration as to what the future would hold before finally committing themselves to divorce. The Commission believed that such a process of facing up to and resolving the consequences of divorce would provide an opportunity to reflect upon the children's best interest and to explore the possibility of reconciliation.

DIVORCE ON CONSIDERATION AND REFLECTION: THE PROCESS

5–12   How would the Commission's aspirations be translated into legislative form? The essence of the detailed legislative package is simple: irretrievable breakdown (which would remain the "ground" for divorce) would be established by the expiry of a minimum period of one year from the filing by one or both spouses of a *formal statement* to the court that the marital relationship was believed to have broken down. At the end of that period, either party would be able to apply for a divorce or separation order to be issued.

The Commission's proposals are worked out with considerable subtlety and sophistication. The *waiting period of one year* is to be "put to good and effective use": the couple would be provided with an *information pack*, and they would be encouraged—with the help of conciliation or other services—to come to agreements about the consequences of their divorce and in particular about the children. If agreement could not be reached, then the issues on which the parties were at variance would be resolved by the court, which would make a *preliminary assessment* of what would be involved, and the court would also have power to make interim orders.

At the end of the period the court would be bound to dissolve the marriage, unless it exercised a closely circumscribed *discretion to postpone the grant of the divorce*. This power to postpone the divorce would only be exercised if—

    (a) The court considered that it was likely that it would exercise its statutory powers in respect of a child of the family but could not yet do so, and the postponement of the divorce would be desirable in the interests of the child.

    (b) *Financial arrangements* had not been made and could not be made before the divorce would normally be made, and postponement would be desirable to allow for such arrangements to be made.

(c) One party lacks legal capacity to act—for example by reason of mental illness—and postponement would be desirable so that steps could be taken to protect the spouse's interest.

(d) The applicant has been guilty of *delay in providing information*, and postponement would be desirable in order to prevent the other spouse from suffering any prejudice as a result.

The Commission was conscious that to allow any grounds for postponement could be a weapon in the hands of an obstructive or vindictive party and made a number of proposals intended to minimise the danger of a stronger bargaining position being exploited. These provisions were intended to meet concern that the process would give rise to bargaining and manipulation and that the grant or withholding of a decree would give one party a potentially powerful bargaining counter.

Conversely, the Commission was concerned that dissolving a marriage against the wish of one party before arrangements had been agreed between the parties could be productive of great hardship to that party. In a particularly controversial proposal, therefore, the Commission proposed that the court should have power to postpone (or even refuse) to grant a decree of divorce if to do so would cause *grave financial or other hardship* to the other party, and that it would be wrong in all the circumstances to grant the divorce.

Proposed cure worse than disease?

These proposals represent a valiant attempt to achieve a consensus **5–13** on the ground for divorce. But it is possible to argue that the cure would be worse—or at least no better—than the disease. For example, it is said that the existing law is difficult for the lay person to understand. But would the process of divorce on consideration and reflection be any easier for the average person to understand? The reader may care to try the experiment of explaining in a sentence or two what precisely would be the ground for divorce under the proposed new law. In theory, of course, it is to be the irretrievable breakdown of marriage. But in practice this is to turn upon the filing of a notice. Is the ground for divorce therefore to be unilateral repudiation? An analysis of the Commission's proposals (discounting the sometimes rather tendentious language in which they are expressed) indicates that they would come very close to this position, since it would only be in the most unusual circumstances that a decree could be withheld on the expiration of 12 months from the lodging of the notice at court.

The Commission would no doubt meet suggestions that the scheme is no more than an elaborate system of divorce by repudiation by saying that the 12 month period is to be used "constructively" for "reflection"; and it is of course possible that in some cases—as no doubt occurs under the existing law—the parties would adopt such an attitude. But it is equally possible that they would adopt an attitude of hostility and recrimination, and use every conceivable forensic device—including applications for postponement of the grant of the decree—in order to inflict an appreciation of their feelings on the other party.

Anyone who doubts the power of emotion to override reason when a relationship has broken down might consider the recent case of *Scott* v. *Scott* [1992] Fam Law 102, CA:

> A husband could not bring himself to accept that his marriage of more than 20 years had come to an end. Although he did not formally contest the divorce, he repeatedly sought to persuade the wife to bring about a reconciliation. He did not use any violence; but the Court of Appeal held that his conduct constituted an interference with the wife such as to justify the grant of an injunction excluding him from the matrimonial home before decree absolute. It seems doubtful whether his attitude—perhaps not uncommon—would have been significantly influenced by giving him an "information pack" and telling him to use the period after the wife initiated the divorce process "constructively."

It is only fair to say that the Commission's proposals have attracted much favourable comment (albeit not always marked by any close scrutiny of the details); but it is suggested that the Report confuses the legal process of divorce (which must inevitably be concerned solely with the legal consequences of the breakdown of a relationship) with the psychological process of adjusting to a change in human relationships. The law should clearly not do anything to hinder the parties from reflecting on their position and acting responsibly and in a mature way; and it can and no doubt should be designed so as not to discourage such an approach. Moreover, conciliation and other services could certainly be made available to the parties, as a matter of social policy, in order to help them to reach agreement about matters such as the arrangements to be made for the children. But such matters are merely incidents of a civilized divorce process. In so far as they disguise the truth about the legal basis for divorce they might well exacerbate the confusion already experienced by those involved in the divorce process.

It is difficult to avoid the feeling that the Law Commission was placed in an impossible situation. The logic of the experience of the working of the existing law, coupled with the apparently strongly held belief that divorce should be based on irretrievable breakdown, would seem inevitably to point to divorce being granted on the request of one or both parties no doubt with some provision (such as a waiting period) to ensure that the parties were not acting frivolously or without proper consideration. But to accept this would appear to make divorce "easy"; and it was made clear that vocal and influential interest groups believed that divorce had already become far too "easy." The Commission—like the 1969 reformers—seems therefore to have felt obliged to disguise the reality of what was being proposed (which, juristically, is little different from the system of divorce by notice practised in Sweden, or the modified Islamic system of *Talak* divorce available in Pakistan under the Muslim Family Laws Ordinance, 1961: see *Quazi* v. *Quazi* [1980] AC 744). The result is a series of proposals whose subtlety and sophistication were evidently intended to make them acceptable to a wide range of opinion—but at the risk of making the divorce law even more confusing to ordinary litigants than it is at the moment. Moreover, the resource and training implications of introducing counselling, conciliation and mediation services on the scale apparently envisaged would be vast; and experience does not suggest any readiness by Government to provide funding on the scale necessary: see para. 5–08 above.

The prospects for reform therefore seem uncertain, not least because the Commission's attempts to achieve consensus do not seem to have succeeded: the Lord Chancellor has said that there is a "strong feeling" that the Commission had not sufficiently recognised the need for a divorce law to strengthen the institution of marriage; and that an element of "fault" should be retained, at least to the extent of denying divorce where one party was innocent of wrongdoing and did not want a divorce: see *Law Society's Gazette* December 4, 1991, p. 8.

SUGGESTIONS FOR FURTHER READING

Hoggett and Pearl, pp. 217–221, 222–247.
Law Commission Report No. 192, *The Ground for Divorce* (1990).
Scottish Law Commission Report Scot. Law Com. No. 116, *Reform of the Ground for Divorce* (1989).
J. Eekelaar, *Regulating Divorce* (1991).
R. Deech, "Divorce Law and Empirical Studies" (1991) 106 LQR 229.
M. Mears, "Getting it Wrong Again" [1991] Fam Law 231.
M. Richards, "Divorce Research Today" [1991] Fam Law 70.

On Conciliation etc.:
Hoggett and Pearl, Chap. 15.
R. Dingwall and J. Eekelaar, *Divorce Mediation and the Legal Process*, Chaps. 1 and 8.
L. Parkinson, *Conciliation in Separation and Divorce* (1986).
L. Neilson, "Solicitors Contemplate Mediation, Lawyers' Perceptions of the Role and Education of Mediators" (1990) 4 IJLF 325.
L. Parkinson, "Mediation Matters" [1990] Fam Law 477.
J. Walker, "Conciliation in the 1990s" [1991] Fam Law 12.

Chapter 6

JUDICIAL SEPARATION AND PROTECTION AGAINST DOMESTIC VIOLENCE

I. JUDICIAL SEPARATION

6–01 Judicial separation is a somewhat misleading term. In theory, the principal effect of a judicial separation decree is to remove the duty of one spouse to live with the other (MCA 1973, s.18(1)); but a decree does not, in fact, require the parties to separate, much less does it mean that the court will compel them to separate—the court will not, for example, necessarily exclude a spouse against whom a decree of judicial separation has been granted from the matrimonial home: see para. 6–12 below. But judicial separation was until very recently surprisingly often used: in 1984 6,098 petitions were presented, and 4,445 decrees pronounced.

What accounted for this popularity? So long as divorce was only available on proof of a matrimonial offence, judicial separation was used by spouses—often wives—who wanted to get a financial provision order whilst denying the husband the right to remarry. Even after the introduction of the reformed divorce law, there were still restrictions on starting divorce proceedings within the first three years of the marriage (see para. 4–01 above), and there is some evidence that judicial separation was widely used as a short-term substitute for divorce. The number of judicial separation petitions fell sharply when the present one year bar (see para. 4–01 above) was substituted for the three year bar, but there is still a significant number of petitions—in 1990 there were 2,900 petitions and 1,794 decrees. It seems probable that judicial separation is used primarily as a form of short-term legal remedy, although it will also be used where the parties have a conscientious objection to divorce but wish to have the financial and other consequences of marital breakdown regulated by a court order.

6–02 The fact that judicial separation is one of the original "matrimonial causes" administered since 1857 by the Divorce Court (along with divorce, nullity and some other forms of relief which have subsequently been abolished) explains why it is still easiest to consider this form of relief separately from the other legal procedures now available to deal with family disputes.

JUDICIAL SEPARATION—THE GROUNDS

6–03 The Divorce Reform Act 1969 amended the law so as to be consistent with the new code of divorce: a petition for judicial separation may be

70

presented to the court by either party to a marriage on the ground that any of the divorce "facts" set out in MCA 1973, s.1(2) 1973 and discussed at paras. 4-05—4-52 above exists: MCA 1973, s.17(1). It is specifically provided that in the case of petitions for judicial separation, the court is not to be concerned with the question of whether or not the marriage has broken down irretrievably: MCA 1973, s.17(2). If one of the relevant facts—adultery, behaviour, desertion, or living apart—is proved, the court is bound to grant a decree.

EFFECTS OF A DECREE OF JUDICIAL SEPARATION

There are three main consequences of a decree of judicial separation: 6-04

(1) Powers over money and children; injunctions

In judicial separation proceedings the court has extensive powers to make orders dealing with financial matters, and with the upbringing of children. So far as financial matters are concerned, the court's powers are virtually identical to its powers in divorce and nullity proceedings (see para. 9-25 below) (although in the exercise of its discretion about the use of those powers the court is not under any obligation to consider the making of a "clean break" order: MCA 1973, s.25A; see para. 9-70 below).

So far as the upbringing of children is concerned, the court is obliged under the provisions of section 41 of the Matrimonial Causes Act 1973 (as amended by the Children Act 1989) to consider the arrangements which are proposed and whether to exercise any of its powers under the Children Act 1989 to make orders in respect of the children: see further para. 14-02 below.

The court may also grant injunctions in the course of judicial separation proceedings, and it is possible that this power is more extensive than the statutory powers under the Domestic Violence and Matrimonial Proceedings Act 1976 and the Matrimonial Homes Act 1983: see para. 6-27 below.

(2) But only limited protection for wife

The Matrimonial Causes Act 1973 provides that where the court 6-05 grants a decree of judicial separation it shall no longer be obligatory for the petitioner to cohabit with the respondent. At one time the removal of this obligation had important legal and practical consequences, but today there is no enforceable obligation on a couple to live together. It remains possible that removal of the duty will still have indirect consequences—for example, after judicial separation neither spouse could be held to be in desertion: see para. 4-29 above.

(3) Succession rights

6–06 After a decree of judicial separation the parties remain husband and wife; but it is now provided that so long as a decree is in force and the separation is continuing the property of the spouses should be distributed on intestacy as if the other were dead: MCA 1973, s.18(2).

USE MADE OF JUDICIAL SEPARATION

Primarily short-term remedy?

6–07 The fact that divorce is now available on the basis of five years' separation means that, after a period, a respondent spouse will almost invariably be able in effect to convert a decree of judicial separation obtained against him or her into a decree of divorce. Hence, judicial separation should now be primarily a short-term remedy which might appropriately be used in the following cases:

(i) where a decree of divorce cannot yet be obtained because one year has not elapsed since the celebration of the marriage;

(ii) where the petitioner wishes to take advantage of the court's ancillary powers to make financial orders, and orders relating to the upbringing of the children, but neither the petitioner nor the respondent wishes to remarry; and,

(iii) where the petitioner does not wish to obtain a divorce, but wants a formal recognition of the separation and the respondent is not yet in a position to establish one of the necessary "facts" for divorce—for example, a wife may obtain a decree of judicial separation on the basis of her husband's adultery or behaviour; he may want a divorce, but not be able to obtain one until he can establish the five year living apart "fact."

Long-term remedy

6–08 There are of course cases in which—for religious or other reasons—neither party to a broken marriage wishes to divorce; and judicial separation may be an appropriate technique in such cases for dealing with the financial and other consequences of the breakdown.

II. DOMESTIC VIOLENCE

6–09 In recent years there has been great concern about domestic violence; and the legal procedures intended to provide a remedy to victims have proliferated. The result is (as Lord Scarman put it in *Richards* v. *Richards* [1984] AC 174, 206) a "hotchpotch of enactments of limited scope passed into law to meet specific situations or to strengthen the powers of particular courts." In an attempt to meet this and other criticisms the Law Commission has provisionally proposed that a single set of remedies should be made available to deal with domestic violence in all the courts which have power to deal with family cases: see Working Paper No. 113, Domestic Violence and Occupation of the Family Home (1989). But before considering the remedies available in the civil courts the relevance of the criminal law should be examined.

The Criminal Law

One spouse is not entitled by reason of marriage to inflict violence on   6–10
the other against his or her will. In appropriate cases, therefore, a spouse can be prosecuted for offences ranging from murder to common assault. And—although it was for long thought that a man could not be convicted of rape against his wife—the House of Lords has recently held that there is no such exemption: R v. R (Rape: Marital Exemption) [1991] 4 All ER 481. (The law on marital rape is examined in detail by the Law Commission in Report Law Com. No. 205, Rape within Marriage, 1992. The Commission recommends that legislation should be enacted to confirm the law as declared by the House of Lords.)

Criminal law not adequate remedy
For a number of reasons the criminal law does not provide an   6–11
adequate response to the problems of marital violence. First, the primary objective of the criminal law is the punishment of the offender, not the protection of the victim. Fining (or even imprisoning) a brutal husband will not necessarily improve things for the wife. Secondly there may be problems in pressing a criminal charge to conviction given the supposed reluctance of the police and other agencies to become involved in domestic disputes—it is too early to assess the effectiveness of recent measures to change traditional attitudes. Thirdly, (as Atkins and Hoggett, Women and the Law (1984), p. 135 point out) a woman may have ambivalent feelings about the fact that she has "shopped" her husband; and these emotions may lead her to withdraw the co-operation with the prosecution which is in practice essential if a conviction is to be obtained. This remains true notwithstanding the fact that a wife can now be compelled to give evidence against her spouse: Police and Criminal Evidence Act 1984, s.80; and see the discussion of the "compellability" rule in the Law Commission's Report on Rape within Marriage (above).

Civil Remedies

It will usually therefore be necessary for a victim of domestic violence   6–12
to seek the assistance of the civil law if he or she is to obtain

reasonably effective protection against violence. The following procedures are relevant:

(a) The victim may seek an injunction under the Domestic Violence and Matrimonial Proceedings Act 1976. A spouse (but not a partner in a non-marital relationship) may also seek an order under the Matrimonial Homes Act 1983.

(b) If divorce or judicial separation proceedings are pending, a spouse may seek an injunction in those proceedings.

(c) A spouse may seek a personal protection or exclusion order from the Magistrates' Court under the Domestic Proceedings and Magistrates' Courts Act 1978.

There may also be circumstances in which orders relating to the children under the Children Act 1989 will be relevant: see para. 6–26 below.

The powers summarised above are extensively used; and in particular the power to grant injunctions is frequently invoked: in 1990 there were 21,023 applications for an injunction.

(a) Injunctions under the Domestic Violence and Matrimonial Proceedings Act 1976 ("the 1976 Act") or under the Matrimonial Homes Act 1983 ("the 1983 Act")

6–13 The advantages of obtaining an injunction are, first, that there is a speedy procedure available; and secondly that there are effective methods of compelling obedience to the terms of the order—breach of an injunction constitutes a contempt of court, and may be punished by fine or imprisonment; whilst in some cases the court has power to attach a "power of arrest" to the injunction: see para. 6–31 below.

The 1976 Act was enacted specifically to give the courts adequate powers to deal with domestic violence; and applications may be made by either party to a marriage or by a cohabitant: see para. 6–16. The 1983 Act—originally enacted in 1967—was intended to provide a remedy for other problems: see para. 7–34; but the House of Lords held that all applications by spouses relating to the occupation of the matrimonial home should be governed by the *principles*—set out at para. 6–25—laid down in the 1983 Act.

The main features of this legislation are as follows:

(i) *No need to seek any other relief*

6–14 The courts have traditionally exercised a wide jurisdiction to grant injunctions, but there were a number of important restrictions on this power. In particular, the courts held that an injunction was ancillary and incidental to a pre-existing cause of action which the applicant intended to assert by legal proceedings so that a wife seeking an injunction in the divorce court would first have to start—or at least undertake to start—proceedings to which the application for an injunction could be said to be incidental. However, the 1976 Act now empowers the county court to grant injunctions in specified terms whether or not any other relief is sought in the proceedings. Accordingly, it is no longer the law that injunctions can only be granted if divorce or other proceedings are imminent; it is no longer the law that a wife must be prepared to petition for divorce or judicial separation in order to confer jurisdiction on the court to grant an injunction against violence.

(ii) No conditions for grant of injunction

The 1976 Act does not specify any conditions which have to be   6–15
satisfied before an injunction can be granted. The decision whether to make an order is in the court's discretion: see para. 6–25 below.

(iii) Applications by cohabitants

The 1976 Act, s.1(2) provides that provisions empowering the   6–16
county court to grant relief on an application by a "party to a marriage shall apply to a man and a woman who are living with each other in the same household as husband and wife as it applies to the parties to a marriage."

This raises certain questions. Most important, what degree of stability is required in a relationship? It is clear that the Act's protection is only intended to be available to men and women who have been living together on a stable basis: the act applies to a man and a woman who are living together "in the same household."

Four elements need to be considered:

(a) Common household

The word "household" refers to people held together by a   6–17
particular kind of tie; and involves some element of community life: see para. 4–34 above. The requirement that the couple be living "in the same household" would therefore exclude cases where a couple had merely shared (however frequently) a sexual relationship.

(b) Existing at time of acts giving rise to complaint

The statutory requirement that the couple "are" living in the same   6–18
household has been interpreted purposively: there is jurisdiction if the couple *have been* living together as husband and wife immediately before the incident which gives rise to the application: see *McLean* v. *Nugent* (1979) 1 FLR 26.

(c) But jurisdiction not dependent on proof of violence

In many cases, of course, the applicant will complain of violence;   6–19
but the Act does not impose any requirement that violence be proved as a condition precedent to the court assuming jurisdiction. Violence goes to the exercise of the court's discretion rather than to the question of whether the court has jurisdiction: *Wiseman* v. *Simpson* [1988] 1 FLR 490.

(d) *As husband and wife*

6–20   Finally, it is necessary to show that the couple were, at the relevant time, living "as husband and wife," rather than as landlord and lodger, for example. The meaning of this expression is discussed below in the context of entitlement to welfare benefits (see para. 8–05); and there is no reported case in which it has given rise to difficulties on an application under the Domestic Violence and Matrimonial Proceedings Act 1976.

Married persons who have been divorced cannot (unless they have subsequently resumed cohabitation) apply under the 1976 Act even if—as is not infrequently the case—they are still living under the same roof.

(iv) *Orders that can be made*

6–21   The Act empowers the county court to grant an injunction containing one or more of the following provisions:

Non-molestation order. The injunction may contain a provision restraining the other party to the marriage from molesting the applicant, or a child living with the applicant: 1976 Act s.1(1)(a), (b). There is no statutory definition of the word molestation. The word certainly extends to physical attacks but molestation may take place without either the threat or use of violence. In 1973 a judge stated that "pester" might be the best single synonym, and more recently it has been asserted that the word molest can properly be regarded as "such a degree of harassment as to call for intervention by the court." For example:

> In *Horner* v. *Horner* [1983] FLR 50, it appears that the husband hung scurrilous posters about the wife on the railings of the school at which she taught.

> In *Spencer* v. *Camacho* [1983] 4 FLR 662, a man's conduct in searching through his partner's handbag was held to constitute molestation.

> In *Johnson* v. *Walton* [1990] 1 FLR 350, a man's action in giving nude photographs of his former lover to the press was held to constitute molestation.

6–22   *Ouster Order.* The 1976 Act provides (s.1(1)(c)) that an injunction may contain a provision excluding the other party from the matrimonial home or a part of the matrimonial home or from a specified area in which the matrimonial home is included. This power enables the court to make what is commonly called an ouster order, *i.e.* that the person against whom the order is made should leave the home and not return. The result of course, may be that one of the parties is put out on the street with nowhere to go. However, an order may be more restricted—for example it may simply exclude one of the parties from part of the family home (*e.g.* the kitchen or a bedroom)—and the court may also order that a party should not go to the street, town or other district in which the family home is situated.

Re-entry orders. The 1976 Act, s.1(1)(d) also empowers the court to **6–23** insert a provision requiring the applicant to be permitted to enter and remain in the matrimonial home or a part of the matrimonial home—an applicant who has been driven from the matrimonial home is thus to be allowed to return in safety.

(v) *Emergency action available*

An application for an injunction can be heard after only a short **6–24** period of notice (two days) to the respondent: see County Court Rules Ord. 13 r. 6(3). Moreover, in a genuine emergency an interim order can be obtained *ex parte*—*i.e.* without notice to the respondent. However an *ex parte* application should only be made or granted if there is a real, immediate danger of serious injury or incurable damage: *Practice Note (Matrimonial Causes Injunction)* [1978] 1 WLR 925; *G v. G (Ouster: Ex Parte Application)* [1990] 1 FLR 395.

(vi) *Principles to be applied in exercising jurisdiction*

As a result of the decision of the House of Lords in *Richards* v. **6–25** *Richards* [1984] FLR 11 it was made clear that applications by a spouse for an ouster injunction would be governed by the principles laid down in the Matrimonial Homes Act 1983. That Act provides (MHA 1983, s.1(3)) that in determining applications the court "may make such order as it thinks just and reasonable having regard to the conduct of the spouses in relation to each other and otherwise, to their respective needs and financial resources, to the needs of any children and to all the circumstances of the case." Case law suggests that the courts will apply similar principles to an application by a person who is not married to the respondent: see *Thurley* v. *Smith* [1984] FLR 875; *Wiseman* v. *Simpson* [1988] 1 FLR 490; but see further below.

It will be noted that the parties' conduct is relevant:

> In *Wiseman* v. *Simpson* [1988] 1 FLR 490 it was held that the action of one person in changing the locks of the council flat of which the parties were joint tenants in an attempt to exclude the other was a serious wrong, and that she should not be allowed to profit from that wrongdoing.

> In *Blackstock* v. *Blackstock* [1991] 2 FLR 308 the court expressed regret that the trial judge had not made any finding as to culpability in a case in which both parties had suffered serious injury. The court clearly considered conduct to be relevant, and thought it inappropriate to exclude a party who had done no wrong.

It will also be noted that the interests of the children are not "paramount," in the sense that they override all other factors (as is the case where the child's upbringing is directly in issue: see para.

11–31 below). However, the children's needs are in practice extremely important, and it will often be desirable for the court first of all to decide where the children are to live so that it can properly assess their needs in accordance with the provisions of the legislation:

> In *T v. T (Ouster Order)* [1987] 1 FLR 181 the court decided that it would first hear an application for custody of the children, and then in the light of the outcome assess their needs and decide an application for an ouster order. In the application for custody, the children's welfare was the paramount consideration, and a decision that the mother should have custody was clearly influential in the decision that the children's needs required that the husband be excluded from the home.

The essential requirement is that the order be *just and reasonable*:

> In *Richards v. Richards* [1984] FLR 11, HL, the wife applied to turn her husband out of the matrimonial home because she could not bear to be in the same household with him. Although the judge found that she had no reasonable ground for refusing to live in the same house, he granted her application in the interests of the three children (who were in the wife's care). The House of Lords held he had been wrong to do so; the order (as the judge had appreciated and indeed said) was not "just and reasonable."

> In *Summers v. Summers* [1986] 1 FLR 343 husband and wife had repeatedly had violent quarrels. The husband would lose his temper, call the wife names, and smash the furniture. On one occasion the wife threw lager over the husband. As a result, the children were frightened and affected by the atmosphere which the judge found to have become "quite impossible." At first instance, the judge ordered the husband to leave, apparently partly "to allow the dust to settle for a time which might perhaps then lead to a fresh reconciliation." It was held that he had been wrong to do so. In particular, the judge had failed to take into account the "draconian nature" of an ouster order expelling the husband and the effect which such an order would have on the husband.

Does the fact that the parties are not married affect the exercise of the discretion to make orders? It is clear that the court will not wish to assume jurisdiction to make the equivalent of the property adjustment orders available on divorce, and it has been said (*Davis v. Johnson* [1979] AC 264, 342, *per* Lord Salmon) that any interference with the owner's occupation of the home should be for a fairly short period while the other partner has an opportunity to look for alternative accommodation. The principle is that the legislation is concerned with personal protection; "first aid but not intensive care." Thus:

> In *O'Neill v. Williams* [1984] FLR 1, CA, M and F had lived together in a jointly tenanted flat. M violently expelled F in August 1982; but (for

various reasons) she did not make an application under the Act until March 1983. The Court of Appeal held that, although the judge had had jurisdiction to hear the application, there was as a matter of law no evidence on which an ouster order could properly be granted. In the words of Cumming-Bruce L.J., "the longer the time elapses the less and less likely it will become that any judge would, or could, find it right to grant the remedy ... because [the 1976 Act] deals with short term relief, not with long term solution of conflicts in matters of property."

It follows that any ouster order in favour of an unmarried applicant will usually be of a temporary character, and a period of up to three months will usually suffice, at least in the first instance; but the order will normally give the parties liberty to apply, so that either party can seek discharge or modification. However, the statute does not impose any fetter on the county court's discretion and, in an appropriate case, an order may be made excluding one partner "until further order." Thus, in *Spencer* v. *Camacho* (1983) 4 FLR 662, CA:

> M had been persistently violent, and had broken the terms of the injunctions on three occasions. On the fourth occasion F asked the court to grant an injunction "until further order"; and the Court of Appeal held that on the facts such an order would be appropriate. This would avoid imposing on F the burden of repeated applications to the court; whilst it would always be open to M to apply for the order to be discharged.

(vii) *Orders under Children Act 1989*

Proceedings under the 1976 and 1983 Act (and the Domestic   6–26
Proceedings and Magistrates' Courts Act 1978: see para. 6–32) are "family proceedings" for the purposes of the Children Act 1989; and it follows that the court may make orders, dealing with the upbringing of children: see further para. 13–06.

(b) Injunctions in pending matrimonial proceedings

The Supreme Court Act 1981, consolidating earlier legislation and   6–27
effectively supplanting what used to be called the "inherent" jurisdiction, empowers the High Court to grant an interlocutory or final injunction "in all cases in which it appears to the court to be just and convenient to do so"; and similar powers are conferred on the county court by section 38 of the County Courts Act 1984 (as now substituted by the Courts and Legal Services Act 1990, s.3). The divorce courts may exercise the power thereby conferred to grant injunctions ancillary to divorce, nullity or judicial separation proceedings, and in practice they frequently make non-molestation and other orders in this way. The principle upon which the courts exercise this jurisdiction is that litigants have a right not to be subjected to undue pressure, and a court may therefore act even after the divorce decree has been made absolute provided that there are still some issues relating to the divorce before the court:

In *Lucas* v. *Lucas* [1992] Fam Law 101, CA, a wife applied to exclude her former husband from the family home two months after their divorce had been made absolute. Since there were still proceedings for financial relief which had not been resolved, the court held that it had jurisdiction to grant the injunction notwithstanding the fact that the parties were no longer husband and wife and were no longer cohabiting with one another.

It is true that in *Richards* v. *Richards* [1984] AC 174 the House of Lords held that applications for ouster injunctions in proceedings between spouses must be made under the Matrimonial Homes Act 1983. However in practice the proceedings will normally be heard by the court dealing with the divorce. The main significance of the *Richards* decision in this context is simply that the principles upon which the court will act in deciding the ouster application are laid down in the 1983 Act: see para. 6–25; and as a matter of procedure the application should include a reference to the Matrimonial Homes Act.

Injunctions in other proceedings

6–28 Injunctions may be granted in support of other legal rights. Sometimes one member of a family may sue another in tort (for example, for trespass to the person or property), and seek an injunction in that action: see, *e.g. Egan* v. *Egan* [1975] Ch 218 (action by parent against son) and *Re S (A Minor)* [1991] 2 FLR 319, CA (below).

Enforcement of injunctions

6–29 There are two main procedures available. First, the traditional remedy of punishing a person who breaks the terms of an injunction; and secondly, the comparatively modern procedure whereby the police may be given power to arrest a person believed to be in breach of the terms of an injunction.

(i) *Punishment for contempt*

6–30 Breach of an order is a contempt of court which may in the last resort be punished by committal to prison for a fixed term of up to two years. It has been said that the object of the exercise is to enforce the order in the sense of getting it working, rather than punishing past behaviour or punishing the offence to the dignity of the court: *Thomason* v. *Thomason* [1985] FLR 214, 216. In many cases, therefore, stern warnings or an adjournment to allow tempers to cool will be the best way of minimising the damage to the family unit (see Ormrod L.J. in *Ansah* v. *Ansah* [1977] Fam 138, 144). Substantial sentences are however passed where it is appropriate to do so. For example:

In *Re H (A Minor) (Injunction: Breach)* [1986] 1 FLR 558 the defendant continued to try to see his daughter and her mother in defiance of an injunction. He smashed his way into the house, waylaid the mother in the small hours of the morning, and assaulted her by putting his hands round her neck and squeezing her throat. He was sent to prison for three months; and the Court of Appeal made it clear that the sentence would have been longer but for the fact that this was the first reported breach.

Again:

> In *Mason* v. *Lawton* [1991] 2 FLR 50, a 20-year-old committed serious breaches of an injunction and although the Court of Appeal considered that the maximum two year sentence imposed by the judge had been excessive in the circumstances, a sentence of nine months detention was substituted.

However, it has to be appreciated that there will inevitably be cases in which the court lacks any effective power to deal with a person who is in breach of an injunction:

> In *Re S (A Minor)* [1991] 2 FLR 319, CA, a woman brought an action against her 15-year-old brother for assault—her primary object in so doing being to give the court jurisdiction to grant an injunction against any repetition of his behaviour (which had included kicking her in the stomach when she was 26 weeks pregnant). The court held that no injunction should be granted. Because the brother was only 15 he could not be imprisoned for breach, and there was no other meaningful sanction which could be imposed on him. The Court of Appeal agreed with the judge that such cases were more appropriate for action by the social services or police than for the civil courts: in all save exceptional cases the right procedure for dealing with unmanageable teenagers was the public, rather than the private, law.

(ii) *The power of arrest*

Breach of an injunction does not constitute a criminal offence, and enforcement action is traditionally for the officials of the court concerned—notably the lipstaff to the Supreme Court and bailiffs in the county court. Until the enactment of the 1976 Act the police had no power to arrest a person merely because he was acting in breach of an injunction: see generally on the limited scope of police duties *R.* v. *Chief Constable of Cheshire, ex parte* K [1990] 1 FLR 70. This caused difficulties for battered wives; and the 1976 Act therefore empowered the court to attach a *power of arrest* to injunctions in certain cases.

6–31

The court may attach a power of arrest to any injunction—whether it was granted under the Domestic Violence and Matrimonial Proceedings Act 1976, the Matrimonial Homes Act 1983, or otherwise—which restrains the other party to the marriage from using violence against the applicant (or against a child living with the applicant) or which excludes the respondent from the family home or from a specified area in which the family home is included: DV&MPA 1976, s.2(1). But a power of arrest can only be inserted if two conditions are satisfied. First, it must be proved that the party enjoined has *caused actual bodily harm* to the applicant (or child); and secondly, the court considers that he or she is *likely to cause actual bodily harm again*. Thus:

> In *Kendrick* v. *Kendrick* [1990] 2 FLR 107 there was no evidence of physical injury to the wife, but she was afraid of her husband to the extent that she felt that she could not return to the family home. The Court of Appeal held that there had been no jurisdiction to attach a power of arrest to the order. Although the court accepted that psychological damage could constitute "actual bodily harm" for these purposes, it considered that "a real change in the psychological condition" of the person assaulted would have to be shown.

Even if these conditions are satisfied the court has a discretion whether or not to attach a power of arrest to an injunction, and it has been said (see Ormrod L.J. in *Lewis* v. *Lewis* [1978] 1 All ER 729) that the power should only be used in exceptional situations "where men and woman persistently disobey injunctions and make nuisances of themselves to the other party and to others concerned."

A power of arrest will be registered at a police station for the applicant's address; and it empowers a constable to arrest, without warrant, a person whom the constable has reasonable cause for suspecting of being in breach of a provision of the injunction: 1976 Act, s.2(3). A person arrested under such a power must be brought before a judge (who may exercise the powers to punish for disobedience to the injunction already outlined) within 24 hours from the time of arrest.

(c) Orders in the Magistrates' Court

6–32 The domestic jurisdiction of magistrates' courts originated in the need recognised by Parliament in 1878 to protect "women of the poorer classes" from physical assaults by their husbands. The legislation is today much more ambitious in scope. Complex, detailed, but in many respects restricted, provisions are now contained in the Domestic Proceedings and Magistrates' Courts Act 1978 ("the 1978 Act"). Under sections 16–18 of that Act either party to a marriage may apply to a magistrates' court for orders usually described as personal protection orders and exclusion orders; and the court has available to it certain emergency powers. But the magistrates' court has no power to grant such orders unless the couple are married.

The main feature of the orders available are set out below.

(1) *Personal protection orders*

6–33 *What the applicant must prove.* To obtain a personal protection order, the applicant must prove two separate matters:

(i) that the respondent had used or threatened to use, violence against the person of the applicant (or a child of the family: see para. 14–03 for the definition), and;

(ii) that it is necessary for the protection of the applicant (or a child of the family) that an order be made: 1978 Act, s.16(2).

Restrictively drafted. This provision is narrowly drafted in three **6–34** important respects. First there must have been *"violence"* either used or threatened. There is no power to act on proof of molestation short of threatened violence even if that behaviour has caused or is likely to cause psychological damage to the applicant or child. Secondly, the violence (or threat) must be *directed against the person of the applicant* or a child of the family. A spouse will be unable to obtain an order merely because violence has been used or threatened against some other member of the family circle or against a child who falls outside the definition of "child of the family." Finally the court must be satisfied that the granting of the order is *"necessary"* for the protection of the applicant or child.

Terms of the order. If these conditions are satisfied the court may **6–35** order that the respondent should not use, or threaten to use, violence against the person of the applicant (or against the person of a child of the family), or incite or assist others to do so. But the magistrates have no power to grant an order against molestation, in the sense of pestering: contrast the powers of the county court: para. 6–21 above.

(2) *Exclusion orders*

What the applicant must prove. The court has power to grant this **6–36** "drastic remedy" only if it is satisfied of two separate matters: 1978 Act, s.16(3):

(i) *Violence by respondent*. It is not sufficient that the respondent has simply threatened to use violence. Even if there is the clearest possible evidence that a spouse or child is in danger of serious physical injury, a magistrates' court will be unable to grant an exclusion order unless the applicant can prove that the respondent has, either:

(a) "used violence against the person of the applicant or a child of the family"; or
(b) "threatened to use violence against the person of the applicant or a child of the family and has used violence against some other person"; or
(c) "threatened to use violence against the person of the applicant or a child of the family" in contravention of a personal protection order.

(ii) *Danger of physical injury*. The applicant must also satisfy the **6–37** court that the applicant or a child of the family is in danger of being physically injured by the respondent (or would be in such danger if the applicant or child were to enter the matrimonial home). It is not sufficient to prove that there is a risk of damage to mental health.

6–38   *Terms of the order.* An exclusion order is the counterpart of an ouster order. The court may (i) require the respondent to leave the matrimonial home; and/or (ii) prohibit the respondent from entering the matrimonial home. The court may also order the respondent to permit the applicant to enter and remain in the matrimonial home. Orders may be for a specified term and subject to exceptions (*e.g.* that the husband be permitted to enter one room) or conditions. But the magistrates have no power to order one spouse to keep away from the area in which the home is situated: contrast the powers of the superior courts, para. 6–22 above.

(3) *Emergency procedures*

6–39   There are two provisions designed to ensure that action can be taken quickly. First, if the court considers that it is essential that the application—whether for a personal protection or exclusion order—should be heard without delay, it may do so in spite of the fact that some of the usual rules about the composition of the court (for example, that it include both a man and a woman) cannot be observed. Secondly, the court (which for this purpose may consist of a single justice) may make an expedited order, lasting for up to 28 days, notwithstanding the fact that the usual procedural safeguards for notice to the respondent have not been complied with. But this expedited procedure is only available in respect of personal protection orders; and the court can only act if it is satisfied that there is "imminent danger of physical injury to the applicant" or a child; 1978 Act, s.16(6). These restrictions make the procedure much less flexible than that available in the superior courts, where orders—even, in exceptional circumstances ouster orders—can be made *ex parte* (*i.e.* without notice to the respondent). Moreover, administrative arrangements have been made in the superior courts to ensure that a judge is always available to hear applications.

Enforcement of Magistrates' Court orders

6–40   The 1978 Act provides two special procedures designed to facilitate enforcement of orders.

(i) *Arrest and punishment for breach.* If an order has been disobeyed, the court on the application of a spouse, can issue a warrant of arrest: 1978 Act, s.18(4). The court may then fine the respondent (up to £50 for every day on which the respondent is in default, but with a maximum of £2,000) or commit him to prison for a period (not exceeding two months).

(ii) *Insertion of a power of arrest.* The court may attach a power of arrest if the respondent has "physically injured" the applicant or a child of the family and considers that he is likely to do so again: 1978 Act, s.18(1). The effect of such an order is comparable to that of an order made under the Domestic Violence and Matrimonial Proceedings Act 1976: see para. 6–31 above.

SUGGESTIONS FOR FURTHER READING

Hoggett and Pearl, Chap. 9.
Law Commission Working Paper No. 113, *Domestic Violence and Occupation of the Family Home* (1989).
L. Smith, *Domestic Violence: an Overview of the Literature*, Home Office Research Study 107, HMSO (1989).
M. Hayes, "The Law Commission and the Family Home" (1990) 33 MLR 222.
S. M. Edwards and A. Halpern, "Protection for the Victims of Domestic Violence: Time for Radical Revision" [1991] JSWFL 94.
C. Williams, "Ouster Orders, Property Adjustment and Council Housing" [1988] Fam Law 438.

PART II—PROPERTY AND FINANCIAL ASPECTS OF FAMILY LAW

INTRODUCTION

Property and financial matters are of great importance when a relationship breaks down and also on some other occasions. The first chapter of this part (Chapter 7) therefore sets out the basic rules governing the entitlement and use of family property. The State also has an interest in family finance—at one level, it has been the policy of the welfare state to promote the welfare of families by providing support through a range of benefits, and these benefits are often of crucial importance to lone parent families. But on the other hand, the State has long been concerned that individuals should not be able to evade their own responsibilities for the upkeep of their families. The relationship between those two policies, and between private and public law approaches to the financial consequences of family breakdown is dealt with in Chapter 8. Finally Chapter 9 summarises the various legal procedures to adjust the financial and property entitlements of the parties and children which are available when a relationship breaks down. This chapter highlights the extensive powers exercisable by the divorce court in matrimonial proceedings, but it also considers the financial position when a non-marital relationship breaks down.

Chapter 7

ENTITLEMENT TO FAMILY PROPERTY

INTRODUCTION—A PROPERTY-OWNING SOCIETY?

In spite of economic policies in the first three-quarters of this century **7–01** which were intended to promote greater equality in the distribution of wealth, 5 per cent. of the population owns 36 per cent. of the country's wealth. The reader may therefore think that questions of whether marriage or other family relationships have any effect on entitlement to property are of interest only to a comparatively small section of the community. But this is not true; and the reason why it is not true is largely connected with the great extension of home ownership financed by building society and bank credit. Approximately one-third of the net wealth of the personal sector consists of dwelling-houses; and this factor has operated progressively to reduce the percentage of marketable wealth owned by the richest groups in society.

The extension of building-society-financed home-ownership, and inflation of house-values over the years, has meant that many families acquire what may be a very substantial capital asset. For example:

> In *Mortimer* v. *Mortimer-Griffin* [1986] 2 FLR 315, a couple bought a home in 1970 for £6,360. They put up £1,350 in cash and borrowed the rest on mortgage. By the time of the hearing the house was worth £70,000 (after allowing for the outstanding mortgage). Although the parties had had to pay interest on the mortgage over the years, a very large sum of capital had accrued.

Do both parties in such a case have any right to share in the gain, or can one of them—typically the husband—say: the house was conveyed into my name, I was in law responsible for paying off the mortgage loan, and so all the gain belongs to me?

For many years, this question would have been answered by **7–02** reference to property law. The divorce court had virtually no powers to readjust the entitlement of family members to capital assets when a marriage broke down, and questions of entitlement had to be solved by reference to the ordinary law of property in which the fact of marital breakdown would be irrelevant. However, since 1971, the divorce court has had wide powers to readjust the parties' property rights—as we shall see in Chapter 9 below; and in divorce proceedings the court now asks the question "to whom shall this be given?" rather than "to whom does this belong?" In deciding how it should exercise its powers, the court is required to give first consideration to the welfare of children, and will also give weight to the interest in the home which the parties have earned by the contributions they have made to the welfare of the family, including contributions by looking after the home and caring for the family.

Lord Denning has graphically described the exercise of the divorce court's modern powers in these words: the court, he said (see *Hanlon* v. *The Law Society* [1981] AC 124, 146):

> "takes the rights and obligations of the parties all together and puts the pieces into a mixed bag. Such pieces are the right to occupy the matrimonial home or have a share in it, the obligation to maintain the wife and children, and so forth. The court then takes out the pieces and hands them to the two parties—some to one party and some to the other—so that each can provide for the future with the pieces allotted to him or to her. The court hands them out without paying any too nice a regard to their legal or equitable rights but simply according to what is the fairest provision for the future, for mother and father and the children."

Property law irrelevant?

7–03   Does this mean that the family lawyer can ignore questions of beneficial entitlement to property? The answer is that it does not. In particular, the divorce court can only exercise its powers to make property adjustment orders "on granting a decree of divorce, a decree of nullity of marriage or a decree of judicial separation." Thus:

> In *Mossop* v. *Mossop* [1988] 2 FLR 173, CA, the applicant had lived with the respondent from 1979 to 1983. In 1985 she applied for an order that the respondent transfer to her such part of his interest in the house in which they had lived together as might be just. The Court of Appeal held that the application had been properly struck out as disclosing no reasonable cause of action. Had the applicant and the respondent been married, the divorce court would have been able to exercise a broad adjustive discretion; but in the absence of a marriage to dissolve, the court could do no more than declare the parties' beneficial interests in the property.

The question of whether the "unmarried housewife" is to be entitled to any share in the home in which she may have brought up a family thus has to be resolved by reference to orthodox principles for determining the beneficial ownership of property. Paradoxically, as will be seen, it is in such cases that the law about the ownership of what may be called "family assets" has perhaps today its greatest relevance. Even more paradoxically the relevant legal principles were developed, at a time before the divorce court had its modern wide adjustive powers, in disputes between married couples.

There are also other circumstances in which the question of beneficial ownership—"the cold legal question" may be relevant in practice:

(i) *Occasionally relevant in exercise of adjustive jurisdiction on divorce.* 7–04
Although as we have seen the court does not "pay any too nice a regard" to the legal or equitable rights of the parties to divorce, there may be cases in which the court needs to know what property is owned by the parties before it can sensibly exercise its discretion: see *Tebbutt* v. *Haynes* [1981] 2 All ER 238, 245.

(ii) *Third party affected.* The dispute may not be between two 7–05
spouses; but between a spouse and a third party—for example, a creditor of the husband. The creditor may be able to enforce his legal rights of recovery against the property of the husband; but he will not generally be entitled to attack property which is beneficially owned by the wife—unless she has joined in the transaction or done something else to render herself liable. In fact, the two recent leading cases in the House of Lords relating to matrimonial property—*Williams & Glyn's Bank* v. *Boland* [1981] AC 487, HL, and *Lloyds Bank plc* v. *Rosset* [1990] 2 FLR 155, HL, have both been concerned with such situations. It is for this reason that questions of beneficial entitlement to property are particularly important when a spouse is adjudicated bankrupt. All the property to which the bankrupt spouse is beneficially entitled vests by operation of law in the trustee in bankruptcy; and it is the trustee's duty to realise the property for the benefit of the bankrupt's creditors. The other spouse's property, in contrast, does not vest in the trustee; and he or she is, in principle, entitled to keep it. However, bankruptcy and debt are not the only situations in which it is necessary to resolve questions of the extent of a third party's interest. For example:

> In *Harwood* v. *Harwood* [1991] 2 FLR 274 a firm in which the husband was a partner contributed to the cost of the matrimonial home. The court could not finally resolve matters until the extent of the partner's interest had been established.

(iii) *Parties do not seek divorce.* There are still people who, for 7–06
religious or other reasons, do not want to divorce; and if a couple choose not to bring matrimonial proceedings the court will have to resolve any questions about the beneficial entitlement to their property without using the divorce court's adjustive powers—although a married couple may use judicial separation as a way of invoking the court's powers.

(iv) *Death.* The majority of marriages are terminated by death, and 7–07
not by divorce. If one spouse dies leaving all his or her property by will to charity, say, or to a lover, the other spouse now has a right to

apply to the court for reasonable provision to be made out of the deceased's estate under the Inheritance (Provision for Family and Dependants) Act 1975; but the court, in deciding such applications, may have to balance the applicant's claims against those of others. In such cases it might be advantageous to the surviving spouse to claim that he or she actually owned the matrimonial home (or other asset) so that it did not pass under the deceased's will at all.

7–08   (v) *Divorce court's powers no longer exercisable.* A divorced spouse loses the right to apply for a property adjustment order on remarriage: MCA 1973, s.28(3). But an application could still be made for a declaration that he or she owned the property in question.

7–09   (vi) *Disputes about use of property rather than its ownership.* Such disputes—for example, as to whether a jointly owned house should be sold—are still sometimes dealt with by reference to property law rather than by invoking the adjustive jurisdiction of the divorce court. This is particularly the case when a third party is involved—for example, if a creditor seeks to enforce a judgment against a spouse's share in property, perhaps by obtaining a charging order against the debtor's interest in the family home.

Rules determining entitlement

7–10   Since 1882, it has been a basic principle of the law that marriage as such has no effect on property entitlement. This rule was adopted by the Married Women's Property Act 1882 in an attempt to protect married women: for example, a married woman's earnings were to be her own to do with as she wished, whereas at common law—under which husband and wife became legally one but (as Lord Denning has put it: see *Williams & Glyn's Bank* v. *Boland* [1979] Ch 312, 332) the husband was that one—her earnings belonged to her husband. Most of the disputes about family assets have centred on the family home and the following rules of land law and equity are particularly relevant.

7–11   (i) *Deed needed for transfer of legal estate.* Section 52 of the Law of Property Act 1925 stipulates that a deed is necessary to convey or create any legal estate in land. Hence, if the conveyance of the family home was taken in the name of one partner it follows (in the absence of any subsequent conveyance) that the other can make no claim to be entitled to the *legal* estate.

7–12   (ii) *Writing necessary for other interests in land.* Section 53 of the Law of Property Act 1925 stipulates that no interest in land can be created or disposed of except by a signed written document. Thus:

> In *Gissing* v. *Gissing* [1971] AC 886, HL, the matrimonial home had been conveyed into the husband's sole name. When the marriage broke up he

told his wife: "Don't worry about the house—it's yours. I will pay the mortgage payments and all other outgoings." However, the wife had no claim on the basis of that statement: there was no deed which could displace the legal estate, and no written document which could give her any other beneficial interest.

(iii) *But interest may be claimed under a trust—express implied resulting*   **7–13** *or constructive trust.* Section 53(2) of the Law of Property Act 1925 creates an important exception to the requirement of writing. It provides that section 53 does not affect the "creation or operation of resulting, implied or constructive trusts"; and a spouse may therefore be able to establish a claim under these equitable doctrines, which are based on the underlying principle that it would in the circumstances be unconscionable to allow the legal owner to continue to assert the absolute ownership which appears on the title documents: see Lord Templeman in *Winkworth* v. *Edward Baron Development Company Ltd.* [1987] 1 FLR 525, 529, HL.

This exception to the general rule has been of the greatest importance, and most claims to share in the ownership of the family home have been established through the medium of an implied resulting or constructive trust imposed upon the owner of the legal estate. But there are also other ways in which a property interest inconsistent with the formal documents of title may be established—in particular, by contract, estoppel and statute. The text therefore analyses in turn:

(i)   claims under implied, resulting or constructive trusts;
(ii) claims based on contract;
(iii) the doctrine of estoppel;
(iv) statutory provisions under which property interests may be claimed.

Finally, the text deals with a number of incidental questions arising in relation to the use and ownership of family property.

I. IMPLIED RESULTING OR CONSTRUCTIVE TRUST

There has, over the years, been considerable difference of judicial   **7–14** opinion about the circumstances in which the court will allow the legal ownership of property to be displaced by the imposition of an implied resulting or constructive trust. At one time it was thought by some that the court could impose a trust whenever it would be "inequitable" for the estate owner to keep the property for himself alone (*Heseltine* v. *Heseltine* [1971] 1 WLR 342, 346), and that the court could impose a trust whenever justice and good conscience required:

see *Hussey* v. *Palmer* [1972] 1 WLR 1286. But as a result of a number of decisions of the superior courts, culminating in the decision of the House of Lords in *Lloyds Bank plc* v. *Rosset* [1990] 2 FLR 155 it is clear that the jurisdiction is in fact much more restricted. In particular, it remains a cardinal principle of the law that the fact that a person expends money or labour on another's property does not of itself entitle him to that property or to an interest in it. As Slade L.J. put it in *Thomas* v. *Fuller-Brown* [1988] 1 FLR 237, 240, CA:

> " ... under English law the mere fact that A expends money or labour on B's property does not by itself entitle A to an interest in the property. In the absence of an express agreement or a common intention to be inferred from all the circumstances or any question of estoppel, A will normally have no claim whatever on the property in such circumstances. The decision of the House of Lords in *Pettitt* v. *Pettitt* makes this clear ... "

7–15   What, then, are the exceptional circumstances in which A's claim will be accepted as valid?

The student should be warned that there is still considerable uncertainty in this area. As Mustill L.J. put it in *Grant* v. *Edwards* [1987] 1 FLR 87, 101, CA, the time has not yet "arrived when it is possible to state the law in a way which will deal with all the practical problems which may arise in this difficult field, consistently with everything said in the cases." The following summary of principles should accordingly be treated with reserve.

In principle, a trust will be imposed only if two conditions are satisfied. First, there must be evidence that the parties *intended* that they should both be beneficial owners of an interest in the property. Secondly, the applicant—the person who would not be entitled if only the documents relating to the legal estate were referred to—must show *reliance* on this intention *to the applicant's detriment.*

(i) Evidence of intention

7–16   In some cases there may be admissible evidence that the parties had discussed the question of ownership of the property and had reached an agreement that both were to share. For example:

In *Grant* v. *Edwards* [1987] 1 FLR 87, CA, the claimant was told that her name was not going to go on the title because if it did there might be problems in her then pending divorce proceedings. The court accepted that this fact, coupled with evidence that the parties treated the house as belonging to them both and that they had a principle of sharing everything, constituted sufficient proof that she was intended to have an interest in the house.

In *H* v. *M* (*Property: Beneficial Interest*) [1992] 1 FLR 229, CA, the claimant was told that "tax reasons" justified the transfer of the family home into the respondent's sole name. The respondent told the claimant not to worry about the future "because when we are married it will be half yours anyway." The court held there was sufficient evidence of the existence of a common intention to own the house jointly.

In many cases, however, the applicant will ask the court to draw an *inference* from all the evidence that there was such an intention; and it is in relation to the circumstances in which the court will draw such an inference that the law has for long been unclear.

It is clear that such an inference may be drawn from the making of *contributions to the acquisition costs* of the property. But such contributions may take a number of forms:

(a) *Financial contributions*. The clearest application of this principle is **7–17** in the case—traditionally classified as a *resulting trust*—where one partner provides all or part of the purchase price for the family home conveyed into the name of the other. If, therefore, a wife pays £100,000, and her husband pays £300,000 of a total purchase price of £400,000, the wife will in principle be entitled in equity to a one-quarter interest in the property. The application of this principle can be seen in the case of *Sekhon* v. *Alissa* [1989] 2 FLR 94—not, be it noted, a case between husband and wife:

A mother contributed £22,500 in cash to the £36,500 purchase price of a house conveyed into the sole name of her daughter; and the mother subsequently made further cash contributions towards repairs and improvements. The daughter funded the balance of the cost by building society loans and a Local Authority improvement grant. It was held that, in the absence of evidence that the mother's contributions were intended to be gifts or loans for a fixed amount, the mother was entitled to an interest in equity in the property by way of resulting trust. That interest was to be quantified by applying the legal presumption that the interests of the parties corresponded with their contributions. (On the facts, the most appropriate way of giving effect to that interest was that the mother should be granted a lease in respect of one of the flats into which the property had been divided.)

(b) *Helping with the mortgage*. Nowadays most houses are bought **7–18** with the aid of a substantial mortgage from a building society or bank. If one of the partners formally assumes liability under the mortgage, or even if he or she makes contributions to the instalments, this fact may provide evidence that the parties, at the time of the purchase, intended that each should have a beneficial interest: see *Marsh* v. *Von Sternberg* [1986] 1 FLR 526, CA; *Bernard* v. *Josephs* (1983) 4 FLR 179, 187; *Re Gorman (a Bankrupt)* [1990] 2 FLR 284, 291. But it must be emphasised that neither the fact that a person assumes liability, nor even the fact that a person makes the payments, of itself gives rise to any beneficial entitlement. The question is to decide whether the facts constitute evidence of the parties' intentions at the time of the purchase: *Re Gorman* [1990] 2 FLR 184, 291, *per* Vinelott J.; and see *Harwood* v. *Harwood* [1991] 2 FLR 274, CA.

7–19   (c) *Non-financial contributions*. In a number of cases, the courts relied on the fact that an applicant has made real and substantial contributions to the property as sufficing to show the necessary intention. For example:

> In *Cooke* v. *Head* [1972] 1 WLR 518 a woman carried out extensive building works, using a sledge hammer and cement mixer ("much more than most women would do," *per* Lord Denning MR at p. 519).

and

> In *Eves* v. *Eves* [1975] 1 WLR 1338 a woman broke up concrete, demolished a shed, and carried out extensive decorations ("much more than many wives would do," *per* Lord Denning MR at p. 1340).

7–20   However, it is worth repeating that the question is not whether a person has devoted time and effort to the acquisition or improvement of the property; the question is whether the evidence indicates that the contributions manifest an intention that the beneficial ownership be shared; and recent cases show a reluctance to allow such an inference to be drawn from the making of non-financial contributions. In particular:

> In *Lloyds Bank plc* v. *Rosset* [1990] 2 FLR 155, HL, a wife carried out and supervised renovation works on a property intended as the family home. She had some skill "over and above that acquired by most housewives. She was a skilled painter and decorator who enjoyed wallpapering and decorating ... " She co-ordinated building work, planned and designed a large breakfast room and small kitchen and papered two bedrooms. Although the judge at first instance thought this was sufficient to justify his drawing the inference that she should have a beneficial interest in the property under a constructive trust, her claim was decisively rejected by the House of Lords. The work which she had done "could not possibly justify" the drawing of such an inference. Indeed Lord Bridge said, "it was common ground that Mrs Rosset was extremely anxious that the new matrimonial home should be ready for occupation before Christmas ... in those circumstances it would seem the most natural thing in the world for any wife, in the absence of her husband abroad, to spend all the time she could spare and to employ any skills she might have, such as the ability to decorate a room, in doing all she could to accelerate progress of the work quite irrespective of any expectation she might have of enjoying a beneficial interest in the property."

So far, the *Rosset* decision may be regarded simply as a rather curious example of the House of Lords being prepared to overrule findings of fact—*i.e.* as to the parties' intentions—made at first instance. But the long-term significance of the case lies in the view, expressed by Lord Bridge (with whom the other Law Lords agreed) that it was "at least extremely doubtful" whether anything short of a direct contribution to the purchase price by the partner who was not the legal owner (whether initially or by payment of mortgage instalments) could justify the drawing of the inference of a common intention to share the property beneficially. *Eves* v. *Eves* (above) was explained on the basis that there was in fact an express agreement that the beneficial ownership be shared.

In the light of these dicta it must be assumed that the courts will not readily draw inferences about the parties' intentions from the fact that the claimant has made contributions (other than financial contributions) to the acquisition of the property.

The presumption of advancement. There is a rule of equity—the so-   7–21
called presumption of advancement—that if a husband makes a payment for or puts property into the name of a wife he intends that this should be a gift to her. In consequence, if property is put into the name of a wife—as is quite frequently done by those engaged in business—the husband would not be able to claim an interest in it by reason of his contributions. However, the presumption reflects out-dated social conditions, and should be applied with caution today: see *Harwood* v. *Harwood* [1991] 2 FLR 274, 294 *per* Slade L.J.

In any event, it is usually open to a party to rebut the presumption of advancement by showing that to apply it would be inconsistent with the parties' true intentions. Does this mean that a businessman, for example, could say that he had only put property into his wife's name in order to keep it from his creditors? It has been held that evidence which involves disclosure of improper or fraudulent motive should not be admitted for this purpose: see *Tinker* v. *Tinker* [1970] P 136. But it may be that this rule is not inflexible (see *Tinsley* v. *Milligan* (1991) *The Times*, August 22) and perhaps, that the exclusionary rule will only be imposed where moral guilt is involved. Thus:

> In *Heseltine* v. *Heseltine* [1971] 1 WLR 342 the wife had transferred property to the husband so that (i) death duty might be avoided if she survived seven years and (ii) the husband could show he was a man of sufficient wealth to become an underwriting member of Lloyd's. The husband argued that the wife should not be allowed to deny the making of an absolute gift, since this would involve revealing that the transactions had been designed to deceive Lloyd's and the Revenue. It was held that she could give evidence of her true intention. The exclusionary rule is based on the principle that a man cannot take advantage of his own wrong; in the present case it did not apply because (in the words of Lord Denning) the "wife here has done no wrong. She only did what her husband asked her. That should not be taken against her."

(ii) Proof of detrimental reliance by the claimant
Case law now establishes that it does not suffice to ground a claim   7–22
for the court merely to infer an intention that both parties should have a beneficial interest in the property. This is because of the

principle that equity will not assist a volunteer. Hence it must also be shown that the claimant *has acted to his or her detriment* in reliance on the intention. It is for this reason that the making of contributions is in practice so important: such contributions will both constitute evidence from which the parties' common intention can be inferred, and also establish that the claimant has acted to his or her detriment in reliance on that common intention. If there has been no such contribution it may be difficult to show the necessary detrimental reliance:

> In *Midland Bank plc* v. *Dobson and Dobson* [1986] 1 FLR 171, CA, the court accepted that husband and wife had a common intention to share the beneficial interest in the matrimonial home; but the wife nonetheless failed in her claim because there was no evidence that she had acted to her detriment on the basis of that intention. She had made no direct contribution to the acquisition costs or mortgage instalments, and her contributions in buying domestic equipment and in decorating the house were unrelated to the intention that the ownership of the house be shared.

Moreover, the detriment must be of some real weight and significance:

> In *Lloyds Bank plc* v. *Rosset* (the facts of which have been given at para. 7–20 above) Lord Bridge said that on any view the monetary value of the wife's contribution to the purchase of a comparatively expensive house "must have been so trifling as to be almost *de minimis*." He went on to express "considerable doubt" whether the work she had done could have constituted sufficient detriment "even if her husband's intention to make a gift to her of half or any other share in the equity of the property had been clearly established or if he had clearly represented to her that that was what he intended."

Significance of marriage

7–23   English law has no special property regime governing matrimonial property. Paradoxically, this fact has made it easier for the courts to develop principles to govern the property rights of the family outside marriage. Lord Upjohn, in *Pettitt* v. *Pettitt* [1970] AC 777, 813 stated that property disputes between husband and wife had to be decided by ordinary principles "while making full allowance" in view of the relationship between the parties. The question therefore becomes "what allowances have to be made?"; and the answer must depend on the content of the parties' relationship rather than on their legal status. The existence or absence of "paperwork" should make no difference; and two couples who have had a similar relationship should find that they have comparable property rights, irrespective of the fact that one couple married and the other never did so.

7–24   But the question does sometimes arise whether the fact that the parties have never married is of any significance in answering questions about their presumed intention in relation to the ownership

of property. The courts have, in some cases, taken the view that, whereas marriage by itself involves a commitment to a permanent relationship, cohabitation can involve very diverse attitudes. Accordingly, it has been said that it is necessary to look carefully at the precise nature of the relationship between an unmarried couple in order to be able to draw appropriate inferences as to the parties' intentions; and the practical result may be that it will be more difficult to satisfy the court that an unmarried couple had an intention to own property jointly than would be the case if the couple were married.
Thus:

In *Burns* v. *Burns* [1984] FLR 216 a couple had lived together for 19 years, and F had given up a job to look after M and their two children. She had also taken his name and obtained a passport in that name; she had put her earnings into the housekeeping, bought fixtures and fittings for the house, bought a washing machine and a tumble dryer, and she had laid a patio and done internal decorative work. It was held that these contributions were insufficient to justify the inference of an agreement to share the beneficial ownership.

In *Thomas* v. *Fuller-Brown* [1988] 1 FLR 237 a bricklayer was provided with accommodation by a divorced woman, and constructed a two-storey extension to her house, created a through lounge, carried out minor electrical and plumbing works, replastered and redecorated the property throughout, landscaped and reorganised the garden, laid a drive-way, carried out repairs to the chimney and the roof and repointed the gable end of the property, constructed an internal entry hall and rebuilt the kitchen and installed a new stairway; but he was held to have no beneficial interest in the property. The court rejected the argument that the only reasonable inference from the parties' conduct was that they both intended that, in exchange for what he was doing, he should have a beneficial interest in the property. Instead, the court accepted that he was living in the house as a "kept man" provided with board and lodging and some pocket money in return for the work which he had carried out.

Going behind the title deeds

So far the text has been concerned almost exclusively with the   7–25
question whether a person whose identity is not revealed on the title documents can claim an interest in the property. But suppose that the legal estate *has* been conveyed to both parties to a relationship. What determines the extent of the parties' beneficial interests? There are two situations. First, where there is in the transfer or in a separate document a declaration quantifying the beneficial interests. In such a case, that declaration will be virtually conclusive in the absence of fraud or mistake. For example:

In *Goodman* v. *Gallant* [1986] 1 FLR 513, CA a house was transferred to a couple "upon trust for themselves as joint tenants." It was held that, in the absence of fraud this declaration was conclusive.

The same principle was adopted by the Divisional Court in *Re Gorman* [1990] 2 FLR 284:

> Property was transferred to a husband and wife as joint tenants. There was no express declaration (such as had appeared in the title documents in *Goodman* v. *Gallant*) but the Land Registry transfer contained a declaration stating that the transferees were entitled to the land for their own benefit and that the survivor of them could give a valid receipt for capital moneys arising on a disposition of the land. It was held that this declaration pointed clearly and unequivocally to a beneficial joint tenancy since it would only be on that footing that the survivor would be entitled to give a valid receipt. (In *Harwood* v. *Harwood* [1991] 2 FLR 274, 287–9, para. 7–04 above, in contrast, the declaration did not have this effect, since it did not exclude the possibility that H and W were to hold the property on trust for X.)

It is obviously desirable, in order to minimise the possibility of dispute, that conveyances of property for use as a family home should deal with the question of beneficial ownership, and it has been said that solicitors who fail to advise their clients on this issue may be guilty of professional negligence: see *Walker* v. *Hall* [1984] FLR 126, CA.

However, in the absence of any declaration, the court may be able to find that the parties had a common intention about the extent of their entitlement, and that may enable the court to impose a constructive trust to give effect thereto.

Severance of joint tenancy

7-26 It is of the nature of a joint tenancy that it can be severed—*i.e.* converted into a tenancy in common. This may be particularly important where a relationship is breaking down: one party may for example want to ensure that his or her half-interest in the family home should on death pass under the will or intestacy (to children by a previous relationship, for example) rather than to the other party. There are a number of ways in which severance can be achieved, of which the simplest is by one joint tenant giving written notice to the other under the provisions of section 36 of the Law of Property Act 1925. (Simply asking for an order in matrimonial proceedings is not by itself sufficient: *Harris* v. *Goddard* [1984] FLR 209, CA.) It is impossible to sever a joint tenancy by will.

II. CONTRACT

7-27 A couple may decide to regulate their affairs by contract; and in appropriate cases the court may be able to infer the existence of a legally enforceable agreement between them. If a contract is to be made out it must be shown that:

   (i)   There was a genuine meeting of minds between the parties— *i.e.* an offer and an acceptance.

  (ii)   The parties intended to create a legally enforceable relationship.

 (iii)   The terms of the agreement are sufficiently precise.

 (iv)   There is consideration (unless the agreement is contained in a deed or document under seal).

  (v)   The terms which it is sought to enforce are not illegal or contrary to public policy.

For the most part there will be no difficulty in applying the ordinary rules of contract to the domestic situation. Two decided cases illustrating the working of the law may be contrasted:

In *Tanner* v. *Tanner* [1975] 1 WLR 1341 the male partner purchased a house for occupation by the defendant and the twin daughters of their relationship. The defendant moved into the house; but subsequently the parties' relationship broke down, and the plaintiff claimed possession on the basis that the defendant was only a bare licensee under a licence which he had revoked. The Court of Appeal held that there was an implied contractual licence under the terms of which the defendant was to be entitled to occupy the house so long as the children were of school age or until some other circumstance arose which would make it unreasonable for her to retain possession.

On the other hand, in *Layton* v. *Martin* [1986] 2 FLR 277 a woman accepted a man's offer that, if she would live with him, he would give her what emotional security he could plus financial security on his death. She failed in an action against his estate after his death notwithstanding the fact that she had lived with the deceased for five years after that offer had been made and that she had been his mistress for 13 years in all. This was because the court refused to find that there had been any intention to create a legally enforceable contract—a decision which seems somewhat harsh on the facts.

If a contract *is* established, questions of public policy may affect its enforceability. The law has long been reluctant to allow a married couple to regulate the consequences of the breakdown of their relationship by private contract. It is, for example, still the law that a married couple cannot by contract preclude the court from exercising its jurisdiction to make financial provision and property adjustment orders: see generally para. 9–82 below. The possible relevance of rules in this category must be considered in any case concerning the enforceability of marital contracts (although in practice the rules are more relevant to cases in which rights are purportedly taken away rather than to cases in which rights are conferred by contract); and in the case of the unmarried, it has to be remembered that there is a general rule that a contract "founded on an immoral consideration" will not be enforced. But it seems doubtful whether this rule would be today considered relevant to cases involving a genuine relationship.

Of much more importance is the provision of the Law of Property (Miscellaneous Provisions) Act 1989 which imposes a general requirement that a contract for the disposition of land or any interest in land should be in writing and signed by the parties. This rule replaces the much more flexible rule formerly contained in the Law of Property Act 1925, which merely required such a contract to be evidenced in writing; and permitted contracts not so evidenced to be enforced if the plaintiff could show an act of part performance such as would render it inequitable for the defendant to rely on the lack of formality. It would seem that the effect of the 1989 Act will do much to restrict reliance on informal contracts as a source of entitlement to property; but the 1989 Act does not affect the operation of implied resulting and constructive trusts and will therefore have no application where a claim can be made under the principles discussed at paras. 7–14 to 7–24 above. Moreover, there will be many cases in which a claimant who might have relied on an informal contract will be able to assert an interest by way of estoppel.

III. ESTOPPEL

7–28   The doctrine of estoppel is of particular relevance in cases where one party has moved into property owned by another. The general principle is that if one party to a relationship incurs expenditure or does some other act to his or her detriment in the belief, encouraged by the other, that the claimant already owns or would be given some proprietary interest in a specific asset, an equity will arise to have the expectations which have been encouraged made good, so far as may fairly be done between the parties—even, in appropriate cases, by requiring the owner of the legal estate in the property to transfer it to the claimant.

This doctrine may therefore enable a court to go some way towards giving effect to the parties' reasonable assumptions if to do otherwise would be unfair or unjust. The scope for the application of the doctrine in the context of a non-marital relationship can be illustrated by reference to the case of *Pascoe* v. *Turner* [1979] 1 WLR 431:

> The defendant and his former housekeeper had lived as man and wife for many years. He then formed another relationship, and told the defendant that the house and its contents were hers. In reliance on that statement the plaintiff made substantial improvements to the house and bought furnishings for it, using for these purposes a large proportion of her small capital. The statement that the property was to be the

defendant's was held to be ineffective because the appropriate formalities had not been observed; but the court held that there was an equitable estoppel by reason of the defendant's encouragement and acquiescence in the actions which the plaintiff had taken in reliance on the defendant's statement, and that this estoppel could only be satisfied by transferring the legal estate in the property to her.

In contrast:

In *Coombes* v. *Smith* [1987] 1 FLR 352, M assured F that he would always provide for her; but it was held that she was not entitled to an interest by way of estoppel since she had not been under any misapprehension about her legal rights.

—and in *Layton* v. *Martin* [1986] 2 FLR 277 the plaintiff failed to establish an estoppel interest because the expectations aroused by the deceased's representations did not relate to any specific item of property.

Estoppel as a defence. Even if one party is unable to establish a proprietary interest under the doctrine of equitable estoppel there may nonetheless be circumstances in which he or she could successfully resist an action for possession on the basis that there has been a representation that the defendant would be allowed to stay in the property for a period, and that the representation was intended to be acted upon and was in fact acted on: see *Maharaj* v. *Chand* [1986] AC 898, PC.

IV. STATUTE

Two statutes (the Married Women's Property Act 1964 and the Matrimonial Proceedings and Property Act 1970) may, in certain circumstances, enable a *married person* to claim a beneficial interest in property, while the Law Reform (Miscellaneous Provisions) Act 1970 confers certain rights in respect of property acquired during an *engagement to marry*. Of much more importance are the Matrimonial Homes Act 1983 (which confers extensive rights in relation to the *occupation* of the matrimonial home) and the Inheritance (Provision for Family and Dependants) Act 1975 (which gives the court extensive powers to order that financial provision be made out of a deceased's estate for his or her "dependants" as statutorily defined). These provisions are examined in turn. 7–29

1. The Married Women's Property Act 1964 was intended to reverse the common law rule under which the husband was entitled to any savings made by his wife out of a housekeeping 7–30 allowance. The (unsatisfactorily drafted) Act provides that such savings shall in the absence of contrary agreement be treated as belonging to husband and wife in equal shares. The Law Commission has recommended repeal of the Act, and that it be replaced by a statutory presumption that property bought for the joint use or benefit of spouses should (subject to certain exceptions) be jointly owned by them. It seems that the provisions of the 1964 Act are rarely invoked.

7–31   **2. The Matrimonial Proceedings and Property Act 1970**, section 37, seeks to clarify the law relating to the effect of one spouse's contributions to the improvement of property. Provided that the contribution is substantial and in money or money's worth the contributing spouse is, in the absence of contrary agreement, to be treated as acquiring a share (or an enlarged share) in the property. In the absence of agreement, it is for the court to quantify the shares according to what it considers to be just. It should be emphasised that the section is not concerned with the effect of contributions to the acquisition or to the maintenance of property.

7–32   **3. The Law Reform (Miscellaneous Provisions) Act 1970** was primarily concerned to abolish the action for breach of promise of marriage. But it was also decided to enact a special code to deal with some of the proprietary problems which may arise from termination of an engagement. The Act applies the rules of law relating to the rights of husbands and wives in relation to property to the determination of beneficial interests in property acquired during the currency of an engagement. In fact this provision is of limited scope: it would seem, however, that the *presumption of advancement* (para. 7–21 above) might be applied to transfers between engaged people and it is clear that the statutory principle embodied in the Matrimonial Proceedings and Property Act 1970 (and explained above) could, in appropriate circumstances, apply so as to create a beneficial interest in favour of a person who has made *contributions to the improvement* of property. Moreover, the Act also gives the parties the right to use the summary procedure available under section 17 of the Married Women's Property Act 1882 if proceedings are instituted within three years of the termination of the agreement.

It is important to note that the provisions of the Law Reform (Miscellaneous Provisions) Act 1970 only apply where there has been a clear agreement between a couple to marry. Vague talk of marriage is insufficient to bring the Act into operation: see *Bernard* v. *Josephs* (1982) 4 FLR 178, 190; (and note that, perhaps, surprisingly, no reliance appears to have been placed on the statute in the case of *H* v. *M* (*Property: Beneficial Interest*) [1992] 1 FLR 229, CA, para. 7–21 above). It is even more important to note that the Act does not give the parties to an engagement any right to apply to the court for the exercise of its discretionary powers to make financial relief or property adjustment orders under the Matrimonial Causes Act 1973 or otherwise, since those powers are only exercisable on or after the granting of a decree: *Mossop* v. *Mossop* [1988] 2 FLR 173, CA.

4. The Matrimonial Homes Act 1983 and the right to occupy the   7–33 matrimonial home. So far in this chapter we have been concerned with questions of beneficial ownership; and the courts have emphasised that facts which might be relevant to ascertaining an intention to *occupy* property are not necessarily relevant to ascertaining an intention that the beneficial *ownership* be shared:

> In *Lloyds Bank plc* v. *Rosset* [1990] 2 FLR 155, 159, HL Lord Bridge made this distinction very clear. "The question" (he said) "the judge had to determine was whether he could find that [Mr & Mrs Rosset] had entered into an agreement, made an arrangement, reached an understanding, or formed a common intention that the beneficial interest in the property would be jointly owned. ... The expectation of parties to every happy marriage is that they will share the practical benefits of occupying the matrimonial home whoever owns it. But this is something quite distinct from sharing the beneficial interest in the property asset which the matrimonial home represents ... "

The ownership of what may be a substantial asset is of course very important, but in practice the right to stay in occupation of a home may, at least in the short term, be of even more significance; and the fact that a spouse cannot establish a beneficial interest in the matrimonial home under the rules set out above does not mean that he or she has no right to stay in occupation. Even at common law a married woman had a right to be provided with a roof over her head (although she would forfeit this right if, for example, she committed adultery). The Matrimonial Homes Act 1967 (now consolidated in the Matrimonial Homes Act 1983, and hereafter called simply "the Act") effectively supplanted the common law; and the Act now codifies the law governing the occupation of the matrimonial home. It is important to note that the Act has no application where a couple are not married.

The Rights Conferred on Spouses by the Matrimonial Homes Act 1983

Rights of occupation
In its original form, the Matrimonial Homes Act was primarily   7–34 concerned with the situation in which one spouse was entitled to occupy the home "by virtue of a beneficial estate or interest or contract" or by statute, and the other spouse was not so entitled. The Act gives the latter—the non-owning spouse who was at common law potentially so vulnerable—"rights of occupation" (s.1(1)):

(a) if in occupation, a right not to be evicted or excluded from the dwelling house or any part thereof by the other spouse except with the leave of the court ... ;

(b) if not in occupation, a right with the leave of the court ... to enter into and occupy the dwelling house."

Duration of rights of occupation
7–35   Broadly speaking, rights of occupation last only as long as the marriage. But the court is given power, "in the event of a matrimonial dispute or estrangement" to override this general principle. If an application is made during the subsistence of the marriage the court may in effect extend the rights of occupation either for a specified period (which could be as long as the applicant's life) or "until further order": MHA 1983, s.1(4), s.2(4).

Application to the court
7–36   So long as one spouse has rights of occupation, either spouse can apply to the court for orders governing the occupation of the home: MHA 1983, s.1(2). Thus, a wife may seek an order excluding her husband from the home (or from part of it, for example her bedroom), and she can do so even though she accepts that as a matter of property law he is the sole beneficial owner. Correspondingly a husband-owner could apply for an order bringing the wife's rights to an end, for example so that he could sell the house with vacant possession.

Joint owners
7–37   As has already been pointed out, the Act was originally concerned with protecting the non-owner; but the procedure was found to be so useful that it is now provided that even where the spouses are jointly entitled they may apply under the Act for an order relating to the occupation of the home: MHA 1983, s.9; s.1(11).

Effect of spouses' rights under Act on purchasers, mortgagees, etc.: rights bind third parties if registered
7–38   In *National Provincial Bank Ltd.* v. *Ainsworth* [1965] AC 1165, the House of Lords had held that the wife's common law right to be provided with housing by her husband was an essentially personal right, intrinsically incapable of binding third parties—even if the third party knew of her claims. The Matrimonial Homes Act therefore introduced a procedure whereby rights of occupation may be made to bind third parties; but if such rights are to bind a purchaser of the land or any interest therein they must be protected by registration as a Class F land charge.

A purchaser who finds that a charge is registered against the property will in practice refuse to complete unless and until it is removed—even though in legal theory the charge will only protect the rights under the MHA 1983 and not other rights (such as a beneficial interest in the property or the sale proceeds):

> In *Barnett* v. *Hassett* [1982] 1 WLR 1385 the parties' marriage had broken down, and the husband and children had left the matrimonial home. He had no wish to return to it, but registered a Class F charge in order to prevent the wife from completing her planned sale of the house until a dispute about money had been settled. The court held that the Act was intended to protect the right to occupy the home, and did not extend to protect other claims. Hence, registration had not been a proper use of the Act; and the charge was set aside.

Effect of spouse's insolvency on occupation rights

What is the position if one spouse is adjudicated bankrupt—can the **7–39** other assert his or her rights of occupation against the bankrupt's creditors? It was originally specifically provided that the spouse's rights were void against the trustee; but under the Insolvency Act 1986 the position has been changed in an attempt to strike a fairer balance between the interests of the family and the creditors. The rights of occupation do now bind the trustee; and it will be for the trustee to apply to the bankruptcy court for an order terminating the other spouse's rights. The court will apply the same criteria to such an application as to an application for the sale of jointly owned property (see para. 7–52 below); and in effect the family will get a year's grace: Insolvency Act 1986, s.336.

Application of act to rented property

During the currency of the marriage, a tenant's spouse will have **7–40** rights of occupation under section 1(1) of the Act. He or she is thus entitled not to be evicted by the other spouse, and can apply to the court to declare and fix the rights to be enjoyed.

The Act also confers special protection:

(a) Any payment by way of rent or rates by the tenant's spouse is "as good as if made or done" by the tenant. Hence so long as the tenant's spouse pays the rent the landlord cannot evict him or her.

(b) A spouse's occupation is treated for the purposes of the Rent Acts as possession by the other spouse. The effect of this provision is to preserve—but only so long as the marriage subsists, *i.e.* not after decree absolute of divorce: see, *e.g. Crago* v. *Julian* [1992] 1 All ER 744, CA—the complex rights of security of tenure conferred by the Rent Act 1977 and by the Housing Act 1988.

Transfer of tenancies

The Act provides that the court may, on granting a decree of **7–41** divorce, nullity or judicial separation, or at any time thereafter order the transfer of tenancies protected by specific legislation to the other party (unless he or she has remarried).

Principles applied by the court in exercising its discretion

7–42   Although the Matrimonial Homes Act does confer rights on a spouse who would not otherwise have them, application to the court is in practice likely to be necessary if there is a dispute between a couple about the occupation of the home.

The Act provides (MHA 1983, s.1(3)) that in determining applications in relation to the occupation of the home the court "may make such an order as it thinks just and reasonable having regard to the conduct of the spouses in relation to each other and otherwise, to their respective needs and financial resources, to the needs of any children and to all the circumstances of the case." The effect of this provision is considered in the chapter on Domestic Violence: see para. 6–25 above.

5. The Inheritance (Provision for Family and Dependants) Act 1975, and succession to family assets on death

7–43   Most marriages are still ended by death (rather than divorce); and marriage does then have a significant effect on the devolution of property. If a married person dies intestate then the surviving spouse will be entitled to the personal chattels and to a "statutory legacy" amounting, if the deceased left issue (whether legitimate or illegitimate) to £75,000. (If the deceased leaves any of certain specified close relatives, but no issue, the legacy is increased to £125,000.) In addition, the surviving spouse will be entitled to an interest in any balance of the estate—a life interest in one-half if there are issue, or half absolutely if there are close relatives but no issue. If there are no other close relatives the surviving spouse takes the whole estate.

An unmarried person has, in contrast—however lengthy the relationship—no rights of intestate succession in the partner's estate.

Freedom of testation

7–44   It seems that comparatively few people make wills: 67 per cent. of a representative sample of the population interviewed in a survey conducted for the Law Commission had not done so, and although some 600,000 people die each year in England and Wales, only some 182,000 wills were probated in 1990. However, English law is unusual in permitting freedom of testation: if there is a valid will its terms override the intestacy rules—English law, unlike many foreign systems, does not stipulate that a spouse has a right to a certain proportion of the deceased partner's estate. This means, of course, that an unmarried person may make whatever provision is wanted for any surviving partner or children.

But court may over-ride will or intestacy provisions

7–45   The Inheritance (Provision for Family and Dependants) Act 1975 permits certain defined categories of "dependant" to apply to the court for reasonable financial provision to be made out of the deceased's estate. If the court considers that the will or intestacy does not make such provision, it may make orders, for example—for periodical income payments, or payment of a lump sum, etc.

How is the court to decide these difficult issues? As Waite J. put it in *Moody* v. *Stevenson* (1991) *The Times*, July 30, the Act contains sophisticated machinery combining elements of fact-finding and discretion and hypothesis in a formula of some elaboration. The court is directed to consider all relevant circumstances, and its attention is specifically drawn to a number of matters.

Applications by widows and widowers

Applications by widows and widowers are, in a number of   **7–46** respects, treated differently from others. In particular, the court is required to consider not only the duration of the marriage, the contribution made by the applicant to the welfare of the family of the deceased (including any contribution made by looking after the home or caring for the family), but also to have regard to the provision which the applicant might reasonably have expected to receive if the marriage had ended in divorce. The "divorce expectation" is "obviously a very important consideration" (Oliver L.J. in *Re Besterman* [1984] FLR 503, 513, CA); and the court is likely to pay particular attention—as would the divorce court—to the needs of the survivor:

> In *Re Clarke (dec'd)* [1991] Fam Law 364 a surviving widow made an application for reasonable provision out of the estate of her deceased husband. The marriage had been a second marriage for both of them. She had investments totalling £60,000. The court refused to make any provision additional to the life interest in the house and in the fund of £25,000 left to her under the husband's will. The judge said that what is required, in respect of both divorce and inheritance, was essentially that the applicant should be housed, that the applicant should have an income upon which to live reasonably, and that there should be something to fall back on to deal with contingencies in the future. On the facts, he considered that those requirements were satisfied.

> Again, in *Stead* v. *Stead* [1985] FLR 16 the court attached particular attention to the applicants' reasonable needs; and the court made a complicated order primarily designed to ensure that the applicant would be properly housed.

Applications by widows and widowers are also treated differently from others in another important respect: where the application is by a widow or widower, "financial provision" is not confined to the financial provision which would be reasonable for the applicant to receive for *maintenance*. Thus:

> In *Re Besterman* [1984] FLR 503, CA, the deceased, after 18 years of marriage, left his wife his personal chattels and an annual income of

£3,500 out of a total estate of £1,500,000. The court made an order that she should receive one-quarter of the estate on the basis that since the estate was large the wife should have sufficient money to ensure that she should not fall into need.

In the case of applications by other dependants, however, the court is restricted to considering provision for the applicant's maintenance.

Position of other dependants on death

7–47   Although the deceased's surviving spouse will, in most cases, be entitled to inherit most of the estate on an intestacy, the deceased's issue and certain other relatives of the deceased have rights on intestacy. But a cohabitant has no rights on intestacy in any circumstances, while there may be circumstances in which the preference given by the intestacy rules to a surviving spouse operates unfairly:

> In *Re Collins (dec'd)* [1990] 2 FLR 72 Mrs Collins had in fact obtained a decree nisi of divorce before her death, but it had not been made absolute. The result was that her husband became entitled on her intestacy to the whole of her estate, and her children—a son of Mr and Mrs Collins and an illegitimate daughter—were entitled to nothing.

In an attempt to provide a remedy for such dependants, the 1975 Act also permits applications for reasonable financial provision—*i.e.* provision for maintenance—to be made by a former spouse who has not remarried, a child (whether legitimate, illegitimate or adopted) and a child of the family (see para. 14–03 below); and the court was therefore able to make an order on the application of Mrs Collins's child. But the real novelty of the Act lies in the provision whereby "any other person ... who immediately before the death of the deceased was being maintained, either wholly or partly by the deceased "may apply as a dependant, since this head may enable the survivor of a cohabiting couple to apply for financial provision from the deceased partner's estate.

For many years, the courts gave a restrictive interpretation to this provision, reflecting the policy that the legislation was not concerned to ensure that the property was distributed fairly on death, but simply to provide a remedy for those who were in a relationship of *dependency* on the deceased. The qualifying condition is not that the survivor had lived with the deceased, but that he or she was being *maintained* by the deceased. Moreover, the Act provides a special definition of "being maintained": a person is to be treated as being maintained if the deceased "otherwise than for full valuable consideration," was making a substantial contribution in money or money's worth towards the applicant's needs; and in answering the question of what provision would be reasonable, the court is specifically directed to have regard to the extent to which and the basis upon which the deceased assumed responsibility for the applicant's maintenance: s.3(4).

Applications by cohabitants—financial dependence necessary

It followed from these provisions that a claimant could only qualify 7-48 under this head if he or she had been financially dependent on the deceased; and if the deceased had assumed responsibility for the applicant's maintenance. What was in issue in deciding whether a cohabitant was eligible to apply was not the emotional relationship between the couple, but whether the survivor had been financially dependent. A woman who—as in *Horrocks* v. *Foray* [1975] 1 WLR 1351—had been provided with a house and an allowance by the deceased would qualify; but the mere fact that a couple lived together and shared a bed and a common household was held not to be sufficient. Indeed, it could have been said that if they each had jobs and contributed more or less equally to the household expenses the survivor could have no claim under the Act because there would be no relationship of dependence. However, in *Bishop* v. *Plumley* [1991] 1 FLR 121 the court suggested that a somewhat more flexible attitude might be appropriate:

A couple had cohabited since 1974, and had been largely dependent on state benefits. However, in 1983, M inherited property, and used it to buy the house in which he lived with F for the remaining nine months of his life. F (it was said) had conferred exceptional benefits on M by devotedly caring for him, particularly during his lengthy illness. At first instance the court held that F was not entitled to make an application as M's dependant. The couple had pooled their benefit income, and although the purchase of the house was a "substantial contribution" to F's needs, this was balanced by the care which she had given to him. In effect she had given as good as she got. But the Court of Appeal rejected this approach. By providing a secure home, M had made a substantial contribution to F's needs, and it would be wrong to engage in fine computations of the value of the support which she had provided. She was not to be deprived of her claim by having the value of the services which she had provided as an incident of the couple's mutual love and support valued in terms of the amount which it would have cost the deceased to purchase those services in the market place.

Time of dependence

The applicant must show that the maintenance relationship existed 7-49 "immediately before the death" of the deceased. It is true that the courts have regard to the settled basis or general arrangement between the parties; and an applicant will not be disqualified merely because there was no factual sharing, for example during the last few weeks of a terminal illness: *Re Beaumont*, dec'd [1980] Ch 444. But the plaintiff in *Layton* v. *Martin* [1986] 2 FLR 277 (see para. 7-27 above) would not have been eligible to apply under this Act in spite of the fact that her lover had promised her financial security out of his estate (which exceeded £350,000 in value) because her relationship had come to an end two years before the death. Even more dramatically, an application failed in *Kourkgy* v. *Lusher* (1981) 4 FLR 65 where the deceased died on August 7 having abandoned his mistress of 10 years' standing on July 29.

INCIDENTAL QUESTIONS

7–50   Property law is a complex subject; and there are many important issues which have to be resolved—beyond the questions on which the text has so far concentrated of rights to beneficial interests in and occupation of family property. The remainder of this chapter summarises the law governing two of the more significant of such issues: (i) in what circumstances will the court *order a sale* of property in which a couple are interested? (ii) to what extent will *third parties* be bound by beneficial interests and other rights about which they may have known nothing.

Will the court order a sale?

7–51   What is to happen if, for example, a wife who has a beneficial interest in property wants to keep it while her husband wants it sold? Such a dispute can be resolved by an application to the court under section 30 of the Law of Property Act 1925. In exercising its discretion under that section the court will take account of the underlying purpose for which the property was acquired: if the parties' relationship has come to an end the court will often regard the purpose as having also come to an end, and order a sale: *Jones* v. *Challenger* [1961] 1 QB 176.

Does the fact that there are still young children for whom a house has to be provided make any difference to the application of this general principle? Conflicting dicta on this point are to be found in decisions of the Court of Appeal. On the one hand, it is said that a purpose of the trust in such a case would be to provide a home for the children during their infancy, so that a sale should not generally be ordered whilst that purpose still exists. In this view, the purpose of the trust is to provide a family home. On the other, it is urged that the children are not beneficiaries of the trust for sale, and that their interests are only to be taken into account "so far as they affect the equities in the matter as between two persons entitled to the beneficial interests in the property": *Burke* v. *Burke* [1974] 1 WLR 1063, 1067, *per* Buckley L.J. In practice there seems to be today little argument that the interests of children are indeed an important factor, and since parents are obliged to support their children it seems difficult to believe that the court would order a sale unless it could be shown that alternative accommodation was available for them: see *Chhokar* v. *Chhokar* [1984] FLR 313.

Sales in bankruptcy cases

On bankruptcy, all the debtor's assets vest in a trustee in 7–52 bankruptcy who has a duty to realize them for the benefit of the creditors. Where the bankrupt had a beneficial interest in property—for example, as joint tenant or tenant in common of the family home—the trustee will usually apply to the bankruptcy court for an order for sale under section 30. That court is by statute (Insolvency Act 1986, s.336(4)) required to have regard to the interests of the bankrupt's creditors, to the conduct of the spouse or former spouse "so far as contributing to the bankruptcy," to the needs and financial resources of the spouse or former spouse, to the needs of any children and to all the circumstances of the case; but after one year from the bankruptcy the court is required (unless the circumstances of the case are "exceptional") to assume that the interests of the bankrupt's creditors outweigh all other considerations: Insolvency Act 1986, s.336(5). In practice, it will be difficult to show that the circumstances are exceptional:

> In *Re Citro (a Bankrupt) and Another* [1991] 1 FLR 71, 78, CA, Nourse L.J. pointed out that there was only a single case in which the welfare of children had been allowed to affect a decision on sale; and that case was unusual because the creditors were likely to receive all that was due to them together with interest in any event. In the typical case, it could not be said that hardship to the children was exceptional: " ... it is not uncommon for a wife with young children to be faced with eviction in circumstances where the realisation of her beneficial interest will not produce enough to buy a comparable home in the same neighbourhood, or indeed elsewhere; and, if she has to move elsewhere, there may be problems over schooling and so forth. Such circumstances, while engendering a natural sympathy in all who hear of them, cannot be described as exceptional. They are the melancholy consequences of debt and improvidence with which every civilised society has been familiar."

Are third parties bound?

In principle it is of the essence of property rights that they bind 7–53 third parties: the vendor who purports to sell the family home cannot give a purchaser a greater interest than the vendor owns. But the interest of the vendor's partner will often be only equitable and in such a case the purchaser is not necessarily bound by the interest. The position can be summarised thus:

(a) If the title is not registered under the Land Registration Act 1925, a spouse's equitable interest under a trust for sale will bind the purchaser of a legal estate in land only if the purchaser has actual or constructive notice thereof. The question is usually whether the purchaser has made such inspections as ought reasonably to have been made (LPA 1925, s.199); and a purchaser will thus normally be treated as having notice of the rights of a spouse who is in occupation at the time of the transaction:

> In *Kingsnorth Finance Co. Ltd.* v. *Tizard* [1986] 1 WLR 783 a purchaser was held to be bound by a wife's constructive trust interest notwithstanding the fact that his surveyor had inspected the property and seen no evidence of occupation by her or any other female. This was because the inspection had taken place by prior appointment on a Sunday afternoon, and the husband had accordingly been able to conceal any evidence of his wife's existence.

(b) If the title to the property is registered under the Land Registration Acts, a wife's beneficial interest will bind a purchaser if the wife was "in actual occupation" at the time of registration unless the purchaser made inquiry of her which failed to reveal her rights: see *Williams and Glyn's Bank* v. *Boland* [1981] AC 487, HL:

> Michael Boland obtained a loan from the bank, to whom he charged the family home as security. The business got into financial difficulties; and the bank brought proceedings for possession. They failed. Mrs Boland had (it was conceded) a beneficial interest in the property, notwithstanding the fact that Michael Boland was registered as sole proprietor. She had been "in actual occupation" at the time when the loan was made; and the bank had made no inquiries of any kind of her about her rights. Hence the bank took subject to her interest which constituted an overriding interest: Land Registration Act 1925, s.70(1)(*g*). The House of Lords emphasised that the words "actual occupation" were ordinary words of plain English, connoting physical presence.

However, even plain English may contain a variety of shades of meaning; and there may well be cases in which it is not easy to say whether a claimant is in actual occupation or not: *Abbey National Building Society* v. *Cann* [1990] 2 FLR 122, 141, in which the point again arose for decision. The House of Lords indicated that some degree of permanence and continuity was required in order to establish "actual occupation," and that "mere fleeting presence" could not suffice: see *per* Lord Oliver at p. 142. It seems doubtful whether this decision clarifies matters.

Waiver of interest

7–54   Because of the risk that someone other than the purchaser of the legal estate in property might be able to assert an interest by way of implied resulting or constructive trust which in certain circumstances could bind a lender, banks, building societies and other mortgage lenders take precautions. They now normally require spouses and other adults who are likely to share the occupation of the property to execute a document authorising the owner of the legal estate to enter into the transaction—for example, mortgaging it to raise money for improvements or other purposes—and giving that transaction priority to the equitable interest:

> In *H* v. *M* (*Property: Beneficial Interest*) [1992] 1 FLR 229 the family home was acquired in M's sole name. He wanted to use it as security for a loan from a bank. The bank required F to join in the charge "to the extent of her beneficial interest if any."

Even in the absence of any such express waiver it has been held that the court may *infer* that the beneficiary has agreed that the property be charged and that his or her beneficial interest be postponed to that charge.

> In *Bristol and West Building Society* v. *Henning* [1985] 1 WLR 778, CA, a couple were living together in a house which they wished to improve with the aid of a loan from the Building Society. It was clear on the evidence that Mrs Henning (who had only an equitable interest) knew and approved of the loan: and it was held that accordingly she must have taken to have agreed to postpone her interest to that of the Building Society.

> In *Abbey National Building Society* v. *Cann and Another* [1990] 2 FLR 122, HL, Mrs Cann's son bought a house for his mother's occupation using the proceeds of sale of another house in which she had lived and a loan of £25,000 from the Building Society. The son falsely told the Building Society that he was buying the property for his sole occupation. The House of Lords held that the mother did not have any beneficial interest which would bind the Building Society. But they also accepted the doctrine of the *Henning* case: on the facts, the mother was well aware that there was insufficient money available to complete the purchase without some outside assistance. Accordingly, it was right to draw the inference that she had permitted her son to raise money on the security of the property without communicating any limitation on his authority to the Building Society. Accordingly, even if she had been held entitled to a beneficial interest in the property, she would not have been entitled to assert it against the Building Society.

In practice therefore, the likelihood of one party to a relationship being able successfully to assert a beneficial interest in property is much reduced, since in many cases the greater part of the funding will have been provided by a lender whose charge will thus take priority over the beneficial interest.

SUGGESTIONS FOR FURTHER READING

Hoggett and Pearl, Chap. 5.
K. Gray, *Elements of Land Law* (1987), Chaps. 22–25.
Law Commission Report No. 175, *Matrimonial Property*, HMSO (1988).

Law Commission Report No. 187, *Distribution on Intestacy*, HMSO (1989).

Scottish Law Commission Report Scot. Law Com. No. 86, *Matrimonial Property* (1984).

Sir Nicolas Browne-Wilkinson, *Constructive Trusts and Unjust Enrichment* (Holdsworth Club, Birmingham (1991).

PART III. FINANCIAL SUPPORT FOR MEMBERS OF THE FAMILY

The common law imposed a duty on a husband to maintain his wife by providing her with necessaries; but today the common law duty to support is of little if any practical relevance in determining the obligations of members of a family to support one another. In practice, there are three—not always well co-ordinated—sets of statutory rules which are relevant. First, the rules governing the provision by the state of welfare benefits. These include rules whereby "liable relatives" may in certain circumstances be required to reimburse benefits which have been paid out to members of their family. Secondly, statute has given the courts extensive powers to make financial orders requiring one spouse to support the other during the marriage and after divorce; and there are procedures which may be available to deal with the financial consequences of the breakdown of a non-marital relationship. Thirdly, statute now gives the court extensive powers to make orders requiring parents to provide financial support for children; and these provisions are to be complemented—or perhaps superseded in the majority of cases—by the provisions of the Child Support Act 1991 which will establish a Child Support Agency responsible for assessing child support obligations and enforcing them. The next three chapters consider these rules in turn.

Chapter 8

WELFARE BENEFITS

Introduction—The Historical and Social Context

Why should the student of Family Law bother about welfare benefits? **8–01** The first, and most obvious, answer to this question is that family breakdown involves the risk of destitution, and that ever since the Elizabethan Poor Law the state has assumed some obligation to provide for those who would otherwise starve. With the coming of the welfare state, the community assumed a broad obligation to help the needy. In particular, the Poor Law was repealed in 1948 and replaced by the Supplementary Benefit system. Every person in Great Britain of or over the age of 16 whose resources (as defined in statute) were insufficient to meet his or her requirements (defined—at a modest level—in statute) became entitled to receive a supplementary allowance. At that time, it was the policy of the law to eradicate the stigma attached to the Poor Law and to insist that supplementary benefits were (as Finer J. put it in *Reiterbund* v. *Reiterbund* [1974] 1 WLR 788, 797) "the subject of rights and entitlement and that no shame attached to the receipt of them."

Over the years, the demand placed on the supplementary benefit system by family breakdown increased enormously. In particular, the number of lone parent families in Great Britain rose to over one million in 1986, and such families now form 14 per cent. of all families with children. These families became increasingly dependent on supplementary benefit which represented the main source of income for many—indeed social security benefits became the *only* source of income for nearly half of all lone mothers. The number of lone parent families dependent on supplementary benefit grew from 330,000 in 1980 to 770,000 in 1989, and over the same period the system of providing family maintenance by private agreement or court order seemed to become less and less relevant. By 1989 less than a quarter (compared with about half in 1981/82) of lone parent families on income support were receiving any periodical maintenance payments from the absent parent.

It has always been an important principle that although the state might provide financial support for a family in danger of destitution, the state should be entitled to recover the amounts disbursed from any person legally bound to support the claimant (that is to say, from the so-called "liable relative"). But with changing attitudes—and specifically the greater emphasis which came to be placed on the duty of parents to support their children—it came to be thought that what the Finer Committee had called the "third system of family law" was

119

ineffective, and that in particular it failed to give effect to the "clear moral duty" which all parents have to maintain their children until they are old enough to look after themselves: see Lord Mackay of Clashfern, *Hansard*, Vol. 526, Col. 775, February 25, 1991.

There has also been a further particularly significant element in the arguments which have influenced policy in this area. One objective of the modern law of divorce is to encourage both partners to put the past behind them and to begin a new life which is not overshadowed by the relationship which has broken down: see *Minton* v. *Minton* [1979] AC 593, 608, *per* Lord Scarman; and one important way of giving effect to this policy was seen to be to encourage women, by maximising their earning capacity, to become economically self-sufficient: see Matrimonial Causes Act 1973, s.25(1)(*a*) and para. 9–70 below. Statistics suggested that the courts were indeed increasingly making so-called "clean break" settlements on divorce, under which the former partners would no longer have any ongoing financial dependence on each other; but paradoxically it was said that the supplementary benefit system discouraged lone mothers from seeking paid employment see, *e.g.* para. 8–16 below. This was inconsistent with government policy that caring parents who wished to work should be enabled to do so as soon as they felt ready and able (*Children Come First*, Cm 1263, (1990) para. 2.1).

The result of these, sometimes conflicting, pressures is that there remains in existence a system of *income support* (which is the modern replacement for supplementary benefit); and this still represents the major source of income for many lone parent families. *Family Credit* is a means tested benefit payable to those in low paid work, and it is intended that this should increasingly be available to encourage lone parents to gain independence by their own efforts—many lone parents "want to work and it is right that we should help them to realise their ambitions": Lord Mackay of Clashfern, *Hansard* HL Vol. 526, Col, 775, February 25, 1991. There are also other benefits which may be of particular relevance to the lone parent family—some, such as widow's benefits, being available only where prescribed contributions have been paid over the years, some (such as Child Benefit) being payable irrespective of contribution. In 1990, new legislation came into force, significantly extending the obligation of the "liable relative" under the Social Security Act 1986 to reimburse benefits paid to the family. Finally, the Child Support Act 1991 (which is not yet in force, but already has an indirect effect on the financial consequences of breakdown) provides that child maintenance should be assessed by a formula intended to produce consistent results, and that these assessments should be made by a Child Support Agency which will also have extensive powers to trace absent parents, investigate their means, and collect and enforce child maintenance payments. Further changes to the Social Security system are also envisaged to give effect to the policies set out above.

The text therefore outlines: 8–02

(a) The *Income Support, Family Credit and Child Benefit* schemes.
     Brief mention is also made of other relevant state benefits—in
     particular, assistance with housing.
(b) The rules governing reimbursement by liable relatives.

The system created by the Child Support Act 1991 is considered in
Chapter 10.

A. ENTITLEMENT TO WELFARE BENEFITS

I. INCOME SUPPORT

Entitlement to benefit
The general principle embodied in the Social Security Act 1986 is   8–03
that a person aged 18 or over who is not engaged in "remunerative
work" (but *is* available for and actively seeking employment) and
whose income and capital do not exceed stipulated levels ("the
applicable amount") is entitled to income support. The legislation—much of it contained in regulations made under statutory
powers—is exceptionally complex, and the following paragraphs can
do no more than highlight the legislative provisions most relevant to
claims in situations of family breakdown.

The claimant—aggregation of a couple's means
A person under 18 is only qualified to apply for Income Support in   8–04
exceptional circumstances (for example, if the claimant is a lone
parent).
The principle is that only one member of a family can claim income
support; and the capital and income of married and unmarried
couples are aggregated for determining entitlement to Income
Support.

Couples—the cohabitation rule
The expression "married couple" is defined to mean a man and   8–05
woman who are married to each other and are members of the same
household. Hence, a separated couple whose marriage has broken
down fall outside the definition, and each spouse is eligible to claim
Income Support.
The expression "unmarried couple" gives rise to much more difficulty. It is defined to mean a man and a woman who are not married
to each other "but are living together as husband and wife . . . "
If it were not for the "cohabitation rule" to which this definition
gives effect an unmarried couple would be significantly better off than

a married couple: the "applicable amount" of two individuals could be some £85 as compared with some £66 for a couple; but the application of the rule is inevitably sometimes controversial. To decide whether a couple are "married" does not involve any investigation of their personal relationship or any value judgment about which of the normal incidents of marriage (such as the use of a common name or the existence of sexual relations) is essential; but to decide whether or not a couple are "living together as husband and wife" does involve precisely such a judgment. The investigations into a couple's private life which are made in order to reach a decision on this issue may seem offensive and cause distress.

The following criteria are amongst those regarded as relevant. First, the couple must be members of the same household, and will (apart from necessary absences) live together. Secondly, the relationship must have some stability. Thirdly, there will often be some financial support provided by one party or a sharing of household expenses. Fourthly, a sexual relationship is regarded as a normal incident of living together as husband and wife, and the presence or absence of such a relationship will be taken into account if information on the subject is volunteered. Fifthly, the fact that a couple are caring for a child or children of their union raises a strong presumption that they are living as husband and wife. Finally, the fact that a couple represent themselves to others is relevant. But no check list can be conclusive:

> In *Crake* v. *Supplementary Benefits Commission* (1980) 2 FLR 264 considerable importance was attached to the couple's intention. The claimant had moved into the household solely in order to care for a sick and incapable person; and the couple were held not to fall within the definition.

Parents and children—aggregation

8-06   The family unit for the purposes of supplementary benefit includes dependent children. A child's income is in principle to be aggregated with the parent's for the purpose of determining whether any Income Support should be paid in respect of the child's needs, and Income Support cannot be paid in respect of a child who has capital in excess of £3,000.

No benefit for persons in full-time work

8-07   A person who is engaged in work for which payment is made or which is done in expectation of payment for not less than 16 hours per week is not entitled to Income Support. The maximum number of hours which may be worked without forfeiting eligibility for Income Support has been sharply reduced over the years; and it seems to have been thought that substituting an entitlement to claim Family Credit would encourage Income Support claimants to "gain independence by their own efforts." But since the Family Credit scheme makes no allowance for the applicant's child care costs, and (unlike Income Support) makes no additional provision to cover the applicant's mortgage payments, it would seem that many lone parents will prefer to remain on Income Support even if this means giving up the possibility of part-time work.

Certain kinds of occupation—notably child minding in the home—are favourably treated in so far as they are excluded from the definition of "remunerative work." This means that a child minder will not lose an entitlement to income support merely by reason of engagement in that activity; and further encouragement is given to child minders by a provision that only one-third of the relevant earnings are to be taken into account as income.

Availability for employment as a condition of eligibility

Eligibility for benefit is generally subject to the condition that the applicant be "available for employment" and "actively seeking employment." But a person who is a lone parent and responsible for a child in the claimant's household is exempt from these requirements.   8–08

Assessment of the applicable amount

The Income Support scheme attributes a so-called applicable amount to each claimant; and in principle the claimant—provided that his or her capital does not exceed a prescribed amount—is entitled to Income Support to bring the income up to the applicable amount. The regulations are complex; and the following summary is highly selective.   8–09

Calculation of the applicable amount

The applicable amount is the aggregate of the relevant personal allowance, premiums, and housing costs.   8–10

Personal allowance

The Regulations prescribe 16 different "personal allowances" depending on such factors as the claimant's age and whether or not he or she is a lone parent (that is to say "a member of a family [who] has no partner"). For example, a single claimant who is not less than 25 has a personal allowance of £42.45 weekly, as does a lone parent who is aged 18 or over. To this is added an amount—ranging from £14.55 for a person under 11 to £33.60 for a person of 18 or over—in respect of any child or young person who is a member of the claimant's family.   8–11

Premiums

The different rates of personal allowance make considerable allowance for individual circumstances, but in further pursuance of the policy of targeting benefits without it being necessary to make detailed inquiries into personal needs, the Regulations provide for the   8–12 inclusion of weekly premiums in the applicable amounts of claimants who satisfy the prescribed conditions. For example, a "family premium" of £9.30 is payable where at least one of the family is a child or young person. In addition, a lone parent is entitled to the lone-parent premium of £4.75; and a claimant who is responsible for a child member of the household who is blind or disabled is entitled to the disabled child premium of £17.80 for each qualifying child.

Housing costs

8–13   A claimant's eligible housing costs are included in the applicable amount; and this is of particular significance in the context of marital breakdown since the definition of housing costs includes mortgage interest payments in cases where the mortgage secures a loan used to "acquire an interest in the dwelling occupied as the home." However, there is no provision to meet capital repayments (including the payment of premiums on a collateral life assurance policy) or insurance. Moreover, only one-half of the relevant interest will normally be paid for the first 16 weeks of benefit entitlement; and there is power not to pay excessive interest—for example if the house is larger than required, or is in an expensive area.

Housing costs other than mortgage interest (such as rent) are now, generally speaking, recoverable if at all through the Housing Benefit scheme: see para. 8–19 below.

The fact that Income Support will often be available to meet mortgage interest liabilities has been a powerful influence in determining the most advantageous settlement of a family's financial affairs on divorce. In particular, it has made the so-called "clean break" a realistic option in many cases where a couple have few assets apart from the family home: see para. 9–70 below.

Calculation of claimant's income and capital

8–14   These calculations are central to the operation of the Income Support scheme, since possession of capital may disqualify a claimant from any eligibility for Income Support, whilst in principle every pound of income goes to reduce benefit entitlement. The fact that the scheme allows for "disregards" is, in this context, of great importance.

Capital

8–15   The regulations lay down a general rule that the whole of the claimant's capital shall be taken into account and assessed at its current market value, save in so far as it is provided that certain specified assets be disregarded; and if the total of a claimant's capital (other than disregarded items) exceeds a specified amount (currently £8,000) the claimant will not be entitled to Income Support. Capital in excess of £3,000 is deemed, regardless of the facts, to give rise to an income of £1 per week for each £250. This is much more than the income likely to be produced by a conventional investment.

Disregards which are particularly relevant include the dwelling occupied as the home or (for a period) occupied as the home by a former partner; personal chattels; and the surrender value of life policies. Once again, these disregards have had a significant impact on divorce settlements: the value of a claimant's equity in the family home will be disregarded, and (as already noted) the cost of servicing any mortgage loan will usually be met by Income Support.

Income

The general principle is that the whole of the earnings and other **8–16** income of members of the family is calculated on a weekly basis and goes to reduce the amount of benefit entitlement. "Earnings" is widely defined (to include, for example, benefits in kind), and although in theory the calculation is based on "net" earnings (so that income tax liability is taken into account) there is no deduction in respect of child care expenses or travelling expenses. However, certain income is disregarded; and in particular the first £15 of earnings—but not of other income—is disregarded where the claimant is entitled to the lone parent premium, and there is thus an incentive to a lone parent to earn this very small weekly sum (but no more).

There is no disregard in respect of maintenance payments received for the support of the claimant's household; and in principle, all payments made by a "liable relative" are taken into account as income. Every pound received will thus go to reduce the amount of Income Support. The combined effect of this rule and the favourable treatment of ownership of the family home (see above) seems likely to have had a significant influence in increasing the number of "clean break" divorce settlements in which the husband is relieved from any continuing obligation to support the wife, and is released from any obligation under the mortgage on terms that his equity in the family home is transferred to the wife.

Lump sum and other payments. There is also a provision which is intended to deal with the fact that periodical payments may be paid in arrears and to ensure that where any lump sum is really a form of maintenance it is used as such before resort is had to Income Support. The rule is that lump sum payments are taken into account as income apportioned over a period of time calculated by reference to the claimant's Income Support entitlement. This rule could operate unfairly where a claimant has received a lump sum as part of a capital settlement on divorce: if her total capital is still less than £8,000 why should she cease to be entitled to Income Support? The rules therefore now provide that a payment "arising from a disposition of property made in contemplation of or as a consequence of divorce proceedings" shall not count as a "payment" for this purpose; and (although the meaning of this provision is not entirely clear) it would seem that a payment which is made in respect of the wife's interest in the former matrimonial home, for example, would be within the exception. However, a payment which is made simply to achieve equity between the partners—for example, out of capital which the husband received by way of redundancy compensation—would apparently not be within the exception. In the result, there would be little point in ordering such a lump sum payment.

Examples of Income Support entitlement in situations of family breakdown are given below: p. 134.

II. FAMILY CREDIT

8–17   Family Credit is a benefit designed to provide some assistance for low-earning families with children; and the scheme has been progressively amended in an attempt to give real incentives to lone parents to take up even low-paid work rather than remaining dependent on Income Support. Moreover, claims are usually processed entirely by post; and, once a claim has been accepted, Family Credit will normally be payable for 26 weeks irrespective of changes in circumstances.

Entitlement to benefit

8–18   The most relevant conditions for entitlement to Family Credit are:

(i) The claimant or the claimant's partner must be "engaged and normally engaged in remunerative work." This condition is only satisfied if the person concerned works for not less than 16 hours weekly; and it should be noted that this minimum period was reduced to this level as one of a number of measures to make paid employment a more attractive option for the lone parent than Income Support.

(ii) The claimant or the claimant's partner must be responsible for a child member of the household. There are complex rules to cover situations in which several people could satisfy this requirement.

(iii) The income and capital of the claimant (and partner) must not exceed certain levels. As with Income Support, a claimant who has capital in excess of £8,000 is not entitled to Family Credit. The general principle is that if the relevant net income of the family (including maintenance payments)—is below an "applicable amount" calculated by reference to the number of children in the family, then "maximum family credits" are payable. If the income exceeds that amount, credit is reduced by 70 per cent. of the excess. The policy is thus that there should always be an incentive to earn more: a pound earned only reduces Family Credit entitlement by 70 pence.

These calculations are based on "net" income; but a great drawback of the scheme from the point of view of the single-parent family is that no allowance is made in respect of child care costs. Accordingly, a single parent with child care responsibilities will still often be better off drawing Income Support and unemployed—or working for less than 16 hours weekly, and earning no more than £15 (that being the sum which will be disregarded for Income Support purposes: see para. 8–16 above). It is significant that some lone parents who wanted to take up full-time work believed that they would need to earn £150 weekly from a full-time job to make working worthwhile: see National Audit Office Report on Support for Lone Parent Families, 1990, para. 3.24.

The fact that there is no allowance for mortgage interest payments or other housing costs must also reduce the attractiveness of the Family Credit scheme from the point of view of a divorced parent.

In pursuance of the Government's policy of making it easier for parents to "gain independence by their own efforts" the rule whereby periodical payments of maintenance were taken into account in full as income has been amended with effect from April 1992: since that date the first £15 of any periodical payments of maintenance have been disregarded for Family Credit—although the full amount of such receipts is still taken into account for Income Support purposes.

Examples of Family Credit entitlement, and comparisons with Income Support, are given below: p. 136.

HELP WITH HOUSING COSTS—MORTGAGE INTEREST RELIEF AND HOUSING BENEFIT

The importance of housing to the welfare of families has long been **8–19** reflected in government policy; and since 1915 central government has provided financial assistance with the costs involved.

The form which that assistance takes is, and always has been, varied and complex. A measure of assistance for those paying mortgage interest in respect of house purchase has been provided through the *tax system*; and in recent years relief has been given under the MIRAS (Mortgage Interest Relief at Source) scheme even to those whose incomes would not involve liability to Income Tax: borrowers are, in effect, allowed to deduct tax at the basic rate (currently 25 per cent.) from payments of mortgage interest (although this relief is not available on interest related to more than £30,000 of borrowing).

Mortgage interest relief takes no account of individual needs, and only benefits those who are buying a house with the aid of a mortgage; but since 1972 *Housing Benefit* schemes have been made available to provide assistance to others with housing needs. The

Social Security Act 1986 made substantial amendments designed to harmonise housing benefit and other welfare benefits; and in particular to ensure that claimants would never be worse off by taking paid employment and would indeed have an incentive to do so.

The main features of the Housing Benefit scheme are that benefit is payable to a person liable to make payments—in practice, of rent in respect of a dwelling occupied as the claimant's home—provided that the claimant's capital and income do not exceed prescribed amounts.

The amount of capital which disqualifies a claimant from Housing Benefit is currently £16,000 (*i.e.* twice the comparable figure for Income Support); and the "lone parent" premium is somewhat higher for Housing Benefit than it is for Income Support purposes. However, the "applicable amounts" of income for the purpose of determining the upper limit of eligibility for Housing Benefit are based on the Income Support system explained above. Since April 1992 the first £15 of weekly maintenance payments are disregarded in computing the claimant's income for Housing Benefit purposes in the same way as for Family Credit: see para. 8–18 above.

A claimant whose income is below the relevant "applicable amount" is entitled to maximum Housing Benefit, *i.e.* 100 per cent. of the eligible rent. If the claimant's income exceeds that amount, Housing Benefit is reduced—by 65 per cent. of the excess income in respect of rent rebate and allowance.

The Housing Benefit scheme used to provide assistance towards the payment of rates, although latterly relief was confined to a maximum of 80 per cent. of the rates payable. On April 1, 1990 household rates were replaced by the Community Charge (sometimes known as the Poll Tax); and a scheme—similar in principle to the Housing Benefit scheme—was introduced to provide relief up to a maximum of 80 per cent. of the sum payable. The Community Charge has itself now been abolished (with effect from 1993) and will be replaced by a property based tax.

IV. CHILD BENEFIT

8–20 The Child Benefit Act 1975 makes provision for the payment in cash of non-contributory benefits in respect of all children in a family. The child benefit scheme has a number of advantages over other methods of benefiting families. First (unlike child reliefs against income tax) it benefits those whose income is below the tax threshold. Secondly, the benefit is tax free. Thirdly, the scheme is flexible; and this flexibility has been used to provide for a special "one-parent benefit," and also to provide an enhanced rate in respect of the first child in a family. On the other hand, child benefit is payable irrespective of need. It is therefore inconsistent with a policy of targeting benefits on the most needy. It is presumably for this reason that in recent years the rate of benefit was not increased even to keep pace with inflation, much less to bear any close relationship with the true cost of child support.

Entitlement

The main principle of entitlement laid down by the Child Benefit Act 1975 (which is supplemented by detailed regulations made by statutory instrument) is that benefit is dependent on "responsibility" for a "child." 8-21

(1) *"Child"*

A person is a child for any week in which he or she is under the age of 16, or under 18 if certain prescribed conditions are met, or under 19 and receiving full-time education. However, benefit is not payable for children receiving "advanced" (*i.e.* above "A" level) education, or certain kinds of training. 8-22

(2) *"Responsibility"*

A claimant is "responsible for a child" if either (a) the child is living with the claimant or (b) the claimant is contributing to the cost of providing for the child at a weekly rate not less than the child benefit rate. 8-23

It will often be the case, particularly after a divorce, that several people qualify for benefit under that test. The Act therefore lays down a code of priorities. A person who has the child living with him is entitled as against one who contributes to his maintenance; and where husband and wife reside together the wife is entitled. Subject to those rules a parent (including a step-parent and an adoptive parent) is entitled as against a non-parent. As between two unmarried parents the mother is entitled. If more than one person is entitled they may elect which of them is to receive the benefit; if they fail to do so, the Secretary of State determines the issue.

There are certain exclusions of those otherwise entitled, *e.g.* where the child is married, detained in legal custody, or where the child is being looked after by a local authority.

One-parent benefit; rates of benefit

The creation of the child benefit scheme coincided with the focusing of attention on the special plight of the single-parent family; and the scheme was therefore adapted to give an additional payment ("one-parent benefit") in respect of the first child in such a family. 8-24

To qualify for one-parent benefit the claimant must show:

(i) the claimant has the child living with him or her; and

(ii) the claimant either has no spouse or is not residing with the spouse; and

(iii) the claimant is not living with any other person as a spouse.

Essentially, therefore, the benefit is payable to anyone (not necessarily a parent) who has sole responsibility for a child. Although the rate of child benefit itself was, as mentioned, "frozen" for a number of years, the one-parent addition has been allowed to rise.

Rates of benefit
8–25 The standard rate of child benefit is now £7.80 for each child; but since 1991 an enhanced rate of £9.65 is payable for the first child. "One-parent benefit" (which is payable only in respect of the first or only child) is an additional £5.85.

Relationship with other benefits
8–26 Child benefit is tax free and not means-tested. It is taken into account in full in determining entitlement to Income Support: see the example at p. 134 below; and it can therefore be argued that it is of more value to parents in full-time work than to those who receive Income Support. To that extent the scheme is consistent with the Government's policies, referred to above, of encouraging reliance on paid employment.

CONTRIBUTORY BENEFITS

8–27 There are a large number of benefits, entitlement to which depends on contributions made by the "insured person" or his spouse—for example, unemployment benefit, sickness benefit, invalidity pension and allowance, maternity allowance, widow's payment, widowed mother's allowance, widow's pension, and retirement pension. The benefits of most direct relevance to family lawyers are widow's benefits and retirement pensions; and their impact on the financial arrangements to be made on marital breakdown is touched on at para. 9–65 below.

B. THE LIABLE RELATIVE PROCEDURE

8–28 As already explained, the legislation has long contained provisions whereby the authorities could recover payments of Income Support from "liable relatives"; and in 1990 these provisions were extended in scope. The text first considers who is under a liability to maintain for this purpose; secondly, it considers the tests applied in deciding whether that liability has been discharged; and finally it considers the procedures available for enforcing the liability in the event of breach.

(i) Liability to Maintain

The Social Security Act 1986 provides that a man is liable, for the 8–29 purposes of Income Support, to maintain his wife and his children, and a woman to maintain her husband and her children. It should be noted that spouses cease to be "liable" for this purpose once their marriage is ended by divorce; but they remain liable to maintain children (but not step-children or other "children of the family").

(ii) Breach of the Obligation to Maintain

The obligation is only enforceable if there has been a claim for Income 8–30 Support in respect of a spouse or child; (and the maximum liability cannot exceed the appropriate Income Support scale rates). However, the maximum liability has been substantially increased by amendments made to the legislation in 1990. It now extends not only to the personal allowance in respect of the children, but also to certain "child-related" premiums (the family premium, the lone parent premium and any disabled child premium or carer premium), and in addition—more controversially—it has been extended to cover a so-called "personal allowance element" (defined as the amount paid by way of personal allowance under the Act to a claimant who has children by the liable person). Benefit paid to a person whom the parent is under no direct obligation to maintain—because the claimant and the relative are not, and perhaps never have been, married—can thus now be taken into account so long as there are dependent children under 16: see Social Security Act 1986, s.24A(1) and Income Support (Liable Relatives) Regulations 1990, reg. 2.

As a matter of routine the DSS seeks to identify and trace a claimant's liable relatives, and aims to ensure that the relative pays the amount which would remove the dependant's need for Income Support or as much as the relative can reasonably afford. In deciding what the relative can afford, the DSS applies an administrative formula which apparently assumes that the relative should be allowed to keep the sum which (after deducting expenses such as housing costs and travel to work) would leave (a) the Income Support payable for a family consisting of the relative and any partner or children living in the same household; plus (b) an "incentive" element which may be 15 per cent. or 25 per cent. of the relative's net earnings: see [1991] Fam Law, p. 32.

If it proves impossible to obtain an effective voluntary payment arrangement, the DSS may seek to enforce the obligation under the procedure summarised below.

It is important to note that the liability to maintain for Income Support cases is not directly affected by any assessment made in matrimonial proceedings. Thus:

> In *Hulley* v. *Thompson* [1981] FLR 53, a consent order in divorce proceedings provided that the husband transfer the matrimonial home to the wife, but that he pay no maintenance to the wife or children. It was held that this did not exclude his liability to maintain for the purpose of the comparable Supplementary Benefit provisions.

(iii) Procedures for Enforcing the Obligation to Maintain

Application by DSS for court order

8–31   If no effective voluntary arrangement is made, the Secretary of State may apply to the magistrates' court for an order directing the liable relative to pay "such sum, weekly or otherwise, as it may consider appropriate." In deciding whether to make an order the court is directed to "have regard to all the circumstances, and in particular to the income of the liable person"; and it is now provided that the order may (provided that the court is satisfied that the relative has the means to pay) include all or some of the "personal allowance element" referred to above: Social Security Act 1986, s.24(4), s.24A(1) and Income Support (Liable Relatives) Regulations 1990, reg. 2.

What factors should the court take into account? In particular, should it take into account the fact that one spouse has agreed to a transfer of the family home to the other in exchange for a dismissal of claims for periodical payments—the so-called "clean break?"

There has been no guidance on this issue since the potential liability was extended to the personal allowance element; but in *Hulley* v. *Thompson* (above) it was held that the "circumstances of the case" did include the fact that a consent order dealing with maintenance had been made, and although the terms of that order were not conclusive in deciding whether a liable person should be required to reimburse benefit, it would seem that the court should have regard to the basis upon which the order had been made: see *National Assistance Board* v. *Parkes* [1955] 2 QB 506.

The 1990 legislation empowers the Department to assign the benefit of any such order (apart from the personal allowance element) to the claimant if Income Support ceases to be payable; but it may also by notice revive any personal allowance element if the claimant subsequently returns to Income Support.

Application by spouse—indirect enforcement

8–32   A parent or spouse may of course take proceedings for financial relief against the other partner. If there is a maintenance order in favour of a parent whose Income Support includes payments for a child, the DSS may now enforce the order on behalf of the claimant (Social Security Act 1986, s.24B); and the DSS has the right to be given notice of and appear in any proceedings to vary, discharge or enforce such an order.

Prosecution

It is a criminal offence persistently to refuse or neglect to maintain   8–33
oneself or any person whom one is liable to maintain: Social Security Act 1986, s.26(1). But prosecutions are rare in cases of genuine separation.

The diversion procedure

It became a common practice for claimants who had maintenance   8–34
orders to authorise payment of the sums due to the DSS, who would then pay the claimant the full Income Support entitlement without deduction for the income receivable under the order. This gave claimants the security of knowing that they would receive a certain amount of money promptly each week; but it seems that the DSS may now be less ready to operate this procedure unless and until there is a record of persistent default by the liable person.

Effectiveness of support for lone parent families

In the light of weaknesses recorded in a Report by the National   8–35
Audit Office, the DSS announced that it was strengthening procedures for recovering maintenance from liable relatives; and that it was intended to increase the total recovered from £155 million in 1988–89 to £260 million in 1990–91. However, a new dimension has been added to this issue by the enactment of the Child Support Act 1991, the provisions of which are summarised in Chapter 10.

WELFARE BENEFITS IN FAMILY BREAKDOWN
I INCOME SUPPORT

Harry and Wendy are divorced. Wendy lives in the former matrimonial home with her three children, Charles (aged 17), Christine (aged 11) and Carl (aged 8), all of whom are at school. There is an outstanding mortgage of £30,000 on the house. Wendy earns £20 weekly by working as a bar-person on Saturday evenings. The Divorce Court ordered Harry (who works abroad) to transfer all his interest in the family home to Wendy on terms that she should assume liability for the mortgage and that her claim for periodical payments be dismissed. The court also ordered Harry to pay £10 weekly to Wendy for each child, but he has never done so. Wendy has no savings or other capital.

Wendy's Income Support entitlement is as follows:

1.	Single Person's Allowance		£42.45
2.	Allowances for Charles (17)	£25.55	
	Christine (11)	£21.40	
	Carl (8)	£14.55	
		———	£61.50
3.	Premiums:		
	Family Premium	£9.30	
	Lone Parent Premium	£4.75	
		———	£14.05
4.	Housing Costs		
	Interest at 11% on £30,000=	£63.46	
	less Miras Tax relief	£15.86	
		———	
	[**NB.** No payment is made in respect of any capital element in the payments Wendy has to make to the Building Society]		£47.60

Total—How much the law says Wendy needs to live on:

£165.60

But **deduct**—sums already coming in:

(i) Child Benefit for Charles (£9.65) Christine and Carl (£7.80 each) *plus* one-parent benefit (£5.85)

£31.10

(ii) Wendy's earnings:

Wendy's earnings (£20) **less** amount disregarded (£15)	£5.00	
	———	£36.10
		———
Entitlement to Income Support		**£129.50**

NB (i) The rates used in the above example are those in force from 6 April 1992.

(ii) As explained at para. 8–28 of the text, Harry (as a liable relative) is under a potential obligation to reimburse these payments of income support.

(iii) Wendy's total weekly spendable income is therefore:

Income Support	£129.50
Child Benefit	£31.10
Earnings	£20.00
	———
	£180.60

It is up to her how she allocates this sum—but note that her obligation in respect of mortgage payments may be substantially higher than the figure of "Housing Costs" by reason of the obligation to pay off the principal of the loan, either by making payments under a Life Policy, or by the traditional instalment method (whereby the borrower pays a sum made up in part of interest and in part of capital every month).

II FAMILY CREDIT

Example 2

The facts are as in Example 1, except that Wendy has found work for 20 hours weekly as a supermarket cashier at a wage of £85 weekly (less tax of approximately £5.40 weekly and National Insurance Contributions of £4) leaving her with a take-home pay of approximately £74.50. She is no longer eligible for Income Support (since she works for more than 16 hours weekly). The first step in working out her entitlement is to calculate the "maximum family credit" applicable to a person in her circumstances. This is:

Adult Credit	£41.00	
Credits for Charles (£21.45)		
Christine (£17.25) and		
Carl (£10.40)	£49.10	
		————
Total ("Maximum Family Credit ["M"])		£90.10

The next step is to work out her weekly income in accordance with the rules. This figure (£74.50) is then compared with a so-called "applicable amount" (now £66.60) laid down under the Social Security Act 1986, s.20(5) (a) and Family Credit (General) Regulations 1987, reg. 47. Since Wendy's weekly income is more than that amount, her entitlement is worked out as follows:

Total weekly income	£74.50
less applicable amount	£66.60
	————
	£7.90
70% of that amount ("X")	£5.53
Family credit payable is	
M minus X, *i.e.* £90.10	
less £5.53	**£84.57**

She will thus have a little more cash available each week (in fact, £9.57) more than when she was on Income Support but this makes no allowance for costs of travel to work or child care. In reality, Wendy may feel that the sort of employment she is likely to be able to obtain does not compensate her for the efforts involved.

Suggestions for Further Reading

Hoggett and Pearl, Chap. 3 and 4.

Chapter 9

COURT ORDERS FOR FINANCIAL RELIEF ON FAMILY BREAKDOWN

INTRODUCTION

We have already seen that marriage creates rights and obligations **9–01** (including financial rights and obligations); and reference has been made to the divorce court's extensive powers in divorce, nullity, and judicial separation proceedings. The various procedures which are available to deal with financial claims by a couple who are or have been married are discussed in greater detail in the first part of this chapter.

If a couple have never been married, the position is very different. In *Windeler* v. *Whitehall* [1990] 2 FLR 505, 506, Millett J. explained the law governing a claim by a woman who had lived with a man for a number of years in these words:

> "If this were California, this would be a claim for palimony, but it is England and is not. English law recognises neither the term nor the obligation to which it gives effect. In this country a husband has a legal obligation to support his wife even if they are living apart. A man has no legal obligation to support his mistress even if they are living together ... English courts exercise a statutory jurisdiction to adjust the property rights of a married person on the dissolution of their marriage, but there must be a marriage to dissolve. The courts possess neither a statutory nor an inherent jurisdiction to disturb existing rights of property on the termination of an extra-marital relationship, however long established a relationship and however deserving the claimant."

What then can be done when a relationship between an unmarried couple breaks down? The law is summarised in the second part of this chapter.

A. BREAKDOWN OF MARRIAGE

There is at common law a duty on a husband to support his wife **9–02** during the marriage. However, the extent of this right was limited, and the methods of enforcing it were inadequate: see *Principles of Family Law*, pp. 323–325. For all practical purposes, the common law duty has been supplanted by statutory procedures which fall into two groups. First, there are those which are only available during marriage. They can be dealt with very briefly, since in practice they are today comparatively little used. Secondly, there are orders which are made in divorce or other matrimonial proceedings. These receive comparatively extended treatment, see paras. 9–25—9–88.

1. COURT ORDERS FOR FINANCIAL SUPPORT DURING MARRIAGE—FAILURE TO MAINTAIN

Applications in superior courts

9–03   MCA 1973, s.27 (as amended), provides that either party to a marriage may apply to the High Court or to a Divorce County Court for an order on the ground that the other party has failed to provide reasonable maintenance for the applicant, or that he has failed to provide or to make a proper contribution towards reasonable maintenance for any child of the family. In deciding whether there has been such a failure, and if so what order to make, the court is to "have regard to all the circumstances of the case" including the matters which are specifically referred to under the divorce legislation (considered in detail at para. 9–39 below). Where an application is made alleging both failure to provide maintenance for the applicant and for a child of the family (see para. 14–03 below) who is under 18 the court must (as in divorce proceedings) give "first consideration" to the welfare of the child while a minor.

If the case is made out the court can make orders for periodical payments (secured or unsecured) and a lump sum; but the court has no power to make the sophisticated property adjustment orders dealing with the family home which are often sought in divorce proceedings: see para. 9–53 below.

Housekeeping orders?

9–04   There is no statutory provision preventing the court from making an order while the parties are living together; and an order may continue whilst they live together.

Not often used

9–05   In practice there are few applications (71 in 1989) to the superior courts under this provision. However, the Magistrates' Court has jurisdiction to make orders on this ground, and this jurisdiction is more widely used—perhaps as a prelude to divorce proceedings, or perhaps because it was for many years the policy of the Supplementary Benefit and Income Support Authorities to encourage separated wives to obtain such orders.

Applications to the Magistrates' Court

Historical evolution

Since 1878 magistrates' courts have had power to make financial 9–06 orders in domestic cases; and their powers are now codified in the Domestic Proceedings and Magistrates' Courts Act 1978—a reforming Act intended to bring the family jurisdiction of the magistrates' courts into line with the reformed law administered in the divorce court, and to remove any justification there might have been for the allegation eloquently voiced in the Finer Report (Vol. 2, App. 5, para. 6) that the magistrates' jurisdiction was a "secondary system" of family law "designed for what were considered to be the special and cruder requirements of the poor."

Powers to make financial orders

The court has power to make financial orders if the applicant can 9–07 establish one of the grounds set out in section 1 of the 1978 Act. Broadly speaking those grounds involve an element of wrongdoing on the part of the respondent. However, the court is also given power to make certain financial orders in cases where the parties are living apart by agreement; and it is given an express power to make orders for payments which have been agreed by the parties.

Grounds for complaint

There are four grounds:
(a) *Failure to provide reasonable maintenance for spouse: 1978 Act, s.1(a)*
This ground is in substance identical to the ground for an 9–08 application to the superior courts: para. 9–03 above. The Act gives no guidance as to what has to be established; but if the ground is made out the court is directed in deciding how to exercise its powers to have regard to certain specified matters such as the income, earning capacity and other financial resources of the parties as well as their conduct if it would be inequitable to disregard it: DP & MCA 1978, s.3(2).

(b) *Failure to provide, or to make proper contribution towards, reasonable maintenance for any child of the family: 1978 Act, s.1(b)*
The term "child of the family" is explained at para. 14–03 below. 9–09 There are special guidelines which may apply in cases where the child in question is, for example, a step-child and not the respondent's own child.

(c) *Respondent has behaved in such a way that the applicant cannot reasonably be expected to live with the respondent: 1978 Act, s.1(c)*
This ground is identical in substance to the "fact" evidencing 9–10 breakdown of marriage for the purposes of the divorce law: see para. 4–16 above.

(d) *Desertion: 1978 Act, s.1(c)*

9–11   Desertion has the same meaning as in the law of divorce (see para. 4–29 above. However, a deserted spouse can apply immediately for a magistrates' order; it is not necessary for there to have been two years' desertion.

Time limits

9–12   Proceedings under the 1978 Act are subject to the general rule applicable in magistrates' courts (Magistrates' Courts Act 1980, s.127) that an application must be made within six months from the date when the cause of complaint arose.

Orders that can be made

9–13   If the applicant satisfies the court of a ground of complaint the court may make any of the following orders:

(a) *Periodical payments*

9–14   There is no formal restriction on the amount of the payments which may be ordered; but the magistrates, unlike the divorce court, have no power to order secured periodical payments.

(b) *A lump sum (not exceeding £1,000)*

9–15   This power was apparently intended to be used to cover payment of expenses such as outstanding hire purchase debts, gas or electricity bills, or removal expenses, and to reimburse a wife for maintenance expenses incurred before the date of the order: see Law Com. No. 77, para. 2.34.

Periodical and lump sum orders may—subject to the restrictions imposed by the Child Support Act 1991, when it is brought into force: see para. 10–21 below—also be made in respect of children of the family.

Guidelines for exercise of discretion

9–16   The 1978 Act, s.3, requires the court to have regard to all the circumstances (including in particular certain specified matters) first consideration being given to the welfare while a minor of any child of the family. These guidelines are now similar to those applicable in divorce—for example, in requiring the court to give priority to the welfare of children, to take account of any increase in earning capacity which it would be reasonable to expect a party to the marriage to take steps to acquire, and to take conduct into account only if it would be inequitable to disregard it: see para. 9–62 below. But the powers of the magistrates are limited, particularly in relation to property; and it may not always be possible for a magistrates' court to do what the divorce court would consider appropriate, for example in relation to the enjoyment of the matrimonial home. In practice in many (perhaps most) of the cases coming before magistrates, the conclusive factor will be the inability of either spouse to provide for all the dependants.

The voluntary separation ground

Section 7 of the Act contains a provision intended to provide 9–17
greater security where husband and wife have separated by consent.
The intention was to give a degree of security and certainty to the
wife, rather than making her wait "for the month when the cheque
does not arrive" (when she would be able to start neglect to maintain
proceedings: see para. 9–08 above). Accordingly the court may
(subject to a number of complex restrictions) make a periodical
payments order if: (i) the parties have been living apart for a
continuous period exceeding three months; and (ii) neither party has
deserted the other; and (iii) one party has during the period of three
months preceding the application been making periodical payments
for the benefit of the other. In practice this provision is hardly ever
used.

Consent orders

Section 6 of the Act empowers the court to make a consent order 9–18
for financial provision for a spouse or a child of the family provided:
(i) there is adequate proof of the agreement and (ii) the court has no
reason to think that it would be contrary to the interests of justice to
do so. At one time, the making of a consent order could result in
significant tax saving, and this provision was much used. However,
changes in tax law have now virtually extinguished this advantage. It
is true that a consent order still gives the payee the advantage of
having a legally enforceable right, and it gives the payer some limited
security against allegations that there has been a failure to provide for
the family. But it seems unlikely that these advantages will be seen to
be sufficient to justify the expense involved in obtaining a court
order.

Duration of orders

The court may make an order for a limited period—for example, for 9–19
12 months from the date of the order. But even if the order is not in
terms limited it will be subject to the following rules:

(a) *Cohabitation*

Although an order can be obtained even if the parties to the 9–20
marriage are living with each other, a periodical payments order will
cease to be enforceable if they continue to live with each other or
subsequently resume living with each other for a continuous period of
six months. The result is that a spouse can go to court and obtain an
enforceable "housekeeping order," but only for a limited period.

(b) *Effect of divorce and remarriage*

Magistrates' orders do not automatically determine on divorce; and 9–21
although the divorce court has a statutory power to direct that a
magistrates' periodical payments order should cease to have effect,
in practice magistrates' orders often continue in force. However

periodical payment orders in favour of a spouse automatically determine if that spouse remarries.

Variation

9–22   The court has power to vary or revoke a periodical payment order but it has no power to vary a lump sum order. In exercising its variation jurisdiction, the court gives effect to any agreement between the parties "so far as it appears just to do so"; and should have regard to "all the circumstances of the case, first consideration being given to the welfare while a minor of any child of the family who has not attained the age of 18, and the circumstances of the case shall include any change in any of the matters to which the court was required to have regard when making the order": DP & MCA 1978, s.20(11). In practice, variation is often sought by husbands who have got into arrears.

Registration of divorce court orders

9–23   A maintenance order made by the divorce court may be registered for enforcement in the magistrates' court. One important consequence of registration is that the magistrates may thereafter vary the order as if it had originally been made by them. Research has shown that 65 per cent. of all orders being enforced in magistrates' courts were cases in which the spouses had in fact been divorced, with the paradoxical result that the major role of the magistrates' matrimonial jurisdiction has thus changed from the intended purpose of making and enforcing maintenance orders for the benefit of the separated to that of an enforcement agency for the divorced.

Enforcement of orders

9–24   For many years, one of the reasons why orders were sought or registered in the magistrates' court was because the legislation provided that maintenance payments should be made to the Clerk of the Court; and this procedure had a number of advantages. First, the Clerk's office kept proper accounts so that it was easy to prove that payments were in arrears. Secondly, the parties were kept at arm's length, but the Clerk's office would be in touch with both. Finally, all matters relating to the making, variation, and collection of orders were centralised in a single building, under the supervision of experienced and responsible officials. Moreover, the Clerk was required, if requested in writing and unless it appeared to him unreasonable so to do, to proceed in his own name for the enforcement of arrears. The Clerk's office therefore played a central role in the enforcement process.

The enforcement machinery has been modernised by the provisions of the Maintenance Enforcement Act 1991: the court may now order that payments be made by standing order or direct debit. But the 1991 Act preserves the central role of the Clerk: the Clerk is still required to take enforcement proceedings in his own name in respect of arrears if requested to do so, and in cases in which the payments are to be made through the Clerk's office, the recipient may give the Clerk standing authority to take such proceedings.

2. COURT ORDERS IN DIVORCE, NULLITY AND JUDICIAL SEPARATION PROCEEDINGS

INTRODUCTION—EVOLUTION OF THE LAW

Money often most important issue in divorce

The judicial statistics suggest that in 1990 some 47,000 orders for **9-25** post-divorce maintenance or property adjustment were made by the County Court, and a further 27,000 orders were made in respect of children. Such orders are usually described as "ancillary relief" because they are ancillary (or subordinate) to the main suit for divorce, etc.; but the reality is that in many cases now it is these financial matters which lie at the heart of the issue between the parties. If either party to a marriage wants a divorce, sooner or later he or she will, unless the case is wholly exceptional, be able to obtain one; and there is thus rarely any point in resisting the grant of a decree. But financial issues loom correspondingly large, and can give rise to long and bitter disputes. It may be that the system is less effective than it might be, and is of little relevance to many spouses: see para. 9–88 below. However, English law is remarkable for the extent of the powers which the court has in divorce proceedings. Virtually all the economically valuable assets of the spouses are put at the disposition of the court; and orders requiring income payments unlimited in amount (and possibly extending until the death of the survivor) may be made. Although the law may be of only limited relevance to those who have low incomes and few assets, it cannot be said that the court is reluctant to exercise these powers: periodical payment orders for as much as £70,000 per annum have been made, as (it would appear) have orders requiring payment of capital sums in excess of £2,000,000.

The text first analyses the powers of the court; it then discusses the principle upon which the court's discretion is to be exercised.

(i) ORDERS THE COURT CAN MAKE

The width of the court's powers exercisable in divorce, nullity and **9-26** judicial separation proceedings—and it seems that no distinction of principle is drawn between them: see *Wagstaff* v. *Wagstaff* [1992] 1 FLR 333 (substantial lump sum award in judicial separation case)— means that it is usually possible to achieve whatever result is regarded as fair, just, and reasonable. The legislation—MCA 1973—distinguishes (s.21) between "financial provision orders" and "property adjustment orders"; and the court also has power to order a sale of property:

1. Financial Provision Orders

(a) *Maintenance pending suit*

9–27   MCA 1973, s.22, empowers the court to order either party to make periodical payments for the other's maintenance for any period (beginning not earlier than the date of the presentation of the petition and ending with the date of the determination of the suit) as it thinks reasonable. Such orders are intended to provide for the petitioner's immediate needs; but in practice there may often be a considerable delay in getting an order, and a spouse without an independent source of income will often have to rely on income support unless maintenance is paid voluntarily.

(b) *Periodical payments—secured or unsecured: MCA 1973, s.23(1)(a), (b) and (e)*

9–28   Orders for regular income payments—for example, £50 weekly; £250 monthly; £8,000 annually—are the traditional way of providing maintenance. The most common form of order is for unsecured payments—and the court now (Maintenance Enforcement Act, 1991) has power to order payment by standing order or direct debit. The court may also make an attachment of earnings order requiring an employer to deduct specified sums from an employee's pay and to pay them over to the court. It is too early to say whether these new procedures will make it less difficult to enforce unsecured maintenance orders.

If the order is secured, a fund of capital (usually stocks and shares) must be set aside. This will usually be vested in trustees. The fund remains the property of the debtor; but if there is default in making the stipulated payments, recourse can be had to the fund to make good the default. A secured order has two significant advantages over an order for unsecured periodical payments. First, the order can be effectively enforced even if the debtor disappears, disposes of other property, or ceases to earn. Secondly, a secured order may continue throughout the lifetime of the applicant. The other partner may die, but the fund remains. In contrast, there is no power to order unsecured payments to continue beyond the parties' joint lives. Secured or unsecured periodical payment orders may be made for either party, and also—subject to the provisions of the Child Support Act 1991: see para. 10–21 below—in respect of children of the family (defined at para. 14–03 below).

Duration of periodical payment orders—joint lives or specified term? Periodical payments order may be for such term as the court directs, and the traditional form of order was for payments during the parties' joint lives. However, under the provisions designed to emphasise self-sufficiency introduced by the Matrimonial and Family Proceedings Act 1984 (see para. 9–70 below) the court may now perhaps be more inclined to make orders for a specified term—*e.g.* three years—in order to give a spouse who has not been in employment time to find a new job or to make alternative arrangements for child care.

Death and remarriage have an automatic effect on periodical payment orders. The death of either party terminates an unsecured periodical payments order; and the payee's remarriage terminates both secured and unsecured orders: MCA 1973, s.28(1). The effect of the remarriage rule may be unfortunate. First, it cannot be in a child's interest that the caring parent should be in straitened circumstances. Secondly, the rule encourages cohabitation in preference to remarriage: cohabitation does not automatically affect the maintenance order, and although the court may reduce or extinguish the order if the new partner is able to provide financially for the couple, the existence of such a relationship does not (in contrast to remarriage) prevent a fresh application for support from the court if circumstances change.

(c) *Lump sum orders: MCA 1973, s.23(1)(c), (f)*

The sums involved may be very large—1.3 million pounds in the case of *Gojkovic* v. *Gojkovic* [1990] 1 FLR 140, see para. 9–37 below. 9–29

The court has power to order payment of a lump sum by instalments. It is also specifically empowered to order payment to cover liabilities or expenses reasonably incurred.

2. Property Adjustment Orders

(a) *Transfer of property: MCA 1973: s.24(1)(a)*

This power enables the court to order that specified property (such as the matrimonial home, or investments) be transferred to the other spouse (or to or for the benefit of a child of the family). 9–30

(b) *Settlement of property: MCA 1973: s.24(1)(b)*

The court may direct that property to which a party to the marriage is entitled be settled for the benefit of the other spouse and/or the children of the family. This power is now often used to make arrangements in connection with the former matrimonial home, in an attempt to ensure that it is available for occupation as a home for dependent children whilst preserving both spouses' financial interest in it: see below para. 9–53. 9–31

(c) *Variation of nuptial settlements: s.24(1)(c), (d)*

The court may make an order varying for the benefit of the parties and/or the children of the family, any "ante-nuptial or post-nuptial" settlement made on the parties to the marriage. This power can, of course, be used to make appropriate variations in those (comparatively rare) cases in which the parties have interests under a 9–32 traditional marriage settlement; but the term "settlement" has been widely interpreted:

> In *E* v. *E (Financial Provision)* [1990] 2 FLR 233 a wealthy man provided support for his son's family. In particular, 10 years or so after the marriage he made funds available for the purchase of a house for them, making use of a settlement on discretionary trusts. The provisions of the settlement no doubt gave effect to the father's view that the wife was profligate, extravagant and neglectful of his grandchildren: the discretionary powers of the trustees were only exercisable with the consent of the father as "protector" of the fund. On divorce, the court ordered that a quarter of a million pounds be removed from the trust and transferred to the wife and children, that the father be removed from his role as protector of the fund, and that new trustees be appointed.

3. Power to Order Sale

9–33   The court now has (MCA 1973, s.24A) an express power, on making an order for financial relief other than an order for unsecured periodical payments, to order a sale. In effect, the power is ancillary to the making of the other orders already considered. This power can be exercised even if a third party also has a beneficial interest in the property (although any such person must be given an opportunity to make representations to the court: s.24A(6)). For example:

> In *Harwood* v. *Harwood* [1991] 2 FLR 274 a firm in which the husband was a partner had an unquantified interest in the matrimonial home. The court ordered that the home be sold and the proceeds paid into court to await ascertainment of the amount to which the husband's partner was entitled.

CONCLUSION ON ORDERS THAT CAN BE MADE—COURT'S POWERS WIDE BUT NOT UNLIMITED

9–34   Although the Court's powers are very wide, it is important to emphasise—as the House of Lords did in *Livesey* v. *Jenkins* [1985] FLR 813—that the powers are not limitless, and that the court may only act in accordance with the provisions of the legislation. It follows for example that the court has no power to order one party to pay insurance premiums on the former matrimonial home direct to the insurers; whilst in *Milne* v. *Milne* (1981) 2 FLR 286 the Court of Appeal held that, since the statute did not permit the court to order payments to be made save to the other party to the marriage or for the children of the family, the court could not order the husband in effect to execute and pay for a life insurance policy and to assign the benefit of the policy to the wife. In practice provisions dealing with insurance, repairs, and payment of mortgage interest and other outgoings are often dealt with by the parties giving undertakings which are then annexed to the court's order in a schedule.

Other limitations
There are three other matters which may affect the court's ability 9–35 effectively to redistribute the family's wealth:

(i) The court has no powers over assets which, by their nature, are not "owned" by either spouse. This may perhaps seem self-evident, but it follows from this principle that the court can have no power to make orders dealing with expectations under many pension schemes. It also follows that the court cannot make orders requiring a company—even a company in which one of the spouses is a majority shareholder—to deal with its assets, and that all that the court can do is to direct the settlement of the shareholding: see *Crittenden* v. *Crittenden* [1990] 2 FLR 361, CA (but compare *Nicholas* v. *Nicholas* [1984] FLR 285).

(ii) The court has no power to deal with the capital of a settlement which is not a nuptial or post-nuptial settlement. If a settlor creates a settlement which is unrelated to any actual or projected marriage—with a view to saving Inheritance Tax, for example—the settlement would not fall within the definition of a nuptial settlement, and accordingly the court could not vary its terms, even though the settlement might make substantial provision for the family.

(iii) The exercise of the court's powers cannot prejudice the rights of third parties not before the court. Thus, if the matrimonial home is subject to a mortgage a transfer of it to the wife cannot affect the mortgagor husband's contractual liability to pay the mortgage instalments, nor the rights of the mortgagee to take action if the mortgage covenants are broken. (In practice mortgage deeds usually contain provisions forbidding the mortgagor from transferring the property without the mortgagee's consent; hence the mortgagee should have notice of the application and be given an opportunity to be heard.)

(ii) HOW THE COURT EXERCISES ITS POWERS

No sex discrimination
The legislation does not discriminate between the sexes. As 9–36 Scarman L.J. put it (*Calderbank* v. *Calderbank* [1976] Fam 93,103) "husbands and wives come to the judgment seat ... upon a basis of

complete equality"; and orders—sometimes substantial—have been made against wives:

> In *Browne* v. *Browne* [1989] 1 FLR 291 CA, a wife was ordered to make payments of some £175,000 to her former husband. Butler-Sloss L.J. said that an application by a husband for redistribution of assets "is not in any way an unusual application ... (and) that it would be a sad reflection if in these times of much vaunted equality of the sexes a husband should be seen to be acting in some way improperly if he exercises the right (to apply for an order) which the law permits and indeed encourages."

However, in practice such orders are the exception; and economic reality often dictates that financial orders be made against the husband in favour of the wife.

Statutory guidelines for exercise of discretion
9-37   The principle upon which the court should exercise its extensive powers has been a matter of controversy. At the time of the Divorce Reform Act 1969, there was considerable concern about the effect of divorce on the economically disadvantaged partner—normally the wife—who might be repudiated and left in severe economic difficulties; and the Matrimonial Proceedings and Property Act 1970 (the provisions of which were subsequently consolidated in the Matrimonial Causes Act 1973) not only gave the courts the extensive powers which have been outlined above but also adopted the so-called *minimal loss principle*: the court, having considered all the circumstances, was "so to exercise its powers as to place the parties, so far as it is practicable and, having regard to their conduct, just to do so, in the financial position in which they would have been if the marriage had not broken down." It was not long before that principle itself came under attack and the legislation was amended by the Matrimonial and Family Proceedings Act 1984. The 1984 Act removed the statutory directive whereby the court was obliged to seek to place the parties in the financial position in which they would have been had the marriage not broken down; and—although it does contain provisions intended to structure the exercise of the court's discretion—it does not substitute any comparable directive. The lack of any clear guiding principle undoubtedly causes a measure of uncertainty, and—although certain trends, based on the interpretation given by the courts to the relevant statutory provisions, can be observed in the case law—the courts have expressed a reluctance to make any gloss on the legislative guidance:

> In *Gojkovic* v. *Gojkovic* [1990] 1 FLR 140, CA, the parties were Yugoslavs who had come to England with almost no money. In what the trial judge described as "a story of high achievement and ... glorious success ... through unrelenting hard work, unlimited self sacrifice and absolute determination" they accumulated assets worth some £4,000,000 almost all of which belonged, in law, to the husband. The court upheld an order

requiring him to pay £1.3 million to the wife, but declined the invitation of the husband's counsel to lay down guidelines to assist in determining the appropriate level of lump sum payments in cases of very substantial assets. Russell L.J. said that such an exercise was not possible, and that the guidelines already existed in the form of the provisions of the statute.

Against this background, the guidance given by legislation and case law must now be examined.

(i) *Maintenance pending suit*

In relation to maintenance pending suit, the legislation contains no **9–38** detailed guidelines at all; it simply directs the court to make such order as it "thinks reasonable." But there is no difference of principle in relation to quantification between this and other orders. The court may therefore take account of all the matters referred to in the guidelines considered below which are known to it: but it obviously cannot make the final settlement of financial matters which is appropriate on final decree, not least because it cannot at this stage deal with the parties' capital—notably the matrimonial home.

The court will usually consider as the most important factor the wife's needs and the husband's ability to meet those needs, having regard to his other needs and obligations:

> In *Peacock* v. *Peacock* [1984] FLR 263 the husband was in fact making a voluntary payment to the DSS under the procedure discussed at para. 8–30 above of £20 weekly out of his take home pay of £82. On investigating the figures, and taking account of the fact that he was about to set up in a new home at increased cost, the court considered that an order for only £15 would be appropriate.

> In *Re T (Divorce: Interim Maintenance: Discovery)* [1990] 1 FLR 1 an order for interim maintenance pending suit of £25,000 per annum was made. The court's view that this would be reasonable was influenced by the fact that the parties had at one time concluded an agreement on that level of support.

(ii) *All other orders*

In contrast to the lack of guidance in relation to maintenance **9–39** pending suit, there are complex provisions which the court must follow in exercising its powers to make other orders. The scheme of the legislation is, in outline, as follows:

(a) It is the duty of the court in deciding whether to exercise its powers and, if so, in what manner to have regard to all the circumstances of the case, first consideration being given to the welfare while a minor of any child of the family who has not attained the age of 18: MCA 1973, s.25(1).

(b) As regards the exercise of the powers to make financial provision orders, property adjustment orders, or orders for the sale of property in relation to a party to the marriage it is provided that the court shall "in particular have regard to" certain specified matters: s.25(2).

(c) The Act also directs the court "in particular" to have regard to certain specified matters as regards the exercise of its powers to make such orders in relation to a child of the family: s.25(3), (4).

(d) Finally, the Act contains a number of provisions designed to direct the court's attention to the principle of self-sufficiency, and to facilitate, in appropriate cases the making of a "clean break" between the parties to the marriage: s.25A.

1. First Consideration to the Welfare of Children

The policy

9–40   In 1987, 149,000 children under the age of 16 were involved in their parents' divorce. The legislation seeks now to "emphasise as a priority" the need to make appropriate financial provision to safeguard the maintenance and welfare of the children by imposing on the court a duty, in deciding whether to exercise its powers in financial matters and if so, in what manner, to "have regard to all the circumstances of the case, first consideration being given to the welfare while a minor of any child of the family who has not attained the age of eighteen."

It is important, first of all, to note that this provision extends to the exercise of the court's powers to make orders in relation to the spouses, and is not solely related to the making of orders relating to the children. In particular, the court has often regarded it as being a priority to seek to ensure that any children have secure housing, and to that end has made orders transferring the family home to the parent with whom the children are to live. Again, the court may think that the requirement to give first consideration to the welfare of the children requires that a mother who has care of the children should have periodical payments for her own support at least until the children no longer need her full-time care: see *Waterman* v. *Waterman* [1989] 1 FLR 380, CA; and it has—as already noted—been accepted that it is not in the children's interest that their mother be in straitened circumstances: *E* v. *E (Financial Provision)* [1989] 2 FLR 233.

It is however obviously important that the court should understand what is really required in financial terms to support a child. The formula to be introduced under the Child Support Act 1991—dealt with at paras. 10–17 to 10–20 below—will provide guidance on this issue; and as already explained, once the legislation is in force the court will only in exceptional circumstances be able to make orders for income payments to or for the parties' children (although its duty to put the children's welfare first will continue to govern the exercise of its powers, and will no doubt continue to influence the orders made in respect of the adults).

In an attempt to provide some basic information about the impact of child care on the parents' available financial resources, the courts are now circulated with information about:

(a) *Income Support Scale Rates* for children's weekly requirements:

Under 11:	£14.55
11—15:	£21.40
16—17:	£25.55
18:	£33.60

[Rates effective from 6th April 1992]

(b) The recommended scale published by *The National Foster Care Association*:

The NFCA Equivalence Income Scale seeks to show how much of a family's income is spent on a child. The following are the figures for April 1989 based on estimated weekly expenditure for an average family (The scale is increased in London, and does not take account of expenditure on the purchase or alteration of the home):

Age	Per Week
—4	£46.66
5—7	£54.43
8—10	£59.62
11—12	£64.91
13—15	£70.03
16—18	£93.46

In addition the court may have access to information about the rates paid by local authorities in respect of children whose accommodation is provided by foster parents. These vary from local authority to local authority, but the NFCA publishes a scale of recommended minimum rates, ranging (in April 1991) from £43.33 weekly for a child aged 4 or less outside London to £102.76 for a 16- to 18-year-old in London. Fostering allowance scales are of particular relevance in the present context because (as Simon Brown J. put it in *Cresswell* v. *Eaton* [1991] 1 All ER 484, 489) "although not insubstantial ... (they are) paid entirely by way of reimbursement of the expense incurred in maintaining children: food, clothing, heating, travel and so forth. The underlying philosophy of the fostering scheme is that it should not be undertaken for gain. There is thus no profit to be made from such payments, no reward for the personal care involved in fostering children."

But these scales merely give general information. In a well presented case the court will be given detailed information about the actual costs incurred in supporting the children of the family involved—by way of expenditure on education and hobbies, for example, as well as on subsistence.

Four significant limitations on the scope of the principle should be noted:

(a) *First, but not paramount*

9–41   In deciding issues relating to the upbringing of children the court regards the welfare of the child as the "paramount" consideration even if that means that the just claims of the child's parents or others affected have to be overridden: see para. 11–31 below. In considering financial matters, in contrast, the court is not required to go so far. It need only give "first" consideration to the welfare of the child in question, so that it must simply consider all the circumstances always bearing the children's welfare in mind; and then try to make a financial settlement which is just as between husband and wife:

> In *Suter* v. *Suter and Jones* [1987] 2 FLR 232, CA, the judge, in the belief that the children's welfare so required, made a periodical payment order to cover the whole of the wife's mortgage outgoings without taking into account any contribution which might be made by the wife's cohabitee. On appeal, it was held that the judge had been wrong to elevate the children's interests so as to control the outcome, and to produce a result which ordinary people might regard as unjust. The cohabitee should be expected to pay his share of the interest.

(b) *Applies only to children of the family*

9–42   The expression "child of the family" is widely defined in the legislation and extends to any child who has been treated by both of the parties to the marriage as a child of their family: see para. 14–03 below. But although this definition is wide, it does not extend to all those children who may, actually or prospectively, be affected by the orders made in the matrimonial proceedings in question. For example, the child born to a husband and his cohabitee after the breakdown of the husband's marriage is unlikely to be within the definition. The legislation thus seems now to embody the principle that the court is to put the interests of the children of a first marriage before the interests of other children affected (although this does not of course mean that the interests of the other children are to be ignored).

(c) *Applies only during infancy of children*

9–43   The court is only required to give first consideration to the welfare "while a minor" of any child of the family who has not attained the age of 18. This has two particular consequences. First, the court is not obliged to give such consideration to the welfare of any child of the family who has at the date of the hearing already attained the age of 18, even if the child is undergoing advanced education or training, or if he or she is (for example) disabled. Secondly, even in the case of children of the family who at the date of the hearing are under 18, the court is only obliged by this provision to give first consideration to their welfare whilst they remain minors. The court is not required by this provision to take account of the fact that children in practice do often stay in their homes until a later age whether because they are undergoing education or training or because they are disabled or unemployed or simply because they prefer to do so, particularly during the early stages of their career. Once again, however, it must be emphasised that this does not mean the court will ignore such interests, but simply that they do not have any priority.

(d) Must take effect subject to limitations imposed by Child Support Act 1991

As already noted, the Child Support Act 1991 does not make any **9–44** relevant amendment to the guidelines governing the exercise of the court's discretion in divorce and other proceedings; but in practice it is likely to have a significant impact on the exercise of the court's powers and duties. The Act will in many cases deprive the court of the power to make any order for periodical payments in respect of a child: see further para. 10–21 below.

2. All the Circumstances—The Specified Matters

MCA 1973, s.25(1), directs the court to consider "all the cir- **9–45** cumstances," and "in particular" to have regard to an elaborate list of specific matters. It follows that the court must not simply confine its attention to those specified matters; it must also (as Scarman L.J. put it in *Trippas* v. *Trippas* [1973] 1 WLR 134, 144) investigate all other circumstances "past, present, and, in so far as one can make a reliable estimate, future" which arise on the facts of any particular case. Examples can be taken from decided cases of such matters:

(i) Wife had remarried at date of financial hearing: *H* v. *H* [1975] Fam 9; and see *Livesey (formerly) Jenkins* v. *Livesey* [1985] FLR 813. In such a case, the court will need to consider how far the financial implications of her new status should affect the distribution of *capital* assets from the first marriage. (As already explained, there can be no periodical payments order in favour of a spouse who has remarried.)

(ii) Wife had made substantial contributions to the husband's business before the marriage: *Kokosinski* v. *Kokosinski* [1980] Fam 72 (*cf.* s.25(2)(f) MCA 1973, para. 9–61 below, applicable to such contributions during the marriage).

(iii) Husband had made his money after the breakdown with the assistance of another woman: *Lombardi* v. *Lombardi* [1973] 1 WLR 1276.

(iv) Husband had brought up the children of the marriage: *Lombardi* v. *Lombardi* (above).

(v) Husband's behaviour disabled the wife from resuming her professional career: *Jones (MA)* v. *Jones (W)* [1976] Fam 8.

(vi) Husband had put the family assets at risk by entering into unwise business transactions: *Martin* v. *Martin* [1976] Fam 335.

The specified matters

9–46   Most of the matters to which the court is now directed "in particular" to have regard in relation to a party to the marriage are substantially unchanged from those originally contained in the Matrimonial Proceedings and Property Act 1970. A vast body of case law has developed. The text seeks to highlight points of particular significance in relation to each of the statutory provisions.

"The income, earning capacity, property and other financial resources which each of the parties to the marriage has or is likely to have in the foreseeable future, including in the case of earning capacity any increase in that capacity which it would in the opinion of the court be reasonable to expect a party to the marriage to take steps to acquire" (MCA 1973, s.25(2)(a)).

This provision directs the court's attention to the parties' assets, in the broadest possible terms. Nothing is excluded:

> In *Schuller* v. *Schuller* [1990] 2 FLR 193, CA, a divorced wife went to work as a housekeeper. Her employer died before the court had settled the financial arrangements to be made on the divorce and left the wife his flat worth £130,000. The court refused to accept the argument that this acquisition was in no way related to the marriage and that it should be disregarded. On the contrary, its value was properly taken fully into account in an order dividing all the parties' property equally, even though this meant that the wife only received £8,500 from the value of the former matrimonial home and a substantial endowment policy. It had been right to achieve parity between the parties, and this was done by ensuring that each of them had housing.

It follows from this approach that the court may also take into account personal injury damages awarded to one of the spouses: *Daubney* v. *Daubney* [1976] Fam 267; *Wagstaff* v. *Wagstaff* [1992] 1 FLR 333. In principle, the court may take account of the likelihood that a party will benefit under the will of a relative who is terminally ill: *Morgan* v. *Morgan* [1977] Fam 122; but in practice inheritance expectations are rarely relevant because they are uncertain: see, for example, *Michael* v. *Michael* [1986] 2 FLR 389 where there was no evidence that the testatrix's death was imminent. But

> In *MT* v. *MT (Financial Provision: Lump Sum)* [1992] Fam Law 99 the husband had indefeasable rights under German law to inherit a share of his elderly father's estate; and he and his wife had conducted their married life on the basis that large funds would be available to them from that source. The court took the inheritance into account.

Common problems include the following:

(a) *Earning capacity*

The court is concerned with what each spouse could reasonably have. For example: 9–47

> In *Hardy* v. *Hardy* (1981) 2 FLR 321 the husband worked in his father's racing stables for much less than he could have earned on the open market. The court saw no reason why he should enjoy this privilege at the expense of his wife and children.

But the question is always one of evidence. It is not sufficient to make general assertions about earning capacity.

(b) *Earning potential*

The requirement of evidence is particularly significant in the light of   9–48
the addition made by the 1984 Act of a reference to "any increase in earning capacity which it would be reasonable to expect" a spouse to take steps to acquire.

This raises two separate issues: The first question is a question of fact: has the spouse in fact any earning potential? As Sir Roger Ormrod said in *Camm* v. *Camm* (1982) 4 FLR 577, 586:

> " ... experience in this court indicates that it is much easier to talk about married women who have not been working for a good number of years getting back into full time employment than it is to get the employment. It is to be remembered that 15 years or more of looking after children and not earning is a serious economic handicap ... "

The second question is one of judgment: what would it be "reasonable" to expect? A comparison of two cases illustrates these matters:

In *Leadbeater* v. *Leadbeater* [1985] FLR 789, CA, the wife, aged 47, had been a secretary, but at the time of the hearing earned only £1,680 per annum as a part-time receptionist. The judge thought she could, by working longer hours, reasonably earn somewhat more; but that it would not be "reasonable" to expect her at that age to familiarise herself with modern office technology.

In contrast:

In *M* v. *M (Financial Provision)* [1987] 2 FLR 1, CA, the wife of a chartered accountant (who himself earned some £60,000 a year) had worked as a secretary prior to her 20-year marriage and done some part-time work during the marriage. When the marriage broke down, she tried "valiantly and persistently" to find some employment, but without success. The judge held on the facts that she was unlikely at her age and with her job experience to achieve more than a "fairly humble job" in the secretarial field and accordingly that her earning potential should not be assessed at more than £6,000 per annum.

It is noteworthy that a recent OPCS Survey (Gregory and Foster, *The Consequences of Divorce* (1990)) found that two-thirds of all divorced wives in their sample had never worked full time during the marriage. Although social conditions are undoubtedly changing—it has been estimated that at the turn of the century women will make up 45 per cent. of the total civilian labour force: Social Trends 22 (1992) pp. 70–74—the reported cases suggest that the courts have resisted any temptation to assume that the statutory provisions should be used to drive "alimony drones" back to work. This does not however mean that pressure may not be used in negotiation. For example:

In *Newton* v. *Newton* [1990] 1 FLR 33, CA, the millionaire husband suggested that his 53-year-old wife, who suffered from agoraphobia amongst other disabilities, should "pull herself together and get a job." However this suggestion was "very properly" abandoned before the hearing.

(c) *New partner's earnings and earning capacity*

9–49   The court has no power to order that a third party—such as the husband's second wife or cohabitee—should provide for the applicant or the children of their family; and it must not make an order which can only be satisfied by dipping into a third party's resources: *Re L (Minors) (Financial Provision)* (1979) 1 FLR 39. But the fact that such a person has means available may be relevant, because thereby the husband can then more readily make appropriate provision: *Macey* v. *Macey* (1981) 3 FLR 7. As the Law Commission put it (Law Com. No. 112, para. 41) the husband is not allowed in such cases to say that he needs all or most of his income in order to provide for the needs of his new family; and in effect the means of the cohabitee are taken into account at what is often the decisive stage of calculating the net effect of the proposed order: see para. 9–88 below.

(d) *Availability of welfare benefits*
Two questions have troubled the courts: **9–50**

(i) *Should an order ever be made against a spouse who is on income support?*
Benefit rates are pitched at subsistence levels which give recipients nothing to spare beyond what is needed for basic support. Hence, although the court will always consider the merits: *Stockford* v. *Stockford* (1982) FLR 58 (and there may indeed be exceptional circumstances—for example a young man living with his parents: *Billington* v. *Billington* [1974] Fam 24, 29—in which an order for payment will be made) the probability is that it will be thought inappropriate to make any order: *Fletcher* v. *Fletcher* [1985] FLR 851. The court may of course make a nominal order (*e.g.* 5p a year) which can be varied if circumstances change: see para. 9–76 below. The court may also make orders dealing with capital assets—in practice usually the matrimonial home.

(ii) *Should the court order a spouse to make payments which will simply*   **9–51**
reduce the recipient's benefit payments?
Obviously the court would not allow a wealthy husband to say: "my former wife is receiving benefit which keeps her alive; why should you expect me to support her?" But the situation is far more difficult where both parties are near subsistence level. Should the court effectively reduce the already low standard of living enjoyed by the husband by compelling him to make payments to the wife when these will merely reduce her entitlement to income support?
The courts apply two coherent principles. First, a husband is not to be allowed to throw onto the state the cost of supporting his dependants. But, secondly, he is to be allowed to keep for himself and his new family at least a subsistence level of income. In practice, therefore, the courts will work out what the husband would get for himself and his new family if he were himself on income support and they will add onto that figure his outgoings for housing and his travelling and other working expenses (and possibly some additional "inducement" allowance) together with a sum to take account of any special circumstances—such as need to establish a new home: *Stockford* v. *Stockford* (above); *Freeman* v. *Swatridge* [1984] FLR 762; *Peacock* v. *Peacock* [1984] FLR 263. Only the balance over that sum will be regarded as available to support the family of the first marriage. The result is to produce rough equality, at more or less income support levels. But the courts have a wide discretion and have rejected suggestions that they should apply the "formula" at one time used by the DSS in calculating whether a liable relative's offer of support was reasonable: Ormrod L.J. in *Shallow* v. *Shallow* [1979] Fam

1, 6. Indeed in recent years the courts, while continuing to assert the salutary principle designed to protect public funds from "feckless or devious" spouses who might seek to escape their proper responsibilities, have been ready to give a really significant inducement to the "genuine struggler" (in the words of Waite J., *Ashley* v. *Blackman* [1988] 2 FLR 278). Thus:

In *Delaney* v. *Delaney* [1990] 2 FLR 457, CA, the husband, after the breakdown of his marriage, took out a £30,000 mortgage to fund the purchase of a house for himself and the woman whom he hoped to marry and with whom he hoped to have a family. The house was also available so that the children of the marriage would be able to come to stay. The court held that this was reasonable, on the basis that the children's welfare was the court's first consideration. That being so, the court was entitled to take into account the fact that the wife would be entitled to single parent benefit and family credit totalling about £50 weekly if there were no maintenance payment. In the circumstances, the Court of Appeal considered that a nominal order would be appropriate for the children. In the words of Ward J., whilst the "court deprecates any notion that a former husband and extant father may slough off the tight skin of familial responsibility and may slither into and lose himself in the greener grass on the other side, nonetheless this court has proclaimed and will proclaim that it looks to the realities of the real world in which we live, and that among the realities of life is that there is a life after divorce. The respondent husband is entitled to order his life in such a way as will hold in reasonable balance the responsibilities to his existing family which he carried into his new life, as well as his proper aspirations for that new future." In the circumstances a nominal order in favour of the children would be appropriate.

In *Ashley* v. *Blackman* [1988] 2 FLR 278, the court adopted a slightly more cautious, but basically similar approach. The periodical payments which the husband had been ordered to pay since the end of his marriage 16 years previously merely reduced the amount of state benefit to which his former wife would otherwise have been entitled, and did not confer any economic advantage on her. Although there would be many cases in which a phased or tapered termination process over a period of time would be an appropriate way of striking a balance between a spouse's obligation to his relatives and his obligation to the community, the present was a classic instance for immediate termination. The judge said: "no humane society could tolerate—even in the interest of saving its public purse—the prospect of a divorced couple of acutely limited means remaining manacled to each other indefinitely by the necessity to return at regular intervals to court for no other purpose than to thrash out at public expense the precise figure which the one should pay the other—not for any benefit to either of them, but solely for the relief of the tax-paying section of the community to which neither of them has sufficient means to belong." (It is however to be noted that on the coming into force of the Child Support Act 1991 there can be no relief from a maintenance obligation in respect of children: see para. 10–16 below.)

"The financial needs, obligations and responsibilities which each of the parties to the marriage has or is likely to have in the foreseeable future" (MCA 1973, s.23(2)(b)).

"Needs"

When assessing financial orders it is in practice usually the "reasonable needs" of the parties and the children of the family, and the "net effect" which the order will have on them, with which the court is primarily concerned: see *Stockford* v. *Stockford* (1981) 3 FLR 58, CA; *Furniss* v. *Furniss* (1982) 3 FLR 46, CA. At the most basic, this involves provision of an income at least sufficient for subsistence, and of a roof over the families' heads. In terms of the low income groups, we have already seen how the courts pay close attention to welfare benefit levels.

9–52

The best way of satisfying "needs" for housing and subsistence has, in practice, assumed a dominant position in dealing with the majority of marriage breakdowns; and in many cases seeking to satisfy the parties' needs is the only factor of any practical relevance. But the legislation does not in fact give "need" any priority, and *all* the circumstances (including in particular the contributions made by the parties) must be considered: *Smith* v. *Smith (Smith and others intervening)* [1991] 2 All ER 306, CA, para. 9–86 below. In any event, if the parties are more affluent, the question of what they "need" inevitably becomes subjective:

> In *Leadbeater* v. *Leadbeater* [1985] FLR 789, CA for example, the court decided that a wife who had during a fairly short (four year) marriage enjoyed a lavish life-style "needed" a two-bedroom house (rather than the three bedrooms she had claimed); and that this would cost £10,000 to furnish—rather than the £20,000 which she had claimed, or the £6,000 which the husband had, on the basis of prices taken from a "Habitat" catalogue, offered. She also needed a Ford Fiesta car (costing some £1,450 to run annually), £2,500 for housing outgoings, and £4,000 for household and private expenses.

What do the wealthy need? Need is a relative term; and the wife of a wealthy man has been held to be entitled to a high and even luxurious standard of living:

> In *Preston* v. *Preston* [1981] FLR 331, CA, the husband had capital assets of £2.3m, and an annual income of £40,000 (which was only subject to a low rate of income tax in Jersey). The court held that "needs" was equivalent to "reasonable requirements," and that in this sense the wife's needs included a house costing up to £300,000, and also to have the reasonable financial security conferred by the availability of a significant sum of free capital. An award of a £600,000 lump sum was upheld.

Again:

> In *Gojkovic* v. *Gojkovic* (the facts of which have already been given: see
> para. 9–37 above) the court held that there was no ceiling on a spouse's
> "reasonable needs." On the particular facts of that case a lump sum of
> £1.3 million was required to enable the wife to buy the hotel which
> would provide her livelihood (as well as adequately reflecting her
> contribution to the acquisition of the family assets: see para. 9–61
> below).

Housing

9–53   The courts have given a lot of attention to the best way of satisfying
the need of the parties for a secure home. There may of course be
cases in which it seems best to transfer the house outright to one
spouse: see for example *Hanlon* v. *Hanlon* [1978] 1 WLR 592 where the
husband had rent-free housing available to him by reason of his
employment as a police officer. Such a transfer can be particularly
advantageous when a wife is likely to be on income support: whereas
any periodical payments paid by the husband would simply reduce
her entitlement to benefit, a transfer of the house would not affect her
entitlement to benefit, while the DSS would pay the interest element
in any outstanding mortgage: see *S* v. *S (Note)* [1976] Fam 18, and
para. 8–13 above.

Mesher orders

9–54   For many years the commonest order made where the wife had
care of the children was the so-called *Mesher* order: (1973) [1980] 1 All
ER 126. In its simple form this would direct a transfer of the
matrimonial home into the joint names of husband and wife on trust
for sale for themselves in (say) equal shares; but it would be provided
that the property be not sold until the youngest child had attained the
age of 17 or ceased full-time education whichever should first occur.
(In practice it would usually be desirable to make provision for a
number of other eventualities—for example, the wife wishing to move
house before the trust for sale had become exercisable—but all
appropriate terms could be included in the court's order under its
power to direct a settlement of property: see generally Hayes and
Battersby (1985) 15 Fam Law 213.)

The decline of the Mesher order

9–55   Subsequently, the tide moved somewhat against *Mesher* orders—partly because in some cases it was not clear how the wife
would be housed when the time for sale came, partly because
(contrary to the "clean break" philosophy: para. 9–70 below) such an
order preserved a financial link between the parties and might
effectively tie her to the former matrimonial home because she lacked
the means to buy another more suitable home. The modern practice,
in cases where outright transfer is not thought appropriate, is to make
a so-called *Martin* order (see *Martin* v. *Martin* [1978] Fam 12) under
which the wife will have the right to occupy the house until her death

or remarriage (or, sometimes, her becoming dependent on another man or living with him as his wife: *Chadwick* v. *Chadwick* [1985] FLR 606; *Clutton* v. *Clutton* [1991] 1 FLR 242). Much the same objective may be achieved (as in *Knibb* v. *Knibb* [1987] 2 FLR 396) by ordering that the house be transferred to the wife on condition that she grant the husband a charge for the appropriate percentage of its value when the charge comes to be redeemed. In this way, it is made clear that the wife is to be regarded as the true owner of the property—with all the burdens and benefits incidental thereto—whilst the husband merely has a financial interest in the process of any sale.

Obligations and responsibilities

How far can a man claim that his income is not as high as it seems   **9–56**
because, for example, he has large travelling expenses, or that he has to service a large mortgage on the house in which he is living with his second wife? The general answer—as is so often the case—is that it depends on what is reasonable:

> In *Slater* v. *Slater* (1982) 3 FLR 364, CA, the court thought the husband had been extravagant in deciding to live in a country house with consequent heavy transport and property maintenance expenses; and he was not allowed to deduct those expenses in working out his available income. But if the husband has reasonably decided to buy a new house with a heavy mortgage, leaving his divorced wife and family in the former matrimonial home, the court will not make an order against him which would make it impossible for him to service the mortgage: *Stockford* v. *Stockford* (1981) 3 FLR 58.

> Again in *Delaney* v. *Delaney* (above para. 9–51) the Court of Appeal considered it reasonable for a man to contract a substantial mortgage in order to provide him with housing suitable for his children's occupation on access visits, as well as providing a home for his intended spouse and the children they planned to have.

Child care responsibilities

Child care responsibilities obviously have an impact on a spouse's   **9–57**
earning capacity. Again the question is largely one of what is reasonable in the light of the facts, and in *Waterman* v. *Waterman* [1989] 1 FLR 380 the Court of Appeal did not dissent from the proposition that a ten-year-old child should not require the same degree or intensity of care as would be necessary for a five-year-old. Perhaps the most striking illustration of the court's pragmatic approach to these issues is to be found in the case of *Fisher* v. *Fisher* [1989] 1 FLR 423, CA:

> A wife had a child by a third party some years after the divorce. The husband argued that by allowing the pregnancy to occur she had voluntarily made herself incapable of self-support, but the Court of

Appeal accepted that it was impossible to ignore the wife's responsibility to her child.

"The standard of living enjoyed by the family before the breakdown of the marriage" (MCA 1973, s.25(2)(c)).

9–58   A wife is not entitled, merely because she has been a wife, to expect to enjoy the standard of living she enjoyed during the marriage, but "adequate recognition" should be given to it in deciding what is reasonable as between the parties:

> In *Leadbeater* v. *Leadbeater* [1985] FLR 789 the wife had been married for four years to a man worth £250,000, and had in consequence enjoyed a "much enhanced" life-style. That factor was taken into account, but so was the modest life-style she had previously enjoyed. Taking all the factors into account (see para. 9–62 below for the facts) a comparatively modest £37,500 lump sum was ordered.

> In *Attar* v. *Attar* [1985] FLR 649 the wife (who had previously been an air hostess with an Arab airline earning some £15,000 per annum net) was married for only six months to a man worth more than £2m. The court ordered a lump sum payment of £30,000 to enable her to adjust over a period of two years (based on an assessment of what she had lived on before the marriage) to the ending of the marriage.

"The age of each party to the marriage and the duration of the marriage" (MCA 1973, s.25(2)(d)).

9–59   It will not often be necessary to consider the parties' ages as a matter distinct from the court's assessment of their needs and resources—if a wife is young and healthy her needs will not be so great because she will be able to work; if she is elderly and infirm her needs will be that much greater. In contrast there is now likely to be much more concern with the duration of the marriage since Parliament has decisively repudiated the notion that a wife is entitled solely by virtue of the status of marriage to be maintained on a scale appropriate to her husband's standard of life. This can be seen by comparing a case decided before the 1984 legislation with cases decided afterwards.

> In *Brett* v. *Brett* [1969] 1 WLR 487 the wife—a childless 23-year-old solicitor, whose marriage had lasted for less than six months—was awarded (in 1990 values) yearly periodical payments of some £20,000 and a lump sum of some £200,000.

In contrast:

> In *Attar* v. *Attar* (referred to above) the court thought a single capital payment of £30,000 was sufficient to enable the wife of an exceedingly wealthy man to retrain after a six-month marriage over a two-year period; and in *Leadbeater* v. *Leadbeater* [1985] FLR 789 the court first of all calculated the wife's reasonable needs along the lines already explained,

and held that they could be satisfied by a payment of £50,000. Since the
marriage had only lasted four years that was reduced by 25 per cent. to
£37,500, to be paid by way of once-for-all settlement of all her claims.

**"Any physical or mental disability of either of the parties to the
marriage"** (MCA 1973, s.25(2)(e)).

This provision seems to add little to the matters which will be   **9–60**
considered under other heads. It does not appear to have been
considered in decided cases.

**"The contributions made by each of the parties to the welfare of the
family, including any contribution made by looking after the home
or caring for the family"** (MCA 1973, s.25(2)(f)).

The law governing property regimes was felt by many not to give   **9–61**
adequate recognition to the contributions which wives made towards
the acquisition of so-called "family assets"—"those things which are
acquired ... with the intention that there should be continuing
provision for (the parties) and their children during their joint lives,
and used for the benefit of the family as a whole," as Lord Denning
put it in *Wachtel* v. *Wachtel* [1973] Fam 72. That case made it quite
clear that such contributions would under the post-1969 law be taken
fully into account, and that where a young couple with little or no
starting capital acquired a home with the help of mortgage finance it
would usually be regarded as their joint investment.

In practice, of course, in most cases any separate consideration of
the parties' contributions will merge into a consideration of their
"needs." For example, the house will often be transferred to the wife
because of the needs of the children and the person with their day-to-
day care, and it will not be necessary to consider separately how far
the wife has contributed to the family's welfare. But there may be
cases in which contributions do need to be regarded as a distinct
matter: see *Smith* v. *Smith (Smith Intervening)* [1991] 2 All ER 306, para.
9–86 below.

The court will equally have regard to a wife's contribution to a
business:

> In *Gojkovic* v. *Gojkovic* (above) the Court of Appeal rejected an argument
> that the wife's claim should be limited to the amount which would satisfy
> her needs. Equally important was the exceptional financial contribution
> which the wife had made to the wealth generated during the parties'
> relationship and marriage.

**"The conduct of each of the parties, if that conduct is such that it
would in the opinion of the court be inequitable to disregard it"**
(MCA 1973, s.25(2)(g)).

The extent to which the conduct of the parties should be relevant in   **9–62**
determining the financial outcome of divorce has been controversial.
The Matrimonial and Family Proceedings Act 1984 was apparently

intended to codify the practice of the courts developed on the basis of the decision in *Wachtel* v. *Wachtel* [1973] Fam 72: the policy of the divorce law was to minimise the bitterness, distress and humiliation of divorce; and accordingly in most cases it would be wrong to allow considerations of what was formerly regarded as guilt or blame to affect the financial orders on divorce. But there would be a "residue of cases, where the conduct of one of the parties had been such that it would be 'inequitable' to disregard it." For example:

> In *K* v. *K (Financial Provision: Conduct)* [1988] 1 FLR 469 the husband suffered from a depressive illness, which made his behaviour unpredictable and suicidal. The wife assisted the husband with suicide attempts not (so the District Judge found) from humanitarian principles but in order that she could set up home with her lover and get as much from the husband's estate as possible. In those circumstances (and also taking into account the wife's wholly deceitful conduct in relation to her association with her lover) it was held that it would be inequitable to disregard the wife's conduct; and that it should be taken into account as one of the relevant circumstances. In the result, the lump sum awarded to the wife was reduced from £14,000 to £5,000.

Again:

> In *Evans* v. *Evans* [1989] 1 FLR 351, CA, a wife obtained a divorce from her husband, after a short marriage, in 1951. Over the next 35 years the husband meticulously complied with court orders for maintenance. In 1985 the wife was convicted of inciting others to murder the husband under a contract-killing arrangement. She was sentenced to four years' imprisonment; and the husband ceased to make the payments. In this case—so the Court of Appeal held—it had been right to discharge the order; since otherwise the public "might think we had taken leave of our senses."

> In *Bailey* v. *Tolliday* (1982) 4 FLR 542 the wife had an adulterous relationship with her husband's father; and that fact was held relevant in assessing the financial provision which should be made for her.

But these cases are exceptional:

> In *Leadbeater* v. *Leadbeater* [1985] FLR 789 the wife (who had an alcohol problem) had committed adultery with several men whilst on holiday; the husband had insisted on a 15-year-old girl moving into the family home, refused to turn her out, and indeed subsequently had a child by her. The court held that it would "not be inequitable" to disregard the wife's conduct; it was a classic case in which (to use Lord Denning's words in *Wachtel*) "both parties are to blame."

These cases are said to give effect to the principle that conduct will only be relevant where there is some imbalance of conduct between the parties so that a right-thinking member of society would say that it would be inequitable to disregard it. But such tests are necessarily subjective as can be seen from the most recently reported case:

> In *K* v. *K (Conduct)* [1990] 2 FLR 225 the husband had a drink problem, which resulted in disagreeable behaviour and neglect of the family home. He was made redundant, and failed to find alternative work—in part (so the judge found) because he did not make sufficient efforts to do so. In contrast the wife continued to work and was highly successful. In those circumstances, it was held that the husband's conduct should be taken into account as a relevant factor; and that his share of the sale proceeds of the home should be reduced so as to leave him with sufficient capital to buy alternative accommodation but only at a rather lower price level than he wanted.

"Conduct" not limited to misconduct

The court will take account of any conduct which it would be **9–63** inequitable to disregard—for example dissipating the family property. As Cairns L.J. put it in *Martin* v. *Martin* [1976] Fam 335, 342, "a spouse cannot be allowed to fritter away the assets by extravagant living or reckless speculation and then to claim as great a share of what was left as he would have been entitled to if he had behaved reasonably."

May be positive factor

In appropriate cases the court will regard conduct as a circumstance **9–64** which should be taken into account as a positive factor in influencing the provision. For example:

> In *Kokosinski* v. *Kokosinski* [1980] Fam 72 the wife (said the judge) had "given the best years of her life to the husband. She had been faithful, loving and hard-working. She had helped the husband to build what was in every sense a family business. She had managed the husband's home and been a mother to and helped bring up a son of whom they were both justly proud." However, all this had occurred before the parties were able to marry; so that it could not be taken into account under s.25(2)(f) (para. 9–61 above); but it would be inequitable not to take those matters into account as "conduct." The wife was held to have earned for herself some part of the value of the family business.

"In the case of proceedings for divorce or nullity of marriage, the **9–65** **value to each of the parties to the marriage of any benefit (for example, a pension) which by reason of the dissolution or annulment of the marriage, that party will lose the chance of acquiring"** (MCA 1973, s.25(2)(h)).

One spouse has substantial rights to succeed to property on the other's intestacy; a widow also has rights to benefit under the National Insurance scheme; while the surviving spouse of a person who belonged to an employer's pension scheme almost invariably has rights—often substantial—under that scheme. If there is a divorce, all those expectations and contingent rights are lost; and the present provision is intended to direct the court's attention to the need to take such matters into account.

The problem of pensions

9–66   In practice it has been the loss of the right to a pension which has caused most difficulty, largely because the court will not usually be able to make orders directly affecting the pension entitlement. This is because the beneficiaries' rights are often merely discretionary; and any assignment or commutation of benefits will be prohibited—either by the terms of the scheme or, in the case of some public sector pensions, by statute: see, *e.g. Walker* v. *Walker* [1983] Fam 68; *Roberts* v. *Roberts* [1986] 2 FLR 152, but *cf. Happe* v. *Happe* [1990] 2 FLR 212. So how can the loss—which may be considerable—be made up?

Sometimes possible to take pension benefits into account

9–67   The "package" of benefits under a pension scheme often includes a lump sum payable on retirement; and the court will sometimes adjourn an application for ancillary relief until the employee receives that lump sum. However, adjournment will only be acceptable for a comparatively short period, such as two or three years: see *Morris* v. *Morris* (1977) 7 Fam Law 244, CA, and contrast *Roberts* v. *Roberts* (above) where the payment was not due until 2003.

Another option is to make an immediate order affecting other assets, in order to compensate for the loss:

> In *Richardson* v. *Richardson* (1978) 9 Fam Law 86 the husband would be entitled on retiring some three years after the divorce to a civil service pension and a lump sum of £9,000; if the wife had survived she would have been entitled to a widow's pension. There was other capital available; and the court ordered the husband to pay the wife an enhanced lump sum to take account of her loss of these expectations.

> In *Milne* v. *Milne* (1981) 2 FLR 286 the husband was ordered to pay a deferred lump sum equal to one-half the amount ultimately received on retirement or death.

Pensioner may undertake to make provision

9–68   The employee spouse may be prepared to undertake to do that which the court could not directly order—for example to pay premiums on a life policy taken out for the other spouse's benefit: see *Milne* v. *Milne* (above). The fact that where the petition is based on five years living apart (see para. 4–56 above) loss of a pension entitlement is capable of constituting grave financial hardship such as to entitle the court to refuse to grant a decree may be an incentive encouraging the spouse beneficiary to agree to such a course: *cf.*

Parker v. *Parker* [1972] Fam 116 (where the court was satisfied that the wife's loss of a police widow's pension could be offset by alternative insurance arrangements secured on the husband's house).

Position unsatisfactory

In spite of these methods of taking pension rights into account, it 9–69 has long been accepted that the situation is not altogether satisfactory. Proposals for reform have recently been made by the Law Society in *Maintenance After Divorce* (1990).

3. Provision Designed to Encourage Self-Sufficiency— The "Clean Break"

In *Minton* v. *Minton* [1979] AC 593, 608, Lord Scarman stated that the 9–70 "clean break" principle informed the modern legislation; and that:

> "the law now encourages spouses to avoid bitterness after family breakdown and to settle their money and property problems. An object of the modern law is to encourage each to put the past behind them and to begin a new life which is not overshadowed by the relationship which has broken down."

The principle of the clean break is now enshrined in the legislation, which contains four provisions designed to facilitate the attainment of this objective. And on one view—stated by Ward J. in *B* v. *B (Financial Provision)* [1990] 1 FLR 20, 26—the new principle has supplanted the status quo or minimal loss as the court's "primary objective":

> "now that the 1973 Act has been amended to delete the goal of putting the parties in the position they would have been in had the marriage not broken down, the [*sic*] objective of the new law is to strive to make the parties self-sufficient."

But it has been pointed out that the expression "clean break" is ambiguous, and that it would be wrong if reference to a so-called "principle" led the court to strive for a so-called clean break regardless of all other considerations: see *Clutton* v. *Clutton* [1991] 1 FLR 242, 245. The correct approach is to follow strictly the—somewhat complex and interlocking—statutory provisions. These are:

(a) *The duty to consider the termination of financial obligations*

If the court decides to exercise its financial powers in favour of a 9–71 party to the marriage, it must consider "whether it would be appropriate so to exercise those powers that the financial obligations of each party towards the other will be terminated as soon after the grant of the decree as the court considers just and reasonable."

This duty arises whenever the court decides to exercise its property adjustment or financial provision powers in favour of a party to the marriage. (It has no application to orders for children.) The question is whether it would be "appropriate" to exercise those powers to terminate the reciprocal financial obligations as soon as the court considers would be "just and reasonable." The duty imposed by this provision is entirely general; and there are three other provisions of the Act which are relevant to its discharge: see (b) to (d) below.

(b) *Court to consider potential increase in earning capacity*

9–72   Self-sufficiency will often be based on an ability to earn a living; and the matters to which the court's attention is particularly directed now include a reference to any increase in earning capacity which it would in the opinion of the court be reasonable to expect a party to the marriage to take steps to acquire: see para. 9–48 above. This factor may be particularly relevant to the duty imposed on the court to consider whether any periodical payments order should be made only for a specified term: see (c) below.

(c) *The duty to consider specifying a term for any periodical payments order*

9–73   The simplest form of "clean break" involves the court ordering capital transfers between the parties, and dismissing all claims for periodical payments. But there will be many cases in which such a once-for-all settlement is not possible and the court feels it appropriate to make an order for periodical payments. If it does decide to make such an order in favour of a party to the marriage, section 25A(2) of the Act then imposes on it a mandatory duty "in particular" to:

> "consider whether it would be appropriate to require those payments to be made or secured only for such term as would in the opinion of the court be sufficient to enable the party in whose favour the order is made to adjust without undue hardship to the termination of his or her financial dependence on the other party."

It follows that in each case in which the court decides to make a periodical payments order it must then consider whether the order should be for a specified term—such as six months or five years; and in making that decision the court is required to consider whether such a period would be sufficient for the applicant to adjust "without undue hardship" to the changed circumstances. Can and should the applicant find a way of adjusting his or her life so as to attain financial independence from the other spouse? Is it possible to predict the time by which such an adjustment will have occurred— for example, because child care responsibilities are likely to have ceased?

In *Waterman* v. *Waterman* [1989] 1 FLR 380, CA, the marriage of a 38-year-old secretary broke down after some three years' cohabitation (of which only 17 months were within marriage). The wife had the care of the five-year-old child; and had moved to live in her mother and sister's "very overcrowded home" in a remote Lincolnshire village. The judge made an order for periodical payments for the wife; and on the basis that she had an earning capacity, that it was in her interests "to get her life on its feet, to obtain an occupation and some source of income for herself," and that by the time the child was ten the mother ought reasonably be able to obtain employment, made an order that the periodical payments should terminate in five years' time. The Court of Appeal held that such an order was not "plainly wrong," and that it should accordingly be allowed to stand.

In contrast:

In *M* v. *M (Financial Provision)* [1987] 2 FLR 1 the court concluded that it would not be appropriate to terminate periodical payments in favour of the 47-year-old wife of a £60,000 a year accountant at the end of any fixed period nor would it be just and reasonable so to do. The court considered that it would be unrealistic to suppose that the wife could become self-sufficient; and that termination would cause undue hardship to a woman who, after 20 years of marriage, was entitled to a "reasonably decent" standard of living.

Power to direct that no application be made to extend specified term
The court will have jurisdiction to vary a specified term order by   **9–74**
extending any term specified in an order at any time during its existence unless the court has exercised the power conferred by section 28(1A) of the Act to direct that no such application be entertained. But it has been said (see *Whiting* v. *Whiting* [1988] 2 FLR 189, CA) that such a direction is "draconian" and is inappropriate in cases in which there is real uncertainty about the future—particularly when young children are also involved. However, unless such a direction is made the paying spouse is left at risk.

(d) *The power to dismiss a claim for periodical payments*
If complete finality is to be achieved, the court must exercise the   **9–75**
power now specifically conferred upon it by statute to dismiss all claims for periodical payments and to direct that the applicant be debarred from making any further application for a periodical payments order. The court will also direct that no application be permitted by a spouse for provision out of the other's estate under the provisions of the Inheritance (Provision for Family and Dependants) Act 1975: see para. 7–45 above.

Significance of nominal order. To understand the need for the   **9–76**
exercise of this power, it has to be remembered that any periodical payments order may be varied at any time during the currency of the order; and that, accordingly, if even a nominal order for

periodical payments of say 5p per annum is made the liable spouse will remain constantly at risk that an application to vary the order will be made. In effect, a nominal order gives one party a "last backstop," *i.e.* some protection against unforeseen changes of circumstances such as ill-health or unemployment, but only at the cost of leaving the other party at risk. On one view, therefore, to make a nominal order is to negate the notion of a clean break; but the courts have refused (see *Hepburn* v. *Hepburn* [1989] 1 FLR 373, 376, *per* Butler-Sloss L.J.; and *Whiting* v. *Whiting* [1988] 2 FLR 189) to hold that such orders are undesirable in principle:

> In *Suter* v. *Suter and Jones* [1987] 2 FLR 232, CA, the wife was cohabiting, but her future was not easy to foresee. A nominal order, unrestricted as to time, was made specifically so that the order could be varied if her financial position were to deteriorate.

The exercise of the discretion to impose a clean break

9–77   It will be apparent that the court has a very wide discretion in these matters. What options are, in practice open to it; and how is it likely that the discretion will be exercised?

(a) *The options available*

It may be helpful first to summarise the various types of order which may be made:

9–78   **(i) Immediate clean break.** The court may consider that it would be appropriate to terminate the parties' financial obligations immediately. In that case it may make a property adjustment order; but it will dismiss any claim for periodical payments, and it will direct that neither party be entitled to make any further application for such an order. It will also order that neither party be entitled to apply for provision under the Inheritance (Provision for Family and Dependants) Act 1975. This would be an example of the "clean break" in its purest form.

The fact that one party may still have entitlements which will only mature in the future—for example, to receive a share of the retirement lump sum payable under an occupational pension scheme, or to receive a share of the proceeds of sale of the family home—is not inconsistent with the clean break policy:

> In *Clutton* v. *Clutton* [1991] 1 FLR 242, CA, the judge considered that it would be appropriate to effect a clean break, and ordered a transfer to the wife of the only significant family asset—the family home. The Court of Appeal accepted that to deprive the husband of any share in the sole capital asset of the marriage would be manifestly unfair; and that an order under which the house was transferred to the wife subject to the husband's right to be paid one-third of its value on her death, remarriage or cohabiting—a so-called *Martin* order: see para. 9–55 above—should be

substituted. It was argued that this would be inconsistent with the "clean break" principle; but the Court considered that such an order—under which matters are settled once and for all, but fully carried into execution at a future date—"could only be said to offend against the principle of the clean break in the most extended sense of that term" (*per* Lloyd L.J. at p. 246).

(ii) Periodical payment order—nominal or specified term? If the court considers that it would not be appropriate to terminate the mutual financial obligations of the parties, it will wish to make a periodical payments order (although this may only be for a nominal amount, with the consequences mentioned at para. 9–76 above). The court must then consider whether it would be appropriate to order the periodical payments for only a specified term.   9–79

(iii) Deferred clean break. If the court decides that it would be appropriate to make a specified term order it must decide whether to direct that the applicant be debarred from applying for any extension of the term. Such an order may be called a "deferred clean break." In the absence of such a direction the applicant will be entitled to apply to have the term extended.   9–80

(b) *The exercise of the discretion*

Is it possible, on the facts of any particular case, to predict how the court will in fact exercise its discretions? It is now clearly established that the Court of Appeal will only interfere with a decision if it is based on some error of law or if it is plainly wrong; and the case of *Whiting* v. *Whiting* (above) is a striking illustration both of the difficulty facing an appellant and of the difficulty of predicting how a particular judge will respond to the facts of a particular case: 9–81

> The wife had retrained as a teacher; and was in full-time employment earning in excess of £10,000 per annum, with pension entitlements. The husband had been made redundant, and earned some £4,000 per annum as a freelance management consultant. The husband applied to discharge the nominal order which had been made against him; but the judge refused to do so on the ground that the wife should have the "last backstop" of a nominal order. The Court of Appeal, by a majority, held that the decision was not "plainly wrong;" but it is perhaps significant that all three Lords Justice indicated that they would, if trying the case at first instance, have reached a different conclusion.

Against this background, can reported cases do more than provide illustrations of how the statutory provisions have been applied to the facts of particular cases? It would seem that at least one general principle can be extracted from them, and this is that where there is substantial capital available (and particularly where the wife is young) periodical payments have become largely obsolescent. Thus:

In *Preston* v. *Preston* [1981] FLR 331, CA, the husband was ordered to pay the wife £600,000 in settlement of all his obligations.

In *Gojkovic* v. *Gojkovic* (above) the husband was ordered to pay the wife a lump sum of £1 million, and to transfer to her a maisonette worth £295,000.

In *Attar* v. *Attar* [1985] FLR 649 the husband, who had assets worth more than two million pounds, was ordered to pay the wife a comparatively modest lump sum (£30,000) after a marriage which only lasted some six months.

At the other extreme, where the parties are likely to have a continuing dependence on welfare benefits, confident prediction is more difficult. In some cases, where no order for continuing provision could confer any real economic benefit on a spouse, the courts have been prepared to sever the maintenance tie altogether. For example, in *Seaton* v. *Seaton* [1986] 2 FLR 398, CA:

The 42-year-old husband had suffered a heart attack and a stroke as a result of which he could barely speak; and he had only limited powers of concentration. After the breakdown of his 14-year marriage to a 36-year-old teacher (who earned some £8,000 per annum) he was cared for by his elderly parents, who contributed to his upkeep. He had no income apart from a state disability pension, and the prognosis was that he would in due course have to go into a state-provided home where provision would be made for his needs. The Court of Appeal upheld a decision that there should be an immediate clean break, largely on the basis that he had no significant needs, and that no periodical payments by the wife could have any material effect in enhancing his life.

But as has been seen, there are difficult problems in deciding whether, and on what terms, a spouse should be relieved from making periodical payments which will not benefit the recipient, but only reduce the amount of income support which is paid. A recent trend had seemed to be that the courts would allow a termination of any ongoing maintenance liability, at least after a period of time: see para. 9–51 above; and it also became common for the husband to agree to a transfer of his interest in the family home to the wife in return for the court releasing him from any ongoing maintenance liability—the fact that the mortgage would be serviced by income support payments being central to the scheme. But recent changes in Social Security law have made it more difficult for a parent to escape from what may be substantial financial obligations to reimburse any income support awarded (see para. 8–31 above).

It is in middle range cases that it is most difficult to predict the outcome; but it is clear that clean break solutions are often sought. For example:

In *Livesey (formerly Jenkins)* v. *Jenkins* [1985] FLR 813, HL, the parties, who had two children aged 15 and 13, were divorced after a 24-year marriage. They agreed to a consent order whereby the husband was ordered to make periodical payments of £7.50 weekly to each child, and to transfer his interest in the former matrimonial home to the wife (who was to be solely responsible for the mortgage and other outgoings). The wife's application for periodical payments was dismissed.

The Judicial Statistics state that 25,663 "clean break" lump sum and property orders were made in the period from April to December 1990; and it appears that 8,235 orders for a specified term in favour of a spouse were made in the same period: see Cm. 1573, 1991, p. 47, para. 18 and Table 5.5. These figures are, in a number of respects difficult to interpret; and a cautious approach to interpretation is indicated. However, it does seem clear that a significant proportion of the divorcing population would prefer to avoid an ongoing maintenance obligation (see *The Consequences of Divorce*, OPCS, 1990. Table 8.14) and that the courts have been prepared to give effect to this preference. But it is difficult to predict how far the introduction of the Child Support legislation will affect the parties' readiness to accept solutions whereby, in effect, the economically more powerful partner "trades in" an interest in the home in exchange for release from future periodical payment obligations. It remains to be seen whether the Child Support Scheme makes sufficient allowance for the value of the provision for children made by giving up an interest in an appreciating capital asset: see para. 10–28 below.

CONSENT ORDERS—THE LIMITS OF PRIVATE ORDERING

A conflict of policy

Textbook discussion often leaves the impression that the financial **9–82** consequences of divorce are usually resolved by the courts in adversarial litigation. But in fact a large number of orders—no less than 39,068 in the period April to December 1990—are made by consent; and it has for some years been the policy of the divorce law to encourage the parties to resolve matters for themselves rather than seeking (to adopt the Law Commission's words) "an unattainable catharsis in a judicial forum." (Law Com. No. 103, para. 37; and note the "no order" presumption in relation to issues of the upbringing of children, para. 13–30 below). But the law has also long taken the view that the community as a whole has an interest in the financial arrangements made by a couple on divorce: a spouse's rights are not to be settled by private agreement, and it is for this reason that statute provides that any provision in a maintenance agreement restricting the parties' right to apply to the court is void: MCA 1973, s.34(1).

A compromise between these two conflicting principles has been found in permitting the parties to seek an order by consent from the court, which will then be decisive—even if it provides for a "clean break" with no right to apply for any subsequent variation—because the order will derive its legal effect from the decision of the court rather than from the agreement of the parties which led up to it: *De Lasala* v. *De Lasala* [1980] AC 546.

(a) *Information to be provided*

9–83   Statute provides that the court may make a consent order on the basis of specified information laid down by Rules of Court: MCA 1973, s.33A. The information required deals with such matters as the duration of the marriage, the age of the parties, the parties' capital resources, the arrangements proposed for the parties' accommodation; similar information about the children; confirmation as to whether either party has remarried or has any present plans to marry or cohabit; and "any other especially significant matters": Family Proceedings Rules 1991, rule 2.61.

(b) *Court's duty to enquire*

9–84   The role of the court in considering an application for a consent order is not reduced to "putting a rubber stamp on the parties' agreement" (Booth Report para. 2.20, echoing Balcombe J., *Tommey* v. *Tommey* (1983) FLR 159). On the contrary, it has a statutory duty to consider "all the circumstances" including those specified in section 25 of the Matrimonial Causes Act 1973 and discussed at paras. 9–39 to 9–69 above; and the parties have a duty to provide all relevant information and to ensure that it is correct, complete, and up-to-date: *Livesey (formerly Jenkins)* v. *Livesey* [1985] FLR 813, HL. For example, it would seem to be necessary to disclose whether the applicant's expectation of life was less than normal (in which case it might not be appropriate for a large lump sum to be paid); or whether the applicant plans to realise a business—since this might put him or her in possession of more liquid funds than would at first appear. It is not sufficient simply to provide the information stipulated in the rule referred to in para. 9–83 above, for that is simply the minimum required to confer jurisdiction on the court.

(c) *Order may be set aside for non-disclosure*

9–85   If it subsequently transpires that the requisite full and frank disclosure has not been made, the court may set aside any order it has made:

> In *Livesey (formerly Jenkins)* v. *Livesey* [1985] FLR 813, HL, the wife agreed with the husband that she would accept a transfer of the husband's interest in the matrimonial home in settlement of all financial claims. On the day before application was made for a consent order embodying these terms she became engaged to be married; and three weeks after the

order was made she remarried. The House of Lords held that she had been under a duty to disclose her engagement since it could have affected the order made; and the consent order was set aside.

The House of Lords was however careful to emphasise that consent orders are not lightly to be overthrown; it is not "every failure of frank and full disclosure which would justify a court in setting aside" such an order. For example:

> In *Edgar* v. *Edgar* [1980] 1 WLR 1410 the wife of a multi-millionaire received proper professional advice and chose to ignore it; she accepted some £100,000 from her husband and agreed not to seek any further provision. Three years later she sought financial relief and at first instance was awarded some £760,000; but the Court of Appeal held that she was bound by the agreement.

(d) *Effect of unforeseen change of circumstances*

What is to happen if there is a change of circumstances after the   9–86 making of the order which was unforeseen by either party? For example:

> In *Barder* v. *Barder* [1987] 1 FLR 480, HL, the court by consent made a "clean break" order under which H was to transfer the matrimonial home to W within 28 days. Four weeks later, W killed her children and committed suicide. All her property would go under her will to her mother. H had not yet executed the documents necessary to transfer the house to W. The House of Lords held that the husband should be given leave to appeal out of time; and, on the appeal, that the order should be set aside.

When should such leave be given? The House of Lords held that where there had been an unforeseen change of circumstances leave should be given if four conditions were fulfilled:

(i) the basis or fundamental assumption underlying the order had been falsified by a change of circumstances;

(ii) such change had occurred within a relatively short time of the making of the original order—usually no more than one year (although it has subsequently been held that this period is not inflexible: *Hope-Smith* v. *Hope-Smith* [1989] 2 FLR 56, CA);

(iii) the application for leave was made reasonably promptly; and

(iv) that the granting of leave would not prejudice unfairly third parties who had acquired interests for value in the property affected.

The question of what would be the appropriate order to make if leave is given may present difficulties. For example:

In *Smith* v. *Smith (Smith and Others Intervening)* [1991] 2 All ER 306, CA, a wife committed suicide, and the court gave leave to appeal against an order which would have given her half the family assets on the basis that this would be sufficient to enable her to purchase a house and thereby meet her needs. The judge hearing the appeal simply set aside the order on the basis that the wife no longer had any needs (apart from a lump sum sufficient to pay certain debts). But the Court of Appeal held that this would be to give "need" excessive weight, and that a lump sum of £25,000—which would in fact pass to her daughter—would reflect the contributions she had made to a long marriage.

CONCLUSION—WORKING OF THE LAW IN PRACTICE

9–87   The legislation originally enacted in 1970 set the courts a specific, albeit elusive, target—that of the "deemed rehabilitation of the marriage"—although the directive to seek to place the parties in the same position they would have been in had the marriage not broken down was virtually negated by the power given to the court to attach as much or as little weight to it as the circumstances justified. This statutory objective has now gone "to an unlamented end" but the amendments made to the law in 1984 do not seek to substitute any comparable principle. Do the changes made in 1984 in practice achieve what the Law Commission described as a "reasonable balance" between the two "intrinsically desirable, but perhaps mutually inconsistent objectives" of certainty and predictability on the one hand and the preservation of the flexibility of approach necessary to enable the courts to achieve justice and fairness between the parties on the other?

Opinions differ on this matter; but in practical terms an examination of the case law suggests that the courts adopt a pragmatic approach along the following lines:

9–88   (i) *Children's needs.* The first step is to consider the needs of the children, and how they may best be promoted. Once the Child Support Act has come into force, the court will not be able to override the Child Support Agency's assessment of the amounts to be paid by way of income maintenance for the parties' children; and it may be that this will have an impact on the making of capital orders intended to secure housing for the children and caring parent: see para. 10–28 below.

(ii) Consideration of *all the circumstances.* The court then considers other relevant circumstances; but in practice the—very subjec- tive—concept of the needs or reasonable requirements of the parties seems often to be the main (albeit not the only) factor determining the outcome.

(iii) *Termination of obligations.* The court applies the statutory directive to consider whether it would be appropriate to terminate the parties' mutual financial obligations as soon as it considers just and reasonable.

In practice, this may lead the court to a provisional view of the appropriate orders; and it then assesses the *net effect* of that order on the parties. Some adjustment may be called for if that provisional order would reduce one party below subsistence level; and there may even be cases in which the once-favoured "one-third" guideline may be used as a bench-mark in respect of income maintenance (see *Wachtel* v. *Wachtel* [1973] Fam 72), or in which an equal division of assets acquired by the parties' joint efforts during the marriage seems to be treated as the conventional starting point: see, *e.g. Trippas* v. *Trippas* [1973] Fam 134. But it has repeatedly been said to be unwise and inconsistent with the legislation to fetter the court's discretion by accepting such presumptions, and that the court should instead follow the legislative guidelines: see *Smith* v. *Smith (Smith and Others Intervening)* [1991] 2 All ER 306, CA.

It is difficult to measure the effectiveness of the private law governing the financial consequences of divorce in practice. On the one hand, the skill of the courts and legal profession in utilising the flexibility of the legislative scheme to maximise welfare benefits (particularly in the context of the family home) is apparent from the reported cases; and it is certainly significant that the Law Society's Family Law Committee—representing those involved in the practical application of the law—has come to favour the retention of the existing broad discretion: see *Maintenance after Divorce* (1990).

On the other hand, empirical evidence suggests serious shortcomings: in particular, there are wide variations in the amount of periodical payments ordered, there are often problems in connection with collecting periodical payments which may be awarded, an increasing number of lone parents have become dependent on income support, and few of these parents receive maintenance (see *Children Come First, The Background,* Cm. 1263, Vol. II; *The Consequences of Divorce* (OPCS, 1990)). Moreover, research at Bristol and elsewhere has indicated a considerable lack of efficiency in the processing of claims, with resultant confusion and alienation.

B. BREAKDOWN OF NON-MARITAL RELATIONSHIPS

It has already been pointed out (see para. 9–01 above) that English   **9–89** law has neither a statutory nor an inherent jurisdiction to order the provision of ongoing income maintenance by one party to a non-marital relationship in favour of the other; but this does not mean that the law provides no remedies relevant to the breakdown of such a relationship.

First, the court now has extensive powers to make *orders for the benefit of children*; and some of these may indirectly ensure for the benefit of the parent with day-to-day care of the children: see para. 10–04 below. These powers extend to the making of capital provision, and it may be that this will be of particular relevance after the coming into force of the Child Support Act 1991 (which will largely remove the jurisdiction of the court to make income orders against parents for support of their child): see para. 10–21 below above.

Secondly, the very fact that English law has no special property regime for married couples means that a cohabitant is at no disadvantage as against a married person in pursuing a claim for a beneficial interest in family property: see para. 7–23 above. Of course, the absence of any provision comparable to those available on the termination of a marriage by divorce enabling the court to re-allocate property is a serious disadvantage (see *Mossop* v. *Mossop* [1988] 2 FLR 173) and it has become apparent that a cohabitant may experience serious procedural difficulties in prosecuting claims to beneficial entitlement: see *H* v. *M (Property: Beneficial Interest)* [1992] 1 FLR 229. But there is, by way of compensation, a number of *statutory provisions* which may be of assistance:

9–90   (a) If there has been an *engagement to marry* the provisions of the Law Reform (Miscellaneous Provisions) Act 1970 will be relevant, as explained at para. 7–32 above.

(b) If the relationship has been terminated by the *death* of one of the partners, the survivor will have no rights of intestate succession, but may be able to claim reasonable financial provision out of the deceased's estate under the provisions of the Inheritance (Provision for Family and Dependants) Act 1975, as explained at para. 7–43 above.

(c) The Court may make orders giving a cohabitant the right to continue in occupation of the family home—albeit in principle only for a short period—under the Domestic Violence and Matrimonial Proceedings Act 1976.

(d) The court may exercise its powers to make financial orders under the Children Act 1989 (see para. 10–04 below) in such a way as indirectly to benefit a cohabitant who has the care of children. Specifically, there is power to make orders dealing with the family home which, in appropriate circumstances, may be used to preserve a home for the children and the parent who is caring for them, at least during the children's minority: see *K* v. *K* (1992), *The Times*, February 21, CA. However, these powers are discretionary (see *e.g. H* v. *M (Property: Beneficial Interest)* [1992] 1 FLR 229 where the judge considered that it would be inappropriate to make a capital order for the couple's child) and in exercising that discretion the court must follow the statutory guidelines: see further para. 10–11 below.

Thirdly, much of the *public law* governing the allocation of *housing* confers rights on parents and others which are not dependent on their marital status: see Partington and Hill *Housing Law: Cases, Materials and Commentary* (1991), Chapter 9.

Fourthly, *other statutory provisions* may assist a cohabitant in obtaining financial compensation for the partner's death from third parties—in particular, the Fatal Accidents Act 1976 now allows a person who was living with an accident victim to sue the person who caused the death for the financial loss suffered provided that certain conditions are satisfied—notably that the plaintiff and deceased had been living together as husband and wife throughout the period of at least two years before the death.

However, it can fairly be pointed out that English law not only falls far short of providing a coherent general framework for dealing with the financial consequences of a non-marital breakdown; but that the issues have not so far received any comprehensive official examination in England and Wales. In this respect, it might be thought that the Law Commission might follow the example of the Scottish Law Commission which (in Discussion Paper No. 86, 1990) has analysed the law and invited comments on a number of options for reform.

SUGGESTIONS FOR FURTHER READING

Hoggett and Pearl, Chap. 7.
Law Commission Report No. 103, *The Financial Consequences of Divorce, The Basic Policy* (1980).
J. Gregory and K. Foster, *The Consequences of Divorce, The Report of the 1984 OPCS Consequences of Divorce Survey* (OPCS, 1990).
E. Clive, "The Financial Consequences of Divorce: Reform from the Scottish Perspective" in Freeman, *State, Law and the Family* (1984).
L. Weitzmann, *The Divorce Revolution* (1985).
J. Eekelaar, *Regulating Divorce* (1991), Chap. 4.
At a Glance (The Family Law Bar Association, 1992) provides much useful financial information in tabular form.

On Cohabitation
Hoggett and Pearl, Chapter 8.
Scottish Law Commission, Discussion Paper No. 86, *The Effects of Cohabitation on Private Law* (1990).
J. Haskey and K. Kiernan, "Cohabitation, some Demographic Statistics" [1990] Fam Law 442.

Chapter 10

CHILD SUPPORT AND THE CHILD SUPPORT ACT

INTRODUCTION

10-01 The legal provisions dealing with support of children are fragmented. So far as the private law is concerned, the court can in divorce or other matrimonial proceedings make financial and property adjustment orders in favour of children of the family; and the court is directed to give first consideration to the welfare of children of the family in exercising its extensive powers to make financial orders: see para. 9–40 above. There are also powers to make financial orders for children in proceedings under MCA 1973, s.27 (neglect to provide reasonable maintenance) and in matrimonial proceedings under the Domestic Proceedings and Magistrates' Courts Act 1978. At one time, there were a number of other procedures under which the court could make financial orders for children—particularly illegitimate children; but the Children Act 1989 has reformed and assimilated those provisions into a comprehensive code. So far as the *public law* is concerned, we have seen the parents are under an obligation to maintain their children; and that the DSS may seek to recover Income Support paid in respect of children under the liable relative procedure: see para. 8–28 above.

The Child Support Act 1991 has been enacted in an attempt to rationalise the law governing the provision for child support; but its ambitious provisions have not yet been brought into force: see para. 10–12 below.

It is therefore necessary to summarise:

   (i) the main provisions governing the exercise of the court's powers to make financial orders for children in matrimonial proceedings;
  (ii) the relevant provisions of the Children Act 1989; and
 (iii) the likely impact of the Child Support Act on the current law and practice.

I. POWERS OF THE COURT TO MAKE ORDERS FOR A CHILD IN MATRIMONIAL PROCEEDINGS

10-02 As already noted, the court has power to make financial provision and property adjustment orders in respect of a child of the family. (For the definition of "child of the family", see para. 14–03 below.)

Financial Provision Orders

The court may make periodical payments orders, secured periodical   **10–03**
payment orders, and lump sum orders. In each case, the court may
order that the payment be made to the child or to such person as may
be specified in the order for the benefit of the child. The powers are
made substantially independent of the outcome of the proceedings
between the parents since it is provided that they may be exercised
before a decree is granted and that they may be exercised from time
to time. If the proceedings are dismissed, an order may be made
within a reasonable period after dismissal, and further orders may be
made from time to time.

Property Adjustment Orders

The court has power to make transfer of property orders in favour   **10–04**
of a child of the family or some other person for the benefit of the
child; it may order a settlement of property for the benefit of children
of the family, and it may vary any ante- or post-nuptial settlement for
the benefit of such a child.

Matters to which the Court is to have regard

It is now provided that as regards the exercise of its powers to   **10–05**
make periodical payment orders, lump sum or transfer of property
orders or orders for the sale of property in relation to a child of the
family, the court shall in particular have regard to the following
matters:

(a) the financial needs of the child;
(b) the income, earning capacity (if any), property and other
     financial resources of the child;
(c) any physical or mental disability of the child;
(d) the manner in which he was being and in which the parties to
     the marriage expected him to be educated or trained;
(e) the financial resources and financial needs of the spouses; and
     the standard of living enjoyed by the family before the
     breakdown, and any disability of either party to the marriage.

Orders against a Spouse who is not the Child's Parent

A spouse may be liable to have financial orders made against him   **10–06**
in respect of a child of the family (such as a step-child) who is not
biologically the spouse's own child. Special criteria apply in such
cases. It is provided that as regards the exercise of its financial powers
against a party to a marriage in favour of a child of the family who is
not the child of that party, the court shall also have regard:

"(a) to whether that party assumed any responsibility for the
child's maintenance, and, if so, to the extent to which, and the
basis upon which, that party assumed such responsibility and to

181

the length of time for which that party discharged such responsibility;

(b) to whether in assuming and discharging such responsibility that party did so knowing that the child was not his or her own;

(c) to the liability of any other person to maintain the child."

Duration of Orders and Age Limits

10–07   The general principle underlying the complex statutory provisions is that periodical financial maintenance should stop once the child is 18; but provision may be ordered beyond that age where the child is, or would be still receiving education or training or there are "special circumstances"—perhaps disablement—which justify the making of a different order. A child who has attained the age of 18 may intervene in matrimonial proceedings (notwithstanding the fact that the decree may have been pronounced many years ago) and claim financial provision, for example to finance further education or training: *Downing* v. *Downing (Downing Intervening)* [1976] Fam 288.

The court has power to order payment of a lump sum or property adjustment for a child irrespective of the child's age; but, it has been held that in the exercise of its discretion, the court will not normally make life-long provision for a child who is under no disability and whose education is secured: see *Lilford (Lord)* v. *Glyn* [1979] 1 WLR 78.

II. FINANCIAL ORDERS FOR CHILDREN UNDER THE CHILDREN ACT 1989

10–08   Matrimonial proceedings can only be brought if the adults concerned have been married, and want a divorce or other legal remedy. The Children Act 1989 establishes a comprehensive code empowering the court to make financial support orders against a child's parents. The text first discusses who is entitled to initiate proceedings in which financial orders may be made, and it then outlines the orders which may be made; and finally the text discusses the principles to be applied by the court in exercising its discretion.

A. *Who can Apply?*

10–09   The following person may apply for a financial order in respect of a child:

(a) **A Parent.** This expression extends to adoptive parents and to both parents of an illegitimate child. The ordinary meaning of the word "parent" is extended so as to "include any party to a marriage (whether or not subsisting) in relation to whom the child . . . is a child of the family." Hence, it will be possible for a child's biological parent to initiate proceedings claiming support for the child against the child's step-parent, or for the step-parent to seek an order against the biological parent.

(b) **A Guardian.**

(c) **Any Person in whose Favour a Residence Order is in force with respect to a child.** A residence order settles the arrangements to be made about where a child is to live; and accordingly everyone who has been given the right to care for a child by court order can now seek a financial order for the child's support.

(d) **An Adult Student or Trainee or Person Who Can Show Special Circumstances** may make an application for an order. However, in this case, there are two restrictions on the court's powers. First, no order may be made if the parents are living together in the same household (so that it is still impossible for a child to compel parents who are living in a conventional relationship to provide support). Secondly, the court's powers on such an application are limited to making periodical payment or lump sum orders.

In addition, there are certain circumstances in which the court may make financial orders even though no application for such an order has been made: it is provided that the court may make a financial order whenever it makes, varies, or discharges a residence order —and a residence order may be made in any family proceedings (whether or not applied for) if the court considers that the order should be made. The court can also make financial orders if the child is a ward of court, whether or not any application has been made for such an order.

B. *The Orders which may be made*

The range of orders available to the court is now wide—the court **10–10** may order a "parent" to make *periodical payments* (secured or unsecured), to pay a *lump sum*, or to *transfer property*.

In an appropriate case these powers may be exercised to deal with the family home. A local authority tenancy might (for example) be transferred to the wife for the children's benefit; or a home belonging to the parents or either of them might be settled on trusts permitting the children to reside there with one of the parents during the children's minority: see *K* v. *K* (1992) *The Times*, February 21, CA.

The general principle adopted by the Children Act is that financial orders are to be made against "parents." However, as explained above, the definition of "parent" is to include step-parents and others: see para. 14–03.

C. *Exercise of the Discretion*

10–11   The Children Act 1989 lays down guidelines for the exercise of the court's powers which are similar (but not identical) to those governing the comparable divorce power. The court (see Children Act 1989, Sched. 1, para. 4(1)) is to "have regard to all the circumstances" including matters such as the income, earning capacity, property and other financial resources which the applicant, the parents and the person in whose favour the order would be made has or is likely to have; those persons' financial needs, obligations and responsibilities; the financial needs income, earning capacity (if any), property and other financial resources of the child; and any physical or mental disability. The court's attention is also directed to "the manner in which the child was being, or was expected to be, educated or trained."

The court is thus given guidelines to structure the exercise of the wide statutory discretion (see *H* v. *M (Property: Beneficial Interest)* [1992] 1 FLR 229 for a case in which it was considered inappropriate to make a capital order in respect of a child). The court must give appropriate weight to all the relevant factors; and it is to be particularly noted that the child's needs are not the only factor to be taken into account:

> In *K* v. *K* (1992) *The Times*, February 21, CA, the judge had ordered that the father's rights as joint tenant of a local authority house be transferred to the mother for the benefit of his children. It was held that, although there was jurisdiction to make such an order, the judge had failed to carry out the balancing exercise required by the statute. In particular, he had failed to consider the father's needs, including the possibility that the father would lose his statutory right to buy the house on advantageous terms. A re-trial was ordered.

The legislation contains provision similar to that in the divorce legislation dealing with the factors to be taken into account where the "parent" against whom the order is sought is (because of the "child of the family" definition (above) a step-parent or someone other than the child's mother or father.

III. THE CHILD SUPPORT ACT

10–12   It has long been recognised that the system of private law maintenance outlined above is, in many respects, ineffective. The problems were subjected to a comprehensive review by the Finer Committee on One-parent Families; and the Committee's report, published in 1974, made far-reaching proposals under which many issues relating to the quantification and enforcement of financial support obligations would be dealt with by an administrative agency rather than by the courts. The Finer Committee also proposed the introduction of a Guaranteed Maintenance allowance intended to provide an income for single parent families significantly higher than supplementary benefit levels. But the Finer Committee's proposals did not find favour with successive Governments. In the late 1990's, the increasing dependence of many lone-parent families on income support, and the gradual reduction in levels of support provided by absent parents for their own children became a matter of concern to the Government; and the Government itself undertook a review of the problem. The White Paper, *Children Come First* (Cm. 1263, 1990) concluded that the present system of maintenance to support children was "unnecessarily fragmented, uncertain in its results, slow and ineffective." The White Paper pointed out that the system was based largely on discretion, and that it was operated through a number of different agencies—notably the courts and the offices of the Department of Social Security. The Government concluded that the "cumulative effect is uncertainty and inconsistent decisions about how much maintenance should be paid"; and that the system was ineffective in providing support for parents who wished to go out to work and become self-sufficient.

The Government considered that legislation was needed to ensure that parents honour their responsibilities to their children whenever they could do so; that a fair and reasonable balance was struck between the liable parent's responsibilities for all the children he or she is liable to maintain; that the system should produce fair and consistent results; that maintenance payments be reviewed regularly to reflect changes in circumstances; that parents' incentives to work be maintained; that the public receive an efficient and effective service; and that dependence on Income Support be reduced.

Legislative effect was given to the proposals by the Child Support Act 1991. The provisions of this Act are revolutionary in scope and in their potential impact; but it is impossible to give a comprehensive account of the new law since many matters—including vital issues such as the extent to which a parent's own housing costs are to be allowed to reduce the extent of the obligation to support children—have been left to be dealt with by delegated legislation, as yet unpublished. Government spokesmen admitted that the Act "contains a rather larger than usual number of regulations making powers" but asserted that the principles and intentions of the scheme are quite clear on the face of the Bill: Hansard HL, Vol. 526, Col. 778. The reader may find some difficulty in accepting this view.

It is envisaged that the Child Support Agency will become operational early in 1993, but its jurisdiction and the use of the maintenance assessment formula will be phased in over a period of years. The courts will retain their existing jurisdiction under the existing law over groups of cases until the Agency is ready to take them on. It seems that the Act's provisions will first be applied in cases in which income support is being paid in respect of a child. Accordingly, only the main principles of the legislation are outlined in the text which follows.

A.   THE CHILD SUPPORT AGENCY

10–13   A Child Support Agency is to be established which will trace absent parents, investigate their means, and assess, collect, and enforce child maintenance payments. The Agency will have extensive powers to collect information, to make legally binding assessments (based on formulae set out in the Act and in Regulations made under it), to determine methods of payment, and to monitor and where necessary collect maintenance.

B.   THE FORMULA

10–14   It is of the essence of the scheme that there will be little or no place for discretion in the assessment of financial obligations in respect of child support. The Act therefore first of all sets out the basic principle governing liability to maintain a child. It then sets out a formula in accordance with which maintenance assessments are to be made by officials called Child Support Officers.

The basic principle of liability

10–15   The underlying principle of the legislation is that each parent of a "qualifying child" is responsible for maintaining the child: s.1(1) A child is, basically, a qualifying child for this purpose if either of his parents is an "absent parent"—that is to say that the parent concerned is not living in the same household as the child—and the child has his home with a person who is "a person with care" (an expression which will normally mean a person with whom the child has his home, or who usually provides day to day care for the child but the words may be given a different sense in accordance with regulations: s.3(3)).

It is important to note that the Act only deals with the liability of persons to provide for their own children; and that a person is not liable, under the Child Support Act, to provide for a step-child. Hence, responsibilities in relation to step-children will still have to be assessed by the court under the provisions discussed at para. 10–02 above.

Meeting the duty to maintain

The Act provides that for the purposes of the Act, an absent parent **10–16** should be taken to have met his responsibility to maintain any qualifying child of his own by making periodical payments of maintenance with respect to the child in accordance with the formula.

The formula: general principle

The underlying principle of the Act is that parents should be **10–17** obliged to contribute from their assessable income to the children's maintenance requirements.

The calculation is to be done in the following way:

First, the absent parent's *assessable income* is to be found: Sched. 1, para. 5(1). The assessable income is basically the absent parent's net income less his so-called exempt income. It is understood—although the details have still to be revealed in Statutory Regulations—that the net income will be effectively the parent's after-tax income (i.e. the "take-home pay"), and that the exempt income will be the level of income support for which he or she would qualify, together with the cost of housing.

It will be immediately appreciated that the calculation of these figures will depend crucially on regulations as yet to be published. For example, will travelling and other work related expenses such as the cost of substitute child care be allowed in calculating net income? What level of "housing costs" will be included in exempt income? For what maintenance obligations to others—children of a subsequent relationship, step-children and so on—will allowance be made?

The assessable income of one parent who has care of a child is then calculated in much the same way, and added to the absent parent's assessable income. The resulting figure is multiplied by a factor (described as "P" in the Regulations) which is "such a number greater then 0 but less than 1 as may be prescribed": Sched. 1, para. 2 (1). In fact it seems likely that this factor will be half, thus adopting the principle that both parents are equally liable for their children. The result of this calculation is to produce the "sum available".

The next step in the calculation is to work out the *children's maintenance requirement.* This is a basic sum likely to be Income Support scale rates for the child and the parent with care.

It is then possible to make the *maintenance assessment.* If the amount of the "sum available" calculation made under Sched. 1, para. 2(1) is less than the maintenance requirement, then the amount of the maintenance assessment will be the absent parent's assessable income multiplied by P.

The Goverment's White Paper gives us an example of how this **10–18** calculation would be applied:

Marie and David have separated. Marie has two children, Sarah (5) and Mark (3) living with her. David has take-home pay of £160 weekly, and pays £31 in mortgage interest:

Assessable income:

Take Home Pay		£160
less IS scale rate of subsistence for adult	39.65	
Housing	31.00	70.65
	———	———
		£89.35 say
		£90.00

If "P" is one-half, the "sum available" is £**45**

Maintenance Requirement:

Child allowance (IS scales)	£26.70
Family Premium	7.95
Lone Parent Premium	4.45
Parental Carer	39.65
	———
	78.75
Less child benefit	16.75
	———
	62.00

In this case, therefore, David pays £45 because the "sum available" is less than the maintenance requirement.(It should be noted that this example is taken from the White Paper without amendment. No account has therefore been taken of subsequent changes in Income Support and other benefits.)

Cases where income available is greater than the maintenance requirement

10–19   The Act is not limited to enforcement of a subsistence level of support. Where the income available is greater than the maintenance requirement an *additional element* is to be payable. This will probably be based on 15 per cent. of parental assessable income, after the basic element above in the maintenance assessment has been calculated; but there will be a maximum liability.

10–20   The White Paper (*Children Come First*, Cm. 1263, p. 19) gives examples of how this additional element might be calculated:

Anna and Paul are divorced and have 2 children, Peter aged 14 and Elaine aged 12. The maintenance requirement for Peter and Elaine is £65.

Anna is living with Peter and Elaine in a house on which she pays £50 per week in mortgage repayments.

Anna's **exempt income** is:

	£ per week
Child allowances	36.50
Family premium	7.35
Lone parent premium	4.10
Personal allowance	36.70
Mortgage	50.00
Total exempt income	**£134.65 per week**
	(rounded £135)

Anna's total net income is £125 per week but as this is below the level of her exempt income, it is not taken into account in the following calculation.

Paul has a net income of £350 per week; and he is living in a house for which he pays £65 per week in mortgage repayments.

Paul's exempt income is:

	£ per week
Personal allowance	36.70
Mortgage	65.00
Total exempt income	**£101.70 per week**
	(rounded £102)

His assessable income is:

	£ per week
Net income	350
Less exempt income	102
Total assessable income	**£248 per week**

The maintenance bill of £65 is met when Paul has paid 50 per cent. of the first £130 of his assessable income.

In addition he pays 15 per cent. of the remaining £118 of his assessable income. This is £17.70 (rounded £18). So Paul pays a total of £65+£18=£83 in maintenance. This is 23.7 per cent. of his total net income.

C. THE ROLE OF THE COURT

10-21   The basic scheme of the Act is that the discretionary jurisdiction of the court should not be exercised in any case in which an assessment under the Child Support legislation could be made. The Act therefore provides (s.8 (3)) that:

> "... no court shall exercise any power which it would otherwise have to make, vary or revive any maintenance order in relation to the child and absent parent concerned"

—in any case in which a Child Support Officer would have jurisdiction to make a maintenance assessment with respect to a qualifying child, even though the circumstances are such that the Child Support Officer would not make an assessment if applied for: s.8 (1), (3).

10-22   In what circumstances therefore may the court exercise the jurisdiction which in theory it will still retain to make orders? It would seem that the court's jurisdiction might be exercised in the following cases:

    i.   Where the maximum assessment which can be made under the Child Support legislation has been made: s.8 (6).

    ii.   The court will also have jurisdiction to make orders in respect of 17- to 19-year-olds who are not in full-time education (s.55 (1)): and it will also have the power to make orders in respect of young persons aged 19 or over.

    iii.   The court will be able to exercise its powers to make orders for step-children and other children of the family who are not covered by the Child Support Agency scheme.

    iv.   The court will still have jurisdiction to make lump sum and property adjustment orders.

    v.   The court will also be able to exercise its jurisdiction in respect of certain disabled children: see Child Support Act 1991, s.8 (8).

D. PRINCIPLES TO BE APPLIED BY THE CHILD SUPPORT AGENCY

10-23   It is provided that where the Secretary of State or any Child Support Officer is considering the exercise of any "discretionary power" conferred by the Act, he shall have regard for the welfare of any child likely to be affected by his decision: s.2. However, the scope for the exercise of any discretion in the actual assessment of liability is, as has been seen, extremely limited. It seems much more likely that the power will be used where the Child Support Agency is considering exercising its powers to compel the disclosure of information.

E. RELATIONSHIP WITH INCOME SUPPORT AND OTHER BENEFITS

The Act contains provisions imposing a duty on a person with care **10–24** of the child who is in receipt of Income Support, Family Credit (or other prescribed benefits) to authorise the taking of action under the Child Support Act to recover Child Support from the absent parent. The Secretary of State has extensive powers to require information to be provided—by the parent with care and others—in order to enable the absent parent to be traced and the relevant financial calculations to be made. If a person in receipt of benefit refuses or neglects to provide that information then the Social Security benefit to which he or she is entitled may be reduced. (This provision reflects existing practice where a person has become unemployed voluntarily, or has lost employment because of misconduct).

The Secretary of State is not to require a parent to authorise such action if he considers that there are reasonable grounds for believing that if the parent were to be required to give that authorisation, or if she were to give it, there would be a risk of her, or of any child living with her, suffering harm or undue distress as a result.

F. REVIEWS APPEALS ETC.

There are provisions for periodical reviews of all child maintenance **10–25** assessments, and there is to be a system of appeals (similar to that applicable in relation to Social Security Appeals) to a tribunal, and thereafter on a point of law to a Child Support Commissioner and to the Court of Appeal.

G. DETERMINATION OF PARENTAGE

It has been pointed out that liability under the Act depends upon **10–26** legal parentage, and it is provided that where a person who is alleged to be a parent of the child denies that he or she is one of the child's parents, then the Child Support Officer concerned shall not make a maintenance assessment on the assumption that that person is one of the child's parents, unless there has been a court order which resolves the question of parentage. The Act provides for the court to make a declaration of parentage for the purposes of the Act: s.27.

H.   COLLECTION AND ENFORCEMENT

10–27   There are far-reaching provisions dealing with the collection and enforcement of maintenance assessments.

CONCLUSION

10–28   In introducing the Child Support Bill into the House of Lords, the Lord Chancellor claimed that the legislation was informed by two central principles or objectives, namely, the giving of priority to the welfare of the child, and the primary reponsibility of parents for securing that welfare even when the parents' own relationship had broken down. The Act was (he said) firmly based upon the principle that parents have a "clear moral duty" to maintain their children until the children are old enough to look after themselves. Events may change the relationship of the parents to each other, but "they cannot change the reponsibility which parents owe to their children": see Hansard HL, Vol. 256, Col. 775.

There can be no dispute that the system of child support which exists prior to the coming into force of the Child Support Act, is seriously defective in many respects, and it is therefore much to be hoped that the new system will indeed prove to be effective. However, there are a number of grounds for concern.

First of all, the Act seems inconsistent with the principle embodied in the Children Act that all issues relating to a child and its family should be capable of being resolved in the same forum and according to the same criteria. The Children Act created a single code for court orders about the welfare of children, which entrusts a wide discretionary jurisdiction to the courts, and allows for cases to be directed to whichever court in the judicial system is best equipped to deal with the issues likely to arise. Moreover, the Matrimonial Causes Act 1973 had established a simple principle in connection with assessment of the financial responsibilities of couples in relation to the children of their family: in exercising the court's extensive powers to make orders following the breakdown of marriage, the court was required to give first consideration to the welfare of any child of the family who had not attained the age of 18.

The contrast between those provisions and those of the Child Support Act 1991 is striking. Although that Act does not remove any power which the court has, it provides that the court must not exercise any of its powers to make, vary or revive any maintenance order in relation to a child and an absent parent. Issues of financial responsibility are therefore severed from those of care; and many will regard this as a serious defect.

Moreover, the division of responsibility between the courts and the Child Support Agency is, in many respects, unsatisfactory. For example, it does not seem sensible that issues relating to step-children should have to be resolved by the court, whereas issues relating to other children should be resolved, according to a rigid formula, by the Child Support Agency.

Moreover, the fact that the Child Support Agency will not be concerned with capital orders is likely to cause significant problems. How far is the Child Support Agency to take account of the fact that a parent has (for example) made provision for his children under a "clean break" arrangement whereby the family home is transferred to the children, or to the parent with care of the child, but no order for periodical payments is made: see para. 9–81 above. No satisfactory answer has ever been given to this question, and confidence in the Government's ability to formulate a rational principle was not increased when the White Paper as originally produced omitted the page containing two vital paragraphs (para. 4.11 and 4.12) which addressed—albeit in extremely vague language—this issue. (The solution tentatively put forward was that the value of the equity given up by the absent parent would be converted into weekly payments for six years and deducted from some or all of the formula amount: para. 4.12. Whether or not this was a hasty afterthought, it seems scarcely convincing.) Meanwhile legislation has been put on the statute book without these issues having been properly addressed. They will therefore have to be determined in regulations which will not be subjected to any great Parliamentary scrutiny. It is not necessary to be a rigid constitutional purist to find this procedure profoundly unsatisfactory.

Many other issues are left to be dealt with by Regulations which could be of broad scope. For example, the Act provides (Sched. 1, para. 9) that the Secretary of State may by regulations provide that in such circumstances and to such extent as may be prescribed . . . a person is to be treated as possessing income or capital which he does not possess; and that income is to be treated as capital and capital is to be treated as income. This Alice-in-Wonderland approach to the conferment of powers on Ministers of the Crown is difficult for those who hold traditional views about the respective roles of the executive and legislature to accept.

It seems inevitable that the delegated legislation will be complex. If the precedents of the Income Support and Family Credit legislature are anything to go by, the inevitable result will be that those lawyers who deal with family matters will find it impossible to familiarise themselves with, or keep abreast of, all the important ramifications. The result will inevitably be that some who desperately need advice will fail to get it.

Underlying the Child Support Act is the assumption that a scheme which is based on a formula worked out in an Administrative Agency is likely to be more efficient than the scheme established by the Matrimonial Causes Act 1973 under which courts make orders in the exercise of a wide discretion after giving the parties full opportunity to be heard. It will be interesting to see whether this assumption will prove to be justified. Nearly five thousand new posts will have to be created to administer the Child Support Agency, and although no doubt substantial resources will be committed to the training of those concerned, the precedent of the Income Support and Family Credit systems does not give any ground for excessive optimism about the working of the scheme. Administrative procedures certainly have advantages, but it is somewhat alarming that as the Child Support Bill was completing its passage through Parliament, the Chief Adjudication Officer's Annual Report pointed out that adjudication standards in the Social Security field remained low, that the officials concerned often failed to apply the law correctly, and that they took decisions on insufficient evidence. More recently, the Comptroller and Auditor General has found mistakes in calculating entitlements in nearly 15 per cent. of cases. The Child Support Legislation is based on principles similar to those governing the Income Support and Family Credit systems, and seems likely to be administered by the same people as are responsible for the failings identified by the Chief Adjudication Officer and by the Comptroller and Auditor General. In those circumstances, it would seem rash to be optimistic about the outcome.

SUGGESTIONS FOR FURTHER READING

National Audit Office, *Department of Social Security: Support for Lone Parent Families* (1990).
Lone Parent Families (1990).
Children Come First, The Government's Proposals on the Maintenance of Children, Cm. 1263, Vols. 1 and 2 (1990).
House of Commons, Social Security Committee, Session 1990–91 (3 Reports) HC 277 (1991).
R. Bird, Child Maintenance, The New Law (1991).
C. S. Gibson, "The Future for Maintenance" [1991] CJQ 330.
J. Eekelaar, *Regulating Divorce* (1991), Chap. 5.
J. Eekelaar, "The Child Support Act 1991" [1991] Fam Law 511.
S. Parker, "Child Support in Australia: Children's Rights or Public Interest" (1991) 5 IJL & F 24.

PART IV—CHILDREN, THE FAMILY AND THE LAW

INTRODUCTION

A new-born child is physically incapable of caring for itself, and mentally incapable of reaching reasoned decisions about its own future. Others must therefore assume the burden of care and of decision-taking for the baby. The growing child may increasingly demand a say in the decisions which have to be taken about such matters as education, and leisure activities. The fact that society casts on the family the function of socialising children—"to tame their impulses and instil values, skills and desires necessary to run society" as it has been said—increases the possibility of conflict, for the child may not want to do what the parents or other carers would wish. Against this background, no one should be surprised that studies of child development and family dynamics often reveal a hotbed of conflict. Yet most of these conflicts are resolved without any reference to the law, much less to the courts: the family is traditionally seen as a private unit (*per* Lord Donaldson MR., *Re M and N (Wards) (Publication of Information)* [1990] 1 FLR 149, 164) constituting a realm which the state cannot and should not seek to enter (*per* Rutledge J., *Prince* v. *Massachusetts* (1944) 321 US 158, 166); and the traditional view is that it is for parents to discipline their children and to make choices on their behalf. Yet there remain cases which cannot properly be resolved by private ordering—not least where parents cannot agree between themselves; while the traditional view has also come into conflict with beliefs, strongly articulated in recent years, which assert children's rights to autonomy and, in particular, to have a say in decisions which affect their future. Increasingly, therefore, the law does have to provide answers to questions about who is to be entitled to take decisions about a child's upbringing, and to provide procedures whereby those issues may be litigated.

Family and state

A further potential source of conflict arises if the parents or other carers are unable or unwilling to adopt the values and child-rearing practices which society generally has adopted—whether because the parents have a different scale of values (a matter of particular significance in a multi-cultural society) or because the parents (through illness, poverty or other factors) are unable to achieve levels of parenting skill which are judged acceptable by contemporary standards. Since the end of the second world war in 1945 the State has assumed increasing responsibilities to provide a wide range of services to benefit children and families and to care for children whose own families are unable or unwilling to provide "good enough" parenting. In many cases, of course, the relationship between the State—acting through Local Authorities—and the family is an entirely consensual one, with no element—or at least no apparent element—of compulsion. But it has for long been recognised that the State sometimes needs to intervene against the wishes of a child's family in order to provide protection for a child against abuse or neglect. The circumstances which justify such intervention have, in recent years—and particularly after the events usually referred to as the Cleveland crisis—become a matter of acute controversy, not least because the result of local authority intervention may be that a child is removed from home and parents and, ultimately, transferred by the process of legal adoption—which destroys all legal links between the child and the birth parents—to other parents.

The Children Act 1989

The law regulating the upbringing of children has been revolutionised by the Children Act 1989, which came fully into force on October 14, 1991. The Act—described by the Lord Chancellor as "the most comprehensive and far reaching reform of child law which has come before Parliament in living memory"—seeks to provide a comprehensive, clear, and consistent code for the whole of child law, and it has undoubtedly effected a considerable simplification and rationalisation. However, the law—not surprisingly, in view of the sensitive issues with which it has to deal—remains complex: the Act is a finely constructed legislative structure, but (as the reader will see) the user needs not only to understand the underlying structure of the legislation, but also to be aware of a substantial amount of detail. Moreover, the Children Act did not make any fundamental change to the law governing legal adoption.

The text of this Part is arranged as follows:

Chapter 11: Legal Parentage: Parental Authority and Parental Responsibility

This chapter deals with the basic questions of the identity of the child's legal parents and outlines the rights and duties which flow from parentage.

Chapter 12: Transfer of Legal Parentage: Adoption

English law recognises adoption as the only institution whereby a child's legal parentage can be irrevocably changed—and adoption has become a technique extensively used by local authorities in an attempt to provide security for a child whose birth parents are unable or unwilling to provide adequate care. The adoptive parents become the child's legal parents, and consideration of how this dramatic change is effected follows logically from the discussion of legal parentage contained in Chapter 11.

Chapter 13: The Courts' Powers to make orders dealing with the upbringing of children

This chapter deals with the main legal structures whereby "private law" issues relating to the upbringing of a child—that is to say, issues which do not directly involve an application by the Local Authority for compulsory intervention—may be resolved by a court.

Chapter 14: Distinctive Features of Different Kinds of Family Proceedings

This chapter describes how the courts deal with different kinds of family proceedings, and explains the distinctive features of divorce, applications for parental responsibility, wardship and other private law family proceedings.

Chapter 15: The Child, The Family and the State

This chapter outlines the circumstances in which the state can intervene in a child's upbringing. It also contains a sketch of local authority powers and duties intended to promote the welfare of children.

Chapter 11

LEGAL PARENTAGE: PARENTAL AUTHORITY AND PARENTAL RESPONSIBILITY

Introduction—What is a Parent?

Words describing family relationships—for example "uncle" and **11–01**
"aunt"—are often used in different senses by different people; and, in
particular, words connoting a relationship are often used to indicate a
social reality, rather than a biological fact. For example, someone
brought up from birth by a man and a woman may well refer to them
as "mother" and "father"; and it is not unusual for a young child to
look on the mother's partner as his or her "father" whether or not the
man concerned is biologically the parent.

For many years, the law rarely had to concern itself with these
ambiguities and differences of linguistic usage. Leaving on one side
legal adoption (which only became possible in this country in 1926:
see Chapter 12 below), the legal theory was that genetic factors
determined the identity of a person's parents; but, in practice, only
very crude procedures were available to answer the relevant
questions. The man and woman who provided the genetic material
—the egg and sperm (or gametes)—which had resulted in conception
and birth were the child's parents; but there were no sophisticated or
reliable methods available to identify those persons. It could robustly
be asserted that motherhood was a biological fact which could be
proved demonstrably by parturition: see *The Ampthill Peerage* [1977]
AC 457, 577; but paternity remained for long almost impossible to
prove; and the law accordingly took refuge in presumptions. For
example, there is a presumption that the father of any child born to a
married woman during the marriage is her husband; and this
presumption could only be rebutted if there were evidence establishing beyond reasonable doubt (as distinct from a mere balance of
probabilities) that the husband could not have been the father. A
husband who could have had intercourse with his wife at the likely
time of conception would thus be held to be the father of her child
even if there were evidence that the wife had also had intercourse
with "one, two or twenty men" (*per* Sir F. Jeune P., *Gordon* v. *Gordon*
[1903] P 141, 142). There is also a presumption that the man named
on the birth certificate is the child's father, but the fact that
restrictions were for long placed on entry of any name other than the
husband's limited the value of this presumption. Finally, the Civil
Evidence Act 1968 creates rebuttable presumptions that findings of
paternity in specified legal proceedings are correct.

In recent years, this comparatively simple state of affairs has been
transformed by two distinct scientific developments:

(i) *Blood and DNA testing*

11–02   Certain characteristics are transmitted from one generation to another in accordance with recognised principles of genetics; and a comparison of the characteristics of the child's blood with the blood characteristics of the child's mother and of a particular man may provide conclusive evidence that the man is not the father of the child. Blood test evidence can thus *exclude* the possibility of parentage; but it can never directly and of itself provide proof that a particular individual *is* the child's parent. However, the practical reality is rather different. First, blood testing may indirectly provide effectively conclusive evidence that a particular man is the child's father. For example, suppose that a married woman has, whilst living with her husband, had intercourse with only one other person, X. The question arises as to whether H or X is the child's father. If blood tests exclude the possibility that H is the father (and do not exclude X) then it follows that X must be the father.

Even in cases where blood tests do not exclude all but one possible man, they will usually provide evidence about the probability of parentage. This is because the blood tests may show that the child has genetic characteristics which he or she is more likely to have inherited from A, rather than from B, C, or D. It is because of the increasing sophistication of blood testing, and of methods for evaluating the probability that certain characteristics have been inherited, that the value of blood testing in establishing, and not merely eliminating, the paternity of a particular man is increasing.

In recent years much more sophisticated methods of determining parentage—notably DNA profiling, or genetic finger-printing—have been developed, and these (it seems) have now largely supplanted blood group comparisons. DNA profiling means that today it is normally possible—if samples of bodily fluid or tissue are available—to establish parentage beyond any reasonable doubt. But blood group testing is, apparently, considerably less expensive than DNA profiling, and may thus still have a part to play.

(ii) *Human assisted reproduction*

11–03   The practice of *artificial insemination* is of some antiquity, and is now widely used—the Government has estimated that some 1,700 children are born annually as a result of artificial insemination by a donor. AID (Artificial Insemination by a Donor) involves a man providing sperm with which the mother's egg is fertilised. The sperm donor is thus unquestionably the genetic father; but the question whether the law should insist on regarding him as the child's legal father, (often in preference to the mother's husband, who might well have suggested artificial insemination as the best way of coping with his infertility) began increasingly to be asked, whilst the development of other techniques in what came to be called Human Assisted Reproduction served—although they were, and are, much less frequently used than AID—to bring the issue to public attention. In particular, techniques for fertilising an egg outside the mother's body (*in vitro*—*i.e.* in a glass, hence the expression "test tube baby") were developed.

The techniques

The main techniques employed in Human Assisted Reproduction **11–04** were described by the Warnock Committee into Human Fertilisation and Embryology (1984, Cmnd 9314) ("Warnock") as follows:

i. *Traditional IVF*

This technique led to the birth of a baby in 1978; and is now widely **11–05** used. It involves a "ripe human egg extracted from the ovary, shortly before it would have been released naturally. Next, the egg is mixed with the semen of the husband or partner, so that fertilisation can occur. The fertilised egg, once it has started to divide, is then transferred back to the mother's uterus." (Warnock, para. 5.2)

ii. *Egg donation*

"A mature egg is recovered from a fertile woman donor, for **11–06** example during sterilisation, and is fertilised *in vitro*, using the semen of the husband of the infertile woman. The resulting embryo is then transferred to the patient's uterus. If it implants, she may then carry the pregnancy to term." (Warnock, para. 6.1)

iii. *Embryo donation*

"The donated egg is fertilised *in vitro* with donated semen and the **11–07** resulting embryo transferred to a woman who is unable to produce an egg herself and whose husband is infertile." (Warnock, para. 7.1)

iv. *Embryo transfer*

" ... the egg is released naturally from the ovary at the time in the **11–08** donor's menstrual cycle. At the predicted time of ovulation she is artificially inseminated with semen from the husband of the infertile woman (or from a donor if the husband is also infertile). Some three to four days later, before the start of implantation, the donor's uterus is 'washed out' and any embryo retrieved is then transferred to the uterus of the infertile woman. If the embryo implants successfully the recipient carries the pregnancy to term." (Warnock, para. 7.12)

Surrogacy

Human Assisted Reproduction and surrogacy are often confused. In **11–09** fact, they are very different. Surrogacy (which simply means substitution) is not a modern development, nor is it necessarily related to the use of artificial fertilisation techniques (see, *e.g. Re an adoption application AA 212/86 (Adoption: Payment)* [1987] 2 FLR 291 where the intending father and surrogate mother had "physical congress with the sole purpose of procreating a child"). A surrogate mother (it has been said) "is a woman who bears and carries a child at the behest of another person with a view to that other person subsequently assuming the parental role: *per* Sir J. Arnold P. in *Re P (Minors) (Wardship: Surrogacy)* [1987] 2 FLR 421. Surrogacy is an emotive subject, and publicity given to the practice — and particularly to the formation of agencies established to arrange for childless couples to have a child born for them by a surrogate mother — led to the enactment of the Surrogacy Arrangements Act 1985. This Act makes it a criminal offence for any person to initiate or take part in negotiations with a view to the making of a surrogacy arrangement, to offer or agree to negotiate the making of a surrogacy arrangement, or compile any information with a view to its use in making, or negotiate the making of, surrogacy arrangements; but these prohibitions apply if (and only if) the actions in question were done on a commercial basis. The Act defines "commercial basis" by reference to the making of "payments"; but it is specifically provided that this word does not include payment to or for the benefit of a surrogate mother or prospective surrogate mother: s.2(3). The intention was therefore to make the Agency criminally liable, whilst leaving the surrogate mother herself free to accept payments whether or not they were confined to expenses.

This legislation left the status of surrogacy agreements unclear; but the Human Fertilisation and Embryology Act (s.36) now provides that no surrogacy arrangement is enforceable by or against any of the persons making it. Hence, for example, the surrogate mother could not sue for any money agreed to be paid to her, whilst any provisions dealing with the future care of the child would be unenforceable.

The legal parentage of a child born to a surrogate mother will be determined under the general rules now laid down in the Human Fertilisation and Embryology Act 1990: see para. 11–11 below. If there is a dispute about the child's upbringing this could be resolved by the court either in proceedings under the Children Act 1989 (see Chap. 13 below) or by making the child a ward of court. The court would resolve the issue by deciding what course of action would best promote the child's welfare: see *Re P (Minors) (Wardship: Surrogacy)* [1987] 2 FLR 421. If the commissioning parents wish to be recognised in law as the child's parents they may apply for an adoption order (see Chap. 12 below) or they may apply for a "parental order" under section 30 of the Human Fertilisation and Embryology Act: see para. 11–12 below.

Legal Parentage
11–10   Legal parentage might reasonably be claimed by at least three separate categories of person:

(i) The *genetic* parents, *i.e.* the persons who have provided the genetic material resulting in the child's conception. On this basis, the sperm donor would be the legal father of an AID child (notwithstanding the fact that he had never had any contact with the child or its mother and that in the great majority of cases he would be wholly ignorant of the fact that a child had been born following his donation).

(ii) The *carrying* parent—*i.e.* the woman who has born the child to delivery (notwithstanding the fact that she may have provided none of the genetic material from which the child's inherited characteristics will be derived, and that she may have agreed to bear the child for a married couple who have provided some or all of the material); and

(iii) The *social* parents—*i.e.* those who arranged for the child to be conceived and born and who intend to care for the child in exactly the same way as would the parent of a child conceived and born in the traditional way.

THE HUMAN FERTILISATION AND EMBRYOLOGY ACT 1990

The Human Fertilisation and Embryology Act 1990 introduced rules **11–11** defining legal parentage in certain circumstances; but the subject is a difficult one and, notwithstanding careful consideration by the Warnock Committee and much parliamentary debate, it cannot be said that the solutions now embodied in the legislation are wholly coherent.

The combined effect of the common law and the legislation can be summarised as follows:

(i) The woman who bears a child will, at the child's birth, always be regarded as the legal mother: HF & EA 1990, s.27(1).

(ii) In principle, the father of a child is the person who provides the sperm which leads to conception. However, this rule is subject to two exceptions relevant to AID:

(a) The husband of a woman who is *artificially* inseminated is treated as the father of the child, unless it is proved that he did not consent to the treatment: HF & EA 1990, s.28(2) and provided he can rebut the presumption that a mother's husband is the father of any child she bears: s.28(5).

(b) Where a woman has been *artificially* inseminated in the course of treatment provided for her and a man under the licensing procedure established by HF & EA 1990 then that man is treated as the child's father: HF & EA 1990, s.28(3).

It should also be mentioned that there are special rules applicable to the situation in which conception has resulted from the use of a man's sperm or an embryo created from it after the man's death: HF & EA 1990, s.28(6)(*b*).

In many cases, the application of exceptions (a) and (b) above will mean that the sperm donor is not treated as the child's father; but the

Act (in an attempt to protect donors from possible legal responsibility as father of a child) goes further. It is provided that a man who donates sperm for the purposes of "treatment services" provided under the HF & EA 1990—in effect, at an officially licensed centre, which is bound to follow certain prescribed procedures—is not to be treated as the child's father. However, the effect of this rule is to create the possibility that a child will be legally fatherless. Suppose, for example, that sperm is donated for treatment services in accordance with the provisions of the Act; and that the donor is accordingly not to be treated as the father. In the usual case, the mother's husband (or partner) will be treated as the father: see HF & EA 1990, ss.28(2), (3) above. But there could be circumstances in which those provisions would not apply—the husband might, for example, prove that he did not consent to the treatment carried out on his wife, in which case he will not be treated as the child's father, or the mother might be a single woman who has received licensed treatment.

The enactment of the rules contained in the Human Fertilisation and Reproduction Act 1990 does not (it would seem) affect the presumptions created by the common law and by statute: see para. 11–01 above. Hence it will be rebuttably presumed that the husband of a married woman is the father of her child; it will be rebuttably presumed that the man whose name is entered as being the child's father in the Register of Births is in fact the father; and the fact that a person has been found to be the father of a child in proceedings under the Children Act 1989 (and certain other statutes) creates a rebuttable presumption that he is indeed the child's father: Child Evidence Act 1986, as amended by Courts and Legal Services Act 1990, Sched. 16, para. 2. Finally, it appears that if the court has exercised the power conferred on it by the Family Law Act 1986 to make a declaration that a named person is, or was, his parent, then that declaration can be controverted only in the most exceptional circumstances: see Family Law Act 1986, s.58(2); *The Ampthill Peerage* [1977] AC 547.

Effect of adoption and of a "parental order" under the Human Fertilisation and Embryology Act 1990

11–12   The effect of an Adoption order is that the child is treated in law as the child of the adopters, and not of any other person; and such an order—considered in detail in Chapter 12 below will effectively—with effect from the date of the order—override the rules set out above: Adoption Act 1976, s.39.

The difficulty of establishing a single coherent set of rules to determine parentage has already been referred to; and the problems to which the rules so far set out could give rise was illustrated while the Human Fertilisation and Embryology Bill was being debated:

In *Re W (Minors) (Surrogacy)* [1991] 1 FLR 385 a married couple were anxious to have children, but the wife had no womb. She provided eggs which were removed and fertilised *in vitro* with sperm provided by her husband. The resultant embryo was implanted in a woman ("the surrogate") who agreed that she would hand the child—in fact twins were born—to the commissioning couple; and she did so. The effect of the rules so far set out above would have been as follows: first, the surrogate would be treated in law as the mother, notwithstanding the fact that she had not provided any of the genetic material which had resulted in the children's conception, that she had never acted as the children's parent, and did not wish to do so; and secondly, the surrogate's husband would, (assuming that he had agreed to the procedure) be treated as the child's father notwithstanding the fact that he had had nothing whatsoever to do with the children's conception or with caring for them.

Adoption could of course have been used in this case to make genetic and social parenting congruent with the legal parentage; but, perhaps not surprisingly, the commissioning parents considered that adoption would be inappropriate.

As a direct result of publicity about such cases the legislation was hurriedly amended whilst it was passing through Parliament and now incorporates a provision (s.30) enabling a married couple who have provided the genetic material which has led to a child's conception to apply for a court order—a so-called *parental order*—which will require the child to be treated in law as their child. Not surprisingly, the legislation appears to be defective in a number of respects: see Douglas, *Law, Fertility and Reproduction* (1991), p. 158 ff; and Hogg [1991] Fam Law 278.

In particular, the court must be satisfied that the surrogate and the legal father of the child "have freely, and with full understanding of what is involved, agreed unconditionally to the making of the order": s. 30 (5). This provision is clearly modelled on the adoption law (see Chap. 12 below); but adoption law makes provision for dispensing with agreement if it is unreasonably withheld and on a number of other grounds. In contrast the 1990 Act only allows the court to dispense with the agreement of a person who "cannot be found or is incapable of giving agreement." Moreover—in another provision clearly influenced by the adoption legislation—the court must be satisfied that no money or other benefit (other than for expenses reasonably incurred) has been given or received by the commissioning parents for or in consideration of the making of the order, the giving of the consent which is required to the making of an order, the handing over of the child to the commissioning parents, or the making of any arrangements with a view to the making of the order, unless such payments have been authorised by the court. This provision seems extremely uncertain in scope—what, for example, are "expenses reasonably incurred" in this context? Finally, it should be noted that at the time of the application and of the making of the order the child's home must be with the commissioning parents (so that the Act will have no application where the surrogate refuses to hand over the child) and that any agreement by the surrogate to the making of the parental order will be ineffective if given by her less than six weeks after the child's birth.

It is difficult to avoid the conclusion that this legislation—which apparently does not deal with the legal status of the child save in respect of his relationship with the commissioning parents—is an unsatisfactory and ill thought-out measure. It is true that the Act provides that regulations may extend provisions of the adoption legislation to applications for parental orders (s.30(9)), and this power will no doubt be used to remedy the most pressing defects in the law; but some will think it unfortunate that matters of such importance should be left to delegated legislation which is likely to escape any detailed Parliamentary or other scrutiny.

The child's right to know about his or her origins

11–13   The modern law has thus accepted that the child's legal parents may not be the child's genetic parents; yet genetic parentage may be seen as a matter of great relevance by the child and others. Should the law give children a right to know the truth about his or her genetic parentage? The question is a difficult one, about which conventional views have changed over the years. The problem first had to be confronted on the context of legal adoption. Although the principle underlying legal adoption in this country was that there should be a complete severance between the adopted child and the birth parents, and that the child should have no legal right to know anything about the birth parents (or other blood relatives), Parliament in 1975 accepted that an adopted child should have the right to access to the register which might reveal the identity of the child's birth parents; whilst provisions of the Children Act 1989 are intended in appropriate cases to promote contact between the child and his birth relatives.

If the adopted child has, in principle at least, the right to know about genetic parentage, can there be any justification for treating the child conceived as a result of human assisted reproduction any differently? After all, it might be argued that such a child has an equal need to discover the truth about his or her inheritance, and that this information may indeed be necessary for medical reasons.

The Warnock Committee considered this issue at some length; but the Committee was evidently impressed by difficulties which it considered stood in the way of giving a right to disclosure. In particular the evidence suggested that parents who had resorted to AID did not in fact disclose this fact to the children. The Committee accordingly rejected suggestions that the child should have an unrestricted right to know the full truth about his or her genetic inheritance; and the Human Fertilisation and Embryology Act adopts something of a compromise.

The Act (s.31) requires the Human Fertilisation and Embryology Authority to keep a register containing information about the provision of treatment for identifiable individuals or which shows that an identifiable individual was or may have been born in consequence of "treatment services." It also entitles a person who has attained the age of 18 to require the Authority to tell the applicant whether or not the information in its possession shows that a person other than a parent of the applicant would or might (but for the provisions of the Act determining the child's legal parentage) be a parent of the applicant. If the information does suggest that the applicant may have been born (in effect) as a result of human assisted fertilisation, it will give the applicant "so much of that information as relates to the person concerned as the Authority is required by regulations to give (but no other information)": s.31(4)(a). The matter is therefore to be left to Regulations; but the Act specifically provides that Regulations cannot require the authority actually to identify the person whose genetic material has been used: s.31(5). In effect therefore it would seem that the position is that donors are entitled to preserve their anonymity, but the child is likely to be given access to information of a general kind about his genetic parentage. The refusal to allow identification of the genetic parent is controversial; and the Act—in an unusual provision—permits Regulations to be made at some future date which will permit identification. However, it is stipulated that no such change in the Law is to take effect retrospectively.

Determining parentage—ancillary powers

The utility of scientific testing to determine parentage had been   **11–14** explained at para. 11–02 above; but it was not until 1969 that the courts were given express powers to direct the taking of blood samples. The Family Law Reform Act 1987 now gives the courts a general power to direct the use of scientific tests to ascertain whether such tests show that a party to the proceedings is or is not the father or mother of a particular person. The report of the test will indicate whether any party to whom the report relates is excluded by the results from being the father or mother of the person concerned; and it will also state the value (if any) of the results in determining whether a person who is not so excluded is the father or mother of that person. If a person refuses to comply with a test direction, the court may draw such inferences from the refusal as seem proper.

LEGITIMACY AND ILLEGITIMACY

Notwithstanding the special rules enacted to deal with the attribution   **11–15** of parentage where a child has been born as a result of human assisted reproduction it has so far been assumed that the question of parentage is essentially one of fact. Whether or not a child's parents are, or ever have been, married ˋhas not been given any special prominence. But most legal systems do in fact draw a sharp distinction between legitimate children (who are regarded as full members of the legal family) on the one hand and illegitimate children (who to a greater or lesser extent are not given full legal recognition) on the other hand; and this distinction usually depends on whether or not the child's parents were married. The general rule was that a child should only be regarded as a full member of the legal family if the parents were lawfully married at the time of the child's birth or conception. Indeed, this principle was carried to an extreme by the common law of England, which classified the illegitimate child as *filius nullius*—"the child of no-one" and thus for legal purposes a stranger not only to his father but also to his mother and to all other blood relatives. In consequence of this doctrine, the illegitimate child (or "bastard") had no legal right to succeed to property or to receive maintenance or to any other benefits derived from the legal relationship of parent and child.

Piecemeal reform: legitimation, etc.

11–16　　Over the years, the legal position of the child born illegitimate was gradually improved; and perhaps the most important reform was to enable illegitimate children to be legitimated—usually by the subsequent marriage of the parents. Even more dramatically, in 1959 Parliament accepted the civil law doctrine—consistently repudiated by the common law — of the *putative marriage* whereby the child of a void marriage would nevertheless be treated as the legitimate child of the parents if at the time of the act of intercourse resulting in the birth (or at the time of the celebration of the marriage if later) both or either of the parties to the void marriage reasonably believed it to be valid: see now Legitimacy Act 1976, s. 1 (1).

But notwithstanding these developments many children remained illegitimate and the law only gradually adopted the policy that children should not be penalised solely because they were not legitimate. For example, legislation culminating in the Family Law Reform Act 1969 greatly diminished the disadvantages of illegitimacy in relation to inheritance: an illegitimate child was given the right to succeed on the intestacy of either parent (although the child still did not count as a relative for purposes of succession to brothers, sisters, or grandparents). Again, if an illegitimate child's parent were killed as a result of the negligence or other wrongful act of a third party, the child could, just like a legitimate child, sue under the Fatal Accidents legislation for loss of financial support.

The Family Law Reform Act 1987

11–17　　Notwithstanding these reforms there remained a number of important areas in which the law continued to discriminate against the illegitimate child (or, as it might less emotively be put, to distinguish between the legal rights of the legitimate and the illegitimate). For example, although the illegitimate child had a right to be supported by the father, that right could be enforced only in a special form of proceedings (called affiliation proceedings) which had to be brought in the lowest court in the judicial hierarchy (the Magistrates' Court) and for long there was a (very low) ceiling on the amount of maintenance which could be awarded. Moreover, affiliation proceedings were surrounded by procedural and other rules which caused the illegitimate child to be treated differently from, and usually less favourably than, the legitimate child in pursuing claims for support.

The Family Law Reform Act 1987.
In 1982 the Law Commission published a comprehensive and detailed report (Law Com. No. 118) which concluded that discrimination against those born out of marriage could not be justified as a general policy. This conclusion was reinforced by the fact that to preserve such discrimination would be inconsistent with this country's international obligations under the European Convention on Human Rights, and under the European Convention on the Legal Status of Children Born Out of Wedlock. The Family Law Reform Act 1987 gave effect to the Law Commission's recommendations, and asserted the general principle that references in legislation

"to any relationship between two persons shall, unless the contrary intention appears, be construed without regard to whether or not the father and mother of either of them, or the father and mother of any person through whom the relationship is deduced, have or had been married to each other at any time."

At first sight, the adoption of this general principle would seem to make any further explanation unnecessary: a child was illegitimate if his parents were not married; the question of whether or not his parents are or were married is now to be irrelevant in determining legal relationships; and hence (it might be thought) illegitimacy has been abolished and the concept of legitimacy or illegitimacy thus rendered, in the context of family law, of only historical interest. But unfortunately this is not the case.

First the principle stated above applies (unless specificially excluded) to legislation enacted after the coming into force of the Family Law Reform Act 1987 on April 4, 1988; but it only affects legislation enacted *before* the coming into force of the Act if express provision is made for that purpose. Accordingly there remain a number of important areas in which the traditional concept of legitimacy is still relevant to the child's legal rights: see para. 11–18 below. Secondly, the Family Law Reform Act accepted the Law Commission's view that the father of an illegitimate child should not, as such, be entitled as of right to parental authority (or "parental reponsibility" to adopt the terminology subsequently introduced by the Children Act 1989: see para. 11–32 below) over the child.

The law therefore still distinguishes between the legitimate and illegitimate (or discriminates against the illegitimate); and it is desirable for the student to be aware of the areas in which the distinction remains legally significant. The text therefore summarises the law under two heads: (a) legal discrimination against the illegitimate child; (b) the position of the father of an illegitimate child. It then considers the statutory language now used to refer to the legitimate and the illegitimate.

A. Discrimination against the illegitimate child

11–18   Although the Family Law Reform Act 1987 made the question of whether a child's parents had been married irrelevant in determining legal relationships for most purposes — so that, for example, brother and sister now have equal rights of inheritance between themselves, whether or not their parents had ever been married — there are two exceptional cases in which the law continues directly to discriminate against the illegitimate child. These are:

(a) Citizenship

11–19   Under the British Nationality Act 1981, the relationship of parent and child exists only between a man and his legitimate child: BNA 1981, s.50(9)(b). An illegitimate child cannot therefore acquire British citizenship through his father; and there are two main factual situations in which a child of unmarried parents will not be entitled to the British citizenship which a child of married parents would take. These are, first, where a child is born in this country to a British father and a foreign mother; and secondly, where a child is born abroad to a British father and a foreign mother or to a mother who is British by descent only.

Although the Law Commission considered that, as a matter of policy, a child who could prove his parentage should be entitled to British citizenship irrespective of the parents' marital status (Law Com. No. 118, para. 11.20) the Government refused to change the law, arguing that further consultation was needed. Five years later, the law remains unchanged.

(b) Succession to the throne, peerages, rights under pre-1988 dispositions, etc.

11–20   Succession to the throne of the United Kingdom is governed by the Act of Settlement 1701, the language of which restricts the right of succession to the legitimate. Because the Family Law Reform Act 1987 does not retrospectively apply the general principle set out in para. 11–17 above to the 1701 Act, the position remains unaltered. Again, hereditary peerages granted before the enactment of the Family Law Reform Act 1987 have all been limited to heirs "lawfully begotten" (see Law. Com. No. 118, para. 8.26) and the right of succession to such peerages, and indeed more generally the right to take property under wills taking effect and settlements made before the implementation of the Act, will be unaffected.

B. The legal position of the father of an illegitimate child

The Law Commission evidently had little difficulty in rejecting the **11–21** proposition that continued discrimination against those born outside marriage was justified as a general policy; but its Report did not take the view which had been put forward in the original consultation paper that the law should be reformed so as no longer to draw *any* distinction based on whether or not a person's parents had ever been married. The reasoning underlying this refusal to carry the principle of non-discrimination to its logical conclusion centred on the question whether it would be acceptable to permit the father of a child born out of wedlock to have parental authority. The position of the father can (as it has been said: see *Re H (Illegitimate Children: Father: Parental Rights) (No. 2)* [1991] 1 FLR 214, 218, *per* Balcombe L.J.) be infinitely variable: "at one end of the spectrum his connection with the child may be only the single act of intercourse (possibly even rape) which led to conception; at the other end of the spectrum he may have played a full part in the child's life, only the formality of marriage to the mother being absent."

It appears that the Law Commission's consultations revealed a considerable division of opinion. In particular, it seems that influential groups—including the groups usually recognised as having the interests of illegitimate children and their parents as a primary concern—considered that automatically to equate the legal position of the father with that of the mother would give rise to considerable social evils. In this view, mothers might be tempted to conceal the father's identity so that he would not be able to exercise any authority; and, secondly, the father's legal right might be exercised in a disruptive way, particularly when the mother had married a third party and established a secure family for herself and the child. An unscrupulous father might (it was said) be tempted to "harass or possibly even to blackmail" the mother at a time when she could be exceptionally vulnerable to pressure.

The Family Law Reform Act 1987 accepted the validity of these concerns, and the Children Act 1989 preserves the principle that the father of an illegitimate child has no "parental responsibility" in respect of that child unless, either; (a) the court makes an order in his favour (see para. 11–37 below); or (b) the child's parents make a Parental Responsibility Agreement in the prescribed form and register it as required by Regulations: see para. 11–38 below.

The result is that an important distinction between children based solely on their parents' marital status remains embodied in the law, since the father of a child born outside marriage will by virtue of that fact have no parental authority over the child. In this respect, therefore, children are still divided by the law into two categories: those with a "normal" relationship with both parents, and others. In the result, although the legal disadvantages of illegitimacy so far as they adversely affect the child have been largely (albeit not entirely: see para. 11–18 above) removed, it cannot be said that the legal concepts of legitimacy and illegitimacy have been removed from the law.

The explanation for what some may regard as a failure of nerve on the part of the Law Commission is to be found in the fact that all law reform is essentially a political process; and the Commission was evidently concerned that opposition from the powerful groups representing single parents and their families would destroy all prospects of purging the statute book of provisions which embodied direct discrimination against children. The Commission candidly explained its position:

> "One of the main purposes of our consultation process is to ascertain whether or not there is a broad consensus on the reforms provisionally put forward in working papers. As we have said, there was almost unanimous support for removing the legal discrimination that presently exists against the illegitimate child: but there was a profound division of opinion amongst both legal and non-legal commentators on the parental rights question. We do not think that it would be right for us to ignore such anxieties where we cannot show them to be without foundation, and where the countervailing advantages of the reform are not clearly demonstrable": see Law Commission Report on Illegitimacy, No. 118, para. 4.48.

The assumption that law reform is such a sensitive area must be by consent, or not at all was part of the conventional wisdom at the time of the publication of the Law Commission's Report in 1982; but it may be that in the changed political atmosphere manifesting itself in British politics in the latter part of the decade, when "conviction politics" become more acceptable, it would have been possible to take a different and bolder view. Certainly, as has already been pointed out, the retention of distinctions based on the marital status of a child's parents makes it difficult to say that English law has in this context rid itself of the concept of legitimacy as a status. Indeed, the statute book provides a procedure whereby an applicant may seek a declaration that he or she is the legitimate child of the parents: see Family Law Act 1986, s.56; but the 1987 legislation does at least mean that the circumstances in which a child will be directly and adversely affected by the fact that he or she is not legitimate will now be comparatively rare.

The question of terminology: "illegitimate" or "born to parents who were not married to one another"

11–22   The Law Commission was concerned to minimise the need for continued use of the expression "illegitimate," with its connotations of unlawfulness and illegality; and in its 1982 Report presented draft legislation which would have substituted the term "marital" for "legitimate," and "non-marital" for illegitimate. However, it was subsequently suggested that to "attach labels" to children in this way would perpetuate discrimination against the "non-marital"; and the Law Commission, having reconsidered the matter, decided that it would indeed be preferable to frame the legislation so that the relevant distinction would depend on whether the child's parents were married to each other at the time of the child's birth: see Law Com. No. 157 (1986). The Family Law Reform Act 1987 adopts that drafting technique, as does the Children Act 1989, and most other subsequent legislation. In effect, the policy is that it should be the parents rather than the child who are labelled; and the legislation accordingly now draws a distinction between cases in which a "child's father and mother were married to each other at the time of his birth" on the one hand, and cases in which the child's father and mother were not so married on the other.

It might be thought that these words—used, for example, in the Children Act 1989 s.2(1) to allocate parental responsibility—are plain words of plain English, which can easily be understood. But in fact the Family Law Reform Act 1987 requires these plain words to be interpreted in a special way; and the student who wishes to understand the legislation should understand, first, why it was thought necessary to give the words a special meaning; and secondly, what that special meaning is.

The reason why it was thought necessary to define plain words so that they actually have a very different meaning from that which the uninitiated reader would expect stems from the fact that the law (as we have already seen: para. 11–16 above) had come to recognise the process of legitimation (whereby the child of a marriage *after* the birth was recognised as legitimate) and the concept of the putative marriage (whereby the child of a couple who had in law *never* been married was entitled to be treated as legitimate). Since there may still be circumstances in which a child who can claim legitimate status will enjoy legal advantages denied to the illegitimate (for example, in relation to citizenship), it was evidently thought desirable to preserve the favoured legal treatment of legitimated children and of children of a putative marriage. But, by definition, the parents of such children were *not* married to each other at the time of the child's birth. (If they had been, the child would have been legitimate and issues of legitimation could not have arisen.)

The solution to this problem put forward by the Law Commission in its Second Report on Illegitimacy (1986) was for statute to provide that references to a person "whose father and mother were married to each other at the time of his birth" should include references to a person who is treated as legitimate by virtue of the putative marriage doctrine, and to a person who is legitimated, or is adopted, or is "otherwise treated in law as legitimate": Family Law Reform Act 1987, s.1(3).

This technique is undoubtedly ingenious; but in the result there may be something of a trap for the unwary user of the statute book:

> Suppose, for example, that a question arises about whether a 15-year-old boy has a parent with parental responsibility for him (a matter which could be relevant to issues of guardianship, for example: see CA 1989, s.5(7), para. 11–40 below). In fact the boy's parents only married when the mother was on her death bed, some few weeks ago. The answer to the question whether the father has parental responsibility for him depends on whether the parents were married to one another "at the time of his birth" CA 1989, s.2(3). Manifestly they were not; but section 1 of the 1978 Act requires the parents of a legitimated child to be treated (contrary to the truth) *as if they were* married to one another at the time of the child's birth.

The statute book has thus been made to exemplify the principle laid down by the author of *Alice in Wonderland*:

> " ... any writer ... is fully authorised in attaching any meaning he likes to any word or phrase he intends to use. If I find an author saying ... Let it be understood that by the word black I shall always mean white ... I meekly accept his ruling, however injudicious I may think it." (C. Dodgson, *Symbolic Logic*, p. 165.)

The reader must judge whether the perversion of language now embodied in the statute book achieves any sufficient compensating advantage in terms of social utility. What the legislation means is that the expression "child whose parents were married at the time of his birth" is to be interpreted as "child who was born legitimate, was subsequently legitimated, or is otherwise entitled to be legitimate." The Law Commission's First Report proposed using the formula "marital child" to describe such a child; and this inelegant word manifestly required reference to the further definition to be found in the relevant section of the legislation. In contrast the words "married to each other at the time of birth" are not such as to cause the unwary reader to seek any further definition.

The words "legitimate" and "illegitimate" continue to be used in this book in the interests of clarity and accuracy—the latter of which could only otherwise be obtained by elaborate periphrases such as "a child whose parents were married to each other at the time of the child's birth, or a child whose parents were not so married but are required to be treated as having been so in accordance with the statutory formula embodied in the Family Law Reform Act 1987."

Unmarried fathers?

One further point about terminology must be made. This relates to the terms apt to describe the parents of an illegitimate child. It seems to have become the practice to use the description "unmarried father" or "unmarried mother" in, no doubt well-motivated, attempts to avoid using the label "illegitimate." This usage is, in the author's view, unnacceptable, because the relevant legal issue is never simply whether the parent concerned is "married" or not; it is whether he or she was *married to a particular person, i.e.* the child's other parent. For example, Charles II, King of England, enjoys a certain notoriety as the father of a number of illegitimate children; yet it would be absurd to describe him, in defiance of the facts, as "unmarried." Accordingly, the potentially misleading expression "unmarried parent" will not be used in this book to describe the parent of an illegitimate child.

THE LEGAL SIGNIFICANCE OF PARENTAGE—INTRODUCTION

Parentage is of importance to the lawyer for two reasons. First, **11–23** legislation frequently confers rights or imposes duties on a child's "parent" or on his "mother" or "father"—for example, a person's mother and father are, in certain circumstances, entitled to share the property of a child who dies without leaving a will; while a child's "parents" may claim damages for bereavement against the person whose negligence caused the death: Fatal Accidents Act 1976, s.1(a).

In terms of duties the social security legislation provides that men and women are liable to maintain their "children" (Social Security Act 1986, s.26(3)), whilst the Education Act 1944 imposes an obligation on parents to ensure that their children attend school. In terms of daily life, it may well be that it is in this area of the creation of statutory rights and duties that the question "who is the child's parent?" will most often be found to be significant. (In this context it should be remembered that the Family Law Reform Act 1987 abolished, in relation to statutes enacted after April 4, 1988 the common law rule (see *Re M (An Infant)* [1955] 2 QB 479) whereby statutory references to a "parent" did not extend to an illegitimate child: FLRA 1987, s.1(1); para. 11–17 above. If Parliament now wishes to distinguish between illegitimate and legitimate children it must do so expressly; and it can be argued that *parentage* is now more important than was the case before 1988 (when status—*i.e.* as a legitimate child—was often of importance).

The second reason for the importance of parentage is that the common law recognises that a child's parent has certain rights and authority in relation to that child—for example, to control the child's movements, to take decisions about the child's residence, schooling, religion and so on—and that those rights may continue throughout the child's minority. The importance and extent of the common law rights—which were vested entirely in the father to the exclusion of the mother—are vividly illustrated by the case of *Re Agar-Ellis* (1883) 24 Ch D 317.

215

Mr Agar-Ellis decided to go back on the promise he had made to his wife that their children should be brought up as Roman Catholics; but the wife nevertheless continued to take the children to Roman Catholic services. Mr Agar-Ellis got an injunction to prevent her doing so; and he subsequently took his daughter Harriet and his other children away from their mother and arranged for them to be looked after by clergymen and others. When Harriet was 16 she asked to be allowed to spend her holidays with her mother instead of being moved about from one lodging to another. An application was made to the court for permission for her to spend the holiday with her mother, and for the mother to be allowed free access to her child; but the court refused the application. In the absence of any suggested fault on the father's part, the court had no jurisdiction to interfere with his legal right to control the custody and education of his children.

This case can—for reasons which will soon appear—be "remaindered to the history books" (*per* Lord Scarman, *Gillick* v. *West Norfolk and Wisbech Area Health Authority* [1986] 1 FLR 224, 248); but it is still necessary to understand the scope and extent of the rights which a parent had at common law, since it is only against this background that recent developments can be understood.

Scope and extent of parental authority at common law

11-24   There is some doubt about the nature and extent of the parental rights which were recognized at common law (see *F* v. *Metropolitan Borough of Wirral DC and Another* [1991] 2 FLR 114, CA) but the specific powers enjoyed by a person with parental authority are conventionally listed as follows:

   (i)   the right to physical possession of the child;
   (ii)   the right to control the child's education and to choose his or her religion;
   (iii) the right to inflict moderate and reasonable corporal punishment and otherwise to discipline the child;
   (iv)   the right to consent to medical treatment;
   (v)   the right to withhold consent from a proposed marriage;
   (vi)   the right to administer the child's property and to enter into certain contracts on his behalf;
   (vii) the right to act for the child in legal proceedings;
   (viii) the right to the child's domestic services (and possibly the right to receive payment for work which the child does for others);
   (ix)   various miscellaneous rights such as the right to choose the name by which the child should be known.

Child's views irrelevant at common law

11-25   Although the law recognised that a wise parent would not seek to enforce his views against the wishes of a mature child, and would refuse to lend its aid to a parent who sought to impose his will on a child who had attained the "age of discretion," the fact that a particular child's intellectual or emotional development was advanced was irrelevant in deciding whether or not parental authority continued: see *R. v. Howes* [1860] 1 E & E 332 and the judgment of Parker L.J. in *Gillick v. West Norfolk and Wisbech Area Health Authority* [1985] FLR 736, CA.

The Gillick decision

This traditional understanding of the common law position of a **11-26** parent was overturned by the decision of the House of Lords in *Gillick v. West Norfolk and Wisbech Area Health Authority* [1986] 1 FLR 224:

> Mrs Gillick, the mother of four daughters under the age of 16, sought an assurance from the Authority that her daughters would not be given contraceptive treatment without her prior knowledge and evidence of her consent. The authority refused to give such an assurance. Mrs Gillick therefore asked the court to declare that DHSS advice to the effect that young people could in some circumstances be given contraceptive advice and treatment without their parent's knowledge and consent was unlawful and wrong, and that it adversely affected Mrs Gillick's right as the children's parent. The House of Lords, by a 3-2 majority, held that her application should have been dismissed.

The Gillick rationale—mature children entitled to take their own decisions?

The basis of the *Gillick* decision seemed to be that—in the absence **11-27** of an express statutory rule (for example, that requiring parental consent to the marriage of a minor child: see para. 1.07 above)—all parental authority "yields to the child's right to make his own decisions when he reaches a sufficient understanding and intelligence to be capable of making up his own mind on the matter requiring decision" (see *per* Lord Scarman at p. 253). The question whether a child had sufficient understanding and intelligence must be an issue of fact in each case, depending on the complexity of the issues involved, and the child's emotional and intellectual maturity. Some decisions—including whether to seek contraceptive advice—require a very high level of maturity and understanding; but less complex issues would require a correspondingly less highly developed intellectual and moral understanding.

The *Gillick* decision did not deal with the question of how the capacity of a child should be assessed if his or her understanding was not stable, but varied from day to day or week to week—perhaps as a result of illness—but this was the issue *in Re R (A Minor) (Wardship: Medical Treatment)* [1991] 4 All ER 177:

> A 15-year-old girl had a history of family problems. Her mental health deteriorated. She threatened to commit suicide and on one occasion attacked her father with a hammer. She was placed in an adolescent psychiatric unit. The question arose whether she had capacity to give a valid consent to the administration of anti-psychotic drugs. The question

was difficult because the patient's condition varied: sometimes she was entirely lucid and rational, but sometimes her rationality and capacity to understand recommendations about medical treatment were severely impaired. The judge at first instance decided that the patient did not have the necessary capacity to take decisions about the medication prescribed for her. The Court of Appeal unanimously agreed that *Gillick*-competence was a developmental concept and required a long-term assessment as distinct from a snap-shot approach. Such competence was not lost or acquired on a day-to-day or week-to-week basis; and the very wide changes in the patient's condition were such that she could not be regarded as *Gillick*-competent.

This test enables a broad and realistic test to be applied, which seems much more sensible than the strictly chronological tests applicable where capacity is fixed by statute—at one minute to midnight on the eve of a young person's 18th birthday he or she cannot make a will, cannot own a legal estate in land, and cannot (generally speaking) make an enforceable contract; but at one minute after midnight, he or she can do all these things.

Right to consent includes right to refuse?

11–28   Unfortunately, the three Lords Justice who constituted the Court of Appeal in *Re R* (above) did not confine themselves to deciding the one point of law which was necessary to their decision; but considered other, much more controversial and difficult issues.

First, if a child had sufficient understanding to be *Gillick*-competent in relation to a particular issue, did it follow that the child had not only the right to consent to medical treatment (which might otherwise be a trespass) but also a right to refuse such treatment? At first glance, it might seem that the answer to this question is so obvious that the question need not be asked. The underlying rationale of the *Gillick* case had seemed to be that an assertion of parental authority could be justified only insofar as it enabled the parent to perform his duties to the child and the other children in the family (Lord Fraser of Tullybelton in Gillick at p. 235); and the practical outcome of this approach seemed to be that once the child had sufficient maturity to understand what was involved, the parent would no longer have authority to take decisions on the child's behalf. It would thus be for the child—assuming he or she understood the relevant issues—to decide whether or not to take a Saturday job, for example, and the parents would have no right to interfere. Again, it would be for the child, subject to the same proviso, to decide whether to live at home or with friends, and the friends will be able to ignore the father's threats that he alone is entitled to decide where the child should live. In particular Lord Scarman in *Gillick* clearly seemed to view the parent's right to take decisions as "yielding" to the child's right to take decisions when he or she had sufficient maturity, and Lord Scarman did in fact in terms state that the parental right to determine whether or not a minor child below the age of 16 would have medical treatment terminates if and when the child achieved a sufficient understanding and intelligence to enable him or her to understand fully what is proposed. But in *Re R*, Lord Donaldson disagreed: although the parents of a *Gillick*-competent child had no right to *determine* whether or not treatment should be given, yet they still retained the right to give a valid consent (thus overruling their child's own decision). He considered that a number of persons—presumably all those with parental responsibility for the child—had a right to give a consent which would be effective to exculpate a doctor from liability for wrongfully carrying out a medical procedure on the child, and that the consent of any of those persons would be sufficient (presumably until the child attained the age of 18).

This seems an extraordinary position. How can it be argued that a young person who has satisfied the demanding tests of comprehension and maturity required to attain *Gillick* capacity to *consent* does not have the capacity to *refuse* to be subjected to treatment? The concept that a person with the necessary degree of maturity can be compelled against his or her will to undergo treatment which he or she has conscientiously decided to reject seems not only inconsistent with principle but likely to be repugnant in its practical administration.

Moreover, this approach seems inconsistent with the policy adopted by Parliament in the Children Act 1989. As will be seen, that legislation clearly embodies the concept that a mature minor has a right to decide (or, to use Lord Donaldson's terminology, to determine). For example, although the court has power under the Children Act 1989 in certain circumstances to make an emergency protection order in respect of a child and to give directions with respect to medical or psychiatric examination or other assessment, the Act (Children Act 1989, s.44(7)) specifically provides that the child "may, if he or she is of sufficient understanding to make an informed decision, refuse to submit to the examination or other assessment"; and there are other similar provisions.

On this point, Lord Donaldson stands alone. The other two Lords Justice did not agree with him, and it is to be hoped that this idiosyncratic view will be rejected by the House of Lords, and that it will not in the meantime be followed.

Has the court power to override a mature minor's refusal?

A much more difficult issue was whether the court in the exercise   **11–29** of its wardship jurisdiction (as to which see para. 14–14 below) could consent to medical treatment when the ward had declined it. All three Lords Justice were agreed that the wardship jurisdiction was derived from the duty of the crown to protect its subjects and particularly children, and that the wardship judge was exercising the authority of the parent "as national parent" (to quote Staughton L.J. at p. 189). It followed that the court in wardship had the right to override the wishes of a child; and the case (to this extent) follows an earlier decision of the court in its wardship jurisdiction in which a young girl was placed in secure accommodation effectively because she was guilty of anti-social behaviour of which her parents disapproved: see *Re SW (A Minor) (Wardship: Jurisdiction)* [1986] 1 FLR 24.

There can, of course, be no question that the state does have a right to override the wishes of its citizens in certain circumstances. Courts exercise the judicial power of the state (Contempt of Court Act 1981, s.19) and coercion is a necessary part of that function. But the question which *Re R* highlights—but does not resolve—is the basis on which the state is entitled to coerce citizens into taking action "in his or her own best interests." It appears to be the view of the Court of Appeal that minority is a sufficient basis for assuming such a power. But if minority, what about senescence? Does it suffice that a person is unable to form rational and well informed views? Where is the line to be drawn? What justification of principle (as distinct from historical explanation) is there for making so much depend on the particular moment at which a person becomes chronologically an adult?

Interference with parental rights—a wrong without a remedy?

11–30   One further point about the nature of parental rights must be mentioned. Mrs Gillick's claim was based on the proposition that the Health Authority's advice "interfered with her parental rights"; but the House of Lords' decision was based firmly on a public law approach. The advice was not erroneous in law, and Mrs Gillick's application for a declaration had properly been rejected. But supposing that, on the facts, the decision had been different and that the advice had been wrong? Supposing that contraceptive treatment had been provided to a child who was not *Gillick*-competent? Could the aggrieved parent sue for damages for interference with parental right?

This question arose—and was resolved—in *F* v. *Metropolitan Borough of Wirral DC and Another* [1991] 2 FLR 114, where a mother claimed damages for interference by a local authority with her parental rights and in particular with the mutual right of parent and child to enjoy one and another's company. The mother claimed that any unjustifiable violation of a legal right committed knowingly gave rise to an action in tort, and that accordingly she was entitled to damages; but the Court of Appeal—in judgments displaying a wealth of erudition and careful analysis—held that her claim had properly been struck out as disclosing no reasonable cause of action. The "parental rights" which the courts recognise stem from the parental duty towards the child to care for and protect the child, and are subservient to the child's welfare; and, for that reason, there is no remedy in damages, for the parents' benefit, for interference with such a right. This conclusion can be justified not only in principle but also historically: whereas a man could, (until those causes of action were abolished by statute in the latter part of the 20th century) sue for the loss of his wife's services or her society, he could only sue for loss of a child's services. There was no cause of action in damages for loss of a child's company or society. In effect therefore, the parental right is a "right" of a very special kind. Although there are legal remedies for interference with the right (for example, in a proper case a parent could use the writ of habeas corpus to reclaim a child: *Lough* v. *Ward* [1945] 2 All ER 338); and although public law remedies may be available in respect of interference by a public agency (such as a local authority) the traditional remedy for interference with a legal right—the action for damages at common law—is denied.

Parental rights and the courts: the welfare principle

The *Gillick* decision—whatever its precise effect—limits the scope **11–31** and extent of parental authority over a mature child but in many ways its practical impact is not as great as might be thought. This is because for many years it had been the law that when a court determined any question with respect to the upbringing of a child, or the administration of a child's property or the application of any income arising from it, the child's welfare was to be the court's paramount consideration: see now Children Act 1989, s.1(1), embodying a principle first given statutory form by the Guardianship of Infants Act 1925. Hence questions of entitlement to parental rights become largely irrelevant if legal proceedings are brought relating to the child's upbringing. The child's welfare overrides the wishes of natural parents, and even overrides considerations of doing justice to the parents.

The leading case is the decision of the House of Lords in *J* v. *C* [1970] AC 668:

> Should a 10-year-old child be returned to his "unimpeachable" natural parents in Spain, or should he continue to be in the care of the English foster parents who had looked after him for most of his life? It was held that to return a child who had been brought up as an English boy with English ways to a strange environment and to parents who would have had difficulty in coping with his problems of readjustment, would be inconsistent with his welfare; and the House of Lords unequivocally accepted that the "welfare" test applied even when the dispute was between unimpeachable parents and someone who had no biological or legal links with the child at all.

Again:

> In *Re B (A Minor) (Wardship: Medical Treatment)* (1981) 3 FLR 117 the parents of a new-born and severely handicapped Down's Syndrome child decided to refuse their consent to the surgical removal of a potentially fatal intestinal blockage. The parents thought that in all the circumstances the kindest thing would be to allow nature to take its course. The Court of Appeal held that it was in the child's interests to be allowed to live. The court was unconvinced that the child's life was "demonstrably going to be so awful that the child must be condemned to die."

—and in fact, it has now become almost commonplace for courts to overrule parental decisions about medical procedures (see, for further examples, *Re P (A Minor)* [1986] 1 FLR 272 (abortion carried out on 15-year-old girl notwithstanding parental opposition); and *Re E* (1990) September 21; blood transfusion to be carried out on 15-year-old boy despite his and his parents' religious objections).

Since no one can now be confident that the parent's "authority" to act on behalf of a child will not be overridden by the court it can fairly be said that to talk of "parental rights" is (as the Law Commission put it) "not only inaccurate as a matter of juristic analysis but also a misleading use of ordinary language" (Report on Illegitimacy, Law Com. No. 118 (1982) para. 4.18).

However, it would be wrong to draw from this the conclusion that parental authority is unimportant. On the contrary, it remains a concept of vital importance for reasons also stated by the Law Commission in its Report on *Illegitimacy* para. 4.19:

> " ... under our law, unless and until a court order is obtained, a person with parental rights is legally empowered to take action in respect of a child in exercise of those rights. It is true that if appropriate procedures are initiated he or she may be restrained from exercising those rights if it is not in the child's interests that he or she should do so; but unless and until such action is taken the person with parental authority would be legally entitled to act. It is self-evident that the court cannot intervene until its powers have been invoked, and in many cases this intervention might well come too late to be effective. ... "

It is true that this statement must now be read subject to certain qualifications subsequently made necessary by statute (see, *e.g.* the provisions of the Child Abduction Act 1984 which impose restrictions on the exercise of a parent's right to remove a child from the United Kingdom) and case law (see, *e.g. Re B (A Minor) (Wardship: Sterilisation)* [1987] 2 FLR 314, 324, *per* Lord Templeman—parental consent not sufficient authority for sterilisation of a girl under 18). But it is still true that the question of who can take legally effective action on behalf of a person under 18 remains significant; and that accordingly questions of entitlement to parental rights cannot be ignored.

11–32　*Parents best for children?* There is also one other—in practice extremely and perhaps increasingly important—respect in which legal parentage is of significance. This is that the courts inevitably seek to give weight to the claims of a parent as the person best fitted to bring up a child. To cite Lord Templeman once again:

> "The best person to bring up a child is the natural parent. It matters not whether the parent is wise or foolish, rich or poor, educated or illiterate,

provided the child's moral and physical health are not in danger. Public authorities cannot improve on nature." (*Re KD (A Minor) (Access: Principles)* [1988] 2 FLR 139, 142, HL).

It now seems clear that this approach is not restricted to cases (such as *Re L (A Minor) (Care Proceedings: Wardship) (No. 2)* [1991] 1 FLR 29) in which there is a dispute between the parent or other relative on the one hand and a public authority on the other, but that it is equally applicable to disputes between relatives: see, for example, *Re K (A Minor) (Custody)* [1990] 2 FLR 64—father and uncle; *Re K (A Minor) (Wardship: Adoption)* [1991] 1 FLR 57—parents and private adopters; *Re C (A Minor) (Adoption)* [1992] 2 FLR 115 (mother, who wanted child to be adopted, and father). The precise formulation of the weight to be given to the parental view is, however, a matter of considerable difficulty.

The new vocabulary—parental responsibility and the Children Act 1989

Words such as "rights" and "authority" have unfortunate connota- **11–33** tions and it had long been accepted that the interests of parents might better be described as "responsibilities," "duties," "authority" or "power." In accordance with this approach, the Children Act 1989 abandons the precedent of earlier legislation framed in terms of "the parental rights and duties" and adopts the term "parental responsibility" in its place. The legislature's use of these words as a key concept emphasised (said the Lord Chancellor) "the reason and sole justification for parental status, namely the duty to raise the child to become a properly developed adult both physically and morally." ((1989) 139 New L.J. 505). However, the Act (s.3) defines "parental responsibility" as meaning "all the rights, duties, powers, responsibilities and authority which by law a parent of a child has in relation to the child and his property." The Children Act therefore does nothing directly to define or alter the scope and extent of parental authority; and the expression "parental responsibility" may in this context be thought to be no more than a useful shorthand expression in the drafting of the provisions identifying those who are to be entitled to act on a child's behalf. Moreover, the Act does nothing at all to meet the criticism that it is "unsatisfactory and unfair to expect people to work with a definition of parental rights which says in effect that parental rights are what the common law says they are, without providing other assistance" [Scottish Law Commission Discussion Paper No. 88, para. 2.10]; and, in a number of detailed respects, the term seems misleading: see paras. 11–44—11–47 below. But—leaving on one side the question of whether it would have been desirable to seek to define the content of parental authority—it is clear that those concerned with the drafting of the Children Act hoped that the use of the expression "parental responsibility" would of itself be beneficial. In this view the perceptions of those who work within the law are vital; and the word "responsibility" was chosen in order to illuminate and reinforce the view of the purpose of parental authority set out above—a perception which is far removed from the concept of parental authority as recognised in this country at least until the end of the last century in which a parent's right could realistically be perceived in absolute and exclusive terms.

Who is entitled to exercise parental authority?

11–34 We have already seen (paras. 11–11 to 11–12) how the law responds to the problems of defining parentage and identifying the persons who are to be regarded as a child's "parents"; but that does not necessarily conclude the issue of who has "parental responsibility" for a child. The Children Act 1989 codifies, clarifies, and in some respects reforms, the law on this subject. Under the Act, the following persons have "parental responsibility":

11–35 1. *Both parents of a legitimate child.* The Children Act provides that where a child's mother and father were "married to each other at the time of his birth" they should each have parental responsibility for a child. In fact, (as explained at para. 11–22 above) the formula "married to each other at the time of his birth" does not mean what it says: the question is in reality whether the child is legitimate or not.

11–36 2. *The mother of an illegitimate child.* The Children Act 1989 provides that the mother of an illegitimate child shall have parental responsibility, but that the father should not have parental responsibility unless he acquires it in accordance with the provisions of the Act: s.2(2). The Act provides two procedures whereby a father may acquire parental responsibility where it would be in the child's interests that he should do so:

11–37 (i) *By the making of a parental responsibility order.* The court may on the father's application order that he "shall have parental responsibility for the child": Children Act 1989, s.4(1)(*a*). The effect of such an order would be to put the father effectively in the same position as if the child were legitimate: see para. 14–12 below.

11–38 (ii) *By the parents making a parental responsibility agreement.* The Act provides that the father and mother of an illegitimate child may by agreement provide for the father to have parental responsibility for the child: Children Act 1989, s.4(1)(*b*). The agreement must be in the form prescribed by regulations, and must be filed in the Principal Registry of the Family Division in accordance with the Parental Responsibility Agreement Regulations 1991 (SI No. 1478).

11–39 3. *The adoptive parents of an adopted child* have parental responsibility; and the making of an adoption order operates to extinguish the parental responsibility vested immediately before the making of the order in any other person: Adoption Act 1976, s.12(3), as amended by the Children Act 1989: see para. 12–01 below.

4. The Children Act provides for parents and guardians to appoint **11–40** other individuals to be the child's guardian by will or written instrument, whilst in some circumstances the court may appoint a guardian: s.5; and it is provided that *a guardian* should have parental responsibility when his or her appointment takes effect. Broadly speaking, an appointment only takes effect on the death of the last person to have parental responsibility for a child: Children Act 1989, s.5(7).

5. *Other persons who have parental responsibility consequent on the* **11–41** *making of a court order.* The Children Act adopts the general principle that the person who is actually looking after a child should have the necessary powers and authority to do so; and the Act provides that in two cases parental responsibility should automatically be given to the person in whose favour an order under the Act has been made:

(a) *Residence order.* Where the court makes a residence order (see **11–42** para. 13–09 below) in favour of a person who is not a parent or guardian of the child, that person has parental responsibility for the child for so long as the order remains in force (Children Act 1989, s.12(2)); and the Act provides (s.12(3)) that the parental authority flowing from the making of a residence order does not include the right to consent to the making of adoption orders or the right to appoint a guardian for the child.

(b) *Care orders and emergency protection orders.* While a care order is in **11–43** force with respect to a child, the local authority designated by the order has parental responsibility for the child: s.33(3)(*a*). But once again, the scope of the parental responsibility is in this case limited in so far as it does not extend to giving agreement to adoption or to the appointment of a guardian, nor does it give the local authority the right to cause the child to be brought up in a different religious persuasion from that in which he would have been brought up had the order not been made: s.33(6).

The Children Act is silent about the situation where the child is a ward of court. The Act does nothing to affect the long-established principle that the court's consent is required to all important decisions about the child's upbringing: see below, para. 14–14. (In practice of course the court will delegate routine decisions to those to whom it entrusts the daily care of the child.)

Divided "parental responsibility"

In many cases there will, as a result of the application of these **11–44** rules, be more than one person who has parental responsibility (and thus parental authority) in respect of a particular child. The Children Act has in fact increased the likelihood of this being the case, because one of the Act's underlying principles is that parental responsibility is not easily lost: in particular, a person with parental responsibility does not lose it solely because another person also acquires parental responsibility: Children Act 1989, s.2(6). For example, suppose the court makes a residence order in favour of the two grandparents of a legitimate child. It follows that they will both have parental responsibility (CA 1989, s.12(2); para. 11–40 above); but the child's parents will have acquired parental responsibility for the child at birth, and they do not lose it merely because of the making of the residence order in favour of the grandparents.

The Act deals with this situation by providing that where more than one person has parental responsibility for a child, each of those persons may act alone and without the other in "meeting that responsibility": s.2(7). This principle—in effect, that parental responsibility is enjoyed jointly and severally—is convenient in practical terms: it will be sufficient to find *one* person with parental responsibility in order to give agreement to emergency surgery, for example. But the convenience is purchased at the cost of creating potential difficulties where those who share parental responsibility are not on good terms. The Act provides a partial remedy for this problem by a provision (s.2(8)) that parental responsibility does not entitle a person to act inconsistently with any order made with respect to the child under the Act. Thus, if the court makes a residence order in favour of one of the parents on divorce, the other—although still possessing parental responsibility—would not be entitled to do anything incompatible with the residence order—for example, removing the child from home.

The most dramatic example of a potential clash is where the court makes a care order. In many cases, the parents will be opposed to the making of the order, and it is not easy to see why a local authority should wish to obtain a care order unless it envisages a real prospect of having to exercise—or to threaten to exercise—compulsion against the parents. But the Act adheres to the philosophy that the fact that a local authority has acquired parental responsibility should not deprive the parents of their responsibility; and it seeks to deal with—the often very real—potential conflict by providing that the local authority should have power "to determine the extent to which a parent or guardian of the child may meet his parental responsibility for the child": s.33(3)(b). In effect, therefore, this provision gives the local authority power to restrict the parents' exercise of parental authority; but it is also provided that the authority may only exercise that power if satisfied that it is "necessary" to do so in order to safeguard or promote the child's welfare: s.33(4); see further para. 15–18 below.

Responsibility not transferable

11–45   The Act (s.2(9)) prohibits surrender or transfer of parental responsibility; but expressly permits arrangements for "some or all of it to be met "by one or more persons acting on behalf of the person with parental responsibility. But the making of such an arrangement does not affect any liability of the person making it which may arise from a failure to meet the responsibility: s.12(11)."

Responsibility without responsibility?

The expression "parental responsibility" is in some respects rather **11–46** misleading. For example, the father of an illegitimate child does not have parental responsibility unless there is a parental responsibility agreement or the court has made an order in his favour. But this does not mean that such a person has no responsibility to support the child: the Child Support and Social Security legislation impose such an obligation on the father, and he may also be subject to orders under the Children Act to make financial provision for the child. It would perhaps surprise a layman, told in one breath that he had no parental responsibility for a child, to be told in the next breath that he did nonetheless have an obligation to support the child.

Again, a step-parent does not (as such) have parental responsibility; and accordingly a step-parent, in the absence of a court order, has no legal authority over the child. Yet the child will almost certainly be a "child of the (step-parent's) family," with the result that the court will have jurisdiction to make financial orders against the step-parent under the Children Act or the divorce legislation: see para. 10–06, above.

Authority without responsibility?

Conversely, in some cases the Children Act confers authority, but **11–47** does not provide any machinery whereby the person with such authority can be made to discharge any duty of support. For example, although a guardian has "parental responsibility" for a child, the Act provides no procedure whereby a guardian can, as such, be required to provide financial support for the child. Again, a person who has parental responsibility as a consequence of having a residence order made in his favour does not thereby come under any obligation to provide financial support for the child.

Emergency action by a person without parental responsibility

The Act (s.3(5)) provides that a person who "has care" of a child **11–48** without having parental responsibility may do "what is reasonable in all the circumstances of the case for the purpose of safeguarding or promoting the child's welfare." This would obviously permit someone caring for a child in the parent's absence to arrange emergency medical treatment; but its scope is unclear.

SUGGESTIONS FOR FURTHER READING

Hoggett and Pearl, Chap. 10 and 11.
G. Douglas, *Law, Fertility and Reproduction* (1991).

Law Commission Report No. 118, *Illegitimacy* (1982).

Law Commission Report No. 157, *Illegitimacy (Second Report)* (1986).

A. Bainham, "When is a Parent not a Parent? Reflections on the unmarried father and his child in English Law" (1989) 3 1JLF 208.

R. Collins and A. Macleod, "Denials of Paternity: The Impact of DNA Tests on Court Proceedings" [1991] JSWFL 209.

An Introduction to the Children Act 1989, HMSO (1989), Chap. 2.

J. Eekelaar, "The Emergence of Children's Rights" (1986) 6 OJLS 161.

J. Eekelaar, "Parental Responsibility: State of Nature or Nature of the State" [1991] JSWFL 37.

Chapter 12

CHANGING FAMILIES BY LEGAL PROCESS—ADOPTION

INTRODUCTION

The legal theory of adoption is simple and dramatic. An adoption **12–01** order irrevocably transfers a child from one family to another. It does this by vesting parental responsibility for a child in the adopters and extinguishing the parental responsibility of the birth parents: Adoption Act 1976, s.12(1). The same Act provides (s.39) that the effect of an adoption order is that the child is thenceforth treated as if he or she had been born as a child of the adopters' marriage, and not as the child of anyone else; and it declares that the legislation prevents an adopted child from being illegitimate: AA 1976, s.39. In principle, therefore, the adopted child is treated for succession purposes as a member of his adoptive family and not of his birth family; and a child adopted by a British citizen becomes a British citizen if he or she was not one already: British Nationality Act 1981, s.1(5).

There are certain statutory modifications of the general principle—for example, the prohibited degrees of marriage between the adopted child and the birth family are unaffected; and although the child is brought within the prohibited degrees in relation to his or her adoptive parents, the legislation does not create any prohibitions on marriage with other members of the adoptive family—so that an adopted child may legally marry his adoptive sister, for example, not to say his adoptive grandmother. But notwithstanding this exception the general principle remains clear; and it is because adoption effects in substance a legal transfer of the child from one family to another that it seems appropriate to outline the relevant legal rules at this stage. Indeed, it might be analytically correct to incorporate the treatment of adoption in the discussion of legal parentage: para. 11–01 above. But logic must sometimes yield to expediency, and—as will become apparent—the subject of adoption requires a chapter to itself.

Changing concepts of adoption. This concept of adoption—with its corollary of a complete severance between the old family and the new (and until 1975 the policy of preserving secrecy so that there the child and his birth parents could never subsequently re-establish contact) may have reflected the social realities when the legal institution of adoption was first created in English law by the Adoption Act 1926, and possibly for many years thereafter. The fact that the institution of adoption filled a need can be seen from the statistics which show that the number of adoption orders made each year increased steadily to a peak of 26,986 in 1968.

It seems that adoption was for long seen primarily as a method whereby a healthy, white (and usually illegitimate) baby would be placed with a childless couple who would bring him or her up as their own child. But adoptions of this kind are no longer typical: in 1986 only 452 adoption orders were made in respect of illegitimate children aged under six months in favour of adopters neither of whom was a parent. Moreover, in recent years there has been a sharp and—until very recently—fairly steady decline in the total number of orders made each year: in 1989, only 7,044 orders were registered.

Adoption increasingly used for children in care: permanency planning. It seems clear that the purposes for which adoption is used are changing: a number of factors—not least the practice of terminating unwanted pregnancies, and the greater readiness of society to accept the lone parent and to support her and her child by welfare and housing benefits—have sharply reduced one source of babies likely to be placed for adoption; whilst at much the same time the concern to achieve permanency and security for children who have come into local authority care because their relationship with their birth parents has broken down (or never existed) has had an important impact. Adoption has come to be seen as the appropriate solution for many children in care, and in particular for those who have traditionally been regarded as difficult to place—for example because they were of mixed race, handicapped or had emotional or behavioural problems. As part of the same trend, adoption is now often used for older children: in 1972, 12 per cent. of adoption orders were in respect of children aged 10 or over; in 1989 the comparable figure was 26 per cent. and more than half of all adoptions were of children aged five or over.

Organisational factors have also been significant. Traditionally adoption services were provided by voluntary agencies—often with a religious inspiration—but the Children Act 1975 imposed on every local authority a duty to establish and maintain a comprehensive adoption service: (see now Adoption Act 1976, s.1); and, although voluntary agencies still play a significant part in arranging adoptions, adoption services are increasingly regarded as merely one facet of Local Authorities' child care work. Certainly, the days when adoption was virtually the exclusive preserve of specialist voluntary agencies have long since gone.

Relative Adoptions. There was another factor which much affected the traditional concept of adoption. This was that in the 1960s and 1970s adoption became widely used by relatives—and in particular, a very large proportion of all adoptions (nearly 70 per cent. in 1975) were in favour of a parent and step-parent. The popularity of such adoptions was founded to a substantial extent on the wish of those who had re-married to integrate the child—usually the mother's child—for all legal purposes into the new family created by her re-marriage.

The factual situation in such cases was far removed from that on which the traditional notion of adoption had been based; and in 1972 a Government Committee—the Houghton Committee expressed concern about the dangers of relative adoptions. In particular, the Committee was concerned that adoption might be used to conceal the truth about the child's parentage (so that the child adopted by her grandparents might be led to think that her mother was her sister). Another important concern was that adoption by a step-parent might be used to sever the child's relationship—in law and in fact—with the birth parent after divorce. These concerns were influential and the Children Act 1975 introduced specific provisions designed to discourage adoptions by step-parents and relatives unless there were special circumstances making adoption desirable in the interest of the child's welfare. But these provisions were, in practice, found to be unsatisfactory and not easy to apply; and they have been repealed by the Children Act 1989: see para. 12–28 below.

Legal transplant desirable?

It will have become apparent that the uses to which adoption has **12–02** increasingly been put create a certain tension between the so-called "total transplant" concept of adoption, firmly embedded in the statutory framework, and practical reality. In particular, it has come to be questioned whether the law should not permit, or even in some cases facilitate, the retention by an adopted person of legal links with the birth family.

The legislation was originally formulated on the assumption that there would be no contact at all. Such contact would (it was thought) be undesirable not only in the child's interest, but in the interests both of the adopting parents (who might find themselves harassed by the birth parents) and of the birth mother who might have agreed to place her child for adoption only on the basis that she could conceal from everyone—including perhaps her husband—the fact that she had ever born a child. The legislation therefore provided—and still provides—a procedure enabling adoptive parents to conceal their identity from the birth parents. But it has for long been regarded as good practice for a child to be brought up in the knowledge of his or her true parentage and of the circumstances leading up to the adoption; and adoptive parents are given written background information about the child and the birth family in an attempt to help them bring up the child in the knowledge of the adoption from an early age: see Annex C to DHSS LAC (84)(3).

This trend which recognises the wish of many adopted people to trace their genetic origins (and also, sometimes, the wish of the birth parents to know what has become of the child) also influenced the enactment of two important statutory provisions. First, on attaining the age of 18, an adopted child is now entitled to access to the original birth records which will reveal his or her original name and parentage in so far as that is recorded: AA 1976, s.51. Secondly, an *adoption contact register* has been established: relatives of an adopted person who wish to contact him or her can have their details recorded in the register, and the information will be passed on if the adopted person has given notice indicating a wish to contact relatives: AA 1976, s.51A (as inserted by Children Act 1989, Sched. 10, para. 21).

No doubt, in many cases it will be beneficial to all concerned to facilitate contact between the adopted person and the birth family; but it appears that some birth parents have suffered grave distress when traced and approached by an adopted person, and the disturbing facts of *R* v. *Registrar General, ex parte Smith* [1991] 1 FLR 255, CA, show all too clearly the dangers which disclosure and openness may create:

> The applicant was a patient in Broadmoor Hospital who had brutally and sadistically murdered a fellow prisoner (apparently under the delusion that the victim was his adoptive mother). Disturbed and unstable, he continued to express hatred for his adoptive parents. He exercised his statutory right to seek the information which would enable him to trace his birth certificate, and thereby to be in a position to trace his birth parents. There were real fears that he would seek to harm the birth parents, whom he blamed for his problems; and the Court of Appeal accepted that, in the circumstances, it had been right to deny him the statutory right of access to his birth certificate.

The provisions designed to achieve what may be described as a clean break between the child and the birth parents are obviously of little relevance in the increasing number of cases where an adoption order is made in respect of an older child. In these cases, the child will often no doubt continue to have links with the birth family: the adoption order cuts the legal tie between the child and his birth family, but it does not and could not necessarily cut the factual tie. All that it can do is to confer on the adoptive parents the same right as any other parent would have to exercise parental authority by restraining (or permitting) contact between the child and others. In some cases the birth parents (and others, such as the child's grandparents) have evidently been concerned that the adopters might prevent contact, and have asked the court to make legally binding provision for continuing contact: see para. 12–28 below.

THE SOCIAL WORK ELEMENT IN THE ADOPTION PROCESS

12-03   The belief that adoption is different from other legal procedures concerned with the upbringing of children is vividly illustrated by the elaborate code of delegated legislation dealing with the preliminaries to the making of an order. Only the court can make an adoption order, but the court cannot itself carry out any adequate investigation of the issues which arise in deciding whether the making of an adoption order would be for the benefit of the child. Accordingly, it is necessary for these investigations to be made by skilled experts whose assessment will be available to the court; and adoption agencies—whether local authorities or voluntary agencies—have a vital part to play in these matters. Their duties are now prescribed in detail by rules (the Adoption Agencies Regulations 1983) while other rules—notably the Adoption Rules 1984—prescribe in detail the content of the reports which must be provided to the court.

It is important to have some understanding of these procedures, not only because a great deal of adoption practice is governed by them, but also to enable the reader to make a comparison with the, generally much less elaborate procedures applicable to other cases concerned with the upbringing of children.

A job for experts: independent placements prohibited

Until 1982 there was nothing to stop private individuals (such as **12–04** doctors or the matrons of maternity homes) from arranging adoption placements; but it is now a criminal offence for anyone other than an adoption agency to make arrangements for the adoption of a child or to place a child for adoption: AA 1976, s.11. For the purposes of the legislation an adoption agency is either a local authority or an adoption society approved by the DOH. (Such societies are usually described as "voluntary agencies.") There are certain exceptions to the general prohibition: in particular there is no prohibition on a private placement being made with a "relative" of the child—the term relative includes the father of an illegitimate child but not—so it has been held—a great-uncle: Adoption Act 1976, s.11(1), s.72; *Re S* [1985] FLR 579.

What is a "placement" for this purpose? It seems that there must be actual physical contact with the prospective adopters. Hence:

> In *Re A (Adoption: Placement)* [1988] 2 FLR 133 an organisation in the USA had organised an adoption by English parents in a court in El Salvador. The child was then brought to England by a representative of the American organization and handed over to the prospective adopters at a point beyond the immigration desk at the airport. It was held that there was no "placement" until that handing over, and that accordingly, there had been an illegal placement. (However, the High Court has a power to dispense with the provisions prohibiting adoptions in cases where there has been an illegal placement, and that power was exercised.)

For the sake of completeness it should also be mentioned that, as a deterrent against the practice of trafficking in children, the making of payments or the giving of rewards in connection with adoption has long been illegal. The legislation is couched in very broad language, and the courts have adopted a restrictive, but purposive, approach to its interpretation:

> In *Re Adoption Application 212/86 (Adoption: Payment)* [1987] 2 FLR 291 a woman, who wanted to help childless couples, agreed to bear a child under a surrogacy agreement. The commissioning parents undertook to pay her £10,000 (representing her loss of earnings and her expenses in connection with the pregnancy). The judge held that this was not a payment or reward for the purposes of the Adoption Act provisions since the parties only began to think of adoption after the payment had been made. Moreover, the legislation empowers the court to authorise the making of payments, (AA 1976, s.57(3)) and it was held that this power could be exercised after the event.

The Adoption Agency's duties

12–05   Statute (AA 1976, s.6) provides that in reaching any decision relating to an adoption of a child the Agency must have regard to all the circumstances, first consideration being given to the need to safeguard and promote the welfare of the child throughout childhood. Agencies are specifically required "so far as practicable" to ascertain the wishes and feelings of the child regarding the decision and give due consideration to them, having regard to the child's age and understanding: AA 1976, s.6. This general duty is elaborated in the specific procedures laid down by the Adoption Agencies Regulations 1983:

(a) *Investigation, reports and counselling*

12–06   The Agency has extensive duties to obtain reports about the child, his birth parents, and the prospective adopters. For example, it must obtain a health history covering the birth parents and their family, giving details of serious or inherited or congenital disease; and the Agency must find out the birth parents' wishes and feelings about adoption. The Agency must make a full investigation into the circumstances of the prospective adopters (including such matters as their financial position, and their previous experience of caring for children), and it must assess their ability to bring up an adopted child throughout childhood. There must be a medical report, which will include details of any daily consumption of alcohol, tobacco and habit-forming drugs. The child must be medically examined, and a detailed account produced dealing with such matters as personality and social development, educational attainment, the extent of the relationship with the birth family, and the child's wishes and feelings in relation to adoption. The Agency must also provide a counselling service for the birth parents, the child, and prospective adopters. (For an example of what this may mean in practice see *Re T (A Minor) (Adoption: Validity of Order)* [1986] 1 FLR 31.)

(b) *The adoption panel*

The Agency must establish a panel including social workers, a   **12–07**
medical adviser, and at least two independent members to consider
proposals for placement. The panel must consider all the information
and reports referred to above, and may seek other relevant
information; and it must obtain legal advice about each case. It is then
for the panel to recommend whether adoption is in the best interests
of the child, whether a prospective adopter is suitable to be the
adoptive parent, and whether he or she is suitable to be the adoptive
parent of the particular child. The Agency can only take decisions on
these matters after taking account of the panel's recommendations;
and it should be noted that, whilst it is for the panel to recommend,
it is for the Agency to decide.

(c) *Placement*

If, but only if, an Agency has decided in accordance with these   **12–08**
procedures, and after considering the recommendations of the
adoption panel, that a prospective adopter would be a suitable
adopter for a particular child, it may make written proposals to the
prospective adopter for a placement. This proposal will be accompanied by written information about the child, his or her personal
history and background, including religion and cultural background,
and the child's health history and current state of health. If the
prospective adopter accepts the proposal, the child may be "placed
for adoption."

When the child is placed, written notice must be given to the
parents of the child. Where the child is already in the care of the
prospective adopters—for example because he has been fostered with
them—they too must be given written notice.

Perhaps fortunately, it has been held (*Re T*, above) that these
complex provisions are directory rather than mandatory, and that
accordingly failure to comply with them will not invalidate the
adoption application.

The Agency also has duties to supervise the placement and to give
advice and assistance. It is then for the prospective adopter to apply
to the court for an adoption order; and if no application has been
made within three months the Agency must review the placement.

Cases where no Agency involved

Notwithstanding the policy that all adoption cases be channelled   **12–09**
through Adoption Agencies, there will still be some adoption
application cases in which no Agency has previously been involved—for example, where foster-parents or relatives apply for
adoption of a child not placed with them by an Agency. In these
cases, a local authority must be notified, and will perform
investigatory and reporting functions along the lines described above.

In recent years there has been a sharp increase in the number of
cases in which children are brought to this country with a view to

adoption, and it seems that the demands on local authorities are, in some areas, imposing considerable strains on the resources available: *R v. Secretary of State for Health, ex parte Luff* [1992] 1 FLR 59.

ADOPTION APPLICATIONS—COURT PROCEDURES

12–10   Adoption orders can only be made by "an authorised court," and proceedings must be started by the issue of an application in the form prescribed by the relevant rules. In fact, in cases not involving a foreign element, the Magistrates' Family Proceedings Court, the County Court and the High Court, all have jurisdiction to deal with adoption applications; but in recent years the great majority of applications have been to the County Court. The Children (Allocation of Proceedings) Order 1991 (SI No. 1677) provides for transfers between the different courts, and opposed applications in the County Court will normally be heard at a specialist "Family Hearing Centre": see para. 13–03 below.

The court will be supplied with a detailed report (commonly called a "Home Study Report") by the Adoption Agency. The report will deal with the child, his natural parents, and the prospective adopters—for example, it must comment on the stability of the prospective adopters' marriage, give particulars of their home and living conditions and details of income and living standards, the prospective adopters' reasons for wishing to adopt the child, and their "hopes and expectations for the child's future": Adoption Rules 1984, Sched. 2. Medical reports will also be before the court.

If it appears that a parent is unwilling to agree to the application (or there are special circumstances) the court may also appoint a *guardian ad litem* (whose duties are laid down in the Rules: Adoption Rules 1984 r.6) to investigate and report.

LEGAL REQUIREMENTS FOR MAKING OF ADOPTION ORDER

12–11   *Who may adopt and be adopted.* The legislation contains certain basic rules about the age and status of adopters:

(i) An adoptive parent must be at least 21 years of age (although a parent adopting his or her own child need only be 18 years of age).

(ii) An adoption order may be made in favour of a married couple, but with that important exception an adoption order may not be made on the application of more than one person. The result is that it is not possible for a brother and sister or an unmarried couple jointly to adopt a child.

(iii) An adoption order may be made in favour of a sole applicant, although in practice the vast majority of adoptions are joint. If a sole applicant is married an order can only be made if the court is satisfied that the applicant's spouse cannot be found, or is incapable by reason of ill health of applying, or that the spouses have separated and are living apart and that the separation is likely to be permanent.

These are the minimum requirements laid down by law about the personal attributes of adopters, but in practice, in the exercise of their discretion in arranging placements, adoption agencies are likely to apply very much more demanding tests. The law does not, for example, set an upper age limit for adopters, but in practice few agencies will accept applicants aged over forty as adopters for a healthy child.

The Act (AA 1976, s.12(5)) provides that the *person to be adopted* must never have been married and must be under 18 years of age—although, provided the other conditions are satisfied, a "child" who is nearly 18 may be adopted. For a remarkable example where an order was made in respect of a child just six days before his 18th birthday see *Re D (A Minor) (Adoption Order: Validity)* [1991] 2 FLR 1215, CA, below para. 12–14. It is not a bar to adoption that the child has been previously adopted.

Child must have lived with the applicants before the making of the order. Although, as we have seen, the court will depend very much on the detailed enquiries into all the circumstances which will have been made by the adoption agency, the legislation (AA 1976, s.13) stipulates that an adoption order must not be made unless the child is at least 19 weeks old, and has at all times during the preceding 13 weeks had his home with the applicants or one of them.

If the child has not been placed with the applicants by an adoption agency (for example, a foster-child or a child brought to this country from overseas) a longer period of 12 months is required unless the applicant or one of the applicants is a parent, step-parent or relative.

These periods are laid down to allow a period for the child to settle in the home, for the applicants to adjust to their new role as parents, and for the court to be able to assess the suitability of the placement; and there is an overriding rule that no order may be made unless the court is satisfied that the adoption agency or local authority has had sufficient opportunities to see the child with the applicants together "in the home environment": AA 1976, s.13(3).

There will thus be many cases in which a child is in the care of   **12–12**
prospective adopters who are not yet in a position to make an application for adoption. What, in such a case, is to stop a birth parent exercising his parental authority by removing the child from the prospective adopters, and thereby preventing them from satisfying the condition that the child should have his home with the applicants? There are three relevant provisions:

(i) A parent or guardian who has once agreed (even informally: *Re T (A Minor) (Adoption: Validity of Order)* [1986] 2 FLR 31, CA to the making of an adoption order is not entitled, so long as an adoption application is pending, to remove the child from the home of the person with whom the child has his home without leave of the court: AA 1976, s.27(1).

(ii) If an application to free a child for adoption (see para. 12–27 below) is pending, no parent or guardian of the child may remove the child from his or her home without the leave of the court: s.27(2). This provision (in contrast to (i) above) applies even where there has never been any parental agreement to the freeing.

(iii) If a child has had his home with a person for five years, and that person starts adoption proceedings or gives written notice of his intention to do so, the child must not be removed without leave of the court: AA 1976, s.28. This provision is widely drawn: for example, it even prevents the local authority which has boarded the child out from removing him or her from foster-parents whose adoption application it does not support.

Adoption must promote child's welfare; and parental agreement necessary

12–13   As explained at para. 11–30 above when a court determines questions relating to the upbringing of a child, the child's welfare is, in principle, the court's *paramount* consideration: Children Act 1989, s.1. Adoption is different.

Although the Act (s.6) provides that, in reaching any decision relating to the adoption of a child, a court is to give *first consideration* to the need to safeguard and promote the welfare of the child throughout his or her childhood, that provision does not override the fundamental principle that an adoption order is not to be made unless each parent or guardian of the child "freely, and with full understanding of what is involved, agrees unconditionally to the making of an adoption order" (AA 1976, s.16(1)(b)). It is true that the court does have power to dispense with parental agreement, but the grounds upon which it may do so are restricted. There is thus a clear difference of legal concept between adoption on the one hand and other methods of providing long-term substitute care for children:

(i)   An adoption order is permanent and irrevocable; other orders dealing with the child's upbringing can be varied at any time.

(ii   Adoption affects legal status—and thus such matters as the child's succession rights and citizenship. Other court orders dealing with upbringing do not have such consequences.

(iii)   Adoption severs the legal family ties with the birth parents and their relatives. Once an adoption order has been made, the parents lose the right even to apply for contact: see *Re R (A Minor) (Adoption: Access)* [1991] 2 FLR 78, CA (although, like anyone else, the birth parents could *seek leave* to apply to the court for contact with the child: see para. 14–10 below).

The result is that the court's decision on whether to make an adoption order involves a two stage process. First, the court must consider whether it would promote the child's welfare to make an adoption order; secondly if, but only if, the court decides that adoption would be in the child's interest, it will consider whether it should dispense with the parent's agreement. These are separate issues which (it has been held) should be dealt with in that order: *Re D (A Minor) (Adoption Order: Validity)* [1991] 1 FLR 48, CA.

(i) The child's welfare
The Adoption Act provides that: 12–14

"In reaching any decision relating to the adoption of a child a court or adoption agency shall have regard to all the circumstances, first consideration being given to the need to safeguard and promote the welfare of the child throughout his childhood; and shall so far as practicable ascertain the wishes and feelings of the child regarding the decision and give due consideration to them, having regard to his age and understanding."

The precise effect of this provision is not easy to state, and consideration of the case law suggests that the courts' attitude to the benefits conferred by adoption vary from time to time. Thus:

In *Re K (A Minor) (Wardship: Adoption)* [1991] 1 FLR 57 the mother became unexpectedly pregnant at a time of particular difficulty and stress in a stormy and unstable marriage. She went to a Greek restaurant, where she met a middle-aged childless couple who wanted to care for a child on a long-term basis. The baby was handed over by the mother six weeks after the birth, but the mother soon decided that she wanted the child back. The Court of Appeal unanimously held that the adoption by the couple would not be in the child's best interest. In particular, their age counted against them: they would be 65 and 57 when the child was 10; and their background—in terms of origins, language and religion—was in every way different from the child's. A factor of crucial importance was that the mother genuinely wanted her child back and that she had cared properly for her other children; and accordingly it would not be in the child's interest to deprive her of any chance of her own family: *per* Butler-Sloss L.J., at p. 62.

This cautious attitude towards the benefits of adoption has been even more forcefully expressed by a Circuit Judge:

> In *Re L (A Minor) (Care Proceedings: Wardship) (No. 2)* [1991] 1 FLR 29 the
> local authority—whose conduct of the case was severely criticised by the
> Judge—considered that a child should be adopted, notwithstanding the
> fact that the child's grandparents wished to care for her. Judge Willis said
> that adoption was a trial and error situation about which too little was
> known. "Many adopted people start looking for their roots, particularly
> in adolescence ... adoption should only be the last resort when no-one
> in the wider family is available and suitable to look after a child.
> Parentage is not always perfect, but parentage in the family is preferable
> to the unknown risks of adoption." The Judge stated that every child had
> a right, whenever possible, to be brought up by its own genetic family,
> and that there must be "strong, cogent and positive reasons" for denying
> that right.

This citation states one extreme of the range of views which may be
held about the desirability of adoption in principle. Of course, any
realistic prospect that the child could be integrated into its birth
family should be explored before a decision is taken to sever all legal
links between the child and the birth family. But the question is
essentially one of evidence; and it will often be possible to
demonstrate that adoption will (as compared with other legal
procedures) confer positive benefits on the child. For example:

> In *Re S (Adoption or Custodianship)* [1987] 2 FLR 331, CA, the Court had
> (under statutory provisions subsequently repealed) to weigh up the
> advantages of adoption against some other form of order which would
> give the child's grandparents long term care. The court considered that
> adoption would give greater legal security for the child's relationship
> with those caring for him and would minimise the risk of disruption.

Again:

> In *Re R (Adoption)* [1967] 1 WLR 34, an adoption order was made in
> respect of a refugee from a totalitarian country notwithstanding the fact
> that he was only a little below the age of majority. Adoption would be
> beneficial in giving the refugee the social and psychological benefits of
> truly belonging to a family as well as the benefit of acquiring British
> nationality.

> In *Re D (A Minor) (Adoption Order: Validity)* [1991] 2 FLR 66, CA, foster-
> parents applied to adopt a severely handicapped child six days before he
> attained his majority. The court rejected an argument that the only
> permissible purpose of adoption was to promote the child's welfare
> during minority.

The question of what would be beneficial to a child may involve
difficult considerations of racial or ethnic identity:

> In *Re N (A Minor) (Adoption)* [1990] 1 FLR 58 a black illegitimate child was
> placed with white foster parents under a private fostering agreement.

The child remained in their care for more than three years, and they applied for an adoption order. The judge considered that adoption would not be in the child's interest because the child's father would have a useful and important part to play in her life when she wanted to seek out her cultural roots. The child should remain in the foster parent's care, but remain legally her birth parents' child.

However, it should be noted that the adoption legislation does not (in this respect in sharp contrast to the Children Act 1989: see para. 13–19 below) contain any direct guidance as to how the child's welfare should be assessed. This issue is in practice left to be dealt with in the reports furnished to the courts. No doubt in making the assessment of the extent to which adoption would be likely to promote the child's welfare the court will now take into account the possibility that the child's future could better be dealt with by orders under the Children Act 1989 dealing with such matters as the child's residence, contact with the child, but having a much less drastic effect on the child's legal status.

Finally, it may be noted that the child's wishes are relevant to the assessment of the child's welfare; but whereas the agreement of the child's parent or guardian is always required (unless dispensed with by the court: see below) the agreement of the child to the making of an adoption order is never required. To some this seems anomalous.

(ii) Parental agreement; dispensing with agreement

Adoption, in principle, requires parental agreement (see para.   **12–15** 12–13); and it should be noted that the agreement of the mother is ineffective until six weeks after the child's birth: AA 1976, ss.16(4), 18(4). The court must appoint a reporting officer to ensure (amongst other things) that the parent understands fully what adoption involves and is willing to agree without condition. The reporting officer is to witness the parents' written agreement: Adoption Rules 1984, r. 5. If it appears that a parent or guardian is unwilling to agree to the making of the adoption order, the court must appoint a *guardian ad litem* to safeguard the child's welfare, and carry out prescribed duties: Adoption Rules, r. 18(1). A parent may withdraw the agreement at any time before the making of the order.

It seems that some parents are reluctant to "sign away" their children, even though in fact they realise that adoption is inevitable and in the child's interests. It also appears that in recent years there has been a greater readiness for agencies to pursue adoption applications notwithstanding the lack of parental agreement.

Who is the child's parent?

The agreement required is that of the child's parent or guardian.   **12–16** The father of an illegitimate child is not for these purposes regarded as the child's "parent" unless the father has parental responsibility for the child: Children Act 1989, Sched. 10, para. 30 (7). Such parental responsibility may flow from the fact that the child's parents have made a parental rights agreement, or that the court has made a parental rights order or a residence order in favour of the father: see paras. 13–09 and 14–12 below. The fact that the making of a parental rights order will give the father a special standing in adoption has been seen to be a factor influencing the court in favour of making such an order in the child's interests: *D* v. *Hereford and Worcester CC* [1991] 1 FLR 205: *Re H (Illegitimate Children: Father Parental Rights) (No. 2)* [1991] 1 FLR 214.

The Act provides six grounds on which the court may dispense with the parent's (or guardian's) agreement to adoption:

(1) Cannot be found or is incapable of giving agreement

12–17   This provision will normally apply to cases where the whereabouts of the person whose consent is required are unknown and cannot be discovered, or where he or she lacks the mental capacity to give consent. But it has been held that a person "cannot be found" for the purposes of this section if there are no practical means of communication, even if the physical whereabouts are in fact known:

> In *Re R (Adoption)* [1967] 1 WLR 34 the parents lived in a totalitarian country and any attempt to communicate with them would involve embarrassment and danger. The court dispensed with their agreement.

(2) Is withholding his agreement unreasonably

12–18   The leading case on the interpretation of this provision (which is much the most frequently invoked ground for dispensing with agreement) is *Re W (An Infant)* [1971] AC 682 in which the House of Lords laid down a number of principles. The case law now seems to establish:

12–19   **(i) Child's welfare not only factor.** There is a clear distinction between adoption and cases merely concerned with the child's upbringing; and the legal relationship of parent and child is not to be sundered lightly and without good reason. The fact that the court is required by statute (AA 1976, s.6, para. 12–13 above) to give "first consideration" to the child's welfare has not altered that principle: *Re P (An Infant) (Adoption: Parental Consent)* [1977] Fam 25. Thus, a parent may in deciding whether or not to agree to adoption, reasonably take into account not only the welfare of the child, but also the parent's own wishes and welfare, and the welfare of other persons (such as siblings and grandparents) who would be affected. For example:

> In *Re V (A Minor) (Adoption: Dispensing with Agreement)* [1987] 2 FLR 89, the mother had left her 21-month-old daughter with foster-parents. At one time the mother agreed that the foster-parents should adopt the

child, but she changed her mind; and by the time of the hearing (when the child had been with the foster-parents for nearly three years) she had decided that in the long term she wanted the child back to live with her and her two younger children. The Court of Appeal held that the court should not have dispensed with the mother's agreement. It was not unreasonable for the mother to hope to reunite her family. The foster-parents should continue to have the care of the child; but the mother should have contact with her.

(ii) Child's welfare relevant to extent that reasonable parent would **12–20**
so regard it. In the words of Lord Hailsham:

" ... the fact that a reasonable parent does pay regard to the welfare of his child must enter into the question of reasonableness as a relevant factor. It is relevant in all cases if and to the extent that a reasonable parent would take it into account. It is decisive in those cases where a reasonable parent must so regard it."

In practice, this way of looking at the issue enables the court to attach considerable importance to its assessment of how far adoption would promote the child's welfare. For example:

In *Re F (Adoption: Parental Agreement)* [1982] FLR 101 a two year-old child who had been ill-treated and neglected by his mother was placed with foster-parents in whose care he remained at the hearing of their adoption application three years later. The mother accepted that the child should remain in the care of the foster parents, but nevertheless genuinely thought that it would be beneficial to the child that she should continue to have some contact with him in the future. On this basis the President of the Family Division held that a reasonable mother could reasonably conclude that she should withhold her agreement to adoption, and refused to dispense with the mother's agreement. On appeal, however, it was held that there were in fact no reasonable prospects of the mother re-establishing contact with the child, and that a reasonable parent would have accepted that it was wrong to deny the child the advantage of eliminating the uncertainty implicit in fostering arrangements.

Again:

In *Re B (A Minor) (Adoption: Parental Agreement)* [1990] 2 FLR 383, CA, foster parents applied to adopt an 11 year-old boy who had been in their care for seven years. It was not in dispute that his future lay with the applicants; and the boy himself strongly favoured adoption. However, the mother refused to agree to the making of an adoption order because she wanted to preserve her legal right to a degree of contact with the child. The Court of Appeal held that a reasonable parent would regard the advantages to the child of the legal security conferred by adoption, coupled with the fact that the child would be "devastated by the result if the adoption did not take place" and that adoption would in all probability not have any impact on continuing contact as outweighing any disadvantages. Accordingly, a reasonable parent would have come to the conclusion that adoption was in the best long-term interests of the child, and an order should be made.

It seems clear from these cases that the question of whether there is any reasonable likelihood of re-establishing a functioning familial link is regarded as crucial in assessing a parental refusal to agree to adoption.

12-21   **(iii) Test is reasonableness not culpability.** Since the test to be applied is the reasonableness of the parent's decision, the court may dispense with agreement even though the parent has been wholly innocent of any breach of parental duty and is in no way responsible for the state of affairs which has led to the adoption application:

> In *Re El-G (Minors) (Wardship and Adoption)* (1982) 4 FLR 589 the mother had been struck down by what Slade L.J. aptly described as "a series of terrible blows which destroyed her health and prevented her from fulfilling her maternal role in spite of her desire to do so." Her inability to care for her children had been entirely the result of misfortune, but the court nonetheless dispensed with her agreement.

12-22   **(iv) Court must not substitute its own view as to what is reasonable for that of parent.** It has been stressed that the court should not substitute its own view for that of the parent. This is because (to quote Lord Hailsham, in *Re W* at p. 700, again):

> "Two reasonable parents can perfectly reasonably come to opposite conclusions on the same set of facts without forfeiting their title to be regarded as reasonable. The question in any given case is whether a parental veto comes within the band of possible reasonable decisions and not whether it is right or mistaken. Not every reasonable exercise of judgment is right, and not every mistaken exercise of judgment is unreasonable. There is a band of decisions within which no court should seek to replace the individual's judgment with its own."

In effect, therefore, a decision should only be held to be unreasonable if no reasonable parent could have taken it: a parent may be wrong or mistaken without being unreasonable (*per* Balcombe L.J., *Re E (A Minor) (Adoption)* [1989] 1 FLR 126). But in practice it may be difficult for the court to avoid applying its own standards, and, indeed, there is evidence that the pendulum of judicial opinion swings between giving greater and less emphasis to the child's welfare: *Re H and W (Adoption: Parental Agreement)* (1982) 4 FLR 614 CA. There is inevitably a balance or tension between the welfare of the child and the interests of the parent; and it is exceedingly difficult to be objective about hypothetical people with hypothetical minds and decide whether they are looking at matters reasonably. As Slade L.J. put it, a parent who loves her children and is not a lawyer may well find it difficult to understand how she can ever be said to be acting unreasonably if she refuses to consent to an adoption which would deprive her of any right to maintain contact with them: *Re El-G (Minors) (Wardship and Adoption)* (1982) 4 FLR 589, 601.

(3) Has persistently failed without reasonable cause to discharge his parental responsibility for the child

In order to satisfy this ground two conditions must be fulfilled. First,   **12–23**
there must have been a persistent failure. This apparently connotes a permanent abrogation of responsibility (see *M* v. *Wigan MBC* [1980] Fam 36)—has the parent "washed his hands" of the child? Secondly, the failure must be "without reasonable cause"—

> In *Re M (An Infant)* (1965) 109 SJ 574 it was held that an unmarried mother's wish to conceal the birth from her parents was a sufficiently reasonable cause.

But *Re M* should be contrasted with:

> *Re P (Infants)* [1962] 1 WLR 1296 where the mother had simply given up the children soon after birth and had no excuse for not having them with her or at least visiting them in their foster home. (This case also establishes that parental responsibility includes both the natural and moral duty of a parent to show affection, care and interest towards the child, and the parent's legal duty of maintenance—the mother had collected welfare benefits in respect of the children but had not supported them to any significant extent.)

(4) Has abandoned or neglected the child

For this purpose the word "abandoned" has to be construed in its   **12–24**
context of neglect or persistent ill-treatment, and thus means such conduct as would expose a parent to the sanctions of the criminal law. It seems that there are few acts (short of leaving a child on a doorstep) which will satisfy the restrictively interpreted ground:

> In *Watson* v. *Nikolaisen* [1955] 2 QB 286 a mother had given her illegitimate daughter over to foster-parents who wanted to adopt her, and in whom she had confidence. The child was in the foster-parents' care for some two years, and during that time the mother made no contribution to her support—indeed, she kept the welfare benefit paid for the child—and saw her only once. The court held that she had not abandoned the child since she genuinely wanted the child to remain her's and not be adopted.

A similarly restricted interpretation has been given to the word "neglected."

(5) Has persistently ill-treated the child

12–25   If this condition is to be satisfied the ill-treatment must be persistent: see for example:

> Re A (A Minor) (Adoption: Dispensing with Consent) (1979) 2 FLR 173 where there had been severe and repeated assaults on an 11 month-old child over a period of three weeks.

But a single attack (however grave) cannot suffice. Moreover, it is the child who must be shown to have been ill-treated; and this condition was not satisfied in:

> Re F(T) (An Infant) [1970] 1 WLR 192 where the father had killed the child's mother and been convicted of manslaughter.

Again, it would seem that the court could not dispense with the parents' agreement to the adoption of one child on this ground merely because the parent had ill-treated another child in the same family.

(6) Has seriously ill-treated the child, and (whether because of the ill-treatment or for other reasons) the rehabilitation of the child in the parent's household is unlikely

12–26   In contrast to the ground of persistent ill-treatment discussed above, there is no need to show a course of conduct: a single act of ill-treatment could suffice provided that it was sufficiently serious. However, the proviso (that agreement cannot be dispensed with on this ground unless, whether because of the ill-treatment or for other reasons, the rehabilitation of the child within the household of the parent or guardian is unlikely) is important, not least because it is independent of the first condition (so that it would apparently suffice if it is the parents' deteriorating mental or physical condition, or even lack of proper housing which makes rehabilitation unlikely).

FREEING FOR ADOPTION

12–27   Until 1984 a parent could only consent to a specific adoption and that consent could be withdrawn after the child had been placed with the prospective adopters and at any time up to the making of the final order. As a result, local authorities who feared that there would have to be a traumatic contest about dispensing with the birth parent's agreement may have been reluctant to place children for adoption. Moreover, the fact that an agreement once given could nevertheless be withdrawn may well have encouraged indecisiveness on the part of the birth parents; and it certainly seems likely to have made the waiting period very tense for almost all prospective adopters.

In an attempt to deal with this problem it is now provided (AA 1976, s.18) that the court may, on the application of an adoption agency, make an order declaring a child "free for adoption"; and an adoption order may then subsequently be made without further evidence of parental consent. The court will of course only make a freeing order if it considers it to be in the interests of the child (AA 1976, s.6; para. 12–13 above); and the Act requires that the court must be satisfied in the case of each parent or guardian of the child that "he freely and with full understanding of what is involved, agrees generally and unconditionally to the making of an adoption order," or that agreement should be dispensed with on one of the grounds considered at paras. 12–17—12–26 above.

The expectation was that the "freeing procedure" would facilitate adoptions, particularly in cases where there was doubt about the birth parents' attitude (or, indeed, where it was known that they would oppose the making of an adoption order which the agency considered likely to promote the child's welfare). But in practice serious difficulties have been experienced with the "freeing" procedure. In part, this is because of the grounds upon which the court may dispense with agreement. Where a child has actually been placed for adoption, it is not too difficult for the parents to weigh up the advantages and disadvantages of adoption by the particular prospective adopters concerned; and it follows that it will not be difficult for the court to decide whether a withholding of agreement to that particular adoption is or is not unreasonable. However, where there has been no placement, the question whether a parent is unreasonable in withholding agreement is much more difficult:

In *Re E (Minors) (Adoption: Parental Agreement)* [1990] 2 FLR 397, CA, a local authority started freeing procedures at a time when the children had been with prospective adopters for only one month. There was no evidence as to how the placement had worked during that month, nor was there any evidence that the mother knew then how the placement had worked. At the time of the hearing, the court considered that the evidence did point to the conclusion that the children's welfare required that their long-term future should be with the prospective adopters, and preferably without any access by the natural mother. But the Court of Appeal held that the mother was not unreasonable in withholding her agreement: she was entitled to say that she should have a proper opportunity to demonstrate that continued contact by her with the children would be of benefit. Her action in refusing consent came within the broad band of decisions which could be regarded as reasonable, notwithstanding the fact that its effect might be to prevent the adoption of her children. It was relevant also to note that the prospective adopters were apparently prepared to continue to care for the children even if they were not able to adopt them.

There are also more technical problems which arise if a freeing order is made. To some extent, the making of a freeing order places the child in a legal limbo.

What, for example, is to happen should it prove difficult or impossible to make a successful placement? The Act provides that, unless the birth parent makes a declaration that he or she does not want to be further involved with the adoption, the parent must be informed after 12 months whether the child has been adopted or is placed for adoption. If the child has not been adopted or "placed" the parent may apply for revocation of the freeing order; but there have been difficulties in deciding whether a child has been "placed" for this purpose: *R. v. Derbyshire County Council ex parte T* [1990] 1 FLR 237. In any event, it is not clear what principle should guide the court in deciding on an application to revoke the freeing order: see Bellamy: Revocation of Freeing Orders [1990] Fam Law 352. Again, what is the position if the child reaches the age of 18 without an adoption order having been made? The effect of a freeing order is to transfer the parental responsibility for the child to the Adoption Agency, but there is no specific provision removing the child from his birth family for such purposes as succession rights. Nor is it clear what duties the Adoption Agency has in relation to the child while a freeing order is in existence.

Research has indicated that Local Authority policies in relation to freeing differ, and the procedure has not been used as extensively as was envisaged. It has been said that the process has not lived up to expectations (see generally [1990] JSWL 220, N V Lowe) and a discussion paper issued by the Department of Health as part of the Government's Review of Adoption Law concluded that freeing has, judged by the criteria originally set, failed. The Discussion Paper suggested a number of options, including the substitution of a more streamlined legal procedure to accommodate the institution of freeing. But the fundamental question is whether the benefits the freeing procedure has for prospective adopters, (who know that the issue of parental agreement has been resolved once and for all), outweigh the disadvantages which in practice the freeing procedure may bring for the birth parents.

ADOPTION AND THE CHILDREN ACT 1989

12–28   The Children Act does not effect any fundamental change in adoption law which continues to be governed by the provisions of the

Adoption Act 1976. However, the Act may indirectly have a significant impact on court decisions. This is because the Children Act classifies adoption proceedings (and freeing for adoption proceedings) as "family proceedings"; and it follows that the court will have power to make any of the orders listed in section 8 of the Children Act 1989 (see para. 13–09, below). For example, the court could, instead of making an adoption order, make a residence order in favour of the prospective adopters, or the child's grandparent. Alternatively, it would seem that it could make a contact order even if it grants the adoption application (see R White (1989) 1 JCL 41. There is, in any event, power to impose conditions on the making of an adoption order (see AA 1976, s.8(7)), and this power has been exercised, in exceptional circumstances, to impose a condition that the adoptive parents permit continued contact with the birth parent or other persons: *Re C (A Minor) (Adoption Order: Conditions)* [1988] 2 FLR 159, HL; and see *Re D (A Minor) (Adoption Order: Validity)* [1991] 2 FLR 66, HL.

REFORM OF ADOPTION LAW

The law of adoption has tended to move very much in isolation from   **12–29** other developments governing the upbringing of children. In particular, it may be questioned whether the "total transplant" concept of adoption is still appropriate in view of the numbers of children adopted by relatives, or adopted at an age when they will have recollections of their birth families. It is said that there is a conflict between the legal concept of adoption and a reality in which adopted persons are increasingly older children who frequently have a knowledge of their own families and background. It may also be questioned whether the emphasis on secrecy which (it has been said) "engulfs the adoption process" is still appropriate: DOH Consultation Paper (1990), para. 73.

Accordingly, as part of the Government's programme of Family Law reform, the Department of Health is undertaking an inter-departmental review of adoption law. The first in a series of papers on the underlying purpose of adoption canvasses the following options for reform of the adoption process:

(i) To retain the basic principle of the existing adoption law, but to provide for some modification to increase the options which are available to those affected and the courts;

(ii) To provide for two different types of irrevocable order—one of which would continue the "total transplant" policy of the existing law, the other of which would provide (effectively) an irrevocable transfer of the right to care for the child, without seeking to transplant the child for all legal purposes in the adopting family;

(iii) To establish a basic form of adoption with a variety of optional alternatives.

SUGGESTIONS FOR FURTHER READING

Hoggett and Pearl, Chap. 14.

Inter-Departmental Review of Adoption Law, Discussion Papers, (No. 1) *The Nature and Effect of Adoption* (1990); (No. 2) *Agreement and Freeing* (1991); (No. 3) *The Adoption Process* (1991).

N. Lowe and others, "The Pathways to Adoption" [1992] Fam Law 52.

Chapter 13

THE COURTS' POWERS TO MAKE ORDERS DEALING WITH CHILDREN'S UPBRINGING: THE CHILDREN ACT 1989

INTRODUCTION—THE ISSUES

Chapter 11 of this book tried to show how the law identifies a **13–01** child's parent and summarised the legal incidents of parentage. Chapter 12 described the process of adoption, which—in terms of legal consequences—means the irrevocable transfer of a child from one family group to another. We now have to explain the circumstances in which the courts—in this as in other respects exercising the judicial power of the state—can interfere in the autonomy of the family unit by making orders regulating the way in which parents bring up a child, without going so far as to deprive them of their legal identity as parents.

There are two central issues of legal policy which need to be kept in mind. First, there is the question of the *basis upon which this judicial power may be exercised*. Is it, for example, sufficient for the court to be satisfied that the child's welfare would best be served by removal from the parents; or is it necessary that some more demanding ground be established if interference and compulsion are to be justified? Secondly, *who is to have the right to initiate court proceedings relating to a child?* For example, can a neighbour who thinks that parents have an unsatisfactory life-style ask the court to make an order about how the parents should bring up their child? Should a pressure group be able to apply for an order overriding parental agreement to some form of medical procedure—perhaps the termination of a daughter's pregnancy? Should a grandparent be able to seek an order that a parent send a child to a particular school? Should a local authority be able to apply for an order that a child be removed to a children's home because the authority considers that the parents' attitude to the child's upbringing is unsatisfactory?

It is important to understand that these are distinct questions. It may, for example, be thought tolerable to allow a parent to bring any dispute about the child's upbringing to the court and to allow the court to resolve that dispute by reference solely to what the evidence suggests would be the child's interests, but intolerable to allow a neighbour or a pressure group to have the unqualified right to put parental decisions into question by a court—with all the attendant tension and uncertainty—even if the court would be guided solely by its perception of the child's interests in deciding the matter. Again, it must be right to allow local authorities—acting as the state's agent in protecting children from abuse—to bring cases before the court in some circumstances; but it does not follow that the court should be empowered to make orders simply on the basis of its perception of the child's welfare, for this would (as Lord Mackay of Clashfern put it: see (1989) 139 New L.J. 508) be to permit children to be removed from their families simply on the basis that a court considered that the state could do better for the child than his or her family.

The enactment of the Children Act makes it less difficult for the student to address these issues, since the Act strips away much of the procedural and structural complexity of the law previously governing these matters, and creates (for the first time in English law) a single and consistent scheme of orders in any "family proceedings." The range of orders available in each court and the criteria applied by the courts are the same; and the Act makes an attempt to clarify the effect of court orders.

Scheme of the Children Act 1989

13–02   The essence of the scheme established by the Children Act is elegant and simple. In its barest essentials it can be seen by asking three questions. First, are there "family proceedings" before the court? Secondly, if so, what orders are available to the court in the proceedings? Thirdly, in the light of the guidelines which are laid down in the Act, should the court in fact make an order, and if so, what should be the terms of the order?

The text adapts this approach: this Chapter first explains the expression "family proceedings"; it then summarises the orders which can be made in any family proceedings under section 8 of the Children Act; and finally it discusses the principles upon which the court will decide whether or not to act. However, the reader should be warned at the outset that the working of the legislation is somewhat more complex than might appear from this introduction, notably in three respects.

First, the fact that there are "family proceedings" before the court means that the court can make orders under the Children Act. It does not mean that the court can ignore rules laid down in the particular legislation governing the type of family proceedings in question. To give a simple example, if divorce proceedings are started by a child's parent, the court will (because divorce proceedings are "family proceedings" under the Act) have power under the Children Act to make orders about the children's upbringing. But the divorce legislation, contained in the Matrimonial Causes Act 1973, also gives the court certain powers, and imposes on it certain duties; and these provisions continue to apply. Hence, the Children Act cannot be seen as an entirely comprehensive codification of the law relating to the upbringing of children. It will often still be necessary to refer to the legislation under which the particular proceedings started; and the relationship between the Children Act and the legislation governing particular "family proceedings" (such as divorce, adoption, etc.) is therefore explained somewhat more fully in Chapter 14.

The second complicating factor is that, although the Act restricts the availability of the jurisdiction (founded on the prerogative of the crown as *parens patriae*) whereby issues relating to a child's upbringing could be resolved in wardship it did not abolish the wardship jurisdiction which still therefore needs to be considered as a separate matter. This issue is also discussed in Chapter 14.

The third complication stems from the Government's decision that a distinction must be drawn between cases about a child involving a dispute between individual citizens on the one hand; and cases where state intervention in the family is proposed on the other. In the former group (where the proceedings are usually described as "private law" proceedings) the court will—as we shall see—be guided by a broad discretion without any defined minimum criteria for intervention beyond the fact that family proceedings have been properly constituted. That, of itself, is sufficient to justify the court making orders on no other basis than that the child's welfare is paramount. But it is a central feature of the legislation that the State itself should not be allowed to intervene in family life in the absence of proof, first, that a child is being or is likely to be positively harmed; and secondly that such harm results from a failure on the part of the family to provide adequate parenting. Hence, before the court can even consider making a public law order (a care order for example) it must be satisfied that certain specified criteria have been met. Public law proceedings are therefore still different in many important respects from private law proceedings; and Chapter 15 seeks to explain the relationship between children, families and the state.

The courts and children—emergence of a specialist family court?

Before seeking to explain the substantive law, something should be said about the courts by which the law will be administered. For long, the administration of the law was complicated by the existence of three courts exercising different jurisdictions; but the Children Act broke new ground by conferring a concurrent jurisdiction exercisable by the High Court (Family Division), the County Court, and the Magistrates' Court. The Children (Allocation of Proceedings) Order 1991 (SI No. 1677) creates the administrative machinery enabling all proceedings relating to the same child and the child's family to be consolidated and heard together; and for ensuring that those proceedings come before the appropriate level of court and judge.

13–03

At the same time, moves have been made to create a specialist judiciary. First, the Magistrates' jurisdiction is to be exercised by a specialist Family Proceedings Court, staffed by trained members of the Family Proceedings Panel. Secondly, the County Courts have been grouped into four categories—in ascending order of specialisation, the county court, the Divorce County Court, the Family Hearing Centre and the Care Centre. In principle, the county court will only deal with injunction applications; the Divorce County Court will deal with routine divorce cases—but if applications relating to a child are contested they will normally be transferred to a Family Hearing Centre; and the Care Centre will also deal with care cases transferred up from the Family Proceedings Court or down from the High Court. Secondly, there is power (Courts and Legal Services Act 1990, s.9) to give directions that cases may only be heard by judges who have been specially designated or nominated to handle cases at the Family Hearing Centre or Care Centre. This power is to be exercised to create a cadre of specialist judges; and extensive administrative arrangements have been made to seek to promote the objectives of the Children Act 1989.

I. ARE THERE FAMILY PROCEEDINGS BEFORE THE COURT?

13–04   Family proceedings are comprehensively defined by the Act (s.8(3)); and the proceedings which fall within this definition are best considered under four groups:

  (i)   Proceedings under the *inherent jurisdiction* of the High Court in relation to children;
  (ii) *Divorce proceedings* and other proceedings under statutes in which relief affecting the family may be sought;
  (iii) Proceedings brought under the *Children Act* itself by someone who is qualified to seek an order relating to the upbringing of a child;
  (iv) Proceedings in which a *local authority* seeks a care order in relation to a child.

At this stage it suffices to give only a brief explanation of the main features of each of these groups. Distinctive characteristics of the various procedures are examined somewhat more fully in Chapter 14.

1. Proceedings Under the Inherent Jurisdiction

13–05   For most practical purposes, the "inherent jurisdiction" in this context refers to wardship proceedings in which the High Court had developed its own wide range of extremely flexible orders. As a result of the classification of proceedings under the inherent jurisdiction as "family proceedings" the court in wardship now has—in addition to its inherent powers—power to make the orders set out in the Children Act, including financial orders.

It remains to be seen whether wardship will continue to be used; and if it is how far the court in wardship will express its orders relating to the upbringing of children in the terms provided in the Act, or whether it will prefer to retain its distinctive and traditional terminology—for example, to give "care and control" of a ward to a named individual. Wardship is discussed further at para. 14–14 below.

2. Proceedings Under Certain Statutes

The statutes in question deal with the following: **13–06**

(a) *Divorce*, judicial separation and nullity of marriage. (The Matrimonial Causes Act 1973.)

(b) *Domestic violence* and occupation of the matrimonial home. (The Domestic Violence and Matrimonial Proceedings Act 1976, and ss.1 and 9 of the Matrimonial Homes Act 1983).

(c) *Application in the Magistrates' Court* by a spouse for financial relief or protection (The Domestic Proceedings and Magistrates' Courts Act 1978).

(d) *Adoption* proceedings (The Adoption Act 1976) and also applications for a *parental order*: see para. 11–12 above.

The way in which the legislation works in relation to these different types of proceedings is illustrated in Chapter 14.

3. Guardianship, Parental Responsibility and other Private Law Applications under the Children Act itself

As mentioned in Chapter 11 of this book the Children Act itself   **13–07** confers jurisdiction on the courts in relation to the appointment of *guardians* for a child; and it contains rules governing the circumstances in which the *father of an illegitimate child* may apply for an order giving him parental responsibility for that child. Of greatest importance are the rules governing what are conveniently described as "free-standing" applications for orders under the Children Act—for example, applications by grandparents to be allowed contact with their grandchild. The question whether a person should have the right to interfere in a child's family life by starting legal proceedings is a difficult one, and the Act contains complex rules designed (as the Law Commission put it: Law Com. No. 173, para. 4.41) to provide a filter protecting the child and the family against unwarranted interference while ensuring that the child's interests are properly protected. These rules are dealt with at para. 14–07 below.

4. Proceedings in which a Local Authority Seeks a Care or Supervision Order in Relation to a Child

As stated above, the Act draws a distinction between "private law"   **13–08** proceedings, and those in which a local authority (or other authorised agency) seeks a care or supervision order giving it compulsory powers to intervene.

The crucial distinction between private and public law proceedings is that, once "family proceedings" are properly before the court the court may make any "private law" order if, on consideration of the guidelines set out in the Act, it considers that it would be for the welfare of the child to do so. But it can only consider making a public law order—a care or supervision order—if two further conditions are satisfied: first that a local authority (or "authorised person") has applied for the order, and secondly that the "significant harm" test embodied in section 31(2) of the Act is satisfied. But it is important at the outset to bear in mind that, once an application for a care or supervision order has been properly made, there are "family proceedings" in existence, and the court will in consequence have jurisdiction to make any of the private law orders discussed below which it considers appropriate in the light of the guidelines set out in the Act. Conversely, the court could make a public law order in any other—private law—family proceedings provided the two additional requirements (application by qualified applicant and "significant harm") were satisfied. For example, a local authority could, if it wished, make an application for a care order in divorce proceedings or in domestic violence proceedings. It is also important to note that, once there are family proceedings before the court, the court may make an order under section 8 of the Act even though no application has been made for it: s.10(1)(b).

The text of this book follows the scheme of the Act by dealing with Public Law orders separately (see Chapter 15) but the relationship between public and private law needs to be kept in mind throughout.

II. WHAT POWERS MAY THE COURT EXERCISE?—THE "MENU"

13–09   The "private law" orders which will usually be relevant in family proceedings are set out in section 8 of the Act: (i) a contact order, (ii) a prohibited steps order; (iii) a residence order; and (iv) a specific issue order. The statutory definition of each of these orders (accompanied by a brief explanation) is as follows:

> **A Contact Order** is "an order requiring the person with whom a child lives, or is to live, to allow the child to visit or stay with the person named in the order, or for that person and the child otherwise to have contact with each other."

This type of order enables the court to give effect to the general principle that it is desirable for a child to preserve links with both parents. It will replace the "access" order in the past commonly made on divorce, and will no doubt often be phrased in terms that the wife allow the husband "reasonable contact." Sometimes, however, it is necessary to be more specific; and now (instead of using expressions such as, for example, "staying access") the court will make a contact order specifying that the child is to be permitted to stay with the parent on (say) alternate weekends, and for specified periods at Christmas and other holiday periods.

Contact may be ordered with any named person (for example, a grandparent) and it is even possible to envisage a teenager seeking an order that he or she be allowed contact with a named friend.

Contact is not limited to face-to-face visits: an order could be made for contact by letter or greetings card.

> **Prohibited Steps Order**: "an order that no step which could be taken by a parent in meeting his parental responsibility for a child, and which is of a kind specified in the order, shall be taken by any person without consent of the court."

A prohibited steps order is the equivalent of an injunction. It might be used, for example, to direct that the child should not be brought into contact with a named person or taken to a particular place, or that the child should not undergo specified medical procedures.

It should be noted that the action prohibited must be of a kind which could be "taken by a parent in meeting his parental responsibility" (defined by CA 1989, s.3; see para. 11–33 above). A prohibited steps order could not, therefore, be granted against a newspaper to restrain it from publishing information about a child (because the publication of newspapers is not something parents do in relation to their children); and it will still be necessary to apply for an injunction where a prohibition of this kind is in issue.

> **Residence Order**: "an order settling the arrangements to be made as to the person with whom a child is to live."

This definition encapsulates the "plain words" approach of the Act. The legislation no longer refers to obscure concepts such as "custody"; instead the order must say in plain English what arrangements are to be made about the child's care. It follows that the making of a residence order does not deprive any other person of his or her parental responsibility—for example, the making of a residence order in favour of the child's mother does not deprive the father of his right to take decisions about education or any other matter (although of course the fact that a person has parental responsibility would not permit him or her to act inconsistently with the terms of any court order—such as a contact order: s.2(8)).

It is envisaged (see s.11(4)) that an order may be made in favour of two or more persons, and that it may specify that the child is to live for a certain period of the year with one of them, and for the rest of the year with the other.

The general policy of the Act seems to be that in principle orders should mean what they say but mean no more than they say. But the making of a residence order does have certain automatic consequences: first, it confers "parental responsibility" on the person in whose favour it is made (if that person does not already have it): s.12(2). Secondly the making of a residence order automatically prohibits change of the child's surname or the child's removal from the United Kingdom (except by the person in whose favour the order is made for a period of less than a month—*e.g.* for a holiday). Finally, the making of such an order also automatically terminates any care order: see para. 15–17 below.

> **Specific Issue Order**: "an order giving directions for the purpose of determining a specific question which has arisen, or which may arise, in connection with any aspect of parental responsibility for a child."

A specific issue order enables the court to resolve disputes about particular matters—for example, about medical treatment or education.

The availability of specific issue orders should enable the court to deal with problems which, in the past, were dealt with by wardship: see para. 14–14 below. The advantage of being able to do so is said to be that the court will be able to deal with the particular matter which requires adjudication without making it necessary to bring all other important matters affecting the child before the court. Thus, it would seem that specific issues orders could properly have been sought in the following cases (which were in fact dealt with in wardship):

(i) *Life or death?*

13–10
In *Re B (A Minor) (Wardship: Medical Treatment)* (1981) 3 FLR 117, CA the court had to decide whether a severely handicapped baby should be allowed to live or die. The court decided in favour of life. Moreover, in *Re C (A Minor) (No. 1) (Wardship: Medical Treatment)* [1990] 1 FLR 252, CA, there was a "prognosis of hopelessness" for a 16-week-old baby, born with massive mental and physical handicaps. In the circumstances, the court accepted that it would be inappropriate for life prolonging treatment to be given; and in effect, that the child should be allowed to die.

In *Re D (A Minor) (Wardship: Sterilisation)* [1976] Fam 185 the court had to decide whether a handicapped child should be sterilised, and, on the facts of that case, decided against permitting such an irreversible step to be taken in relation to an 11 year-old girl; but in the case of *Re B (A Minor) (Wardship: Sterilisation)* [1987] 2 FLR 314, HL, (where the ward was nearly 18, and quite unable to cope with pregnancy) the House of Lords held that it would be in the patient's best interest to be sterilised so that she might lead as full a life as her intellectual capacity allowed.

(ii) *Abortion?*

13–11
In *Re P (A Minor)* [1986] FLR 272 the court had to decide whether an abortion should be carried out. The ward, Shirley, who was 15, had a baby (born when Shirley was only 13) for whom she was caring in a

mother and child unit with schooling facilities. Shirley became pregnant again, and wanted an abortion. Shirley's parents were opposed to this on religious grounds and because they thought Shirley would live to regret having her child aborted; and they offered to care for Shirley's existing baby so that she could herself care for the new-born child. The court decided that Shirley's pregnancy be terminated to avoid risk of injury to her mental health and to avoid her own growing-up being endangered.

(iii) *Living abroad?*
In a number of cases the court has allowed a divorced parent to take   **13–12**
a child to a distant country, even though this would inevitably mean the severance of the child's links with its other parent: see, *e.g.* *Lonslow* v. *Hennig (formerly Lonslow)* [1986] 2 FLR 378; *Re F (A Ward) (Leave to Remove Ward Out of the Jurisdiction)* [1988] 2 FLR 116.

(iv) *Submitting to police caution?*
The following case illustrates the wide variety of issues which have   **13–13**
traditionally been dealt with in wardship, but on which a specific issue order might now be sought:

> In *Re A (A Minor) (Wardship: Criminal Proceedings)* [1990] 1 FLR 86 a 16-year-old boy, who was a ward of court, admitted a number of sexual offences; and the prosecution service proposed that a verbal caution be given. This would involve an admission of guilt, recording of the caution in police files for reference in any subsequent proceedings, and possibly the taking and retention of fingerprints.

On the other hand, this and other similar cases only arose because of the rule that any important issue affecting a ward of court should be referred to the court. The normal rule was that the guardian must consent to a caution; and the court acting in wardship as the child's parent, therefore had to agree to the caution being administered. It may be, therefore, that this case better illustrates the sort of issue which will in practice no longer be brought to the court at all, because wardship is expected to be used much less frequently: see para. 14–28 below.

Restrictions on power to make specific issues and prohibited steps orders.
The Act contains a provision of rather uncertain scope which prohibits a court from exercising its powers to make a specific issue order or prohibited steps order "with a view to achieving a result which could be achieved by making a residence or contact order." It seems probable that this provision (s.9(5)(a)) was intended simply to prevent local authorities circumventing the policy of the Act, which is to debar a local authority from taking a child into its care unless the "significant harm" threshold criterion (see para. 15–12 below) is satisfied. Hence the Act prohibits the court from making a residence

order in favour of a local authority, and requires that a care order be obtained; and it would obviously be unsatisfactory if a local authority could instead seek a specific issue order (*e.g.* that the child reside in house A with local authority foster parents) or prohibited steps order (*e.g.* that the child be not moved from the foster parent's house). But the scope of the prohibition is not restricted to the local authority context, and it could be potentially wide. Suppose, for example, that the court wishes to prevent a third party having contact with the child. Were it not for the existence of the prohibition contained in s.9(5)(a) it would be possible to make a prohibited steps order to that effect; but it could conceivably be argued that the same result could be achieved by making a residence order on condition that the child be not allowed to have contact with a named individual.

The Act also prohibits the making of specific issue or prohibited steps orders (in effect) which would require a child to be in the care of a local authority or accommodated by it: s.9(5)(b); see further below p. 15–07.

Conditions and directions

13–14 The Act contains a useful provision empowering the court to give directions about how any section 8 order is to be carried into effect, and to impose conditions—for example, that the child be allowed to live with A provided that A does not bring B within a mile of the house, or that the child live with A provided that A continues to reside in a specified house or town, or (perhaps) that the child reside with A, provided that A surrenders into the custody of a third party the passport issued by a foreign government which might be used by A to remove the children from the jurisdiction.

OTHER ORDERS

The Act empowers the court (subject to certain conditions) to make a *Family Assistance Order*—*i.e.*: an order requiring a probation officer or officer of a local authority to be made available to advise, assist and (where appropriate) befriend the child, or any parent or guardian or any person with whom the child is living or in whose favour there is a contact order in force: s.16(1).

The Act also confers power to make a wide range of *Financial Orders*: (periodical payments, lump sum and transfer of and settlement of property, variation of settlement) in some cases subject to special conditions. These are dealt with in Chapter 10 above.

Finally, it should be remembered that there is power in certain circumstances to make a *Care Order* or a *Supervision Order*. These public law orders are dealt with at paras. 15–10 below.

THE ACT IN OPERATION

A brief example of how the orders might be used may be helpful at this stage:

> H and W start divorce proceedings. They cannot agree on the arrangements to be made for the upbringing of their child, Caroline; and W's mother is concerned that she will lose touch with her granddaughter. The court might order that Caroline reside with W (*Residence Order*) but that she be allowed to stay with H at Christmas and Easter, and on alternate weekends, and with her grandmother for a week once a year (*Contact Order*). It could also order that Caroline be educated at a named convent (*Specific Issue Order*), that H should not take her outside England and Wales for even a short period (*Prohibited Steps Order*); and the court might also order H to pay maintenance for Caroline, and to pay her school fees (*Financial Order*). It could make these orders whether or not any application had been made: s.10(1)(b).

III. SHOULD THE COURT MAKE AN ORDER?—THE WELFARE PRINCIPLE

5 The overriding consideration in determining whether to make an **13–15** order, and if so what terms the order should contain, is whether the child's welfare would thereby be promoted. However, the Act also contains two specific provisions—one seeking to minimise harmful delay, and the other embodying the so-called "no-order" presumption—which are relevant to the court's decision. This section of the text therefore deals, first with the welfare principle, and secondly with the specific guidance. The section concludes with a brief account of the role of the welfare officer.

A. Child's Welfare Paramount

6 The Children Act 1989 reasserts the principle that when a court **13–16** determines any question with respect to the upbringing of a child or the administration of a child's property or the application of any income arising from it, the child's welfare shall be the court's paramount consideration: s.1(1).

Principle applied in all family disputes
7 We have already noted some dramatic examples of the application of **13–17** the welfare principle in cases dealing with decisions about whether a handicapped child should be allowed to die (see para. 13–10 above)

but the same principle applies to the resolution of all disputes within the family about the upbringing of a child. The question of whether there should be continued contact between a divorced parent and a child of the family, and if so, the frequency of that contact, is routinely litigated, for example. In this context, case law—whilst emphasising (see *M* v. *M* [1973] 2 All ER 81, CA) that continued contact is a basic right of the child rather than a basic right of the parent—suggests that preservation of the links of both divorcing parents with their child is usually considered to be in the child's interests, and some ongoing contact will normally be allowed, even if this causes temporary distress to the child: see *D* v. *M* *(Minor: Custody Appeal)* [1983] Fam 33. For example:

> In *Re H (Minors) (Access)* [1992] 1 FLR 148, CA, the father had no contact with his children for more than three years. The Court of Appeal held that the relevant question was whether there were any cogent reasons why the children should be denied the opportunity of access to their natural father; and an order was made (and see *Re B (Minors: Access)* [1992] 1 FLR 140, CA).

On one view there may even be a general principle that a parent has a claim to contact with a child: *Re KD (A Minor) (Access: Principles)* [1988] 2 FLR 114; but it is possible to explain most of the cases on the basis of an assessment of what is in the child's interests. However, it has to be said that the courts sometimes seem less impressed by the benefits of continued contact between an illegitimate child and the father: see *Re C (A Minor) (Access)* [1992] 1 FLR 309; *Re SM (A Minor) (Natural Father: Access)* [1991] 2 FLR 333; but see also *Re A (Minors: Access)* [1992] Fam Law 67 (where the parents were married).

Limitations on application of welfare principle

13–18   It is important to note, first, that the principle that the child's welfare is the paramount consideration only applies where the child's upbringing (or the other matters referred to at para. 13–16 above) is directly in issue; and that the child's welfare is not the governing factor where the child's upbringing arises only incidentally—for example, in an application relating to the occupation of the family home: see *Richards* v. *Richards* [1984] AC 174, HL, para. 6–25 above.

Secondly, the child's welfare cannot justify the court making an order which is outside its jurisdiction. In particular—as already pointed out—there is no jurisdiction to make care or supervision orders unless certain specific criteria are satisfied: see para. 15–12 below.

The welfare checklist

13–19   How is the court to determine what is in the child's interest? The Act contains a checklist of matters; and it was hoped in this way to achieve greater consistency and clarity in the application of the law.

But the court is only *obliged* "to have regard in particular" to the matters specified in the checklist in two cases. First, where the application is opposed; and, secondly, where the application relates to a care or supervision order. Hence in these two cases the court's order would apparently be liable to be set aside if the court had not made sufficient findings of fact about the specified matters, and directed itself about the weight to be attached to each of them.

The fact that the court is not *required* to consider the checklist does not mean that it will not, in practice, wish to do so; and certainly it is to be expected that courts and advisers will find it useful to use the checklist as an aide-mémoire.

The matters to which the checklist specifically draws attention are as follows:

(a) *The ascertainable wishes and feelings of the child concerned (considered in the light of his age and understanding)*

The relevance of a child's own wishes has been re-enforced by the *Gillick* decision: see para. 11–26 above. However, the courts have in the past emphasized that in custody cases the decision is for the court, and not for the child; and in particular the court has been aware of the dangers of putting the burden of making a choice on the child—in *Adams* v. *Adams* [1984] 5 FLR 768, for example, Dunn L.J. remarked that the pressures on children were "quite sufficient when the marriage has broken down and one of the parents has left home without putting on the additional burden of being made to feel that they have to decide their own future." Hence, in an appropriate case, the court will override the expressed wishes of the children:

13–20

> In *Clarke-Hunt* v. *Newcombe* (1983) 4 FLR 482 an 11-year-old boy was said by the reporting welfare officer to be quite unequivocal in his wish to live with his mother rather than his father, whereas his elder brother apparently preferred to live with the father. The judge decided to make an order under which the children would live with the father.

The age of the child may be of crucial importance in determining the weight to be given to a child's wishes:

> In *Re P (A Minor) (Education)* (1991) *The Times*, October 1, CA, divorced parents disagreed about whether their 14-year-old son should go as a boarder to a public school or as a day pupil to an independent day school. The boy himself decided, after the first instance hearing, that he would prefer the day school; and the Court of Appeal held that this view should be respected. The courts (said Butler-Sloss L.J.) have "become increasingly aware of the importance of listening to the view of older children and taking into account what children say, not necessarily agreeing with what they want nor indeed doing what they want, but paying proper respect to older children who are at an age and have the maturity to make their minds up as to what they think is best for them, bearing in mind that older children very often have an appreciation of

their own situation which is worthy of consideration by, and the respect of, the adults, and particularly including the courts...." Had the boy been 11 she would not have hesitated "to pack him off to boarding school" but his age meant that his views carried greater weight.

How is the court to ascertain the wishes of the child? There are occasions when judges have themselves interviewed children in private, but this practice may give rise to difficulties, and normally the court will rely on the investigation made by a welfare officer: see para. 13–34 below.

(b) *The child's physical, emotional and educational needs*

13–21 The need to provide for a child's *physical* care is self-evident: the court would not make a residence order in favour of a parent who was homeless, and who had no prospect of obtaining housing. It is true that it has been said that in most cases "disadvantages of a materials sort must be of little weight" (*Stephenson* v. *Stephenson*) [1985] FLR 1140, 1148; but a basic minimum of physical provision is required.

In considering questions of *education*, the court will often be primarily concerned with the dangers of uprooting a child from a school where satisfactory progress is being made (and see the facts of *Re P (A Minor) (Education)* (above). But there may be cases in which there is a clash of values to be resolved:

> In *May* v. *May* [1986] 1 FLR 325 the question was whether two boys, aged six and eight, should live with their father or their mother. There was no conflict about the competence of either parent, but there was a conflict of values between them. The father attached importance to academic achievement, punctuality, tidiness, and giving assistance in the household. The mother and her cohabitee had, in contrast, a much freer and easier approach to life and to such issues as the amount of time that the children should spend working, the time they should spend watching television and so on. The Court of Appeal refused to upset the trial judge's decision that the children should live with the father.

In recent years the courts have attached very great weight to the children's *emotional needs*: see, for example, the facts of *J* v. *C* [1970] AC 668, HL, set out at para. 11–27 above, and contrast the attitude taken by the court 45 years earlier in *Re Thain*, para. 13–22 below. Judges have been receptive to the findings of child psychiatrists. In particular, they have accepted the need for continuity of care; and they are accordingly reluctant to interfere with the *status quo* (*i.e.* the existing arrangements) unless there is clear justification for doing so. This is not to say that the courts will never move children from the home where they have been living perhaps for some years (see for example *Clarke-Hunt* v. *Newcombe* (*above*) where the children had been with their mother for five years).

There was a time when the courts tended to apply presumptions—for example that young children should be with their mother, that girls approaching puberty should be with their mother, and that boys over a certain age should be with their father. But the more modern approach (*Re S (A Minor) (Custody)*) [1991] 2 FLR 388, 392, CA is not to make any such presumption. It may be (said the Master of the Rolls) natural that young children should be with their mothers, but there has been a change in the social order as a result of which more men care for children; and it must (he said) follow from this that fathers were more equipped to do so than formerly.

(c) *The likely effect on the child of any change in his circumstances*
In a case decided in 1926 (*Re Thain* [1926] Ch 676) the question was   **13–22**
whether a six-year-old girl who had been brought up from infancy by an uncle and aunt should be returned to the care of her father. The judge admitted that "the little girl will be greatly distressed and upset ... but, at her tender age, one knows from experience how mercifully transient are the effects of partings of other sorrows ... and I cannot attach much weight to this aspect of the case." It is inconceivable that a judge should today express himself in these terms: the danger of psychological harm arising from a change in care is now widely recognised and forms part of the general knowledge and experience of the judges. Indeed, it has been said that the fundamental rule of child care is that *stability* is all important, and the courts will accordingly (as already mentioned) be extremely cautious in disturbing an arrangement which is well-established.

(d) *The child's age, sex, background and any characteristics of his which the court considers relevant*
It has already been mentioned that the courts no longer follow   **13–23**
presumptions to the effect that very young children should be in the care of their mother, for example. Nevertheless, the children's age and sex obviously affects their needs; while the statutory reference to "background" may involve the court in a consideration of the child's cultural and religious background:

> In *Re P (A Minor) (Adoption)* [1990] 1 FLR 96 the mixed-race child had been cared for from infancy by a white European. The Court of Appeal held that the judge had been entitled, on the evidence presented to him, to conclude that the advantages to a child of mixed race of being brought up in a black family outweighed the importance of preserving the existing well-settled arrangements.

For many years custody disputes were often concerned with religious issues—with the soul, rather than the body, of the child: see *Re J M Carroll* [1931] 1 KB 317, 331, *per* Scrutton L.J. But in recent years the courts have become reluctant to pass judgment on the parents' belief; and religion only becomes relevant where, for example, adherence to a particular religious sect could cause the child emotional disturbance or physical harm: see *Wright v. Wright* (1980) 2

FLR 276 (where the Court of Appeal held that there was ample evidence that the father would use any contact with the child actively to indoctrinate him with the beliefs of the Jehovah's Witnesses and, in the particular circumstances of the case, to do so would cause emotional disturbance.

(e) *Any harm which he has suffered or is at risk of suffering*

13–24   In recent years, allegations that one parent has been guilty of *sexual abuse* have increasingly been made; and it seems that Family Division judges may be "sated with circuit sex abuse" cases: see, *per* Ward J., *Ravenscroft* v. *Rederiaktiebølaget Transatlantic* [1991] 3 All ER 73, 76. The court will have to weigh up the evidence as to whether such behaviour has occurred or not, and then determine the risk of harm on the basis of evidence. There is a danger that in seeking to protect children from sexual abuse, society may cause other, and possibly greater, harm to the children it seeks to protect, *per* Balcombe LJ., *Re H (Minors) (Wardship: Sexual Abuse)* [1991] 2 FLR 416. Hence, the court must exercise its discretion, weighing in the balance all the relevant factors in order to assess the relative weight of advantages and risks to the child of the possible courses of action. For example:

> In *Re B (A Minor) (Child Abuse: Custody)* [1990] 2 FLR 317 the Judge found that it was "overwhelmingly likely" that a four year-old boy had seen sexual behaviour between his parents which he ought not to have seen, that he had seen indecent videos and that there was a serious lack of awareness on the part of the child's parents as to "quite where boundaries are to be drawn." However, notwithstanding the fact that the judge held that there was an unacceptable risk that the child had been subjected to sexual abuse and that on balance there was a risk of further abuse, the risk of harm to the boy did not outweigh the advantage of preserving links with a "warm playful father" who had a good relationship with his son.

In several recent cases the courts have had to consider whether the fact that a parent has an homosexual orientation and relationship should affect his or her right to care for the child.

> In *C* v. *C (A Minor) (Custody: Appeal)* [1991] 1 FLR 223 the Court of Appeal held, on the facts, that a judge had been wrong to allow a mother (a prison officer who had formed a lesbian relationship with a prisoner) to have the care of a young girl rather than entrusting care of the girl to the father (who had re-married and was living in a "classic husband and wife relationship.") However, the court emphasised that the decision depended on evidence, and that a court might well decide that a "sensitive, loving lesbian relationship is a more satisfactory environment for a child than a less sensitive or loving alternative."

In contrast:

> In *B* v. *B (Minors) (Custody, Care and Control)* [1991] 1 FLR 402, expert evidence about the impact of the parental relationship was available, and

that evidence enabled the judge to deal with the concerns expressed by the Welfare Officer and in some of the earlier cases about the likely outcome. The mother, who was living in a lesbian relationship, was given the care of a two-and-a-half year-old child.

(f) *How capable each of his parents, and any other person in relation to whom*   **13–25**
court considers the question to be relevant, is of meeting the child's needs

For example:

In *Dicocco* v. *Milne* (1983) 4 FLR 247 the court had given custody of a one   **13–26**
year-old boy to his father. The welfare report indicated that the mother had low standards of hygiene and mixed with what the health visitor believed to be the "wrong sort" of people; and that the child was often left unwashed and unprovided with clean or adequate nappies by an immature and, by implication, lazy mother. However, the Court of Appeal considered that there was no lack of love and affection on her part, no finding that she had neglected or ill-treated the child, and that the father's proposals would involve the child's care being divided between at least three and possibly four adults. Taking into account the fact that the child had been in the care of the mother and that accordingly should not be removed unless there were strong reasons for doing so, it was ordered that the child remain with the mother.

(g) *The range of powers available to the court under the Children Act in the*
proceedings in question

This provision is novel. It requires the court to consider what it can   **13–27**
achieve by exercising the powers which it has under the legislation. In particular, the court may want to consider imposing *conditions* on the making of a residence order, it may want to consider the desirability of making contact orders with other relatives—particularly bearing in mind the fact that the Act expressly permits the court to make an order if it considers that it should do so "even though no ... application has been made" for the order (s.10(1)(b)—and it may want to consider the possibility of making *financial orders*. The court may also think it appropriate to consider the making of a *Family Assistance Order*: (see para. 13–15 above, and CA 1989, s.16). The object of a Family Assistance Order (which replaces the Supervision Order formerly available in divorce and other custody proceedings) is to provide the family with some skilled short term social work support—for example, to help the family come to terms with new arrangements for the children or to help with arrangements for contact between the parents and children.

B. The Welfare Principle: Specific Provisions

The Children Act contains two further important provisions designed   **13–28**
to safeguard the welfare of children in family proceedings: the first is

concerned with the effect of delay on children, and the second—the so-called no-order presumption—requires the court to ask precisely how the making of an order could promote the child's welfare.

1. Delay harmful

13–29 The Act provides (s.1(2)) that in any proceedings in which any question with respect to the upbringing of a child arises the court shall have regard to the "general principle" that any delay in determining the question "is likely to prejudice the welfare of the child." This general statement of principle is fleshed out by rules (s.11(1)(2)) requiring the court to draw up a timetable for determining the question and to give appropriate directions to ensure that the timetable is followed; and the Family Proceedings Rules 1991 (SI No. 1247) contain provisions enabling the court to discharge these duties—for example, where the rules lay down a time within which things should be done such as filing expert evidence) that time cannot be extended by consent of the parties but only by court order; and the court is, in principle, to fix dates for resuming hearings which have been adjourned rather than leaving this to the parties: see Rules 4.14–16. In these ways, the legislation—as the Official Guide to the Children Act puts it—recognises that "the child's sense of time may be more acute than an adult's and that delay in determining the proceedings may in itself be harmful to the child" (para. 3.23), and that delay in court proceedings may put stress on all those involved which may rub off generally in damage to the child.

However, it is important to note that the legislation merely states a principle. It certainly does not seek to prescribe that a case should never be adjourned, or to prevent the court from a deliberate decision that delay might be beneficial. Not only would any such attempt be futile, it would in fact be harmful to children's welfare. In particular, where the situation is still volatile after the breakdown of the parents' relationship, there may well be a strong case for moving slowly and carefully:

> In *S* v. *S (Minors: custody)* (1991) *The Times*, June 7, CA, the stability of a new relationship formed by the mother was not yet established; and the Court of Appeal considered that she had still to demonstrate that she was a stable parent, in the sense of being a mother willing to remain in one place and not move at whim from one part of the country to another "according to the ups and downs of any relationship she happens to be maintaining." It had therefore been wrong to make a custody order in her favour; and the Court substituted what was in effect a temporary order with a view to review in three months time.

There may also be cases in which taking time (perhaps through conciliation) in exploring the possibility of a settlement may well be time well spent, particularly if contested court proceedings can thereby be avoided. The Act is surely aimed at minimising mere "drift." For example:

> In *Re G (A Minor)* (1991) *The Times*, February 6, the parties had asked that a custody case be adjourned because they wanted more time. The judge however held that there was ample evidence, no indication that the hearing at a later date would produce a different decision, and that the need to decide children's cases within the shortest possible time would outweigh the importance of obtaining parental consent.

2. The "no order presumption"

The Law Commission in its Report on Guardianship and Custody   **13–30** (Law Com. No. 172, 1988, para. 3.2) expressed concern over what it believed to be a common tendency to assume that some order about children should always be made in divorce and other matrimonial proceedings—in effect, as "part of the package" provided for litigants and clients. The Commission thought that there was a risk that orders allocating "custody" and "access" would polarise the parents' roles, and perhaps alienate the child. As Waite J. put in in *S* v. *S (Minors: custody)* (1991) *The Times*, June 7, CA, "once a father or a mother is given custody, they regard themselves as clothed with parental authority and a new chapter begins"—notwithstanding the fact that in principle orders relating to the care of children are never "final" in any technical sense.

In an attempt to meet this concern, the Children Act provides:

> "where a court is considering whether or not to make one or more orders under this Act with respect to a child, it shall not make the order or any of the orders unless it considers that doing so would be better for the child than making no order at all." (s.1(5)).

In effect, the court therefore, needs to justify a decision to make an order, rather than making no order and leaving matters to be resolved from time to time if and when a court decision is required. The court must ask itself what, precisely, would be the effect of making an order, and whether this would or would not be positively in the child's interests. The court should only make an order if it reaches a decision that an order would be *better* for the child than making no order.

There will obviously be many cases in which the court will find no difficulty in satisfying itself that the making of an order would be better for the child than not to do so. For example:

(a) *If there has been a dispute* which the court has had to resolve, the   **13–31** case for making an order would seem to be almost unanswerable. The dispute might be between divorcing parents about who should have the daily care of the child; or it might be between unmarried parents about whether or not the father should have any contact with his child. There are undoubtedly cases in which the court will feel it appropriate to make an order requiring one parent to do what the court considers to be in the child's interest, notwithstanding that parent's opposition. For example:

> In *Re S (Minors: Access)* [1990] 2 FLR 166, CA, a Sikh mother was terrified of her husband who (she alleged) had beaten and attacked her. One child was living with the father, and the other with the mother; and the mother was "implacably opposed to any access which might lead her into contact with the father." The judge made no order for access. The Court of Appeal held that this decision was clearly wrong. It was wrong in principle for a court to abrogate responsibility and not even try to ensure the continued contact with the child's welfare required merely because of the mother's implacable attitude.

Again the court may have been asked to resolve a single specific issue—for example, whether an abortion should be carried out on a young girl—and in such a case the need for its decision to be expressed as an order would seem to be self-evident.

13–32   (b) *Giving formality to an agreement.* Even when there is no dispute, an order may be desirable so as—in the Law Commission's words (para. 3.2):

> "to confirm and give stability to the existing arrangements, to clarify the respective roles of the parents, to reassure the parent with whom the child will be living, and even to reassure the public authorities responsible for housing and income support that such arrangements have in fact been made."

In particular, it would be usual to make an order if the court resolves financial matters, and particularly if it is thought necessary to exercise the court's powers to make a transfer of property or settlement of property order. Again, it is often the practice of Housing Authorities to require a parent seeking public sector housing to produce a court order dealing with the child's residence; and perhaps courts will feel it right to make a residence order in such a case.

13–33   (c) There are other more *technical factors* which might incline the court towards making an order. For example, court orders may be useful if a child is removed to a foreign country, and indeed may be essential if recovery of the child is sought under the provisions of the European Convention on Recognition and Enforcement of Custody Decisions (as embodied in the Child Abduction and Custody Act 1985). Again, we have seen that the effect of making a residence order is to confer parental responsibility on the person in whose favour that order is made. To allow a child to live with someone who has no parental responsibility—and thus effectively no clearly defined legal authority in relation to the child—might be unsatisfactory.

It should be noted that the "no order presumption" relates to the making of *any* order under the Act—not only an order from the "menu" set out in section 8, but the making of a Care or Supervision Order under Part III of the Act, or indeed the making of emergency orders. These topics are considered in detail in paras. 15–17—15–28 below.

Ascertaining the relevant issues—Provisions relating to Welfare Reports

Civil litigation in England is usually conducted on the basis of the so-called adversarial system in which the court merely listens to such evidence as the parties choose to put before it. It is self-evident that such a procedure would be quite unsuitable for ascertaining what is truly in a child's interests, not least because in many cases the voice of the child would not be heard at all; and the legislation has for many years provided procedures designed to ensure that investigations can be made, and the court be put in possession of the material needed to make an informed decision. The Children Act (s.7(1)) now provides that a court considering any question with respect to a child under the Act may ask a probation officer or local authority to arrange for a report to be made to the court "on such matters relating to the welfare of that child as are required to be dealt with in the report."

Extensive use was made of the comparable power in the divorce legislation; and surveys found that a report was called for in more than half of contested custody cases, and in a significant number of uncontested cases—where, for example, the child has not been in the care of the same person between the date of the parents' separation and the date of the divorce petition, or if a change in the child's residence seems likely to be in issue. The mere fact that there is a contest between the parents often leads the court to order a welfare report. Sometimes—partly in order to avoid overloading the available resources—the reference will specify particular matters on which a report is required; but this does not prevent the reporting officer from bringing to the notice of the court any other relevant matters: *Practice Direction (Divorce: Welfare Report)* [1981] 1 WLR 1162.

What the welfare officer does. The primary function of the welfare officer is to assist the court by providing the court with the factual information on which it can make a decision: *Scott v. Scott* [1986] 2 FLR 320. The welfare officer (who may be a member of a specialist team, or a probation officer doing other work as well) has power to inspect the court file; and he or she will then usually interview all the parties and visit the parent's home, see the parent's children and others involved, see the children with their parents in their homes, and see doctors and teachers if that would be appropriate in the circumstances. The welfare report should contain a statement of the

13–34

different proposals made by the parties for the future care of the children: *Re H (Conciliation: Welfare Reports)* [1986] 1 FLR 476. It should also contain:

> a statement of the conditions, both material and otherwise, in which the children are living or in which it is proposed that they should live;

> a reference to, or summary of, any relevant reports on the family and the children by independent persons such as doctors, school teachers, social workers, probation officers and police records;

> a statement of the relations of the children with each of their parents, including, when the children are old enough, a summary of their own views about their respective parents and their homes, and their own wishes as to the future.

Welfare reports and conciliation

13–35   Welfare officers are concerned to promote the welfare of families; and many individual welfare officers have a strong commitment to the ideals of conciliation. But the courts have emphasised the difference between the functions of a conciliator and a welfare officer: see para. 5–06 above.

Confidentiality

13–36   The welfare officer's report can be inspected by the parties, but it is to be treated as confidential and must not be shown to anyone other than the parties and their legal advisers. The court may, if it thinks it appropriate, order the officer to attend the hearing and submit to cross-examination.

Recommendations

The welfare officer's report may (and usually will) contain a recommendation; and this may be of great significance because it has been held (*Clark* v. *Clark* (1970) 114 SJ 318) that if courts do differ from the welfare officer's report, it is essential for them to explain their reasons. However, the decision is for the court, not for the welfare officer.

Hearsay evidence

13–37   Welfare reports almost by definition contain "hearsay"—that is to say they give an account of what the reporter has been told by other persons such as the child's school teacher. The Children Act contains a general provision that the court may, regardless of the normal rules of evidence, take account of statements contained in the report, and evidence given in respect of the matters referred to in the report so far as they are considered to be relevant: s.7(4). But this does not mean that the court should be uncritical; and it should obviously exercise caution in accepting the truth of untested statements made by someone not before the court: *Thompson* v. *Thompson* [1986] 1 FLR 212.

SUGGESTIONS FOR FURTHER READING

Hoggett and Pearl, Chap. 12.
Law Commission Report No. 172, *Guardianship and Custody* (1988).
An Introduction to the Children Act 1989 HMSO, (1989).
The Children Act 1989, Guidance and Regulations, Vol. 1, Court Orders, Department of Health (1991).
M. King, "Playing the Symbols—Custody and the Law Commission" (1987) 17 Family Law 186.
M. King and C. Piper, *How the Law thinks about Children* (1990).

Chapter 14

DISTINCTIVE FEATURES OF DIFFERENT KINDS OF FAMILY PROCEEDINGS

14–01 Although the Children Act 1989 introduces a code which enables all proceedings relating to a child to be brought before the same court, and empowers the court to make orders on the basis of the coherent and comprehensible principles discussed above, there remain important distinctions between different "family proceedings." This Chapter seeks to highlight the more significant characteristics of the "private law" proceedings. The "public law" proceedings (in which a local authority seeks a care or supervision order) are dealt with in Chapter 15.

This Chapter deals with

    (i)   Children in divorce;
   (ii)   Children in other matrimonial proceedings;
  (iii)   Children and domestic violence;
  (iv)   Adoption;
   (v)   Freestanding applications under the Children Act 1989;
  (vi)   Applications by a father for parental responsibility;
 (vii)   Other proceedings under the Children Act 1989;
(viii)   Wardship.

1. Children in Divorce

14–02 There were 148,000 children aged under 16 in the families of couples who divorced in 1989; and more than half the couples divorced in that year had children aged under 16. Divorce is statistically by far the largest class of "family proceedings"; and widespread concern about the welfare of children involved in parental divorce has led to the divorce court being given a special inquisitorial and protective role, in an attempt to ensure that satisfactory arrangements are made for the upbringing of children to be affected by a parental divorce.

Until the coming into force of the Children Act 1989 the court was—save in exceptional cases—prohibited from making any decree absolute unless and until it had made a declaration that the arrangements for the welfare of every "child of the family" under 16 were "satisfactory or the best that can be devised in the circumstances," or that it was impracticable for such arrangements to be made. A circuit judge would look into the arrangements for the children at a special "children's appointment," thus bringing at least one parent into direct contact with a judge even if the parties were agreed on the divorce and all the consequential arrangements.

In spite of the symbolic accordance thus attached to the children's welfare, this procedure was unsatisfactory in a number of respects—for example, the court was often in practice left without important information, and the hearings themselves tended to be short or even cursory. At a more theoretical level there were suggestions that the court's duty under section 41 was not an adjudicative function and that it smacked of paternalism: Booth Committee Report, para. 2.24. The Children Act 1989 took account of these criticisms; and the section 41 procedure has now been radically altered.

The court is no longer required to consider whether arrangements are "satisfactory." Instead it is to consider whether "in the light of the arrangements which have been, or are proposed to be, made for the upbringing and welfare" of children of the family under 16 (or over that age if the court directs that the section shall apply) it should exercise any of its powers under the Children Act 1989—in effect, whether it should require a welfare officer's report (para. 13–34 above), whether it should direct an investigation by a local authority into the child's circumstances with a view to an application being made for a care order or other action (CA 1989, s.37, para. 15–11 below), or whether it should make a "menu" or family assistance order: para. 13–09 above.

The system of routine children's appointments has been abolished. Instead the court's functions are initially allocated to the District Judge who will consider in private the—very detailed—information which the Rules require the petitioner to provide (and if possible agree with the respondent): see Family Proceedings Rules 1991, Form M4, and rr. 2.2 and 2.39. No doubt in the vast majority of cases the District Judge will certify that the court need not exercise its powers in respect of the children; but the Family Proceedings Rules do allow the District Judge to direct that further evidence be filed, that a welfare report be obtained, or that the parties attend a hearing: Family Proceedings Rules 1991, r. 2.39(3). Only in "exceptional circumstances" may the court, in the interests of the child, direct that the making of the decree absolute be postponed.

It may well be that this new procedure will prove more efficient in filtering out cases in which active intervention by the court is needed to safeguard the welfare of children than the old children's appointment system. But it can certainly be argued that the change effects a more significant change in the underlying philosophy of the law—for example, by removing from the court the task of deciding whether arrangements are "satisfactory" and substituting a requirement that the court consider whether to exercise its powers to make orders, and by enabling parents to obtain a divorce in most cases without any appearance of any kind before a judicial officer—than should properly have been effected by a provision almost hidden in the schedule of "Minor Amendments" effected by the Children Act 1989: see Sched. 12, para. 31. In this view, the changes are an important example of an underlying philosophy which some have seen as being directed towards "privatising the family."

Children over whom court's powers exercisable on divorce

14–03   The court's powers and duties in divorce proceedings—as has been mentioned—arise in respect of the "children of the family." This expression is widely defined by the Matrimonial Causes Act 1973, s.52(1) which provides that:

> "child of the family," in relation to the parties to a marriage, means:
>
> (a)   a child of both of those parties; and
>
> (b)   any other child, not being a child who has been placed with those parties as foster-parents by a local authority or voluntary organisation, who has been treated by both of those parties as a child of their family."

Hence all children—whether they be legitimate, legitimated, illegitimate, or adopted—of the two parties to the marriage are included within the definition of "child of the family"; but the extension of the definition to all children "treated" as a child of the family by both parties makes the existence of a biological—or even a formal legal relationship (such as adoption)—between the child and the parties irrelevant.

The most obvious example of a child of the family who is *not* the child of both spouses is a step-child living with the spouses. The step-child will of course remain a child of the family in respect of his birth parents. The definition thus accurately reflects the erosion of traditional kinship patterns which is incidental to increasing divorce and remarriage, as a result of which a child may have links (biological and/or factual) with several different marriages.

But the definition of "child of the family" is very wide; and it seems clear, for example, that a child who is being looked after by relatives on a long term basis will be a child of their family; as will a child who is privately fostered by them. (A child who is placed by a local authority is excluded, no doubt because it is thought that the local authority would make appropriate arrangements in such a case.)

But not an unborn child. It has been held to be impossible to treat an unborn child as a child of the family: if a man marries a woman who is pregnant by someone else the baby will be a child of their family if the husband treats it as such after birth—even if the wife has deceived him into thinking that he is the father—but if the relationship breaks down *before* the birth the child will be outside the definition whatever the husband may have said about his intentions to treat the baby as his own: see *A* v. *A (Family: Unborn Child)* [1974] Fam 6.

2. Children in Other Matrimonial Proceedings

Judicial Separation and *Nullity* proceedings are governed by the rules,   **14–04** outlined above, which apply in divorce. Proceedings under the Domestic Proceedings and Magistrates' Courts Act 1978—seeking maintenance, for example—are within the definition of family proceedings, and the court will thus be able to exercise the powers conferred by the Children Act and outlined above in respect of any child of the family. Moreover, the Domestic Proceedings and Magistrates' Courts Act 1978 contains a provision that once an application is made under the provisions of that Act dealing with financial orders (see para. 9–06 above) the court must not dismiss or make a final order on the application until it has decided whether to exercise any of its powers under the Children Act: see s.8. No doubt the policy underlying this provision is similar to that reflected in MCA 1973, s.41: the fact that an application has been made of itself suggests that the court should be alive to the possibility that the welfare of children may be at risk, and the court should consider the matter—whether the parties want it or not.

3. Children and Domestic Violence

The statutory provisions under which orders excluding one spouse   **14–05** from the family home or otherwise providing legal protection against molestation and violence have been discussed at para. 6–09 above (Domestic Violence and Matrimonial Proceedings Act 1976), para. 6–13 above (Matrimonial Homes Act 1983), and para. 6–32 above (Domestic Proceedings and Magistrates' Courts Act 1978). It is self-evident that situations in which there is thought to be a need for protection by an adult may involve a risk to the children, but in the past the superior courts have had no powers to make orders in such proceedings dealing with the children's upbringing, and no power to require a welfare report or local authority intervention.

This gap in the law has now been filled by the Children Act 1989. By classifying the relevant proceedings as "family proceedings" the Act gives the court all the powers referred to above which it previously lacked. It is particularly to be noted that the court may act if it considers that a section 8 order should be made even though no application for such an order has been made: CA 1989, s.10(1).

It seems probable that the powers to make short term private law orders, and to seek a welfare report, and the public law powers dealt with in Chapter 15 below to direct investigation by the local authority—and to make interim orders—in cases in which it appears that it may be appropriate for a care or supervision order to be made (CA 1989, s.37(1)) will be particularly useful in practice.

4. Adoption

14–06   All proceedings under the Adoption Act 1976 (*e.g.* applications to *free a child for adoption* as well as an application for an adoption order) are brought within the Children Act definition of "family proceedings," with the result that the court may exercise its powers to make orders under the Children Act as described above. It would seem that the court could make any of the section 8 orders, whether or not it makes an adoption order—so that it could (for example) make a residence order in favour of a foster-parent or grandparent rather than making an adoption or freeing order if it considered that to do so would *better* serve the child's welfare—even if the conditions for making an adoption order, outlined in Chapter 12, have been satisfied. Moreover, it would seem that it could make a contact, specific issue or prohibited steps order as well as making an adoption or freeing order.

Two points should be kept in mind, however. The first is that the fact that the court has jurisdiction to make an order does not mean that it will frequently wish to exercise its powers. In particular, adoption has traditionally been seen as a technique for putting the adoptive parents fully in control, and it is reasonable to suppose that the courts will continue to view the imposition of restrictions on the adopters' parental authority as being exceptional: see *Re C (A Minor) (Adoption Order: Conditions)* [1988] 2 FLR 159, HL, and *Re R (A Minor) (Adoption Order: Access)* [1991] 2 FLR 78, CA. Secondly, the fact that the court has power to make Children Act orders in adoption proceedings does not, of course, mean that the court could make an adoption (or freeing) order in any other Children Act proceedings however much it considered adoption to be the best solution for the child, and however much some or all of those involved might agree: as already pointed out, adoption remains juristically distinct from all other orders relating to children and the procedures laid down by the Adoption Act 1976 must be followed if the court is to have power to make an adoption or freeing order.

5. "Freestanding" Applications under the Children Act 1989

14–07   So far, we have been looking at situations in which the fact that there are other "family proceedings" already in being is thought to be sufficient justification for allowing the court to exercise its powers of intervention by making orders. It would obviously be absurd to restrict the court's powers to these cases, and yet to allow *anyone* to apply to the court for *any* order relating to any child would equally obviously be unacceptable in a society which accepts claims for the autonomy of the family.

The Children Act resolves in an ingenious way the question of how it is to be decided whether a person has a sufficient interest to be allowed to bring proceedings: certain people are to be *entitled* to apply for *any section 8 order*; certain people are *entitled* to apply for *specified section 8 orders*; certain people are in effect *debarred* from seeking orders; but *anyone else may apply to the court for leave* to make the application, and the Act lays down guidelines for the court in deciding such applications for leave:

(i) *Persons entitled to apply for any section 8 order*

The Act provides (s.10(4)(a)) that any *parent or guardian* and any *person* **14–08** *in whose favour a residence order* is in force is entitled to apply for any order.

This provision, in effect, defines those who are deemed to have a legitimate interest in seeking the court's intervention, irrespective of the particular circumstances of the case. Thus, for example one spouse should be able to apply for a residence order even if he or she does not want to bring divorce proceedings. Again, although the father of an illegitimate child does not, in the absence of a court order or parental responsibility agreement, have parental responsibility for the child, it was thought reasonable to give him the right to apply to the court for a residence order, a contact order—and in practice such applications may well be numerous—or any other order (for example a specific issue order). A person who has a residence order has thereby parental responsibility, and may thus need to seek a specific issue order or a prohibited steps order to enable that responsibility to be properly met.

Of course, the fact that a person is entitled to apply for an order does not mean that it will be appropriate to grant it; and the legislature was conscious that vexatious or harassing applications might be made, even by a parent. Hence the court is given power (s.91(14)) on disposing of any application to make an order that a named person be debarred from making any application for an order under the Act without leave of the court. For example, the court might direct that no further application for contact be permitted by the father of an illegitimate child in cases where the father's obsessive attitudes led him to persist in making hopeless applications—and, of course, the court could also exercise the power to make an order of its own motion prohibiting the father from contacting the child (and presumably the court would have jurisdiction to prohibit the father from coming within a specified distance of the child's home).

(ii) *Persons entitled to apply for residence or contact orders*

Some people may have—or have had—a sufficiently close link with **14–09** the child to justify their being entitled to apply for contact, or to justify their seeking to have care of the child in their home, without it being appropriate for them to have the right to make applications which would interfere with the specific decision—taking powers of those who have "parental responsibility" for the child. The detailed provisions (contained in s.10(5)) are complex; but the scheme may be summarised. Any of the following persons is entitled to apply for a *residence* or for a *contact* order:

(a) Anyone to whom the child has ever been a "child of the family" (as defined above: para. 14–03), *e.g.* any step-parent of the child.

(b) Anyone with whom the child has lived for three or more years. The period need not necessarily be continuous, but must not have ended more than three months before the application: s.10(10).

(c) Anyone who has the consent of all those who have a residence order, or (if the child is in care under a care order) anyone who has the consent of the local authority or (provided there is *no* care order) the consent of everyone who has parental responsibility: s.10(5).

(iii) *Persons who require leave to apply*

14–10   The Act adopts what is sometimes described as the "open door" policy. The court may make a section 8 order if an application for the order has been made by a person who has *obtained the leave of the court* to make the application: s.10(1)(a)(ii). The Rules (Family Proceedings Rules 1991, r. 4.3) stipulate that an applicant must make the request for leave in writing setting out the reasons for the request and providing a draft of the application in respect of which leave is sought. In effect, therefore, anyone—unless debarred under the rules summarised in para. 14–11 below—may bring an issue to the court's notice; and the decision whether to allow the application to proceed is dependent on the exercise of a judicial discretion.

In deciding whether to grant leave the court will, of course, apply the principle that the child's welfare is paramount (s.1); but more specific guidance is also given.

First, where the application is made *by the child concerned* the court must be satisfied that he or she has sufficient understanding to make the proposed application (s.8(8))—but it seems that the court need not apply the further guidelines set out below.

Secondly, where the applicant is someone other than the child, the court must have "particular regard" to:

(a) the nature of the proposed application for the section 8 order;
(b) the applicant's connection with the child;
(c) any risk there might be of that proposed application disrupting the child's life to such an extent that he would be harmed by it; and

(d) where the child is being looked after by a local authority—(i) the authority's plans for the child's future; and (ii) the wishes and feelings of the child's parents.

It is fairly easy to see how these provisions might be applied in many cases; and if the matter is clear cut the court might well make use of the power to deal with applications for leave on the papers without a hearing: Family Proceedings Rules 1991, r. 4.3(2)(a).

Some examples may be given. Consider, first, an application by grandparents who are estranged from the child's mother to the extent that she returns birthday presents and letters. The grandparents want to resume the contact which they had with their grandchildren while the father and mother were married, and which the grandchildren want. In such a case, the nature of the application would be to re-establish well-settled conventional family links; the applicants would have a well-established connection with the children, and the disruption caused by the application would probably be slight. It therefore seems likely that the court would grant an application for leave to apply for a contact order.

Again there may be cases in which the importance of the issue raised might outweigh all other considerations:

> In *Re D (A Minor) (Wardship: Sterilisation)* [1976] Fam 185 the mother of an 11-year-old handicapped girl was concerned about the possibility that the girl might be seduced and give birth to an abnormal child. On the advice of a consultant paediatrician and gynaecologist she made arrangements for the child to be sterilised. But an individual who was concerned for the daughter's welfare made the child a ward of court so that the court could decide whether the mother's decision was really in the girl's interest. The court held that the operation should not be carried out: it would be wrong irreversibly to deprive the girl of the basic human right to bear children.

It seems probable that the court would today grant an application for leave to seek a specific issues order because of the importance of the issue—all the more so in the light of the court's policy that sterilisation of minors should be court-approved. Again, no doubt the fact that the applicant could show that she was motivated by genuine concern for the particular child would weigh with the court (whereas, perhaps, an application by a pressure group seeking primarily to advance a particular course would be less likely to be granted). But there is no doubt that some applications for leave might cause difficulty. Consider, for example, the facts of *B v. W (Wardship: Appeal)* [1979] 1 WLR 1041:

> A wealthy businessman hoped that his grandson would succeed him in business and arranged for the grandson to go to boarding school. The boy's mother (who resented her father's domination and thought he was seeking to gain control over her son's upbringing) decided to take the

boy away from the school. The grandfather made the boy a ward; and it was held that he had behaved properly in so doing.

Should the grandparent in such a case be given leave to seek a specific issues order dealing with the child's education? It might well be that the grandparent would in practice still prefer to invoke the wardship jurisdiction (as he or she would be entitled to do: see para. 14–14 below) because, first, he would not need to seek leave to make the child a ward; and, secondly, making the child a ward would mean that *all* important issues affecting the child should be taken to the court.

It seems inevitable that there will be many cases in which different views might reasonably be held about the weight to be attached to the listed factors; but that is of the nature of a discretionary jurisdiction. The very uncertainty of the outcome of an application for leave may, however, defeat the policy that the statutory jurisdiction be preferred to wardship; since it is not clear why an applicant should seek leave so long as he or she can, without leave, make the child a ward of court.

(iv) *Persons debarred from applying for leave*

14–11   The Act is concerned to give local authorities control over the discharge of their responsibilities to children in care; and it is therefore provided that a person who has been the child's local authority foster parent within the last six months may not seek leave to apply for any section 8 order: s.9(3). There are exceptions—notably relatives, or someone with whom the child has lived for three years.

As already pointed out, the Act adopts the philosophy that the state can only intervene in the upbringing of a child if the child is at risk because of a failure in the family. It would completely defeat this policy if local authorities were to be entitled to apply for residence orders on the basis simply that the child's welfare would be best served in this way; and accordingly the Act provides that no local authority may apply for a residence or contact order and the court is prohibited from making such orders in favour of a local authority: s.9(2). There are other provisions in the legislation designed to achieve this objective, but they are best considered in the context of the court's jurisdiction to make care orders: see para. 15–09 below.

6. Application for Parental Responsibility by Father of an Illegitimate Child

14–12   The father of an illegitimate child does not as such have parental responsibility for that child unless:

> (i) the father and mother make and file a "parental responsibility" agreement as explained at para. 11–37 above; or

(ii) the court makes an order (under Children Act 1989, s.4(1)(a)) conferring parental responsibility on him.

A parental responsibility order may be made in two different procedures. First, the Act (in pursuance of its general policy that anyone in whose favour a residence order has been made should also have parental responsibility) provides that where the court makes a residence order in favour of the father it must also make a parental responsibility order in his favour: s.12(1). The parental responsibility order cannot be brought to an end at any time while the residence order remains in force. In such a case the parental responsibility order reflects the fact that the father will be engaged in caring for the child, and needs parental responsibility to do so.

The Act (s.4(1)(a)) also provides for the court to make a parental responsibility order on the application of the father. It has been said that the undoubted aim of the legislature was, in an appropriate case, to equate the position of the father of a child born out of wedlock to that of the father of a legitimate child *Re H (Illegitimate Children: Father: Parental Rights) (No. 2)* [1991] 1 FLR 214, 220, *per* Balcombe LJ; and the decision whether to make an order on such an application depends on the court's assessment of whether it would in the circumstances be in the child's interests to do so (CA 1989, s.1(1)); and on whether the court considers that it would be better to make the order than to make no order at all: s.1(5), para. 13–30 above.

The court may make an order even in cases in which the father is not in a position to exercise any parental authority over the child — for example, where the court has decided that it would not at the moment be in the child's interests for the father even to have contact with the child.

> In *Re C (Minors) (Parental Rights)* [1992] 1 FLR 1, CA, the court considered that it would be in the child's interests that the father should have a right to withhold agreement to adoption.

Again:

> In *D v. Hereford and Worcester CC* [1991] 1 FLR 205 the court made an order giving the father parental responsibility notwithstanding the fact that the child was in care and the local authority did not intend to include the father in its plans for the child's future.

And in the particularly striking case of *Re H (Illegitimate Children: Father; Parental Rights) (No. 2)* [1991] 1 FLR 214, CA:

> — the court made an order giving a father parental responsibility although it also dispensed with his agreement to the making of an order declaring the child free for adoption: see para 12–27 above. The father's

"rights" would only be of practical value if, for some reason, no adoption order were made.

It is obvious that the exercise of the discretion to make a parental responsibility order requires a close analysis of the precise effect which a parental responsibility order would have; and an assessment of how far the making of such an order would benefit the child. It has been said that the extent of the father's commitment, the state of his current relationship with the children and his reasons for applying are matters which the court will regard as being of particular relevance; but the court should also ask:

> "Was the association between the parties sufficiently enduring, and has the father by his conduct during and since the application shown sufficient commitment to the children, to justify giving the father a legal status equivalent to that whch he would have enjoyed if the parties had been married, due attention being paid to the fact that a number of his parental rights would, if conferred on him by a [Parental Responsibility order] be unenforceable under current conditions": *Re C (Minors) (Parental Rights)* [1992] 1 FLR 1, 8, *per* Waite J.

But this guidance was given (and the three decisions referred to in the text were taken) under the comparable (but not identical) provisions of the Family Law Act 1987. It could be argued that they reflect a concern to do justice to the claims of the father rather than the structured approach to the child's welfare which will be required under the Children Act 1989.

Finally, it should be remembered that an application by a father for a parental responsibility order constitutes "family proceedings"; and accordingly the court may make any of the section 8 orders referred to in para. 13–09 above if it considers that to do so would be the best way of promoting the child's welfare. For example, it could in an appropriate case make a contact order in favour of the father whilst rejecting his application for a parental responsibility order; or it would, whilst granting the application for a parental responsibility order also make a contact order in favour of the child's maternal grandparents.

7. Other Applications Under The Children Act 1989

14–13   It should not be overlooked that "family proceedings" are defined to include a number of miscellaneous proceedings under the Children Act itself, which are dealt with elsewhere in this book—for example, applications by an individual to be appointed a guardian (CA 1989, s.5), and applications to terminate guardianship (CA 1989, s.6). In all these cases the court may exercise its powers to make any appropriate section 8 orders.

8. Applications under the Inherent Jurisdiction of the High Court in Relation to Children—Wardship, Museum Piece or Essential Safeguard?

The main (but not the only manifestation of the courts' inherent   **14–14**
jurisdiction over children is the wardship jurisdiction; and it is
necessary to deal with wardship at some length. This is because,
although the Children Act 1989 restricts the availability of the
jurisdiction, founded on the prerogative of the Crown as *parens
patriae*, whereby issues relating to the upbringing of a child could be
resolved in wardship, it does not abolish it. Most of the restrictions
relate to "public law" cases, and it is still open to individuals to
invoke the wardship jurisdiction. The policy of the legislation appears
to have been—in the "private law" context—to seek to provide most
of the advantages of wardship in proceedings under the Children
Act—notably in the freestanding applications discussed above. In
order to enable the reader to form a view as to whether this policy is
likely to be successful, the text outlines, first, the main features of
wardship. It then summarises the restrictions placed on the
availability of wardship (first by the courts themselves, and then by
the Children Act). Finally, it again poses the question whether
"freestanding" proceedings under the Children Act are in practice
likely to supplant wardship in those cases in which it remains.

The background
The wardship jurisdiction was developed on the basis that it was   **14–15**
the Crown's prerogative as *parens patriae* to have the care of those
who could not look after themselves. For long, wardship was used
almost exclusively by the wealthy; but (in the words of the Law
Commission; Working Paper No. 101, para. 3.2) over the years
wardship "came to be regarded not so much as a refuge for orphaned
heiresses and a bulwark against predatory adventurers but rather as a
means of resolving all kinds of disputes over children ... " The
increased popularity of wardship can be seen from the statistics: in
1951, there were only 74 originating summonses issued to make a
child a ward. By 1971, the figure had risen to 622, by 1981 to 1,903,
and the numbers have continued to rise: in 1990 there were 4,721
applications to make a child a ward.
The reason for this increased recourse to wardship was, in part at
least, its great flexibility. There was no need to establish any
"ground" before a child could be made a ward: the issue of a
summons had the immediate effect that the child became a ward, and
thereafter (so long as the wardship continued) no important step in
the child's life could be taken without the court's consent. Moreover,
in deciding questions relating to the child's upbringing the court
would apply the principle that the child's welfare was paramount;
and the flexibility and wide range of powers at the courts' disposal

made wardship a remarkable example of the successful adaptation of a long standing institution to modern circumstances. However, for a number of reasons—including the considerable burden which its use placed on scarce judicial resources—wardship became unpopular with those responsible for the administration of the courts; and the Children Act 1989 accordingly imposed significant restrictions on the use of wardship by local authorities.

1. Characteristics of Wardship

14–16 The salient characteristics of wardship are: (a) any individual may make a child a ward of court; (b) all important issues affecting a ward must be referred to the court; which (c) has wide, flexible and effective powers to safeguard and promote the ward's welfare; and (d) a careful and inquisitorial procedure to assist in getting at the truth.

(a) *Any individual may make a child a ward of court*
14–17   Any individual—even a concerned neighbour or friend, as in *Re D (A Minor) (Wardship: Sterilisation)* [1976] Fam 185, above para. 14–10 may, without leave, issue a summons making a child a ward of court; and in cases of urgency orders can be made even before the summons has been issued by a judge sitting at his home, or even over the telephone.

(b) *All important issues affecting a ward must be referred to the court*
14–18   The principle underlying the wardship jurisdiction was that "custody" of the ward—*i.e.* the bundle of rights and duties attributed by law to parents relating to their child's upbringing: see *Hewer* v. *Bryant* [1970] 1 QB 357, 373, *per* Sachs L.J.—remains in the court, which delegates aspects of custody (for example, "care and control" to others). It followed from this that the court would exercise an extensive and, if necessary, detailed control over its ward. Making a child a ward of court immediately "freezes" the situation, and inhibits anyone from taking action relating to the child without the court's consent. This is indeed one of the main reasons for the popularity of wardship and it is not clear that any procedure available under the statutory code contained in the Children Act 1989 is equally efficacious. Conversely, of course, the need to apply to the court to decide all "important" issues about a child's upbringing increases, perhaps unnecessarily, the burden placed on the legal system.

(c) *The wardship court has wide flexible and effective powers to safeguard the child's welfare*
14–19   The effectiveness of wardship as a means for protecting children stems, to a substantial extent, from the court's readiness to grant injunctions, breach of which would be a contempt punishable by fine,

imprisonment, or other means; and from the fact that the court's wide powers may be exercised in very flexible ways. The width of the powers assumed in wardship is well illustrated by the fact that in wardship the court has—contrary to the normal principle that injunctions only bind the parties—granted an injunction operating against the world at large:

> In *Re AB (Wardship: Jurisdiction)* [1985] FLR 470 the court held that it had power to grant such an injunction prohibiting publication of facts which would have revealed that the ward's mother was a person who, at the age of 11, had been found guilty (after a trial involving much publicity) of killing two small boys. The court considered that if the mother's true identity were disclosed, it would "damage the fragile stability she had achieved and thereby endanger the well-being of her own infant child": *per* Balcombe L.J.: *Re C (A Minor) (No. 2) (Wardship: Publication of Information)* [1990] 1 FLR 263, 271.

No precise limit has ever been placed on the wardship jurisdiction. Indeed, it has been said that the "wardship judge has 'limitless power" to protect the ward from any interference with his or her welfare, direct or indirect: *Re K (Wards: Leave to Call as Witnesses)* [1988] 1 FLR 435, 442 and (as noted at para. 11–29 above) consistently with this view in *Re R (A Minor) (Wardship: Medical Treatment)* [1991] 4 All ER 177, the Court of Appeal held they were not limited to the powers of a parent over the parent's child.

Not only were the court's powers wide, they were flexible; and extremely sophisticated orders could be made. For example:

> In *Re B (A Minor) (Child Abuse: Custody)* [1990] 2 FLR 317 a therapist and a social worker concluded that the way in which a four year-old had played with anatomically correct dolls suggested awareness of masturbation and oral sexual intercourse, and that the child had been sexually abused by his parents. The parents—who denied that there was any substance in these allegations—retained a close and happy relationship with the boy who was upset and tearful when removed from them. Although the Judge concluded that there was a strong likelihood that the child had been subjected to some form of sexual abuse, he considered that it would be in the child's best interest to return to his parents. An order was made that the child should remain in the care of the local authority with a view to his return to the care and control of his family as soon as possible. The Judge continued the wardship and directed that the case be brought back before him in six months time for further consideration. A method was to be worked out whereby there would be continuing supervision of the child after his return to the parents.

Since wardship proceedings are within the definition of "family proceedings" (see para. 13–04 above) the court will now be able to make any order—for example a contact or residence order—from the "menu" of orders set out in section 8 of the Children Act; and it will have the wide powers to make financial orders which are conferred by the Act on courts in family proceedings; but it would seem that the court may still in wardship make detailed and flexible orders, which may not be within—or perhaps could only with difficulty be brought within—the statutory framework. If that is true, there will remain a case for invoking wardship in preference to seeking orders under the statutory code where to do so is still permitted.

(d) *Court makes use of careful and inquisitorial procedure*

14–20   The wardship court's jurisdiction is said to be essentially parental and administrative, and the procedure is extremely flexible. In particular wardship proceedings are not subject to the normal rules of evidence and procedure applicable in ordinary legislation. The judge may see the child and perhaps one or other or both parents in private if it is considered desirable to do so. It is the practice to admit hearsay evidence if that is the best available, and the judge may take into account the contents of a confidential report (*e.g.* by the Official Solicitor who sometimes represents the ward) without disclosing its contents to the parents (even though the ordinary rules of natural justice might require the disclosure of any adverse allegations against them): see *Official Solicitor* v. *K* [1965] AC 201, HL: *Re C (A Minor)* (1990) *The Times*, December 21, CA—but it is not clear whether the Court of Appeal regarded this practice as an incident of the quasi-administrative wardship jurisdiction or considered that it was applicable in all cases relating to children. The distinction may be important in the context of the Children Act: are there in this respect, wider powers available in wardship than in other procedures dealing with the upbringing of children?

The fact that wardship ensured a detailed, thorough and skilled judicial enquiry was one of the factors which, prior to the enactment of the Children Act 1989, accounted for the increased recourse to wardship by some local authorities—even although the case might have been dealt with under the statutory code then contained in the Children and Young Persons Act 1969. For example:

In *Re E (A Minor) Child Abuse: Evidence* [1991] 1 FLR 420, the local authority had removed a happy, well adjusted child, from his parents on the basis of allegations that he had been sexually abused by his parents. The child showed no signs which might suggest that he had been abused, and the allegations were founded on what other children (aged four and three) had said. The court, in a judgment extending over 35 pages, carried out a detailed enquiry into the allegations, held that they were without substance, that the parents had been subjected to considerable injustice by having such allegations made and pursued against them, and that accordingly it would be unthinkable to remove the child from the care of his parents or to require him to be supervised by the local authority. The judge considered that the social worker primarily involved in the case had become so emotionally involved as to be incapable of exercising a dispassionate judgment; and the prolonged interviews to which the children had been subjected might well have damaged the child. It was true that the parents were unconventional about nudity and sexual matters, that they lived apart during the week, smoked cannabis, and lived in "development corporation housing"; but the judge said that the world "would be a dull place if everyone were the same," and that the parents' life style was not so unusual as to require them to be asked to justify it.

(e) The courts with jurisdiction

Traditionally, the wardship jurisdiction was exercisable only in the **14–21** High Court; and it is still only the High Court which can make an order that a minor be made a ward of court, or that a ward of court should cease to be a ward. However, the judges of the High Court no longer have a monopoly over wardship cases:

Proceedings must be *started* in the High Court; and only the High Court can *terminate* wardship; but, subject to that, wardship proceedings may be transferred to the County Court: M & FPA 1984, s.38. Moreover, even if the case is still being dealt with in the High Court, that jurisdiction (as a result of the flexible system introduced by the Courts Act 1971 and by the Courts and Legal Services Act 1990) may be, and in some parts of the country is in practice, often exercised by a circuit judge sitting as a High Court judge (or indeed sometimes by a barrister sitting as a deputy High Court judge).

2. Restrictions on the Availability of Wardship

One of the great advantages of wardship has always been that it is **14–22** characterised by the "golden thread" (as Dunn J. described it in *Re D (A Minor) (Justices' Decision: Review)* [1977] Fam 158) that the welfare of the child is considered "first, last and all the time." But—although the courts have been reluctant to define the boundaries of the wardship jurisdiction—it was never unlimited in availability or scope. The text first outlines the restrictions which the courts have themselves created; it then outlines the restrictions imposed by the Children Act 1989.

(a) *Judicially imposed restrictions*

The courts have long been cautious about the exercise of the **14–23** wardship jurisdiction. It was said, for example, that "great care must be exercised in invoking that jurisdiction in situations in which third parties are involved and in which a statutory code or framework for dealing with the matter has been established": *Re K (Wards: Leave to Call as Witnesses)* [1988] 1 FLR 435, 441. Hence, in *Re H (Minors) (Wardship: Surety)* [1991] 1 FLR 40 the Court of Appeal held that a judge had been wrong to order that the father of children who had been removed to Pakistan by their grandfather should provide a surety of £25,000 to be forfeited if the children were not returned within 21 days: the court considered it to be obvious that far-reaching limitations in principle on the exercise of this jurisdiction must exist; and the jurisdiction is habitually exercised within those limitations": see *per* Sir J. Pennycuick, *Re X (A Minor) (Wardship: Jurisdiction)* [1975] Fam 47, 61.

Some examples of limitations which the court has accepted can be given:

(i) *There is no jurisdiction in respect of an unborn child:*

14-24   In *Re F (in utero) (Wardship)* [1988] 2 FLR 307, CA—a pregnant woman who had a history of severe mental disturbance disappeared shortly before the expected date of her child's birth. An application was made to ward the unborn child; and it was intended to ask the court to make orders to help trace the mother and to ensure that she lived in a suitable place until the birth. The Court of Appeal held that, for three reasons, the wardship jurisdiction was not available. First, a foetus has no right of action, and is incapable of being a party to an action. Secondly, the only practical consequence of warding the foetus would be to control the mother, and in such a sensitive field which affected the liberty of the subject, it was for Parliament (rather than the courts) to take any necessary action. Finally, conflicts of interest could arise between the foetus and the mother—for example, if a mother wanted her pregnancy to be terminated; and the wardship jurisdiction was not appropriate for the resolution of such conflicts since wardship was concerned to promote only one of those interests, the welfare of the child.

(ii) *Public interest sometimes overrides child's welfare*

14-25   In deciding whether (and how) to exercise its powers over a ward the court may need to consider not only the child's interests but also the rights of outsiders and indeed the public interest: compare *In Re X (A Minor) (Wardship: Jurisdiction)* [1975] Fam 47 (where the court refused to prohibit publication of a book about the ward's father, notwithstanding the psychological damage she would be likely to suffer when she discovered its contents); and *Re C (A Minor) (No. 2) (Wardship: Publication of Information)* [1990] 1 FLR 263, CA, where the court refused to permit the publication of information (including photographs) of the doctors and nurses who had been involved in the treatment of a handicapped child, because the baby's welfare required that those caring for her should not have to cope with the massive personal publicity which would be likely to follow.

(iii) *Wardship supplanted by legislative code*

14-26   The most important of the restrictions which the court has itself imposed on the availability of wardship stems from the well settled principle of administrative law that the inherent jurisdiction of the courts is not to be allowed to interfere with action properly taken under a comprehensive legislative code. Thus:

> In *Re JS (A Minor) (Wardship: Boy Soldier)* [1991] FLR 7 a boy soldier, who was unhappy in the army, went absent without leave in order to live with his parents. The boy's mother made him a ward of court, and sought an order restraining the Secretary of State for Defence from arresting her son. The court refused: even if a soldier could be warded, questions of military control would be left to the military authorities.

Again:

> In *Re Mohamed Arif (an infant)* [1968] Ch 643 two men started wardship proceedings to stop children being deported as illegal immigrants. The court struck out the applications: the court (said Denning L.J. at p. 662) "will not exercise its jurisdiction so as to interfere with the statutory machinery set up by Parliament. The wardship process is not to be used so as to put a clog on the decisions of the immigration officers or as a means of reviewing them."

But the most important application in the years prior to the coming into force of the Children Act 1989 of the general principle that a prerogative jurisdiction should not be allowed to interfere with a legislative code is to be found in the refusal of the courts to allow the wardship jurisdiction to be invoked to supervise or review the merits of decisions taken by local authorities within their statutory powers:

> In *A v. Liverpool City Council* (1981) 2 FLR 222, HL, a mother made her child, who was the subject of a care order, a ward of court in an attempt to challenge the local authority's decision to reduce her access to him from once weekly to once monthly. The House of Lords—influenced to some extent by the cost and delay caused by excessive use of wardship jurisdiction—held that the courts could not exercise that jurisdiction in order to review the merits of the authority's decision. This was because Parliament had, in the child care code, marked out an area in which, subject to the enacted limitations and safeguards, decisions for the child's welfare were removed from the parents and from supervision by the courts.

This restrictive approach was reinforced by the House in *Re W (A Minor) (Care Proceedings: Wardship)* [1985] FLR 879, HL:

> Grandparents and other relatives wanted to get care and control of a child whom the local authority intended to free for adoption. They issued a summons making her a ward, but the House of Lords held that it would be wrong to use the wardship jurisdiction in such a case. Decisions about where the child was to have its home had been entrusted by Parliament to the local authority. It was irrelevant that the relatives had at that time no right to be heard in freeing, access, or other legal proceedings.

(b) *Restrictions imposed by the Children Act 1989*

14–27 The result of *A* v. *Liverpool City Council* was to prevent the use of wardship by parents and others who considered that local authority decisions would not promote a child's welfare; but it did nothing to prevent local authorities invoking wardship even in circumstances in which the statutory child care procedures could have been used—or even if those procedures had been unsuccessfully invoked by the local authority.

The Children Act 1989 introduced specific, and much more extensive, restrictions on the availability of the wardship jurisdiction, apparently with two objectives in view. First, there is what may be described as the rule of law/civil liberties argument: it would be wrong to allow local authorities to circumvent the requirements now imposed by statute in order to define and restrict the circumstances in which the state may intervene in family life by invoking the broad inherent jurisdiction based solely on an assessment of the child's interests. But, secondly, if those requirements are met, and the court has—in the exercise of its statutory discretion—decided to make a care order, then it should not be possible to have the court supervise the day-to-day exercise of the local authority's discretion.

14–28 The main restrictions imposed by the Children Act are summarised here, although they will be better understood in the context of the statutory scheme governing local authority powers embodied in the Children Act 1989 and discussed in Chapter 15 below.

(i) A local authority cannot invoke the wardship jurisdiction (or seek any other exercise of the court's inherent jurisdiction with respect to children) unless it has obtained leave of the court. The court may only grant such leave in defined and restricted circumstances: Children Act 1989, s.100(3), (4).

(ii) The court cannot exercise its wardship (or other inherent) jurisdiction with respect to children so as to require a child to be placed in care or put under the supervision of a local authority or to be accommodated by a local authority: Children Act 1989, s.100(2)(a), (b).

(iii) The wardship jurisdiction must not be exercised so as to make a child who is the subject of a care order a ward of court; and the statutory power which the court formerly enjoyed of committing a child to care in wardship has been abolished: Children Act 1989, s.100(1).

(iv) Wardship is brought to an end if a court makes a care order under the provisions of the Children Act 1989: Children Act 1989, s.91(4).

(v) Finally it is provided that the wardship or other inherent jurisdiction with respect to children shall not be exercised "for the purpose of conferring on any local authority power to determine any question which has arisen, or which may arise, in connection with any aspect of parental responsibility for a child": s.100(2)(d).

It will be noted that there are no specific restrictions on recourse to wardship by private individuals (unless a child is already the subject of a care order); and it follows that, subject to the limitations which the court has itself imposed, discussed above, wardship is still available to private citizens. The "open door" policy, whereby anyone may, with leave apply to the court for a Children Act order, coupled with the fact that courts will, in principle, be able to make specific issue and prohibited steps orders in Children Act proceedings, evidence an intention that wardship should be allowed to wither away. Is this situation likely to be achieved?

3. Conclusion—life in the corpse?

In summary, there would seem to be a number of circumstances in which wardship is likely still to be invoked: **14–29**

(i) It is still the law (see Supreme Court Act 1981, s.41(2) as **14–30** amended by CA 1989, Sched. 13, para. 45(2)) that a child (unless he or she is already subject to a care order) becomes a ward on the issue of a summons making the application; and that thereafter no important step may be taken in the ward's life without leave of the court. It is not easy to see how this result can be achieved—at any rate so simply—in any procedure under the Children Act 1989. Hence, unless and until further restrictions are imposed on the right to invoke the wardship jurisdiction, individuals concerned that potentially irreversible damage might be done to a child's welfare are likely to prefer to use wardship in preference to making an application under the Children Act.

(ii) It has already been noted that many people with a legitimate **14–31** interest in a child's upbringing have no *right* to bring proceedings under the Children Act, but only a *right to seek leave*. It is not easy to see why such persons should prefer to seek leave rather than exercising the right (still unfettered, unless the child is the subject of a care order) to ward the child.
It is true that this argument needs to be treated with caution for three reasons. First, the availability of legal aid may have a strong influence on the practicability of starting legal proceedings; and it could be that applications for legal aid to invoke the wardship jurisdiction will be treated unfavourably. Secondly, it is not beyond the bounds of possibility that the courts will, on the basis of the principle of *A* v. *Liverpool City Council* (para. 14–26 above), hold that

the Children Act is intended to form a comprehensive code governing applications in connection with the upbringing of children; and only allow the wardship jurisdiction to be invoked in exceptional circumstances. Thirdly, the ready availability of wardship is to some extent a consequence of the procedural rules; and those rules might be made much more restrictive without requiring further primary legislation.

14–32   (iii) There will remain cases in which an applicant does not merely wish to apply for an order which will determine the outcome of a particular dispute, but wants the court to be empowered to exercise a detailed supervision over decisions relating to the child—for example, consider the case of the handicapped baby whose future was in issue in *Re C (A Minor) (No. 1) (Wardship: Medical Treatment)* [1990] 1 FLR 263, CA, para. 13–10 above. In this, and similar cases, it might well be thought that in view of the possibility of controversial media coverage (see *Re C (A Minor) (No. 2) (Wardship: Publication of Information)* [1990] 1 FLR 263, CA) and further dispute about the treatment of the child it would be desirable for the court to remain formally seised of the case without it being necessary to make a fresh application for a particular specified issue or prohibited steps order as and when this was thought desirable.

Unfortunately, it seems likely that many of these cases—and particularly those concerned with child abuse—will involve a local authority and it is in such cases that the restrictions imposed by the Children Act seem likely to have the greatest impact: see further Chapter 15 below.

Chapter 15

THE CHILD, THE FAMILY AND THE STATE

Introduction—the scope and purposes of state intervention

The community has always assumed some limited duties to **15–01** orphans and other deprived children—for many years primarily through the medium of the poor law; and in 1948, as part of the creation of the modern welfare state after the second world war, the Children Act 1948 imposed a general duty on local authorities to provide care for children deprived of a normal home life. The Act created the concept of "voluntary care": local authorities had a duty to *receive* certain children into care—for example orphans, the abandoned, or children whose parents were prevented from providing for the child's proper accommodation, maintenance and upbringing. It is important to emphasise that this was a duty to receive, not a power to take: the local authority was under a positive duty to seek to rehabilitate the family unit, so far as this was consistent with the child's welfare.

Reinforced by duty to provide help

The emphasis of the legislation was thus clearly on preventing the **15–02** need for children to be kept away from their families: and this was reinforced by the enactment of the Children and Young Persons Act 1963. That Act imposed a duty on local authorities to make available guidance and assistance (including "in exceptional circumstances" cash assistance) in order to diminish the need to receive children into care or keep them in care.

Compulsion. There may, of course, be circumstances in which a family is unwilling or unable to accept help; and there have long been provisions allowing the community to take over the parents' authority and to impose its own standards—for example, in cases where the parents were deemed unfit to care for a child "by reason of ... vicious habits or mode of life" (Poor Law Act 1899, s.1). Sometimes the assumption of parental authority was effected by administrative process—latterly by the so-called parental rights resolution under the Child Care Act 1980, s.3—albeit the parents had in effect a right of appeal to the magistrates' court; sometimes it was done by means of a court order—most often by the making of a care order under the provisions of the Children and Young Persons Act 1969 on the basis that the child's health was being avoidably impaired and that the child was in need of care and control which he or she was unlikely to receive unless the court made an order.

The Criminal Law. Sometimes the child's problems resulted from **15–03** parental abuse; and in such cases the parent concerned might well be prosecuted for criminal offences ranging from the general offence of child cruelty (Children and Young Persons Act 1933, s.1), through a wide range of sexual offences (such as incest), to the very specific

295

(such as allowing a child to be in a room containing an unguarded heating appliance: Children and Young Persons Act 1933, s.11). The fact that a parent's behaviour might be the basis for social services action whilst at the same time constituting the basis on which the parent might be prosecuted gives rise to many difficulties (relating, for example, to the differing standards of proof in criminal and civil litigation, and to the right of an accused person to remain silent); and much media comment on the law relating to children confuses the two issues of whether compulsory measures should be taken to safeguard the child's welfare on the one hand and whether a parent should be prosecuted and (if convicted) punished on the other. It is important for the reader to avoid this confusion, and to remember that this text is concerned solely with civil proceedings designed to protect the child.

15–04   *Background to the Children Act 1989.* Between 1948 and the enactment of the Children Act 1989 there were many shifts of opinion in relation to the proper balance to be struck between protecting the child on the one hand and preserving the right of parents to bring up children in accordance with their own philosophy without interference from social workers or other agents of the state on the other hand. There were also many developments in social work philosophy and in the administration of local authority social services departments. The result was that the legislation governing the relationship between the child, the family and the state became complex, confused and sometimes inconsistent. For example, the Children Act 1975 was heavily influenced by the belief that children were being allowed to "drift" in voluntary care; and the Act therefore provided that a Parental Rights Resolution could be founded simply on the fact that a child had been in care for three years. The 1975 Act was also concerned to protect children against the risk that they would be precipitately removed from voluntary care, and it therefore required a parent to give 28 days' notice of intention to remove a child who had been in care for six months. All these measures might be thought to evidence a policy of emphasising the child's welfare even—as some thought—at the cost of interfering with the parents' legitimate rights. Yet at the same time it remained the law that a local authority could not institute care proceedings in respect of a child who was not in care merely because the authority considered that the child was at risk (however well-founded that concern might be); since it was held that a care order could only be made under section 1(2)(a) of the Children and Young Persons Act 1969 on the basis of something which had already occurred. Things were not made any more coherent by the fact that a local authority could make the child a ward of court and seek compulsory intervention simply on the basis that this would best serve the child's interests, even if it was clear that the local authority would fail if it sought a care order in the Magistrates' Court under the 1969 Act.

Against this background, a series of widely publicised disasters—in which children in local authority care met their deaths as a result of neglect or abuse—led to considerable (if not always well-informed) public and media interest.

In 1983, the Law Commission began a comprehensive review of the private law relating to the upbringing of children; and at much the same time the House of Commons Select Committee on the Social Services began the process which led to a comprehensive Inter-Departmental *Review of Child Care Law* (1985).

The public attention given to events in Cleveland in 1987—when a large number of children were removed from their homes by the local authority because of suspicions of sexual abuse—led directly to the establishment of a wide-ranging enquiry under the chairmanship of Mrs Justice Butler-Sloss (Report of the Enquiry into Child Abuse in Cleveland 1987, 1988, Cm 412). The publication of this report did a great deal to create strong pressure for legislation; and the Children Act 1989 was the outcome.

Impact of the Children Act. The Act not only—as has been **15–05** seen—rationalises and codifies the private law relating to children; it also has a revolutionary impact on the public law. First, it codifies and reforms the legal rules governing the powers and duties of local authorities in relation to the provision of support for children and families. Secondly, the Act makes sweeping changes affecting the legal position of children who are being looked after by local authorities. Thirdly, the Act makes radical changes in the law governing the circumstances in which a local authority may intervene compulsorily in the upbringing of a child—perhaps by removing the child from its parents; and the new legislative code governing the circumstances in which compulsion may be exercised is skilfully integrated with the provisions of the Children Act 1989 governing private law disputes between a child's parents and other members of the family circle.

It is this third area—*i.e.* the circumstances in which the state may exercise compulsion—which traditionally receives most attention from lawyers and in student text books. But it would be wrong to ignore the other aspects of child care legislation—in particular, the duty of local authorities to provide support—since the legislation quite clearly espouses the doctrine that the development of a working partnership with parents is usually the most effective route to providing supplementary or substitute care for their children, that there are unique advantages for children in experiencing normal family life in their own birth family, that every effort should be made to preserve the child's home and family links, and that family links (with the wider family as well as with parents) should be actively maintained even if a child is being cared for by others.

The text therefore considers in turn:

i.   the powers and duties of local authorities to children;
ii. the legal position of children who are being looked after by a local authority;

iii. the circumstances in which a local authority can exercise compulsion—for example to remove a child from the parents, and place the child with foster parents with a view to adoption by them.

I. LOCAL AUTHORITIES' POWERS AND DUTIES

15–06 The Children Act draws together local authority functions in respect of children, and imposes a significant range of new duties. The legislation contained in Part III of the Children Act imposes a general duty to safeguard and promote the welfare of children in the authority's area who are "in need." The term "in need" is widely defined (section 17(10), and each local authority has a general duty to provide a range and level of services appropriate to the needs of children in their area so as to safeguard and promote the welfare of such children; and, so far as is consistent with that duty, to promote their upbringing by their families.

The requirement that local authorities should promote children's upbringing by their families (CA 1989, s.17(1)) is significant, and is supported by a duty to make appropriate provision for services (ranging from advice, through home help, to travel and holiday facilities or assistance) to be available for children in need while they are living with their families: Sched. 2, para. 8. There is a general duty to take reasonable steps to reduce the need to bring care or other family proceedings in respect of children in their area; and a similar duty to "take reasonable steps through the provision of services to prevent children in the area suffering neglect or ill-treatment": CA 1989, Sched. 2, para. 4(1).

The Act also contains provisions dealing with Family Centres, Day Care Services (such as Day Nurseries, Play-Groups, Child-Minding, and Out-of-School Clubs and Holiday Schemes); and it is impossible in a short students' textbook to elaborate all the extensive powers and duties of local authorities under these provisions. But they are significant not least because an authority which seeks a care order is likely to find that it is asked questions about whether the child's welfare could not better be promoted by support furnished under the Act.

II. CHILDREN WHO ARE BEING LOOKED AFTER BY A LOCAL AUTHORITY

15–07 The Act abolishes the concept of "voluntary care" which had been a feature of child law and social policy since 1948. Instead local authorities are placed under a duty to "provide accommodation" for children who require accommodation as a result of their being abandoned or there being no person who has parental responsibility, or as a result of the person who has been caring for the child being prevented from providing the child with suitable accommodation or care (s.20(1)); and the local authority *may* provide accommodation for *any* child in their area if it would safeguard or promote the child's welfare.

Such children are described as being "looked after" by the local authority; and the authority of parents is expressly recognised in so far as the local authority is prohibited from providing accommodation for a child if a person who has parental responsibility objects and is able and willing to provide (or arrange for the provision of) accommodation: s.20(7). (There are certain exceptions to this power of veto where private law residence orders have been made, and more significantly, perhaps, if the child has reached the age of 16.) Of even greater significance is the provision (s.20(8)) that "any person who has parental responsibility for a child may at any time remove the child from accommodation provided" under the legislation. This constitutes a remarkable shift from the provision of the Children Act 1975 which required notice to be given (see para. 15-04 above); and seems to give little—if indeed any—weight to the child's own feelings. If a local authority is concerned that such a removal will be injurious to the child, application could be made for an Emergency Protection Order (para. 15-25 below) and a Care Order.

With the exception of this startling acceptance of parental authority, however, the Act generally speaking, strengthens the emphasis on the need to promote the welfare of children whom the local authority is looking after, if at all possible by a *partnership* between the authority and the others concerned. The Act imposes on local authorities a specific statutory duty to safeguard and promote the welfare of such children, and it is also the local authority's duty

> "so far as is reasonably practicable to ascertain the wishes and feeling of (a) the child; (b) his parents; (c) any other person who has parental responsibility for him; and (d) any other person whose wishes and feelings the authority considers to be relevant..."

Before making any decision with respect to a child whom they are looking after or proposing to look after, the local authority is obliged to give due consideration to the wishes and feelings of such persons as well as to the wishes and feelings of the child ("having regard to his age and understanding"), and to the child's "religious persuasion, racial origin and cultural and linguistic background" in making the decision: s.22(5).

Provision of accommodation. There are various ways in which a local   **15-08** authority may provide accommodation, of which the most important for present purposes is perhaps the so called "family placement" which means placement with a local authority foster parent—*i.e.* a family, relative or other suitable person: s.23(2). Regulations lay down detailed provisions requiring the approval of foster parents, and for the decision-taking procedures leading up to a placement of a child: see the Arrangements for Placement of Children (General) Regulations 1991, and the Foster Placement (Children) Regulations 1991. There are also detailed provisions governing placement in children's homes.

III. Compulsion—Acquisition of Parental Responsibility by Local Authority

Court order essential for compulsory intervention

15–09   There are two basic principles underlying the Children Act 1989. First, a court order is necessary to vest "parental responsibility"—and with it parental authority: see para. 11–33 above—in a local authority. The days when a local authority could assume parental authority by passing a resolution have gone. This means that there must be a court hearing, however willing the parents may be to accept the vesting of parental responsibility in the local authority.

The policy of the legislation is that compulsory intervention can only be justified if:

"there is evidence that the child is being or is likely to be positively harmed because of a failure in the family."

It is not sufficient to show that state intervention would be in the child's interests. It may be the case (as the Lord Chancellor, Lord Mackay of Clashfern, put in defending the Government's decision to debar local authorities from having recourse to the wardship jurisdiction (see para. 15–23 below)) that a broad discretion

"guided by the principle of the child's best interests (would) be appropriate and defensible where a court is deciding a dispute between warring members of a family. However, once the court becomes involved in intervention from outside the family, and especially where state intervention is proposed, I do not believe that a broad discretion can be justified."

He went on:

"The integrity and independence of the family is the basic building block of a free and democratic society and the need to defend it should be clearly perceivable in the law ... to provide otherwise would make it lawful for children to be removed from their families simply on the basis that a court considered that the state could do better for the child than his family. The threat to the poor and to minority groups, whose views of what is good for a child may not coincide closely with that of the majority, is all too apparent ... " (1989) 139 New LJ 505, 507.

The text therefore considers the grounds upon which the court may authorise such intervention. (It should be noted that in practice, compulsory local authority intervention often begins by the taking of so-called emergency measures, but it is convenient to deal with those separately: see para. 15–25 below.)

GROUNDS FOR INTERVENTION

The court can only make a care order or supervision order if: **15–10**

(i)   there is an application by a local authority or ("authorised person");
(ii) the court is satisfied that the "threshold criteria" set out in section 31 of the Children Act are met;
(iii) the court, having directed itself by reference to the matters to which section 1(3) of the Act requires it to have "particular regard," considers that the making of the order would promote the child's welfare—that being the paramount consideration; and the court is satisfied that making an order would be better for the child than making no order at all: CA 1989, s.1(5).

These are considered in turn; and the text then outlines the effect and duration of care and supervision orders.

1. Application by local authority or authorised person
[i.e. the NSPCC or any of its officers]

The Act adopts the principle that care orders are not to be made   **15–11** unless those who have the responsibility for dealing with the welfare of children consider that such an outcome would be desirable.

Consistently with this principle, the Act removes the jurisdiction of the divorce and other courts to make care orders because there were exceptional circumstances making it impracticable or undesirable for the child to be entrusted to a parent or other individual: MCA 1973, s.43. (The retention of this provision would also have conflicted with the principle that there should be a single comprehensive ground upon which orders should be made.) Instead, if a court in any family proceedings considers that it might be appropriate for a care or supervision order to be made, it has power to direct the local authority to make an investigation of the child's circumstances and to consider whether to apply for a care or supervision order (or to take other action): CA 1989, s.37. If the local authority concludes that it does not wish to seek such an order it must make a report to the court, but the court cannot require the authority to seek an order.

Although it is a prerequisite to the making of an order that an application should have been made by a local authority or authorised person, it does not follow that the authority (or authorised person) should have initiated the proceedings: the court may—*provided* that the relevant conditions are satisfied—make a care order in any family proceedings. For example, a local authority could intervene in a "freestanding" application by the father of an illegitimate child, and seek a care order: see s.31(4).

2. The threshold criterion

15–12   The court may only make a care or supervision order if it is satisfied that the conditions set out in section 31(2) of the Act are satisfied. The statutory rules are complex, and the drafting caused considerable problems (as became apparent during the passage of the Children Act through Parliament). It seems appropriate, therefore, to set out the rules exactly as they appear in the statute:
The court must be satisfied:

"(a)   that the child concerned is suffering, or is likely to suffer, significant harm; and

(b)   that the harm, or likelihood of harm, is attributable to—

(i)   the care given to the child, or likely to be given to him if the order were not made, not being what it would be reasonable to expect a parent to give to him; or

(ii)   the child's being beyond parental control.

The Act further defines certain elements in this test: for example, *harm* means "ill-treatment or the impairment of health or development"; *development* means "physical, intellectual, emotional, social or behavioural development; *health* means "physical or mental health"; and *ill-treatment* "includes sexual abuse and forms of treatment which are not physical."

Apprehended harm suffices

One thing is clear: the condition may be satisfied if the court is
satisfied that there is a *likelihood* of significant harm; and it need no
longer be satisfied that such harm has already occurred. But much
else is obscure; and it seems certain that "every word will require
(judicial) interpretation and analysis" (see M. D. A. Freeman, in
Children and the Law, ed. by D. Freestone (1990) p. 135, an essay to
which the reader may be referred for a stimulating discussion of
many of the difficulties of interpretation).

In many cases—for example, where a child has been severely
injured or neglected—the question of whether he or she has suffered
"significant" harm may not be controversial. The Act seeks to provide
some assistance by including a gloss that "where the question of
whether harm suffered by a child is significant turns on the child's
health or development, his health or development shall be compared
with that which could reasonably be expected of a similar child
(s.31(10)), and this would seem to be an invitation for the local
authority to lead expert evidence comparing the child's development
with that which would be expected on the basis of statistical data
about such matters as weight, size, and so on. And it seems clear that
the reference to a "similar" child is intended to compare like children
with like children—a blind child with a blind child, a Down's
Syndrome child with a Down's Syndrome child, for example. But
although there will be many cases in which the "significance" of the
harm cannot really be questioned, it seems likely that there will be
problems in cases nearer the border line, as will be immediately
apparent to anyone who has heard such expressions as "just a few
cuts and bruises," "a nasty shock but she'll soon forget about it,
won't she?" The underlying problem is that the test of "significance"
involves answering the question "What can a child be expected to
tolerate? What do adults believe to be tolerable?"—necessarily highly
subjective issues. However, the question may turn out not to be as
important as could be feared, since any court left in doubt about
whether the harm suffered might truly be described as "significant"
would be unlikely to be satisfied about the benefits of making an
order, see para. 15–14 below.

The difficulties of deciding whether significant harm is being, or is
likely to be suffered, pales into insignificance in deciding whether the
second requirement—*i.e.* that any such harm be "attributable" to the
matters set out—has been satisfied. What is it reasonable to expect
"a" parent to provide? In seeking to answer that question, how far
should the court take into account the fact that the particular parent is
disadvantaged and perhaps not able to do what a better educated,
more intelligent, or more affluent parent would do? It would be
possible to make tentative predictions about these matters (for
example, the Act refers to "a" parent rather than "the" parent,
which might be thought to suggest some objectivity of approach); but
since these provisions are certain to be litigated it would seem

303

appropriate, in an elementary student text, simply to advise the reader to keep an eye on the Law Reports.

3. Court only to make care or supervision order if to do so would promote child's welfare

15–14   It is essential to understand that, under the Children Act, the court *cannot* make a care or supervision order *unless* the threshold criteria are satisfied; but it does not follow from the fact that the threshold criteria have been satisfied that the court will make a care or supervision (or indeed any) order. If the criteria are met, the court has a discretion whether to make a care order or not; and if it decides not to make a care order it may either make a section 8 "menu" order, or it may decide to make no order at all.

This is because, in deciding on the exercise of the discretion, the court must apply both the principle that the child's welfare is paramount, and the "no order" presumption. In cases in which the court is considering whether to make, vary or discharge a care or supervision order, the court is required to have regard "in particular" to the matters listed in the statutory checklist (see s.1(3), and para. 13–19 above), so that the court is required, for example (s.1(3)(g)) to consider the range of powers available to the court under the Act. Accordingly, it will need to consider whether there is any other order (such as a residence order in favour of a relative) which might be more appropriate to promote the child's welfare. Having considered the specified matters, and any other considerations relevant to the child's welfare, the court must ask whether making the care or supervision order (or indeed any other order) would "be better for the child than making no order at all": s.1(5). The court will therefore need to ask precisely what benefit the making of a care order will give the child, and this inevitably means that the court will need to have details of the local authority's plans for the child—for example, do the authority plan to place the child in a residential home? Do they plan to place the child with foster parents? Do they envisage that the child will have contact with the parents, or do they envisage that the child will be placed for adoption?

In order to enable these and other matters to be probed, the Rules (Family Proceedings Rules 1991 Form CHA 19) require the authority to state its plans for the child if a final order is made, and to make specific reference to the arrangements it envisages for contact with the child: see para. 15–19 below. Furthermore, in order to assist the court, the *guardian ad litem* (see below para. 15–16) is specifically required to advise the court on the options available to it in respect of the child and the suitability of each such option, including what order the guardian considers should be made in determining the application: Family Proceedings Rules 1991, r. 4.11 (4)(e).

The majority of care cases are likely to be heard by magistrates sitting in the Family Proceedings Court. Traditionally, magistrates have not given reasons for their decisions (see *Re B(A Minor) (Justices' Reasons)* [1990] 1 FLR 344); but the rules (*e.g.* The Family Proceedings Courts (Children Act 1989) Rules 1991, r. 21(6)) now require the court to state any findings of fact and the reasons for the court's decision. It is to be expected therefore that the courts will have to give a structured account of the matters the court has considered.

Procedures. The Act contains important provisions designed to **15–15** *minimise delay* in dealing with care cases. Apart from applying the general presumption (s.1(2)) that delay in determining questions is likely to prejudice the child (para. 13–29 above), the court is specifically required (s.32(1)) to draw up a *timetable* with a view to disposing of the application without delay, and to give appropriate directions. The Rules (*e.g.* The Family Proceedings Courts (Children Act 1989) Rules 1991, r. 15) spell out these duties in detail, and empower the court (or justices' clerk) to give *directions*.

The guardian ad litem

The expression *guardian ad litem* means a guardian "appointed for **15–16** the purpose of litigation," and such guardians were traditionally appointed to defend actions brought against infants and other persons under disability. Social workers began to be involved as *guardians ad litem* in adoption cases (where the guardian was given special duties) and the concept thus became a familiar one in the Family Courts. There may be some who regret that the Children Act 1989 did not substitute English words (such as "Children's Representative"); but it may be that—rather like the Swedish word "Ombudsman"—the term has come to have its own significance in the English language. Be that as it may, building on experience gained under provisions introduced by the Children Act 1975 and intended to ensure that the child's voice was properly heard in care and related proceedings, the Act provides that the court shall appoint a *guardian ad litem* in care and some other proceedings "unless satisfied that it is not necessary to do so in order to safeguard" the child's interests: s.41(1).

The guardian is to be independent of the local authority involved; and will be appointed from panels established under the Act: s.41(7). To facilitate the guardian's investigatory rôle, the Act gives the guardian specific rights to examine and copy local authority records: s.42.

The guardian plays a central role in care proceedings, and has wide-ranging and important duties—for example, to appoint a solicitor for the child (unless one has been already appointed), advise the child, carry out investigations and commission expert reports, give instructions to the child's solicitor, attend all directions appointments and all hearings, and to advise the court on a wide range of matters—including the wishes of the child, the appropriate forum for the hearing (Family Proceedings Court or County Court Care Centre, for example: see para. 13–03 above), the appropriate timing for the proceedings, the options available to the court, and any other matter concerning which the court seeks the guardian's advice or concerning which the guardian considers the court should be informed: the Family Proceedings Courts (Children Act 1989) Rules 1991, r. 11.

The guardian is required to *file a report* not less than seven days before the final hearing (the Family Proceedings Courts (Children Act 1989) Rules 1991, r. 11(7)) and that report will be served on all the parties. It is to be expected that the guardian will be asked to justify the recommendation made in the report by any party who is dissatisfied with it. The recommendation will obviously be of great importance, not least because it has been held that the court must give clear reasons if it decides not to adopt the guardian's recommendation: *Devon County Council* v. *G* [1985] FLR 1159, CA.

In most cases, the child will be represented by a *solicitor*—normally a specialist who is a member of the panel established by The Law Society. Normally the *guardian ad litem* will instruct the solicitor on the child's behalf; but the solicitor will conduct the case in accordance with the child's instructions if those instructions conflict with the *guardian ad litem*'s (provided that the solicitor considers the child is capable of understanding the matter). But if there is no guardian and the child is not capable of giving instructions the solicitor must do what he considers will further the child's best interests: the Family Proceedings Courts (Children Act 1989) Rules 1991, r. 12.

EFFECT AND DURATION OF CARE AND SUPERVISION ORDERS

Care Orders

15–17   Where a care order is made, it is the duty of the local authority to receive the child into their care "and to keep him in their care while the order remains in force": s.33(1). The local authority will have "parental responsibility" for the child—although the authority cannot give the parental consent necessary in adoption or freeing for adoption, cannot appoint a guardian, and must not cause the child to be brought up in any religious persuasion "other than that in which he would have been brought up if the order had not been made": s.33(6)(a). The child will be "looked after" by the local authority, which will in consequence have the powers to provide accommodation and other services as set out above: para. 15–06.

Before the enactment of the Children Act, the position of the child's parents was dramatically affected by the making of a care order. It is true that the local authority could not terminate access to the child without giving the parents the right to apply to the Juvenile Court for an access order; but there was no legal procedure whereby parents could question decisions to *restrict* access: see *A* v. *Liverpool City Council* (1981) 2 FLR 222, HL (wardship not available to question decision to restrict mother's access to two-year-old child to one monthly supervised visit at day nursery). In effect, therefore, once a care order had been made all power over the child's future seemed to pass to the local authority, who could restrict access; and then, when the bond between parent and child was adjudged to have become sufficiently tenuous, the authority could place the child for adoption (or seek an order freeing the child for adoption): see, for example, *Re D (A Minor)* [1987] 1 FLR 422, HL, in which drug addicted parents resisted—unsuccessfully—the making of a care order, not because they considered themselves fit to care for the child, but because they wanted the opportunity which would have been available to them if the child's future had been dealt with in wardship to be heard whenever an important decision (such as an adoption placement) was being considered. It is, as already explained, true that no adoption order could be made unless the parent agreed (or the court dispensed with the parent's agreement), but if the links between parent and child had become such that rehabilitation seemed unlikely the court might well consider the parent to have withheld agreement unreasonably: see para. 12–18 above.

What is the impact of the Children Act on this scenario? The Act contains a number of provisions which—to some extent—strengthen the parents' right to keep in touch with their child. Thus:

(i) The parents (and others) *retain parental responsibility;* and this **15–18** provision might suggest that the local authority would never be able to act against the parents' wishes. But the Act provides that while a care order is in force the local authority has the power "to determine the extent to which a parent or guardian may meet his parental responsibility for" the child (s.33(3)(b))—albeit only if the authority is "satisfied that it is necessary to do so in order to safeguard or promote the child's welfare": s.33(4).

It is impossible to predict how these provisions will operate. In particular the word "necessary" is obviously capable of many different interpretations; and it may be that many authorities will wish to ensure that they remain "in the driving seat" (as the government spokesman put it in the parliamentary debates). The methods whereby parents who disagree with a local authority decision to deny them the right to exercise their parental responsibility—for example, by stipulating that the child receive a certain kind of medical treatment—might question the matter are dealt with below.

(ii) The Act deals with the question of *contact* with a child who is **15–19** subject to a care order by requiring the authority to allow the child "reasonable contact" with the parents (and some others): s.34(1). The authority may only deny such contact if they consider that to do so is "necessary" to safeguard or promote the child's welfare, and the refusal is decided on as a matter of urgency, and does not last for more than seven days: s.34(6).

But what is "reasonable" contact? The Act enables a dispute to be resolved by a provision that the parent or the authority may *apply to the court*, which may make such order as—applying the welfare principle—it considers appropriate: s.34(3).

These provisions mark a radical change from the existing law—not only in creating the right to contact, but in giving the court almost complete power to make detailed provisions about contact. To some extent this provision negates the policy that the local authority be put "in the driving seat," and reinforces the increasing legalisation of the care process. The only apparent fetter on the right to have the matter constantly re-opened is that a person whose contact application has been refused is not to be allowed (without leave of the court) to apply again for a period of six months.

Apart from these provisions, which seem to give parents considerably more extensive rights than in the past whilst the care order is in force, a parent may apply to *discharge* an order. This subject is considered below (para. 15–21), and then the general issue of how far local authority decisions may be questioned is considered.

15–20   **Supervision orders.** A supervision order places the child under the supervision of a designated local authority or of a probation officer (s.31(1)) whose duty it is to "advise assist and befriend" the child and to take such steps as are reasonably necessary to give effect to the order: s.35(1). The supervisor may give directions to the child as to where he or she should live, or to participate in activities. Directions—for example, that all reasonable steps be taken to ensure that the supervised child complies—may also be given to the person with whom the child is living or those who have parental responsibility. The order may require the child to undergo psychiatric or medical examinations or procedures subject to a number of conditions—notably that a child who has the understanding to make an informed decision must consent: see generally Sched. 3.

15–21   **Duration of orders**. A supervision order is a short term measure and will normally come to an end after one year: Sched. 3, para. 6(1). The supervisor may apply to extend the order, but it cannot be extended beyond three years from the date when it was made. A care order, in contrast, will last until the child attains 18, if not brought to an end earlier: s.91(12).

There are provisions whereby the child, any person with parental responsibility for the child, and the supervisor or local authority may apply to the court for the *discharge* of a care or supervision order (or for the variation of a supervision order): s.39. If an application for discharge is rejected, no further application may be made for six months unless the court grants leave to do so: s.91(15).

There are also circumstances in which these public orders are *automatically terminated* because another court order is made: the most important is that the making of a residence order automatically discharges a care order: s.91(1).

Questioning local authority decisions

15–22

A person who disagrees with the local authority's decisions about a child in care may therefore seek to discharge the care order. But suppose that, say, a parent does not wish the order to be discharged—perhaps because it is clear that the parent could not personally care for the child. Is there any way in which a particular local authority decision can be questioned?

Wardship and judicial review?

15–23

Disputes about contact, as we have seen, are in a class of their own: application may be made to the court to settle the matter. But the position about other decisions is less satisfactory from the point of view of the dissatisfied person. In particular, it seems clear that *wardship will not be available* to question a particular decision (CA 1989, s.100(2)(c) and see generally para 14–28 above); and *judicial review* would only be available if it could be shown that the local authority had misdirected itself in law, failed to consider relevant matters, or conducted the decision-taking process in a way which was un-fair—perhaps "manifestly" unfair—or unreasonable in the sense that no reasonable authority, properly directed, could have reached it. (It is perhaps necessary to show the decision to have been "utterly unreasonable," *per* Butler Sloss L.J. *R* v. *Harrow LB ex parte D* [1990] 1 FLR 79, CA, or even "verging on the absurd": *R* v. *Parole Board ex parte Bradley* [1990] 3 All ER 828, 839).

Representations procedure

15–24

The scope for invoking the legal process to question local authority decisions thus seems limited; but in an attempt to provide some redress, the Act stipulates that local authorities must provide a procedure for *considering any representations* "(including any complaint)" made to them about the discharge of their functions under Part III of the Act (which covers Local Authority Support for Children and Families) by any child in care or otherwise being looked after by them, any parent or person with parental responsibility for such a child, any local authority foster-parent, and any other person thought to have a sufficient interest in the child's welfare: s.26(3). This machinery must include an independent element: s.26(4). The Representations Procedure (Children) Regulations 1991 (S.I. No. 894) allow a person who is dissatisfied with a local authority's response to the representations to have the matter referred to a panel, which will make recommendations to the local authority: reg. 9.

EMERGENCY PROCEDURES

15–25   However streamlined the procedure for dealing with applications for care orders, it is self-evident that there will be cases in which emergency action needs to be taken before the requisite full judicial hearing—a child cannot for example be left with parents who are starving him or her, and care must be given for a child whose parent has been arrested and detained in respect of a criminal offence. Moreover, there may be cases in which the parents refuse to allow the child to be examined, even though there is considerable ground for concern about the child's welfare.

Under the law in force before the Children Act 1989 application could be made for a *"place of safety order"* in such circumstances; but the Report of the Butler Sloss Inquiry into Events in Cleveland (Cm. 412) revealed many disturbing features of the use to which that procedure had been put—in particular, applications were made *ex parte* without any notification to the parents, applications were made to a single magistrate sometimes sitting in his or her home (notwithstanding the fact that the hearing took place during court hours), record keeping was defective, and—of most importance—there was little understanding of the legal rights of those concerned, so that access by the parents was often improperly denied, medical examinations were (perhaps improperly) carried out, and, generally, the procedure seemed to be used in an attempt to obtain control over the situation for the local authority.

The Children Act 1989 seeks to balance the conflicting interests involved by providing that courts may make *Emergency Protection Orders* and *Child Assessment Orders*. (The police also have limited powers to remove and protect a child: s.46.)

15–26   An *Emergency Protection Order* requires any person who is in a position to do so to produce the child, and authorises the applicant to remove the child (or prevent the child's removal from a hospital or other place—for example, a foster home—in which the child was being accommodated). The order gives the applicant parental responsibility, but imposes severe limits on its exercise: in particular, the applicant may only take action reasonably required to safeguard or promote the welfare of the child. Moreover, the court may give directions about the parental and other contact to be allowed with the child, and about medical examination or other assessment procedures—although a child of sufficient understanding may refuse to undergo such procedures. An Emergency Protection Order is not to continue beyond eight days (although the court may order one extension of no more than seven days). Application may be made to discharge the order after 72 hours.

Application for an Emergency Protection Order may be made by anyone who has reasonable cause to believe that the child is likely to suffer significant harm if the child is not moved (or if the child does not remain where he or she is); and application may be made by local authorities or authorised persons on somewhat broader grounds: s.44(1).

Any application must be made to a court; and the court will apply the *welfare principle* and the *"no order"* presumption.

The Child Assessment Order is intended to provide for cases in which　　**15–27**
there is reasonable concern about the child, the people caring for him or her are unco-operative, yet there are insufficient grounds to obtain an Emergency Protection Order or Care Order: see *An Introduction to the Children Act 1989*, (HMSO, para. 6.41). The applicant must satisfy the court that there is reasonable cause to suspect that the child is suffering or is likely to suffer significant harm; and the applicant must also satisfy the court that an assessment of the child's health or development is necessary to enable the applicant to determine whether or not the child is in fact suffering or likely to suffer significant harm.

A Child Assessment Order permits the making of an assessment; but the child may only be kept away from home in specified circumstances, and may (if of sufficient understanding) refuse to submit to any assessment.

Interim Orders. Notwithstanding the improvements in court proce-　　**15–28**
dures, there may well be circumstances in which an application for a care or supervision order cannot be dealt with at once. The Act (s.38) permits the court to make an Interim Care or Supervision Order if it is satisfied that there are reasonable grounds for believing that the threshold criteria set out in section 31(2) of the Act are met. Orders may be made for up to eight weeks, but may be extended for a further four weeks. It is not clear whether they may be further extended.

SUGGESTION FOR FURTHER READING

Hoggett and Pearl, Chap. 13.
Report of the Inquiry into Child Abuse in Cleveland 1987, (Chairman: The Hon. Mrs Justice Butler-Sloss DBE), Cm. 412, (1988).
N. Parton, *Governing the Family* (1991), particularly Chapters 6 and 7.
N. Parton, "The Contemporary Politics of Child Protection" [1992] JSWFL 100.
The Care of Children, Principles and Practice in Regulations and Guidance, Department of Health (1989).
The Children Act 1989, Guidance and Regulations, Vol. 2 (*Family Support, Day Care and Education Provision for Young Children*), 3 (*Family Placements*), 4 (*Residential Care*), and 7 (*Guardians ad litem and other Court Related Issues*), Department of Health (1991).
Working Together under the Children Act 1989, Department of Health and Others (1991).

INDEX